The Authoritarian Commons

Based on six-year fieldwork across China including over 200 in-depth interviews, this book provides an ethnographic account of how hundreds of millions of Chinese homeowners practice democracy in and beyond their condominium complexes. Using interviews, survey data, and a comprehensive examination of laws, policies, and judicial decisions, this book also examines how the party-state in China responds to the risks and benefits brought by neighborhood democratization. Moreover, this book provides a framework to analyze different approaches to the authoritarian dilemma facing neighborhood democratization, which may increase the regime's legitimacy and expose it to the challenge of independent organizations at the same time. Lastly, this book identifies conditions under which neighborhood democratization can succeed.

Shitong Qiao is Professor of Law and Ken Young-Gak Yun and Jinah Park Yun Research Scholar at Duke University. He also taught property and comparative law at the University of Hong Kong and New York University and was Law and Public Affairs Fellow at Princeton University. He received his law degrees from Wuhan (LLB), Peking (MPhil) and Yale (LLM and JSD). He has published numerous articles in the top Chinese and US law journals and a prize-winning book about law and marketization, *Chinese Small Property: The Co-Evolution of Law and Social Norms* (Cambridge University Press, 2017).

Law in Context

Since 1970, the Law in Context series has been at the forefront of a movement to broaden the study of law. The series is a vehicle for the publication of innovative monographs and texts that treat law and legal phenomena critically in their cultural, social, political, technological, environmental and economic contexts. A contextual approach involves treating legal subjects broadly, using materials from other humanities and social sciences, and from any other discipline that helps to explain the operation in practice of the particular legal field or legal phenomena under investigation. It is intended that this orientation is at once more stimulating and more revealing than the bare exposition of legal rules. The series includes original research monographs, coursebooks and textbooks that foreground contextual approaches and methods. The series includes and welcomes books on the study of law in all its contexts, including domestic legal systems, European and international law, transnational and global legal processes, and comparative law.

Books in the Series

Acosta: *The National versus the Foreigner in South America: 200 Years of Migration and Citizenship Law*
Alaattinoğlu: *Grievance Formation, Rights and Remedies*
Ali: *Modern Challenges to Islamic Law*
Alyagon Darr: *Plausible Crime Stories: The Legal History of Sexual Offences in Mandate Palestine*
Anderson, Schum & Twining: *Analysis of Evidence, 2nd Edition*
Ashworth: *Sentencing and Criminal Justice, 6th Edition*
Barton & Douglas: *Law and Parenthood*
Baxi, McCrudden & Paliwala: *Law's Ethical, Global and Theoretical Contexts: Essays in Honour of William Twining*
Beecher-Monas: *Evaluating Scientific Evidence: An Interdisciplinary Framework for Intellectual Due Process*
Bell: *French Legal Cultures*
Bercusson: *European Labour Law, 2nd Edition*

Birkinshaw: *European Public Law*
Birkinshaw: *Freedom of Information: The Law, the Practice and the Ideal, 4th Edition*
Blick: *Electrified Democracy: The Internet and the United Kingdom Parliament in History*
Broderick & Ferri: *International and European Disability Law and Policy: Text, Cases and Materials*
Brownsword & Goodwin: *Law and the Technologies of the Twenty-First Century: Text and Materials*
Cane & Goudkamp: *Atiyah's Accidents, Compensation and the Law, 9th Edition*
Clarke: *Principles of Property Law*
Clarke & Kohler: *Property Law: Commentary and Materials*
Collins: *The Law of Contract, 4th Edition*
Collins, Ewing & McColgan: *Labour Law, 2nd Edition*
Cowan: *Housing Law and Policy*
Cranston: *Making Commercial Law Through Practice 1830–1970*
Cranston: *Legal Foundations of the Welfare State*
Darian-Smith: *Laws and Societies in Global Contexts: Contemporary Approaches*
Dauvergne: *Making People Illegal: What Globalisation Means for Immigration and Law*
David: *Kinship, Law and Politics: An Anatomy of Belonging*
Davies: *Perspectives on Labour Law, 2nd Edition*
Dembour: *Who Believes in Human Rights?: Reflections on the European Convention*
de Sousa Santos: *Toward a New Legal Common Sense: Law, Globalization, and Emancipation*
Diduck: *Law's Families*
Douglas-Scott: *Brexit, Union, and Disunion: The Evolution of British Constitutional Unsettlement*
Dowdle: *Transnational Law: A Framework for Analysis*
Dupret: *Positive Law from the Muslim World: Jurisprudence, History, Practices*
Emon: *Jurisdictional Exceptionalisms: Islamic Law, International Law, and Parental Child Abduction*
Estella: *Legal Foundations of EU Economic Governance*
Fortin: *Children's Rights and the Developing Law, 3rd Edition*
Garnsey: *The Justice of Visual Art: Creative State-Building in Times of Political Transition*
Garton, Probert & Bean: *Moffat's Trusts Law: Text and Materials, 7th Edition*
Ghai & Woodman: *Practising Self-Government: A Comparative Study of Autonomous Regions*
Glover-Thomas: *Reconstructing Mental Health Law and Policy*
Gobert & Punch: *Rethinking Corporate Crime*
Goldman: *Globalisation and the Western Legal Tradition: Recurring Patterns of Law and Authority*
Haack: *Evidence Matters: Science, Proof, and Truth in the Law*
Harlow & Rawlings: *Law and Administration, 4th Edition*
Harris: *An Introduction to Law, 8th Edition*
Harris, Campbell & Halson: *Remedies in Contract and Tort, 2nd Edition*
Harvey: *Seeking Asylum in the UK: Problems and Prospects*
Herring: *Law and the Relational Self*
Hervey & McHale: *European Union Health Law: Themes and Implications*
Hervey & McHale: *Health Law and the European Union*
Holder & Lee: *Environmental Protection, Law and Policy: Text and Materials, 2nd Edition*

Jackson & Summers: *The Internationalisation of Criminal Evidence: Beyond the Common Law and Civil Law Traditions*
Jeutner: *The Reasonable Person: A Legal Biography*
Kennedy: *Inducing Intimacy: Deception, Consent and the Law*
Kostakopoulou: *The Future Governance of Citizenship*
Kreiczer-Levy: *Destabilized Property: Property Law in the Sharing Economy*
Kubal: *Immigration and Refugee Law in Russia: Socio-Legal Perspectives*
Lewis: *Choice and the Legal Order: Rising above Politics*
Likosky: *Law, Infrastructure and Human Rights*
Likosky: *Transnational Legal Processes: Globalisation and Power Disparities*
Lixinski: *Legalized Identities: Cultural Heritage Law and the Shaping of Transitional Justice*
Loughnan: *Self, Others and the State: Relations of Criminal Responsibility*
Lunney: *A History of Australian Tort Law 1901–1945: England's Obedient Servant?*
Maughan & Webb: *Lawyering Skills and the Legal Process, 2nd Edition*
McGaughey: *Principles of Enterprise Law*
McGlynn: *Families and the European Union: Law, Politics and Pluralism*
Mertens: *A Philosophical Introduction to Human Rights*
Miller: *An Introduction to German Law and Legal Culture: Text and Materials*
Moffat: *Trusts Law: Text and Materials*
Monti: *EC Competition Law*
Morgan: *Contract Law Minimalism: A Formalist Restatement of Commercial Contract Law*
Morgan & Yeung: *An Introduction to Law and Regulation: Text and Materials*
Nash: *British Islam and English Law: A Classical Pluralist Perspective*
Ng: *Political Censorship in British Hong Kong: Freedom of Expression and the Law (1842–1997)*
Nicola & Davies: *EU Law Stories: Contextual and Critical Histories of European Jurisprudence*
Norrie: *Crime, Reason and History: A Critical Introduction to Criminal Law, 3rd Edition*
O'Dair: *Legal Ethics: Text and Materials*
Oliver: *Common Values and the Public–Private Divide*
Oliver & Drewry: *The Law and Parliament*
Palmer & Roberts: *Dispute Processes: ADR and the Primary Forms of Decision-Making, 1st Edition*
Palmer & Roberts: *Dispute Processes: ADR and the Primary Forms of Decision-Making, 3rd Edition*
Picciotto: *International Business Taxation*
Pieraccini: *Regulating the Sea: A Socio-Legal Analysis of English Marine Protected Areas*
Probert: *The Changing Legal Regulation of Cohabitation, 1600–2010: From Fornicators to Family, 1600–2010*
Radi: *Rules and Practices of International Investment Law and Arbitration*
Reed: *Internet Law: Text and Materials*
Richardson: *Law, Process and Custody*
Roberts & Palmer: *Dispute Processes: ADR and the Primary Forms of Decision-Making, 2nd Edition*
Rowbottom: *Democracy Distorted: Wealth, Influence and Democratic Politics*
Sauter: *Public Services in EU Law*

Scott & Black: *Cranston's Consumers and the Law*
Seneviratne: *Ombudsmen: Public Services and Administrative Justice*
Seppänen: *Ideological Conflict and the Rule of Law in Contemporary China: Useful Paradoxes*
Siems: *Comparative Law, 3rd Edition*
Stapleton: *Product Liability*
Stewart: *Gender, Law and Justice in a Global Market*
Tamanaha: *Law as a Means to an End: Threat to the Rule of Law*
Taylor: *Fortin's Children's Rights and the Developing Law, 4th Edition*
Tuori: *Properties of Law: Modern Law and After*
Turpin & Tomkins: *British Government and the Constitution: Text and Materials, 7th Edition*
Twining: *General Jurisprudence: Understanding Law from a Global Perspective*
Twining: *Globalisation and Legal Theory*
Twining: *Human Rights, Southern Voices: Francis Deng, Abdullahi An-Na'im, Yash Ghai and Upendra Baxi*
Twining: *Jurist in Context: A Memoir*
Twining: *Karl Llewellyn and the Realist Movement, 2nd Edition*
Twining: *Rethinking Evidence: Exploratory Essays, 2nd Edition*
Twining & Miers: *How to Do Things with Rules, 5th Edition*
Wan: *Film and Constitutional Controversy: Visualizing Hong Kong Identity in the Age of 'One Country, Two Systems'*
Ward: *A Critical Introduction to European Law, 3rd Edition*
Ward: *Law, Text, Terror*
Ward: *Shakespeare and Legal Imagination*
Watt: *The Making Sense of Politics, Media, and Law: Rhetorical Performance as Invention, Creation, Production*
Wells & Quick: *Lacey, Wells and Quick: Reconstructing Criminal Law: Text and Materials, 4th Edition*
Woodhead: *Caring for Cultural Heritage: An Integrated Approach to Legal and Ethical Initiatives in the United Kingdom*
Yeung and Ranchordás: *An Introduction to Law and Regulation: Text and Materials, 2nd edition*
Young: *Turpin and Tomkins' British Government and the Constitution: Text and Materials, 8th Edition*
Zander: *Cases and Materials on the English Legal System, 10th Edition*
Zander: *The Law-Making Process, 6th Edition*

International Journal of Law in Context: A Global Forum for Interdisciplinary Legal Studies

The *International Journal of Law in Context* is the companion journal to the Law in Context book series and provides a forum for interdisciplinary legal studies and offers intellectual space for ground-breaking critical research. It publishes contextual work about law and its relationship with other disciplines including but not limited to science, literature, humanities, philosophy, sociology, psychology, ethics, history and geography. More information about the journal and how to submit an article can be found at http://journals.cambridge.org/ijc

The Authoritarian Commons

Neighborhood Democratization in Urban China

SHITONG QIAO
Duke University

CAMBRIDGE
UNIVERSITY PRESS

CAMBRIDGE
UNIVERSITY PRESS

Shaftesbury Road, Cambridge CB2 8EA, United Kingdom

One Liberty Plaza, 20th Floor, New York, NY 10006, USA

477 Williamstown Road, Port Melbourne, VIC 3207, Australia

314–321, 3rd Floor, Plot 3, Splendor Forum, Jasola District Centre, New Delhi – 110025, India

103 Penang Road, #05–06/07, Visioncrest Commercial, Singapore 238467

Cambridge University Press is part of Cambridge University Press & Assessment, a department of the University of Cambridge.

We share the University's mission to contribute to society through the pursuit of education, learning and research at the highest international levels of excellence.

www.cambridge.org
Information on this title: www.cambridge.org/9781108840279

DOI: 10.1017/9781108885416

When citing this work, please include a reference to the DOI 10.1017/9781108885416

First published 2025

A catalogue record for this publication is available from the British Library

Library of Congress Cataloging-in-Publication Data
Names: Qiao, Shitong, 1985– author.
Title: The authoritarian commons : neighborhood democratization in urban China / Shitong Qiao, Duke University, North Carolina.
Description: Cambridge, United Kingdom ; New York, NY : Cambridge University Press, 2025. | Series: Law in context | Includes bibliographical references and index.
Identifiers: LCCN 2024023518 | ISBN 9781108840279 (hardback) | ISBN 9781108885416 (ebook)
Subjects: LCSH: Rule of law – China. | Right of property – China. | Authoritarianism – China. | COVID-19 (Disease) – Government policy – China. | Democratization – China. | Democracy – China.
Classification: LCC KNQ2020 .Q53 2025 | DDC 323.4/60951–dc23/eng/20240904
LC record available at https://lccn.loc.gov/2024023518

ISBN 978-1-108-84027-9 Hardback

To my family

Contents

Figures

Tables

Acknowledgments

The initial spark for this book was a series of messages that my former classmates at Peking University (PKU) Law School posted in late 2017 on their WeChat accounts and in online groups. These former classmates were typical middle-class professionals: averse to most activism and politically reticent. Such traits are common among Chinese of my generation. Having been born in the mid 1980s, we grew up in the midst of China's economic boom and experienced an awakening of rights consciousness but also witnessed an increasingly constrained political environment in the post-1989 context. Thus, we learned to enjoy our growing economic freedoms while carefully avoiding any activity that might be regarded as a confrontational stance against the party-state. And thus, I was surprised to learn, in these online posts, that several of my former classmates were willing not only to establish homeowners' associations (HoAs) but also to take on local government officials in the process. Just for fun, I conducted individual calls with several of the classmates and was amazed by how much such a seemingly trivial matter – the establishment of HoAs – had occupied their attention. Six years later, with more than 200 interviews with homeowner activists, local government employees, and real estate management professionals and dozens of neighborhood visits under my belt, I have come to accept a very different view of Chinese citizens.

Over the past six years, I've done research on this project at various institutions, and I owe my greatest debt of gratitude to the following: I began my academic career and indeed started this project at the University of Hong Kong (HKU) Faculty of Law, where my position enabled me to secure critical research funding from the Research Grants Council of Hong Kong (project number: 17617921). It was also a fortune to be in a faculty with so many Chinese law experts and benefit from daily conversations with them. I finished this book at the Duke University School of Law, where I have received tremendous encouragement and feedback from many wonderful colleagues. Indeed, I first presented this project in the spring of 2019 at the Duke Law School faculty workshop, where attendees posed a stream of insightful questions. One went like this: "So, your paper is about parking?" When I responded in the affirmative, the whole room burst out in approving laughter. At that moment, I knew that Duke would be a lovely place to work. This book also benefited greatly from my experience as a visiting professor at New York University (NYU) School of Law in the spring semester of 2020. On March 2, 2020, I presented this project at the NYU Law School faculty workshop. With COVID rapidly spreading around the world at the time, I had been concerned that the workshop would be cancelled or, at best, would draw a tiny number of attendees. My fears turned out to be unfounded, and the many thoughtful individuals in attendance inquired into my research both during and after the workshop. These questions and related comments have profoundly shaped the present book. Finally, I would like to mention the immensely helpful one-year fellowship that I enjoyed in the Law and Public Affairs program at Princeton University. Owing to the COVID pandemic, I spent much of that year attending numerous virtual meetings held by the Princeton program at noon, New Jersey time (but at midnight, Hong Kong time).

There are too many individuals to thank for their input on this project. For reasons of space, the list below is incomplete, so if your name is not mentioned, please know that I value your contributions nonetheless.

I am extremely grateful for the fieldwork help provided by Bingwan Xiong, Zhiqiang Wang, Jinhua Cheng, Jingping Jin, and Yun Zhao. My interviewees, with many of whom I still communicate regularly, deserve the most thanks, but need to be kept anonymous.

Professor Rick Hills encouraged me to work on such a "boring" subject when there were so many exciting things, good or bad, happening in China all the time, and helped me think through the book's theoretical framework. Professor Frank Upham patiently read my draft chapters and even praised my devotion to details. In an era of big data, it is easy for even an author to doubt the meaning of his ethnographic work such as this book. Professor Bob Ellickson's pioneering work on HoAs in the US context inspired this book. I also benefited directly from a conversation with him about the differences between HoAs in China and the US and his feedback on the theoretical framework of this book. Professor Paul Romer brought to my attention the general implications of my project on the political economy of entitlements. Chapter 6 is based on a paper I coauthored with Professor Yu Zeng at the PKU School of Government. I thank him for consenting to my use of the paper in the chapter.

I'd also like to thank the following professors for serving as commentators on this project at various institutions: Avinash K. Dixit and Rory Truex at Princeton University, Jacques deLisle and Jiangyu Wang at National University of Singapore, Laura Underkuffler at Cornell University, Ya-Wen Lei at The University of Michigan, and Chun Peng at PKU. I'd also like to thank Professor Don Clarke who – when a family health emergency forced me to cancel a talk at an annual meeting of the American Association of Law Schools – volunteered to serve as both a presenter of and a commentator on Chapter 7 of this book.

This book has also benefited from the input of the following individuals: Kerry Abrams, José Alvarez, Katharine Bartlett, Vicki Been, Stuart Benjamin, Margaret Boittin, James Boyle, Curtis Bradley, Richard Briffault, Rick Brooks, Yun-chien Chang, Hao Chen, Weitseng Chen, Jerry Cohen, Nestor Davidson, Kevin Davis, Deborah A. DeMott, Michael Dowdle, Andrew Elmore, Richard Epstein, Cindy Estlund, John M. de Figueiredo, Eleanor Fox, Hualing Fu, David Garland, Brandon Garrett, Clayton Gillette, Sara Greene, Paul Haagen, Shenjing He, Xin He, Larry Helfer, Xiaoqian Hu, Sam Issacharoff, Mitchell Kane, Mike Klausner, Dan Klerman, David Law, Maggie Lemos, Daryl Levinson, Ji Li, Benjamin Liebman, Ralf Michaels, Claire Priest, Wendell Pritchett, Jed Purdy, Arti Rai, Susan Rose-Ackerman, Bill Sage, Adam Samaha, David Schleicher, Richard Schragger, Steven Schwarcz, Nadav Shoked, Neil Siegel, Stewart Sterk, Rachel Stern, Cathy Strandburg, Scott Veitch, Jeremy Waldron, Chris Webster, Susan Whiting, Saul Wilson, Yu Xie, Daniel Xu, Xu Xu, Taisu Zhang, and participants of the China Law Conference at the University of Michigan, the annual State & Local Government Law Works-in-Progress Conference, the PKU–HKU Annual Law Conference, the HKU Chinese Law Research Group Meeting, the Duke Law School Faculty Workshop, the NYU Law School Faculty Workshop, the Massachusetts Institute of Technology (MIT) Urban China Seminar, and the Inaugural Asian Law Junior Faculty Workshop (National University of Singapore).

Sifan Jiang, Junye Guo, Yuriko Harimoto, Ruona Qi, Xingfang Li, Tianyi Yang, Xiaobin Huo, Xiling Zheng, and Zhixing Liu provided superb research assistance.

For his guidance and patience in the publication process, I'd like to thank my editor at Cambridge University Press, Jog Ng. Relatedly, I'm also very grateful for constructive feedback provided by three anonymous reviewers of this book project. Needless to say, any remaining errors in this book are solely mine.

This book is dedicated to my family for their company and love. In the past six years, Carol and Ellie have moved with me multiple times across three cities before, during, and at the end of the COVID pandemic. We even spent an entire month in a Manhattan apartment without getting out once in the spring of 2020, when COVID was peaking in that city. Together with this book, such experiences have given me a deeper understanding of the meaning of home, including homeownership. I thank Carol, my wife and best friend, for her advice, patience, understanding, and unwavering support and love; my parents, who are the best parents I've ever known and who have set such a high bar for being parents; and Ellie, my seven-year-old, for being interested in her dad's book project.

Abbreviations

ACME	average causal mediation effect
BBA	Beijing Bar Association
BJHC	Application Committee for Beijing Association of Homeowners' Associations
CCP	Chinese Communist Party
CCTV	China Central Television
CtR	cooperating to resist
DoJ	Department of Justice
EIE	environmental impact evaluation
GMAO	grassroots mass autonomous organization
HoAs	homeowners' associations
HoCs	homeowners' committees
MCs	management companies
MHC	Ministry of Housing and Construction
MoC	Ministry of Construction
MoCA	Ministry of Civic Affairs
NGO	nongovernmental organization
NIMBY	not in my backyard
NPC	National People's Congress
NPCSC	National People's Congress Standing Committee
PCSC	People's Congress Standing Committee
PRC	People's Republic of China
RCs	residents' committees
RMB	renminbi
SEZ	special economic zone
SHDHC	Shanghai Department of Housing and Construction
SoE	state-owned enterprise
SPC	Supreme People's Court
SZHC	Shenzhen Center of Promoting Transparent and Harmonious Communities

Introduction

As Morris Cohen rightly pointed out in his classic essay, property is sovereignty.[1] Could associations of property owners pose a competitive threat to the sovereign Chinese state? Using Cohen's vocabulary, homeowners' *dominium* over their property could potentially challenge the state's *imperium* over individual citizens. In particular, one might expect the authoritarian Chinese state to be especially suspicious of such competition for the people's loyalties. The conventional wisdom is that the *imperium* must be held in check for a robust property system of neighbors and sharers to operate.[2] In Tocqueville's words, local community autonomy ("town liberty," in his New England-centered account of "community") is rare and fragile because local institutions can "scarcely resist a strong and enterprising government."[3]

It is widely asserted that authoritarian regimes are hostile to the development of self-governed, autonomous civic organizations, and thus often pit neighbors and groups against one another.[4] On the face of it, China is no exception in this regard, with civic organizations routinely suppressed, eliminated, marginalized, or assimilated.[5] Their only chance for survival in China, if any, is said to be the fragmentation of the authoritarian state.[6] This conventional wisdom, however, is challenged by the apparent durability and prevalence of homeowners' associations (HoAs) in China. Given that China has one of the highest homeownership rates in the world,[7] its 400 million middle-class homeowners constitute the most numerous – and mainstream – group in the country. Homeowners' associations have participated in the national legislative process,[8] litigated in the Supreme People's Court (SPC),[9] and, most importantly, combated powerful government and real estate interests nationwide to take control of their own neighborhoods. This ongoing democratic revolution taking place in hundreds of thousands of neighborhoods across China is as yet incomplete. Nevertheless, it is fair to say that the development of HoAs has already fundamentally changed how Chinese neighborhoods and cities are governed.

Condominium ownership arose in Shenzhen, China, in the late 1980s and is the major legal form of urban housing ownership under China's Property Law and Civil Code, as well as the primary asset of the country's 400 million-strong middle class.[10] It consists of the individual ownership of units and the joint ownership of the common areas and facilities in condominium complexes,[11] creating hundreds of thousands of commons in urban China.[12]

How is the party-state to react to the emergence of such urban commons? Theoretically, it has three options: (1) direct administration: local governments can themselves provide public services to and govern urban neighborhoods[13]; (2) corporatist authoritarianism: local governments can grant real estate management companies the *de facto* power to manage them[14]; and (3) homeowner self-governance: local governments can grant homeowners the power to govern themselves.[15] The first two options appear more consistent than the third with the party-state's tradition of monopolistic control, as both government agencies and real estate management companies have hierarchical structures that can be readily commanded and controlled by the state. However, direct administration has proved to be costly, and corporatist authoritarianism suffers from a principal–agent problem: management companies tend to abuse their power in the absence of effective supervision. In fact, the number of disputes between management companies and homeowners has exploded in the past three decades.[16]

HoAs emerged as a market practice to empower homeowners to resolve common problems and were quickly picked up by the government for the purposes of protecting housing consumers' rights, and relieving itself of the burden of neighborhood governance, such as the disciplining of developers and their management companies.[17] From the 1990s until very recently, city governments across China rely on revenue they collect from selling land to developers who then build and sell apartments to hundreds of millions of housing consumers whose rights need to be honored to a certain degree to sustain the market.

Homeowner self-governance constitutes a form of basic democracy, which means collective self-government without committing to conventional liberal values,[18] and poses a tricky dilemma for the party-state. On the one hand, it can relieve the party-state of the burden of trying to govern hundreds of thousands of complex neighborhoods that, if badly handled, could undermine the party's legitimacy simply through incompetence. On the other hand, independent civic organizations may threaten the party leadership both within and beyond residential neighborhoods. How is the party-state to empower homeowners while maintaining control?

The national authority has adopted two approaches. First, national law can control the cost of homeowner decision-making by regulating voting procedures such as adjusting voting quorum and majority requirements. Second, as it has happened since 2019, the party has tried to establish its organization and leadership in HoAs.[19] The party-state's ideal for HoAs is to "have the cake and eat it too." The conundrum, however, is that too much control would deprive HoAs of the capacity to govern neighborhoods effectively.

At the local level, I have discovered divergent paths of neighborhood democratization. In Shanghai, 94 percent of condominium communities have established HoAs,[20] compared with 41 percent in Shenzhen[21] and only 12 percent in Beijing.[22] What is the reason for the stark differences in HoA development across the three cities? National law grants local governments the power to "guide and assist" (指导和协助) the establishment of HoAs,[23] and yet local governments in Beijing, Shanghai, and Shenzhen have exercised that power very differently owing to the differing degrees of risk to social stability posed by homeowner self-governance and varying degrees of state capacity in urban governance. Correspondingly, what property rights homeowners claim and how they claim those rights are a function of the effectiveness, or lack thereof, of the local states and laws in supporting neighborhood self-governance.

The previously mentioned tale of the three cities also demonstrates that a highly capable local state that has the administrative capacity to discipline its frontline employees and the judicial capacity to adjudicate neighborhood disputes, facing an intermediate degree of risk, can make institutional reforms to accommodate grassroots democracy.

Whether a community can be allowed freedom and choice while the party-state retains its monopoly on power is "the key question in China's central dilemma."[24] It is posited in this book that even the party-state demands neighborhood democracy due to its own limits in informational, financial, and human resources in governing a society based on individual property rights and a market economy.[25] Chinese neighborhoods satisfy all of the three factors that David Stasavage attributes the emergence of early democracy in human history to[26]: (1) such neighborhoods are small-scale settings that enable regular meetings of their members, though as I will discuss in this book, the cost of holding such meetings and the rules regulating the cost vary and contribute to the different HoA rates in different Chinese cities; (2) the party-state has inadequate information about residential neighborhoods as they are often gated communities and has not succeeded in establishing its own organizations in each HoA; and (3) homeowners can do without the party-state in their neighborhoods, whereas the party-state needs homeowners to contribute human and financial resources to deliver public services in such neighborhoods.

On the other hand, neighborhood democratization has indeed posed risks to the party-state's monopoly of power. It seems that the party cannot achieve two goals simultaneously: improving its legitimacy through effective neighborhood self-governance and controlling such self-governance by imposing on it the party's leadership and containing it to the boundaries of neighborhoods and the spheres of real estate management.

This book is divided into three parts. Part I includes two chapters laying out the theoretical arguments of this book. Chapter 1 defines the authoritarian commons. Chapter 2 defines neighborhood democratization, identifies its challenges, and argues that the success or failure of neighborhood democratization depends on how the party-state balances its demand for effective governance and the risk posed by homeowner mobilization and association.

Part II presents a tale of three cities, which represent three different paths of neighborhood democratization in urban China. Chapter 3 reveals the striking contrast across Beijing, Shanghai, and Shenzhen, introduces a framework of risk and capacity in understanding this contrast, and discusses the three styles of authoritarianism: repression in Beijing, fragmentation in Shenzhen, and coordination in Shanghai. Chapter 4 addresses one essential aspect of state capacity: the judicial capacity, and argues that local courts in Shanghai are more capable than national authorities (including the SPC), local courts in Beijing and Shenzhen, and other branches of the Shanghai municipal government in supporting neighborhood democracy. Chapter 5 examines the different dynamics of the homeowner movement in the three cities, focusing on the scope of homeowners' claims and the concomitant ways in which they claim those rights.

Part III presents further empirical evidence, both qualitative and quantitative, on the benefits and risks of HoAs to the party-state. Based on survey data, Chapter 6 reveals that democratized neighborhoods have better governing outcomes than do non-democratized ones, as evidenced by more effective homeowner control over neighborhood affairs, greater respect for democratic principles, and a higher degree of community identity. Owing to these positive outcomes, homeowner activists in democratized neighborhoods develop higher trust in their local government than do their counterparts in non-democratized neighborhoods. Most pointedly, this chapter suggests that an authoritarian regime may support neighborhood self-governance in the interest of building political trust. Chapter 7 examines the benefits of homeowner self-governance to the party-state in the context of China's COVID lockdowns, and, more importantly, the risk of the party-state's dependence on homeowners and the latter's capacity to shape key party-state policies in the same context. Chapter 8 investigates how homeowners nationwide have shelved the party-state's plan to institute party leadership in HoAs. Can the party-state "have the cake and eat it too" in neighborhood governance? It seems that the party cannot achieve two goals simultaneously: improving its legitimacy through effective neighborhood self-governance and controlling such self-governance by requiring the party's leadership. Chapter 9 discusses how homeowners' democratization efforts have gone beyond both the physical boundaries of condominiums and the virtual boundaries of property rights and real estate management, and the party-state's varied responses to such "trespasses."

The Conclusion of this book addresses the implications of this research on democracy in China and its limitations.

Part I
Theory

1

Defining the Authoritarian Commons

The extant literature on the liberal commons takes as granted secure property rights, freedom of association, and the rule of law, all of which have been the exception rather than the rule throughout human history[1] and therefore fails to explore the origin of the liberal commons (from an illiberal regime). Authoritarianism poses a fundamental challenge to, but also an opportunity to explore the origin of, the liberal commons. This chapter defines the authoritarian commons[2] by examining the tension between authoritarianism and the liberal commons – both theoretically and in the specific context of neighborhood governance in urban China.

1.1 From Liberal Commons to Authoritarian Commons

More than two decades ago, Hanoch Dagan and Michael Heller coined the term "liberal commons," which they envisioned as comprising three spheres: the sphere of individual dominion, the sphere of democratic self-governance, and the sphere of cooperation-enhancing exit.[3] In this liberal commons, the law "can help generate social expectations supportive of trust and cooperation" but only if it operates as a set of background norms and as a safety net.[4] Condominium associations, as Dagan and Heller acknowledged, constitute a typical example of the liberal commons, encompassing condominium owners' ownership of their individual units, that is, the sphere of individual dominion; their right to make decisions concerning matters beyond the walls of their own apartments but within the building and the surrounding neighborhood, over which they exercise common ownership, that is, the sphere of democratic self-governance; and, of course, their right to exit by selling their units, that is, the sphere of cooperation-enhancing exit.

Dagan and Heller did not investigate the origin of the liberal commons, probably because they assumed the freedom of association and right to vote typical of liberal democracies.[5] Similarly, although several generations of property scholars have written about homeowners and their covenants and communities, they have taken such covenants and communities as given, paying no attention to their origin. The extant literature on homeowners' associations

(HoAs) focuses on conflicts between homeowner autonomy and legal intervention.[6] It is usually only when homeowner self-governance generates negative externalities that legal intervention is justified.[7]

We cannot, however, take the liberal commons as given. Authoritarianism describes a system in which "all decisions can potentially be made by a single decision-maker, whose decisions are both formally and practically unregulated by law."[8] In line with this definition, the challenge of authoritarianism is threefold. First, it poses a challenge to secure property rights. Authoritarian regimes are known for their exploitative and extractive nature,[9] and the idea that they would protect property rights has been described as something of a cruel joke.[10] Second, authoritarianism poses a challenge to the freedom of association, the decentralized nature of which seems to be inherently incompatible with the centralized, top-down nature of authoritarianism.[11] Third, the unconstrained nature of power under authoritarianism challenges the rule of law. The conventional view is that authoritarian states are lawless.[12] Although the burgeoning literature on authoritarian legality[13] points in a different direction, it fails to explain why and when authoritarian states do or do not obey the law.

Considering the foregoing tripartite challenge, the term "authoritarian commons" sounds like an oxymoron: If the state's authority prevails over and penetrates the commons, there is no commons to speak of; if democratic self-governance prevails in the commons, there is no authoritarianism. However, with respect to the aforementioned opportunity that authoritarianism presents for our purposes, we can better understand the origin of the liberal commons if we examine its emergence in an authoritarian regime.

There are two traditions in the economic analysis of property rights: one focuses on the choice of different property forms and the other on the political institutions that define property rights. We can call the former tradition "private property law" and the latter "public property law." The pioneers of the economic analysis of property rights, as represented by Douglass North[14] and Yoram Barzel,[15] had their own theories of the state that paralleled their theories of property rights. In the past two decades, the economic analysis of property law has focused primarily on the choice of different forms of property rights,[16] with insufficient attention paid to the politics of property rights or the development of various contemporary property arrangements.[17] It is no wonder that Katrina Wyman has advocated for a supply-side theory of property rights[18] and that Roderick Hills and David Schleicher have recently proposed an "institutional turn" in property theory.[19] The theoretical ambition of the exploration of the authoritarian commons herein is to accelerate the institutional turn in property theory by returning the state to the economic analysis of property rights.

Study of the authoritarian commons also has profound implications for our understanding of development, to which both the provision of public goods and services and the establishment of a basic point of entry into the political system at the local level are essential.[20] Recent research by prominent scholars indicates that authoritarian regimes are effective at managing critical junctures in their countries' development.[21] Growth-favoring authoritarian regimes can be even better at promoting economic development than weak democracies.[22] However, these scholars still hold quite a pessimistic view of democratic development in authoritarian regimes, China, in particular, with a number of prominent legal scholars[23] and economists[24] actually predicting the failure of that country's democratic transition. Like the seemingly oxymoronic nature of the term "authoritarian commons," the democratization of a successful authoritarian regime such as China's party-state is on the face of it a self-defeating mission.[25] Understanding the dynamics of the authoritarian commons and the interaction between state and society in such a setting might help us to understand the role of the authoritarian state in political transition.

1.2 Residential Neighborhoods as Commons

Condominium ownership in China consists of the individual ownership of units and the joint ownership of the common areas and facilities in condominium complexes,[26] creating hundreds of thousands of urban commons[27] in Chinese cities. To be clear, Chinese residential neighborhoods under the condominium ownership regime are not open-access commons, "in which anyone at all may use a resource and no one may be excluded,"[28] as described in Garrett Hardin's seminal paper "The Tragedy of the Commons."[29] It is clear in such neighborhoods who shares the power to decide and the right to benefit from the use of the resources therein. At the same time, however, similar to Elinor Ostrom's "common pool resources," the resource system is "sufficiently large ... to make it costly to exclude potential beneficiaries from obtaining benefits from use."[30] Using Carol Rose's terms, it is a commons to insiders and private property to outsiders.[31] What happens to such urban commons? Despite the robust literature on the self-organized management of natural resources, scholars have paid insufficient attention to polycentric governance in the urban context.[32]

Common property rights in China's condominium neighborhoods include not only the right to manage common space and facilities but also the right to govern the neighborhood, including owners' rights to establish their own associations, elect their own committees, and manage such common affairs as maintenance funding, changing management companies and fees, and regulating community members' behavior.

More specifically, there are three aspects of residential neighborhood governance. The first concerns control over the common space and facilities in the neighborhood, such as parking space and elevators. A single parking spot in the megacities under study can sell for up to half a million RMB (about US$62,500).[33] Parking spaces are thus valuable assets and have been subject to contest both in and out of court, particularly in Shenzhen.[34] Local governments have a direct interest in maintaining control over the common space in neighborhoods, some of it for use for municipal facilities and, in some instances, for the construction of a municipal road running through a neighborhood.[35] The second aspect of control is building regulations. In Chinese cities, most condominium buildings are towers that are pre-built before buyers move in. The major issue here is the so-called illegal construction, including enclosed balconies and rooftop (built by apartment owners on the top floor) or underground (built by apartment owners on the ground floor) structures.[36] The final aspect is behavior regulation, including the regulation of residents' activities within their own apartments and those in the neighborhood's common space. Examples of the former activities include making nonresidential use of residential apartments, ranging from running a children's play/study group for profit to establishing a corporate office to engaging in paid sexual transactions.[37] Examples of the latter are square dancing in common areas, a common cause of noise complaints, and unleashed dogs that can pose a threat to safety, particularly for children.[38]

All three aspects concern not only homeowners' property rights and daily life but also the major functions of local governments and the state's spatial control. They concern how Chinese homeowners live with one another and with the authoritarian state. In this sense, HoAs pertain to both the social contract among homeowners and that between homeowners and the state. It is no wonder that Chinese people sometimes refer to HoAs as the "government in the neighborhood,"[39] and the covenants passed by homeowners as "neighborhood constitutions."[40] Chinese homeowners establish HoAs through majority resolutions, which also create a covenant, decision-making rules, and elect a homeowners' committee ("HoC").[41] In general, each housing unit has one vote.[42]

All legally established HoAs have gone through democratic election procedures, and the validity of such procedures is regularly contested in local courts.[43] Local governments can hinder and slow down such democratic processes,[44] and occasionally manipulate such processes,[45] but they are not able to force homeowners to vote if homeowners do not believe that the elections are genuine. An example of the government's inability to mobilize homeowners to vote and to participate without giving them authentic autonomy is residents' committees (居民委员会, RCs), which are supposed to be elected according to the Chinese Constitution. However, genuine elections and resident participation are rare.[46]

It is this legally sanctioned right to vote and to form associations that makes HoAs the most exciting form of grassroots democracy in China.[47] As one leading homeowner in Beijing said to me, "'One person, one vote' is really implemented in only two situations [in China]: villagers' committees and homeowners' associations …, in rural China, conventional authority and [clan-like] organizations … are still powerful and might control villages. The best hope to develop a civil society is through homeowners' associations of the urban middle class."[48]

Theorists from Tocqueville to Putnam generally agree that the daily practice of autonomous associations and democratic decision-making is important to developing and maintaining democracy at the national level.[49] Since the 1990s, scholars and policymakers have applauded village elections in rural China, which have actually turned out to be more complicated than originally, and rather rosily, imagined.[50] Needless to say, such grassroots elections are just the beginning of a long-winded process of democratization.[51] Nevertheless, such election practices and self-governance are particularly valuable in an authoritarian regime to nurture the hearts and minds of citizens for a future democracy.[52] As evidence of their value, my questionnaire survey reveals that homeowners who have actively participated in neighborhood self-governance have greater respect for democratic principles and are more likely to comply with a legally passed majority decision even if they were on the losing side of the voting process, than homeowners who have not.[53]

2

Neighborhood Democratization

Neighborhood democratization refers to homeowners' efforts to create liberal commons in an authoritarian state, or, more specifically, to their wresting of control over their neighborhoods through democratic elections from management companies (MCs) and developers, whose neighborhood dominance local governments often acquiesce in for a variety of reasons. This chapter defines neighborhood democratization, identifies its challenges, and argues that the success or failure of neighborhood democratization depends on how the party-state balances its demand for effective governance and the risk posed by homeowner mobilization and association.

2.1 Institutional Setting and Choice in Neighborhood Governance

There are three major categories of stakeholders in the governance of China's urban residential neighborhoods: homeowners and their associations, MCs and developers, and the street-level governments and residents' committees (RCs) under their control. A street-level government (街道办, *jiedaoban*) is established by each district government (区政府, *quzhengfu*), which is in turn created by the city government, to administer public affairs within its designated territory.

Such administration often requires coordination with other departments and agencies within the government. Multiple agencies are involved in neighborhood governance, including functional agencies, particularly those in charge of urban planning and land administration and those in charge of social stability, and territorial agencies, primarily street-level government offices. All such agencies are under the leadership of the city government.

The territory and population governed by street-level government offices vary both within and across cities. The small offices that I visited govern around 50,000 people within a territory of 2–3 km^2,[1] whereas large ones can govern up to half a million people over a territory of more than 25 km^2.[2] One residential neighborhood in a Chinese megacity includes, on average, 1,000–2,000 apartment units in multiple towers resulting from a single development project, although large such neighborhoods can include more than 10,000 apartment units. The land use rights certificates of these development projects determine the boundaries of residential neighborhoods,[3] which constitute the basic units of street-level governments.

How should a street-level government manage the residential neighborhoods under its control? A street-level government can be analogized to a firm that needs to deliver public goods to homeowners in return for social stability and loyalty. It can provide such services through direct administration, by granting the power to do so to MCs, or by granting homeowners the right to self-governance.

First, a street-level government can opt for direct administration, generally by establishing governmental branches at or near the neighborhood level. This is the approach that the party-state has taken since 1954, establishing RCs to govern one or several residential neighborhoods, depending on the neighborhood size.[4] Although the PRC Constitution promises RCs as a form of direct democracy,[5] apart from a few exceptions such democracy has rarely been fulfilled. Most of the time, the government has no intention of holding real elections,[6] and neither are residents seriously interested in running for RCs.[7] Although legally defined as "mass autonomous organizations" (群众自治组织), RCs rely on the government for funding and personnel, and are essentially the lowest tier of the party-state's bureaucratic pyramid.[8] Direct administration results in typical authoritarian governance at the neighborhood level. Residents' committees are therefore not accountable to the residents under their jurisdiction, but rather to the street-level governments immediately above them. They can help the government to monitor and control homeowners' associations (HoAs) but are not capable of direct governance owing to their limited financial and personnel resources and limited influence among homeowners.

The second option is to rely on the market to manage residential neighborhoods. Management companies charge management fees and provide services ranging from the cleaning of communal areas and building maintenance to neighborhood security and the enforcement of parking rules and building codes. These corporate entities are well organized and resourceful and can provide public services and maintain social order within residential neighborhoods. They are often subsidiaries of the developers that originally built the condominium complexes. I characterize this alliance between the local state and MCs as a corporatist authoritarian regime. In Chinese cities, MCs often profit more from their control over the common space in a neighborhood, by, for example, leasing parking spots, operating swimming pools, and sometimes even running for-profit schools or other businesses, than from collecting management fees. As a result, their primary concern is generally retaining their control over common property, meaning they have little incentive to provide neighborhood services. Developers and their appointed MCs also have little incentive to form HoAs, whose main responsibilities are supervising and monitoring MC performance or, even worse, replacing them with another MC.[9]

Even when they have to acquiesce in HoA establishment, they often manipulate the process and dominate the association through bribery and even violence.

This leaves the government with the third choice: granting homeowners the power to govern themselves, which can avoid the cost of direct administration and the principal–agent problem in the corporatist authoritarian regime. However, HoAs and their organizations are independent of the party-state and potentially pose a threat to its monopoly on power.

Figure 2.1 illustrates the governance structure in urban China in conjunction with the three governance options available to street-level governments. Before homeowners successfully exercise their legal rights to establish HoAs and elect homeowners' committee (HoCs), urban residential neighborhoods

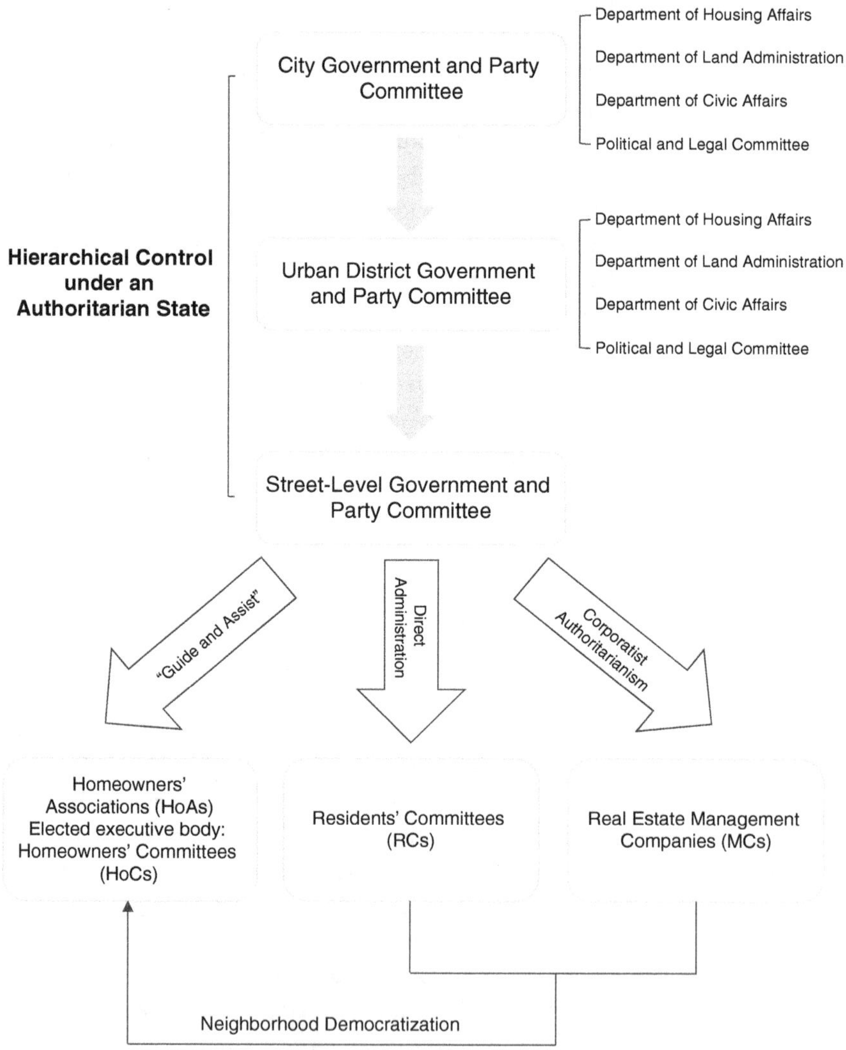

Figure 2.1 The neighborhood governance structure in urban China

are controlled by MCs with the acquiescence and implicit support of the RCs and street-level government concerned.

2.2 The Definition and Process of Neighborhood Democratization

Neighborhood democratization refers to homeowners' wresting of control of their neighborhoods from MCs and developers, whose neighborhood dominance formal street-level governments often acquiesce in for a variety of political, economic, bureaucratic, and, at times, corrupt reasons.

The lack of control over their living space frustrates and angers many homeowners. Theoretically speaking, homeowners have two options if they are unhappy with the governance of their neighborhood: they can leave the neighborhood or protest and change the management regime.[10] The first option, that is, to exit, is costly, and alternative residential opportunities are limited.[11] With respect to the second, that is, voice, homeowners cannot claim their communal property rights individually. Management companies refuse to deal with individual homeowners, as "a single homeowner cannot represent all [homeowners]."[12] According to the law, however, they do have to respond to HoAs and HoCs.[13] In other words, the establishment and operation of HoAs constitute the main way for homeowners to take control of their neighborhoods. Democratization takes place in China's urban neighborhoods where homeowners "are forced to get along"[14] to fight for their property rights.

Prior to HoA establishment, the developer controls the neighborhood and appoints a so-called "preliminary MC," which is often affiliated with the developer. Once the total area of delivered apartments exceeds 50 percent of the total housing area in the development, the developer is required by law to submit a roster of homeowners and other relevant information on the neighborhood to the street-level government in preparation for the first homeowners' assembly.[15] A group of homeowners, if they represent more than 5 percent of the total number of homeowners in the development, can also apply to the street-level government for an election to establish an HoA.[16]

The street-level government, in conjunction with its RCs on the ground, decides whether and when to establish a preparatory committee and appoints the committee members subject to a number of legal constraints. The director of the preparatory committee is often a street-level government official or party secretary of the corresponding RC. The developer has one official representative on the committee. At least two-thirds of committee members should be homeowners.[17] After a preparatory committee holds a successful homeowners' assembly and election, the HoA and the elected HoC still need to register with the street-level government. Figure 2.2 summarizes the overall process from real estate development to HoA establishment.

Figure 2.2 The process of neighborhood democratization

In reality, developers rarely initiate the process of establishing HoAs as required by law. Before such establishment, developers and their affiliated MCs control the neighborhood, whereas afterward they can be "fired" and kicked out of the neighborhood. Noncooperation and resistance from developers and their MCs mean that the first requisite information, a roster of homeowners, is usually unavailable. Homeowners thus need to find their own way of collecting such information. The government can require the developer to submit the information, as the law requires. Whether it is willing to do so, however, is an open question and context-specific, as is whether the government establishes a preparatory committee, as the law requires, and which members it chooses for that committee. Sometimes, there may be an insufficient number of capable homeowner volunteers, and the government may need to search the neighborhood for volunteers. Even if a preparatory committee is established, there is still a big question mark over whether homeowner activists can obtain sufficient votes to pass a resolution/charter and elect an HoC in the face of opposition from the MC and its homeowner supporters. The government can either encourage division among homeowners or coordinate various forces in the neighborhood to establish an HoA. Even after the assembly and election, the government still holds the key to the official recognition of the elected HoC. According to law, HoCs need to register with the government, which can decline the registration and/or challenge the validity of the election or the qualifications of HoC members.[18]

At every step, frontline government officials have a choice about whether to support or hinder the process of neighborhood democratization. Their choice depends on two things: first, their estimation of the risk involved, which depends on what homeowners claim and how they claim it, and, second, their ability to execute their choice.

The foregoing process does not touch upon what HoAs can do after their establishment. Are HoAs legal persons? Can they participate in litigation, suing and being sued?[19] Can HoAs own property, open a bank account, and become a member of other associations? The national law has these questions unaddressed. The Supreme People's Court (SPC) has allowed HoAs to participate in litigation, but only to sue others, not to be sued.[20] The rationale is that HoAs cannot own property and therefore have no capacity to take on legal liabilities. The lack of legal capacity in external civil and social interactions, not to mention political participation, limits the potential of HoAs as independent organizations. In the face of such legal ambiguity, different cities empower HoAs to differing degrees.

2.3 Challenges to Neighborhood Democratization

The establishment of HoAs faces two challenges. The first is the collective action problem among homeowners: Neighborhood governance is a public good and many, if not most, homeowners prefer free riding to devoting themselves to the tedious, unpaid, and often thankless job of neighborhood organization. The party-state could alleviate the collective action problem by identifying and supporting homeowner volunteers if homeowners prove themselves trustworthy and deserving of institutional support by accepting the legal boundaries of their property rights. More importantly, the party-state can reduce the cost of collective action by changing the legal rules of homeowner decision-making and disciplining its frontline agents to follow law and regulations to support HoAs rather than colluding with MCs to oppose HoAs.

The second challenge is the coordination problems among homeowners and between homeowners and the party-state. The party-state faces the choice of whether to accommodate homeowners' self-governance demands, whereas homeowners need to decide how far they want to go with their claims. Both prefer to push the boundaries and maintain as much control as they can. On the other hand, both prefer cooperation to conflict in this mixed-motive game of neighborhood governance. The question is which form of cooperation to coordinate upon. Homeowners also need to coordinate with one another about the scope of their rights claims: Some are primarily concerned with the preservation of the value of their home, to which management service is crucial, and are thus happy to adhere to the law, whereas others are politically driven and seek to challenge the legal boundaries and even the authoritarian state.

2.3.1 The Collective Action Problem

Although subsidies of up to RMB 500 per month are available in some cases,[21] membership of HoCs, the executive body of HoAs, is generally unpaid. It is also quite common for HoC members to refuse any available subsidies, no matter how small, because they do not want others to think that they are working for money.[22] Further complicating the situation, many homeowners work as volunteers or even lead neighborhood democratization efforts without being officially HoC members. Given the collective action problem and the option of free-riding, one might ask, as Nobel Laureate Elinor Ostrom did in Beijing in 2004, why so many Chinese homeowners have participated in a movement to democratize their neighborhoods despite the significant monetary and non-monetary costs involved, as well as how any condominium neighborhood has succeeded in forming its own association and electing its own HoC.[23]

Homeowner activists often get involved without fully realizing the scale of sacrifice required: long hours of work, sometimes at night, and even risks to personal security. Once a homeowner becomes involved, however, he or she usually finds neighbor comrades, who, although they may constitute only a small percentage of homeowners in the community, offer support to one another.

Some homeowner activists have connected with their peers in other communities within their city and even nationwide. They have formed homeowners' forums online and WeChat groups in which they debate one another, share knowledge, information, and expertise, and provide one another with emotional support. These outlets and forms of mutual support afford homeowner activists – who often refer to themselves as "lonely heroes" – the strength to carry on serving the community without pay, and sometimes without perceived understanding or support from their communities.[24] Homeowners in Shanghai refer to the overall process as a "pit": Once you jump in, it is difficult to get out.[25]

Nevertheless, the majority of homeowners remain a passive audience, or what their activist neighbors call "keyboard revolutionaries," who rarely show up for rallies or take real action but are very generous with their praise and sometimes even money. Voluntary donations are routine and necessary in the process of establishing HoAs because, before their establishment, MCs control all income from the community (in the form of management fees and revenue from parking lots and other common-property facilities).

In other words, the free-rider problem is still a major challenge to the growing homeowner movement in China. On average, less than 10 percent of homeowners in a given neighborhood are activists for self-governance; about 30 percent are their followers and cheerleaders.[26] The remaining 60 percent include the silent majority and, sometimes even worse, homeowners who are connected to or bought out by the MC.[27] However, establishing an HoA requires majority approval from all homeowners in the neighborhood.

2.3.2 The Coordination Problems

Coordination is different from cooperation, though they constitute two facets of collaboration.[28] Cooperation focuses on commitment and alignment of interests, but even in a situation of perfect alignment of interests, partners still need to coordinate effectively to complete their joint or individual tasks.[29] In the classic game of Prisoner's Dilemma, the two players face the problem of *cooperation* that fails because of their misaligned incentives.[30] Driving on the right or the left side is a pure *coordination* game. The problem in coordination games is not misaligned incentives, but the fact that there are multiple ways to match behavior in a way that is best for both or at least better than some alternative each wants to avoid.[31]

There are two coordination problems in neighborhood democratization. That between homeowners is finding a way to coordinate with one another to claim the same rights and adopt the same strategy. Only united homeowners have the potential to force the local government to compromise. The second coordination problem is this: What property rights claims can be acceptable to both homeowners and the local party-state? For the latter, granting homeowners the right to govern themselves is a double-edged sword: Although doing so can improve neighborhood governance and relieve the state of the burden of direct administration or dealing with conflicts between MCs and homeowners, homeowner mobilization can also threaten its authority.

For homeowner activists, the challenge is to mobilize ordinary homeowners to join their efforts. Only by forming a consensus among the majority of homeowners in the neighborhood can they pass a resolution to establish an HoA and gain some bargaining power with the local state.[32] It is not unusual for homeowners to disagree with one another over the scope of their rights and the proper strategy to adopt in the face of an unsupportive government official. Whether they can successfully coordinate with one another to reach a consensus is thus key to the success of homeowner self-governance.

According to HB, a leading activist in Shanghai, you need to "demonstrate your power" to force the government to cooperate and implement the law. Power, in HB's view, is the ability to mobilize and organize homeowners to take uniform action. QB, a leading activist in Beijing, also emphasized the importance of organizing homeowners to claim their rights. The citywide homeowner organization in Shenzhen, too, saw bridging the gaps with homeowners and promoting conversation among them as its core tasks.[33]

How do homeowners know whether the local party-state is actually willing to support neighborhood self-governance? How does the local party-state ensure that homeowners want nothing more than quality neighborhood services? For example, homeowners might believe that they need to engage in as much mobilization as possible to become sufficiently powerful to force the local party-state to recognize their right to self-governance. However, the local party-state might view mobilization beyond the neighborhood level as a political threat, and therefore be unwilling to make any compromise. Similarly, homeowners might believe their claims to the parking space and roads within their neighborhoods to be perfectly legal and reasonable, whereas the local party-state might be concerned that its influence in the neighborhood is being undermined by greedy homeowners. If homeowners and the local party-state cannot coordinate successfully to reach a consensus, it would be difficult indeed to achieve neighborhood democratization.

2.4 The Authoritarian Dilemma

Homeowner self-governance poses a dilemma for China's party-state. On the one hand, the party-state has traditionally opposed the creation of mediating institutions that could act as rivals to the party-state, both within the boundaries of individual neighborhoods and beyond them at the city or even national level. On the other hand, homeowner self-governance can relieve the party-state of the burden of trying to govern hundreds of thousands of complex neighborhood problems that, if badly handled, could undermine party-state legitimacy simply through incompetence. The party-state wants to maintain control over governance free from any resistance from competitors. At the same time, it wants to deliver services effectively to ensure that middle-class residents do not become dissatisfied with the party-state's performance.[34] The problem is that total party-state control risks eroding party-state legitimacy simply through incompetence, whereas delegating service delivery to independent-minded middle-class residents can endanger party-state control. Homeownership is a common identity that has the potential to unite Chinese people across different backgrounds and sectors.[35] A home is the primary investment for most Chinese households,[36] which can motivate hundreds of millions of them to demand protection of their property rights and good governance both within and beyond neighborhoods.

Within residential neighborhoods, even if the party-state is willing to support homeowner self-governance, it still wants to maintain a certain degree of power for such practical reasons as securing neighborhood space for electricity lines, water pipes, roads,[37] and other municipal facilities and implementing municipal policies such as recycling.[38]

Beyond residential neighborhoods, the party-state is concerned that independent-minded homeowners may move from within-neighborhood mobilization and organization to cross-neighborhood, citywide, and even nationwide mobilization, a nightmare scenario for the party-state. Homeowner mobilization beyond the neighborhood level has already occurred in China. As Lee Fennell and other property law scholars have noted, the value of residential property has become unbound from the four corners of property, and homeowners pay close attention to the space beyond their property boundaries.[39] Property owners' concerns over property values have contributed to the rise of the NIMBY (Not in My Backyard) movement in China. It has become increasingly common for middle-class property owners to challenge urban planning decisions, such as those related to the construction of nearby chemical factories, public transit facilities, and garbage-disposal sites, sometimes through public protests.[40] Needless to say, an independent organization with 400 million middle-class members would pose a fundamental challenge to the party-state's authority, and therefore must be killed in the cradle. Homeowner activists have already attempted to run for local people's congresses in both Beijing and Shenzhen. Leading homeowner activists in Beijing even got involved in unrelated areas of political mobilization, such as an unprecedented attempt for a *real* election of the Beijing Bar Association in 2008.[41] It is out of concern over homeowner mobilization beyond neighborhood boundaries that the Beijing city government has refused to approve the establishment of a citywide homeowner organization. Such an organization once existed without legal authorization and mobilized hundreds of thousands of homeowners across the city to challenge the Beijing city government directly[42] and across the country to change the Property Law.[43]

The authoritarian dilemma in balancing the benefits and risks of HoAs was well reflected in the promulgation of China's first national regulation that legalized HoAs in 2003. Since then, the party-state has fully recognized HoAs in its first Property Law in 2007 and first Civil Code in 2020. In the meantime, to maintain control of HoAs, Chinese law has left the legal personality of HoAs unspecified, limiting their ability to engage in external civil, legal, and political activities, and increased the cost of decision-making for HoAs from 2003 onward.

Real estate development is a crucial part of the land-based local finance system in China. It originated in Shenzhen in the 1980s and remains the dominant model of local government finance until the recent housing market crisis. China first started selling publicly owned housing to individuals in the early 1990s,[44] and it then launched a full housing market by leaving both housing supply and demand to the market in 1998.[45] Since then, the real estate industry has become a "pillar industry" of the Chinese economy.[46] Homeowners' associations first emerged as a market practice to empower homeowners to solve common problems in condominium buildings in Shenzhen, and were then quickly picked up by local governments in Shenzhen and Shanghai as a way to discipline developers and their MCs in the 1990s.[47] To promote the development of a "mature" real estate market by allowing housing consumers to discipline real estate companies through their market power, the Ministry of Construction (MoC) moved to legalize HoAs from the 1990s to the early 2000s.[48]

The 2003 Regulations on Real Estate Management (The 2003 Regulations) for the first time fully recognized HoAs and granted homeowners the power to govern their own neighborhoods by establishing HoAs, electing HoCs, and making decisions through majority voting, including on which MC to hire. The purpose of the 2003 Regulations, as laid out in Article 1, was to "regularize neighborhood management activities, protect the legal rights of homeowners and MCs, and improve the people's living and work environment."[49] To clarify, the 2003 Regulations were about the real estate management market, not concerned with local government reform. Nevertheless, it indeed accelerated a revolution in neighborhood governance by recognizing homeowners' right to govern their own neighborhoods through democratic mechanisms.

The Ministry of Civic Affairs (MoCA), which was in charge of RCs, lodged a protest, arguing that HoAs constituted a new kind of "grassroots mass autonomous organization (GMAO),"[50] which is a term used by the PRC Constitution to describe RCs, therefore competing with RCs for political power. It further argued that the 2003 Regulations either had no authority to create HoAs or that they should be part of RCs, the only GMAO in urban areas recognized by the PRC Constitution.[51] This MoCA's protest posed a fundamental challenge to the existence of HoAs. As the sociologist Michael Mann has argued, the state is merely and essentially a place and a territorially centralized form of organization.[52] The very definition of the state is concentrated in its authoritative power over a delimited territory.[53] By asserting and exercising control over a given neighborhood, HoAs are indeed contesting the power of the authoritarian state.

The MoC made an effort to distinguish HoAs from RCs. It argued that their responsibilities were fundamentally different: RCs were the product of residents exercising their political rights, whereas HoAs were concerned with real estate management and property rights. The latter were a necessary organization to enable homeowners to exercise their collective property rights. The MoC acknowledged that the exercise of property rights by homeowners might exert an impact on public affairs and gave public safety as an example. Homeowners can make arrangements to protect the safety of their apartments, but neighborhood security falls within the scope of power of both RCs and the police. Accordingly, HoAs should work with RCs and the police on matters related to neighborhood security. It was left unclear, however, how HoAs should work with RCs and other government agencies such as the police.[54] Some homeowners have argued that HoAs should replace RCs.[55]

The MoC might be right that RCs and HoAs are different in nature, the former being political and the latter economic. Nevertheless, they govern the same neighborhoods on the same neighborhood affairs, and therefore HoAs pose a threat to RCs, and more broadly, the party-state's rule and control in urban neighborhoods. Until today, the relationship between RCs and HoAs is yet to be fully resolved.

At the time, however, the priority was to promote the development of the real estate industry, which required the preservation of market incentives, including the protection of housing consumers' rights. The industry's development gave rise to an explosive increase in neighborhood management conflicts. The MoC and leaders of the State Council, that is, the Chinese central government, viewed HoAs as a way to protect homeowner rights, promote the balanced development of the real estate market by empowering consumers, and relieve local governments of the burden of governance. Accordingly, the solution to the MoCA's challenge was not to abolish HoAs but to recognize the tension between HoAs and RCs. The final version of the 2003 Regulations added two articles: Article 19 stated that HoAs should not make any decision or conduct any activities unrelated to real estate management,[56] and Article 20 that HoAs should work with and support RCs and accept their supervision and monitoring.[57]

The party-state has had different priorities at different stages of development. In the early 2000s, the priority was clearly economic development, of which real estate was a pillar industry. Later on, the party-state started to emphasize the importance of a harmonious society and HoAs' role in promoting social stability.

The 2007 Property Law, which is a private law and was the first property law in the PRC to protect individual property rights and promote economic development, incorporated the main content concerning HoAs in the 2003

Regulations in Chapter 6, with minor revisions.[58] The 2007 Property Law, which underwent seven drafts before being passed amid a widely circulated debate about both its general direction, such as whether it was constitutional/socialist,[59] and specific institutions, such as the scope of homeowners' common property rights, was a landmark legislation in the PRC history.[60] The Property Law's legislative status as a basic law is much higher than that of the 2003 Regulations, which is an administrative ordinance. The 2007 Property Law therefore granted HoAs the highest legal recognition possible and had since its passage become a foundational document of the homeowner movement until the passage of the Civil Code in 2020.

The 2007 Property Law does not, however, clarify whether HoAs have a legal personality and, correspondingly, whether they can own property, open bank accounts, participate in litigation, and even form their own associations.[61] It turns out that for HoAs to prosper, such organizational rules are as important as legal recognition. In other words, the 2007 Property Law specifies how homeowners can form their own associations but leaves blank the legal status of those associations, and therefore the leeway the government has to control such associations' ability to play an independent role in external civil, legal, and political activities.

Moreover, despite its full recognition of HoAs, the 2007 Property Law increased the cost of decision-making of HoAs. The 2003 Regulations required over half of HoA members to participate in a vote and over half of the participating members to agree on a resolution.[62] The 2007 Property Law took a stricter approach by requiring over half of HoA members to agree on a resolution,[63] which made the establishment of HoAs quite difficult but for local deviations in cities such as Shanghai and Shenzhen.[64]

The Civil Code of China, which was promulgated in 2020 and replaced the 2007 Property Law, failed in its mission-on-paper to reduce the cost of homeowner decision-making,[65] reflecting the party-state's mutually conflicting considerations in governing HoAs.

Part II
A Tale of Three Cities

3

The Three Styles of Authoritarianism

My fieldwork uncovers the differing dynamics of the homeowner self-governance movement in three cities over the past two decades: in Shanghai, 94 percent of condominium communities have established homeowners' associations (HoAs),[1] compared with 41 percent in Shenzhen[2] and only 12 percent in Beijing.[3] These figures are especially intriguing given that the Chinese homeowner movement originated in Beijing and Shenzhen, culminating in such path-breaking achievements as the organization of a nationwide campaign to shape the content of the Property Law in 2007[4] and litigation in the Supreme People's Court (SPC) in 2013,[5] respectively. Homeowners in both cities have even attempted to run for seats in the local people's congresses, a move that was widely applauded for its democratic implications both inside and outside China.[6] In contrast, such overtly political events have rarely occurred in Shanghai. What, then, does the exceptionally high percentage of HoAs in that city mean? Are those associations inactive or – as some critics both inside and outside Shanghai have contended – puppets of the Shanghai government? My empirical investigation reveals that, on the contrary, the HoAs in Shanghai are the most active and capable in terms of neighborhood self-governance among the three megacities under study.[7] In summary, in both percentage and capacity/vitality terms, Shanghai homeowners have taken the lead in neighborhood democratization and self-governance, with Shenzhen coming a distant second, and Beijing lagging far behind.

What is the reason for the stark differences in HoA development across the three cities? There is always a possibility that independent civic organizations will challenge the party-state's authority, and there is no way to eliminate that possibility at a theoretical level. On the ground, however, repeated interactions between local officials and homeowner activists may result in some degree of trust and a reciprocal relationship whereby local officials support homeowner self-governance in exchange for homeowners' support for the party-state and adherence to legal boundaries. Accordingly, the solution to the dilemma of authoritarian governance lies in the local interpersonal relationships between frontline party cadres and homeowners. If frontline party cadres can develop a long-term reciprocal relationship with homeowners, then an equilibrium of a cooperative relationship may arise: Frontline officials help homeowner activists to overcome the collective action problem and support neighborhood self-governance in exchange for homeowners being "good citizens."[8]

This solution of reciprocal governance is inherently local and subject to constraints on the ground. The first constraint is how the city government perceives the risk of homeowner self-governance. In Beijing, China's political center, government officials are likely to be more sensitive to social stability concerns than their counterparts in the two other cities under study. This is not to say that Beijing city government officials cannot see the benefits of burden relief through neighborhood self-governance but rather that in their preference social stability weighs more heavily than it does in the other cities. Accordingly, the Beijing city government may well adopt a more hostile approach to neighborhood self-governance and be less likely to support it than the governments in the two other cities.

The second constraint is whether frontline city government agents have an incentive and the capacity to develop a long-term reciprocal relationship with homeowners.[9] Frontline agents often collude with management companies and oppose neighborhood democratization. The success of reciprocal governance depends on to what extent a city government can change incentives of such agents to support HoAs, which requires structural reform and judicial capacity, and depends on the financial and human resources a city government has.

In this chapter I present a framework with two variables, the risk to social stability and state capacity, to explain the different types of authoritarianism, and examine three aspects of the role of the local state in the development of HoAs. First, how does the local state handle homeowners' initiatives in establishing and operating HoAs? Second, how does it deal with inter-community associations and cooperation in the city? Third, has it devoted any effort to providing an institutional infrastructure for HoAs, and if so how?

With respect to the first aspect, in Beijing, the government does not in general support the establishment of HoAs and, accordingly, creates obstacles at each stage of their establishment. Because the street-level government actually has the legal power to chair a preparatory committee to initiate the whole process and to screen potential candidates, it intervenes in community self-governance at a very early stage. In Shanghai, the city government has created an institutional infrastructure to ensure various government agencies to obey the law and to support and monitor the development of homeowner self-governance. It also facilitates coordination among different parties and groups in neighborhood governance. In Shenzhen, in contrast, the government is generally fairly hands-off but often finds itself stuck in the middle of conflict with no clear strategy to move forward. When disputes or conflicts arise within the neighborhood, the street-level government often lacks the capacity to resolve them and sometimes goes back and forth without any clear decision.

With respect to the second aspect of the state's role, Beijing is not at all supportive of inter-community associations; Shanghai is in the process of building an official platform for homeowners to communicate with one another. In Shenzhen, the city's housing administration supports the development of citywide inter-community associations of homeowners, whereas the authority tasked with stability maintenance is against it.

Finally, with respect to the third aspect, the Beijing city government perceives a high risk of homeowner mobilization, and its departments and agencies at all levels view homeowner activists and their organizations as troublemakers. Repression takes the form of noncooperation. In Shenzhen, the city government believes in "small government, big society" but fail to coordinate government agencies in either the development of institutional infrastructure for HoAs or the development of inter-community associations. One department's progressive effort often ends up being futile owing to a lack of coordination with other departments. The city government's ability to discipline government offices at the street level is weak, resulting in corruption and abuses of power in neighborhood governance. In contrast, the Shanghai city government has successfully coordinated departments and agencies at various levels to support HoAs, and has centralized the power and resources of neighborhood governance within its street-level offices while implementing the effective monitoring and disciplining of these offices. In the following sections, I further specify the risk-capacity framework and examine the three cities in detail.[10]

3.1 Risk and Capacity

The primary concern for an authoritarian state is to maintain authoritarian rule. A related concern is ensuring that the state has the capacity to do so. There are two ways of maintaining authoritarian rule. The first is through the exercise of what Michael Mann terms "despotic power," and the second is through "infrastructural coordination power."[11] Despotic power refers to the state's capacity to undertake actions without routine, institutionalized negotiation with the society, such as through violence.[12] Infrastructural power refers to the capacity of the state to *penetrate its territories and logistically implement decisions,*[13] and reflects in, for example, a state's capacity to discipline its frontline agents to force them to obey the law, its courts' capacity to apply rules consistently and neutrally even against state agencies. There is no question about the Chinese state's despotic power to crush any rebellion if it wishes so. My focus here is on the governments' infrastructural power, although I refer to their exercise of despotic power occasionally.

In the Chinese context, social stability is a major concern at every level of the authoritarian state, and the risk to social stability can be used to measure (or be considered a synonym for) the threat to authoritarian rule. The risk to both social stability and authoritarian rule posed by social mobilization is high in Beijing, China's capital. In Shenzhen, which is far from Beijing and lies at the "margin of the empire," in contrast, there is much greater tolerance for social instability and social mobilization. The central government designated Shenzhen as the country's first special economic zone in 1979 because its failure would have no impact on the authoritarian rule of China as a whole.[14] Shenzhen, and to a certain degree Guangdong province of which it is a part, is demonstrated herein to have more space than the two other cities for nongovernmental organizations (NGOs), the media,[15] labor unions,[16] and social mobilization in general. Finally, Shanghai is the economic powerhouse of China, and in China, political landscape is more important than in Shenzhen but less important than in Beijing. Social mobilization poses less of a threat to authoritarian rule in Shanghai than in Beijing, but more of a threat than in Shenzhen. I therefore characterize the social stability risk in Shanghai as medium.

How can we measure a government's infrastructural power, that is, the capacity to penetrate its territories and logistically implement decisions? It is a complex concept, and different scholars have adopted different approaches to defining and measuring it.[17] To be clear, I make no attempt to exhaust all of the variables influencing state capacity, and I am well aware of the argument that state capacity can be a "moving target."[18] In this study, I follow the Weberian tradition, as recently elaborated upon by Fukuyama,[19] and focus on the autonomy of a government, how well its bureaucratic system is structured, and how well such a system formulates and carries out policies.[20] In the following, I examine the autonomy, revenue, and size of the bureaucratic systems in the three cities under study. I then move on in subsequent sections to investigate what the local states in those cities do with respect to neighborhood governance to further gauge their state capacity.

One widely accepted criterion for measuring government autonomy is whether there is a competing authority within the given jurisdiction.[21] In this regard, the Shanghai city government enjoys complete autonomy over urban governance. The Beijing city government, in contrast, despite being at the same administrative level as its Shanghai counterpart, is subject to central government control in urban governance. Over the years, its primary function has been to serve the central government, including hosting such international events as the 2008 Beijing Olympics. Given Shenzhen's status as a special economic zone, the Shenzhen city government enjoys a fair degree of autonomy in urban governance but remains subject to the Guangdong provincial government's rules and regulations to some extent. With respect to the presence of a competing authority, it is clear that Shanghai has the highest degree of autonomy, whereas both the Beijing and Shenzhen city governments face a certain degree of interference from upper-level governments.

Financial capacity is a crucial aspect of state capacity. The three cities do not differ significantly from one another in this aspect as measured by government revenue per person, that is, annual city government revenue divided by the total number of permanent residents, including those without *hukou* (i.e., legal residency) status (Beijing: RMB 27,100; Shanghai: RMB 29,500; Shenzhen: RMB 28,200).

Table 3.1 Population, revenue, and size of government in Beijing, Shanghai, and Shenzhen (2019)

	Permanent residents (常住人口)	Permanent residents without Hukou (常住非户籍人口)	Revenue (RMB)	Number of street-level governments	Number of resident committees
Beijing	21.5 million[22]	7.5 million[23]	581.7 billion[24]	338[25]	2,918[26]
Shanghai	24.3 million[27]	9.8 million[28]	716.5 billion[29]	215[30]	6,034[31]
Shenzhen	13.4 million[32]	8.5 million[33]	377.3 billion[34]	74[35]	810[36]

The three cities do differ significantly with respect to the reach of the state to residential neighborhoods, as measured by the average number of residents governed by residents' committees (RCs), the lowest tier of the party-state's bureaucratic hierarchy. Shanghai has only a slightly larger population than Beijing (24.3 million vs. 21.5 million), but its number of RCs is more than double that of Beijing (6,034 vs. 2,918).[37] Shenzhen performs even worse in this respect: Its population (13.4 million) is more than half that of Shanghai's population, and yet it has only about one-eighth the number of RCs (810).[38] On average, each RC in Shanghai governs 4,000 residents, whereas the figures for Beijing and Shenzhen are 7,000 and 16,000, respectively.[39] The relatively small size of the Shenzhen government is due to its short history as a city. Since 1979, Shenzhen has grown from an agricultural county of 300,000 people to a megacity it is today, resulting in an exceptionally high percentage of residents without a *hukou* (63.4 percent vs. 40.3 percent in Shanghai and 34.9 percent in Beijing). In China, the size of a city government is determined by the size of the population it governs.[40] Migrants with no *hukou*, or legal residency, are thus not taken into account in the central government's decisions about the size of the Shenzhen city government. In Table 3.1, I present detailed data on population, revenue, and size of government in Beijing, Shanghai, and Shenzhen.

Taking these factors into consideration, I characterize the state capacity of the Shenzhen city government as low, that of the Beijing city government as medium, and that of the Shanghai city government as high. Table 3.2 shows the state capacity and risk to social stability in the three cities.

One note before we move onto the details of the three megacities: Is culture an independent factor that differentiates the three megacities from one another? Culture may impact homeowners' ability to work with each other and their attitudes toward law. The problem with culture is its endogenous interactions with institutions.[41] It is said that citizens in Beijing are politically charged,[42] in Shanghai are rule-following,[43] and in Shenzhen are adventurous.[44] But why is that? Populations in these megacities are highly mobile, though Shenzhen features a much higher percentage of migrant workers than the two other cities. Why would somebody become adventurous after moving to Shenzhen,

Table 3.2 Risk and capacity in Beijing, Shanghai, and Shenzhen

	Beijing	Shanghai	Shenzhen
Risk to social stability	High	Medium	Low
State capacity	Medium	High	Low

rule-following after moving to Shanghai, or politically active after moving to Beijing? Citizens in the three cities may differ in education and wealth, but not in religion or ethnicity, both of which are inherently cultural,[45] and they are free to move from one city to another, subject to economic and welfare constraints such as *hukou*. The answer lies primarily at institutions, mainly the government's perception of risk and its ability to take actions, including building infrastructural institutions. In other words, I do not take culture as an exogenous factor outside my framework of risk and capacity in examining the homeowner movement in the three cities. On the other hand, homeowners' trust of the government is positively correlated with the effectiveness of infrastructural institutions.[46]

3.2 Beijing: Repression (through noncooperation)

Unlike the repression of more politically sensitive political, religious, or human rights organizations,[47] that of HoAs primarily takes the form of noncooperation, including intentional neglect, non-recognition, and the withholding of institutional support even when required by law, with punishment taking place only in the severest cases. Monitoring, which falls somewhere between proactive repression and noncooperation, provides the government with information to determine whether homeowner activism has gone too far and whether any action is needed in response.

3.2.1 Repressing the "Neighborhood Revolution"

It was clear from my interviews with both street-level government officials and housing administration officials at the urban district level in Beijing that they do not welcome the establishment of HoAs. In their view, homeowner activists are driven by profit and fame, often resort to *weiquan* (defending one's rights through petitions, protests, litigation, etc.), and create endless trouble for them. If they cannot afford to manage neighborhoods by themselves, they still prefer management companies (MCs) to homeowner activists because they consider the former to be more responsible.[48]

One district-level housing administration official explained: "After all, management companies (MCs) are entities and they have bottom lines in doing bad things. Homeowners have no bottom line at all because they can vote with their feet, selling their apartments and moving out!"[49] The establishment of an

HoA often means homeowners taking control over the neighborhood from the MC. Conflicts are often unavoidable in the process, and violence is not uncommon.

Contrary to the previous comment from the government official, however, it is often MCs that threaten and harm homeowner activists, engaging in behavior that ranges from placing nails in their car tires,[50] throwing feces at their door,[51] and filling their locks with glue[52] to beatings[53] and, in the most extreme cases, murder.[54] In response, homeowner activists often feel forced to resort to violence to take control of their neighborhoods even after successfully establishing HoAs, electing homeowners' committees (HoCs), and selecting new MCs. In one interview, an HoC chairman in a neighborhood of 1,629 apartments with an average price of RMB 100,000/m^2 (US$14,787), who is a veteran of the People's Liberation Army, described how he had planned the "battle" to evict the old MC by force.[55] It is quite common for HoCs to evict their old MCs by force, normally using security guards from the newly selected MC.[56]

Regardless of who is more prone to violence in the end, from the perspective of street-level government officials, it is the effort to establish HoAs which triggers conflict and violence. And once there is violence, which is intolerable to a regime emphasizing social stability, officials have no choice but to respond. One street-level government official complained: "Our society became much more chaotic after there were HoAs; it was quiet and peaceful before that."[57] As a result, he said, his office has many "restrictive measures" for dealing with them.[58]

What are those restrictive measures? Once such measure is for government officials to delay the process of establishing an HoA as long as they can, as happened in Sunshine Manhattan, a condominium complex of 2,532 apartments that had an average sales price of RMB 88,000/m^2 (US$13,013) in 2018. Homeowner activists in the complex submitted their application to establish an HoA, which had been signed by more than 20 percent of homeowners, in November 2016. As of December 2018, however, a preparatory committee for the election had yet to be established despite the law stipulating that the relevant government body must establish such a committee within 60 days of an application's receipt.

The law also mandates that a preparatory committee comprises members of the government, the current MC, and homeowners, with an official from the street-level government in whose jurisdiction the neighborhood lies acting as chair. Homeowner members can be recommended or designated. In the case of Sunshine Manhattan, the current MC backed five homeowners for committee membership, none of whom showed up for meetings, which the street-level government used as an excuse to delay the whole process.[59]

Many neighborhoods get stuck in this very first step on the long march toward establishment of an HoA. Even if they are successful, many points of dispute lie ahead, including election procedures, how to calculate the total housing space of the neighborhood and the number of eligible votes, whether the homeowners' charter is contrary to laws and regulations,[60] etc. Furthermore, the need to mobilize half of all homeowners to vote constitutes a huge challenge, if not mission impossible. In the worst cases, the developer and MC still own a substantial portion of real estate in the neighborhood: apartments, facilities, and sometimes even hotels. In such cases, the developer/MC wields enormous influence, holding close to de facto veto power in community elections.

Even after homeowners have overcome all of the challenges and managed to establish an HoA, the government may find multiple reasons to prevent them from changing their MC. In one community I investigated, the government invalidated an HoA's resolution with the reason that homeowners could not combine firing the old MC and selecting a new one in the same resolution. Instead, they would have to organize two homeowners' meetings to deal separately with the two issues.[61]

3.2.2 Repressing Inter-Community Association

Homeowners in Beijing tried to establish a citywide inter-community association of HoAs.[62] Even in an authoritarian state such as China, the government does not tell homeowners that they cannot have a citywide association. However, setting up any organization in China requires approval from and registration with the government.[63] The founders of a main citywide platform for Beijing homeowners tried to register with the Beijing Department of Civic Affairs. A departmental official responded positively and said that they just needed approval from the city housing administration to do so. The founders submitted their application to the city housing administration in August 2006, and in December of that year received an indirect but negative reply.[64] The official answer was that the government needed to further study the issue as it was unprecedented. Without the legal registration, the platform does not have legal rights and cannot hold meetings under its own name.

In the years since, the platform has sent formal invitations to the housing administration for most of its public events, including its annual meetings and homeowners' forums. However, the administration has never acknowledged receipt of the invitations and has never mentioned the existence of any citywide HoA, although, in private, government officials have followed its development.[65] One or two of the founders have even been invited to attend government meetings, but the invitations are always addressed to them as chairmen of their HoCs instead of as founders of the citywide association.[66]

Although the platform held annual meetings in the years after 2006, it has stopped doing so since 2016. According to CB, one of the four founders, no one told them to stop, but they heard worrying things from various sources. For example, they were told that someone in a governmental meeting had said that the platform was illegal and should be banned. The decision to suspend annual meetings was a joint decision made by the four founders after evaluating the overall situation.[67]

3.3 Shenzhen: Fragmentation

The Shenzhen city government perceives the risk of independent civic organizations low and is receptive to the development of NGOs,[68] including HoAs, but fails to take systematic efforts to craft an institutional infrastructure for the development of HoAs due to its limited administrative capacity. As one evidence, the city housing administration employs only six people[69] to monitor the city's 1,500 MCs[70] in 3,597 neighborhoods.[71]

In Shenzhen, the party-state is fragmented at both the horizontal level (i.e., agencies at the same level of government, such as the city's housing administration and the political and legal committee in charge of social stability) and vertical level (i.e., different levels of government, such as the city's housing administration and the street-level government offices). The vertical fragmentation between the national and city governments is also reflected in the inconsistency between national laws and local regulations. Further, I present two case studies: the first to illustrate how the fragmentation of the state at the local level led not only to the failure of self-governance in one neighborhood but also to the near death of a citywide homeowners' organization, and the second to demonstrate how such fragmentation of authority led to explosive conflicts over parking space across the city.

3.3.1 Fragmentation in Governing HoAs

TYJ is one of the largest condominium complexes in Shenzhen, covering a total area of 1.16 km^2 and home to more than 14,000 apartments and 60,000 residents. The real estate developer and its MC, both of which and their employees still owned real estate in the neighborhood, had dominated the neighborhood for a long time, as a result of which the management service was deteriorating and the developer was using the neighborhood maintenance fund elsewhere. The developer had manipulated the election of the first two HoCs in the community, which thus served as the developer's puppets. In 2010, the MC had even manipulated the homeowners' meeting to ensure passage of a resolution to increase the management fee. Homeowners who refused to pay the higher fee were beaten up by employees of the company, which triggered a large-scale protest that ended up blocking a national highway nearby. The government sent in an anti-riot force to remove the homeowners and restore the traffic flow.[72]

The city housing administration would like to resolve neighborhood conflicts and supervise MCs with homeowners' help. However, it is difficult for several thousand homeowners to agree to pass a given resolution. It takes months to organize a meeting of all homeowners, and the resolutions passed in such meetings are also heartily disputed by the losing side. WeChat has become widely adopted in China for social and work communications over the past five years, and currently has over one billion active users.[73] The city housing administration decided to use this new communication technology to make homeowners' meetings more convenient and transparent. It developed a system that allows homeowners to vote online via their WeChat accounts after verifying those accounts with their cell phone numbers.[74]

However, because the department lacked the human resources to mobilize homeowners across the city to register their WeChat accounts and train them in the system's use, it paid the a citywide homeowner organization to do the ground work. At the same time, it was the street-level government offices, lacked human resources and expertise, which guided and monitored the elections and meetings of HoAs, and they therefore had the power to decide whether voting would take place through the new system or via traditional paper ballots.

The citywide homeowner organization and the city housing administration eventually persuaded the street-level government in whose jurisdiction TYJ fell to experiment with the new WeChat voting system to resolve the long-term governance problems in the community. The system initially appeared to be a success. Within one week, 8,041 households had registered and voted with the system, and 4,600 had voted for the proposed HoC. The votes in this instance would enable the homeowners in TYJ to set up their own association for the first time in the neighborhood's history.[75] No previous efforts had succeeded in getting more than half of homeowners to vote. Without the cooperation of the street-level government and the MC, it had even been difficult to obtain a complete roster of homeowners and their contact information, let alone to contact, identify, and persuade sufficient numbers to vote.

At this point, everything changed. The MC petitioned the government, objecting that the new WeChat voting system deprived some homeowners of their right to vote because they did not use WeChat. It further claimed that some of the phone numbers used to verify the WeChat accounts were not those of real homeowners. The MC organized a group of "old party members of TYJ" to send a petition letter about the system to the party secretary of Shenzhen and governor of Guangdong province.[76] In the letter, they claimed that the citywide homeowner organization had manipulated the election, and thus posed a threat to both social stability and the party's leadership in Shenzhen.

To exaggerate the threat, they claimed that the leader of the citywide homeowner organization, FGZ, had posted a message on his WeChat page stating that most government officials in Shenzhen were corrupt, a claim that FGZ proved to be untrue during the subsequent government investigation.[77] The petitioners also questioned why the citywide homeowner organization had provided training on the WeChat voting system to homeowners on behalf of the city housing administration.

The election preparatory committee comprising homeowners, an MC representative, and street-level government officials had actually discussed the issue of whether to allow both paper votes and votes submitted on the WeChat system, but the street-level government official in charge insisted that only the latter should be allowed and promised that he would be responsible for any problems that arose.[78] However, after "the old party members" sent their petition letter to the city and provincial leaders, who ordered an investigation of the election over social stability concerns, the street-level government refused to publish the election results and never accepted any responsibility.

The investigation, which lasted several months and cost RMB 0.6 million, revealed that 491 accounts had been registered without homeowners' cell phone numbers. It should be clarified, however, that this does not mean that these 491 accounts were fraudulent, simply that household members whose names were not on the corresponding real estate certificates had used their own phone numbers to register the certificate holders' WeChat accounts on the system and vote online.[79] It is pretty common in neighborhood elections for a wife to vote on her husband's behalf or an elderly father to vote on his son's behalf. Nevertheless, this technical inconsistency was taken as evidence in support of the claim that the election had been manipulated. The street-level government therefore declared the election results invalid, leaving the homeowner activists in despair.[80] It is worth noting that even if the 491 problematic votes had been deducted, the remaining valid votes would still have been sufficient to establish an HoA.[81]

Even worse than the decision to invalidate the election was that the petitioners' claim that the citywide homeowner organization was manipulating community elections and threatening social stability in neighborhoods across the city now seemed to have foundation. The city Department of Civic Affairs sent a team to investigate its finances and operations, although it found nothing illegal. The political and legal committee of the city requested a meeting with FGZ during which they warned that the citywide homeowner organization should not get involved in any neighborhood affairs without advance approval in the future, essentially preventing it from fulfilling its original purpose.[82]

This whole episode started with the city housing administration's ambition to facilitate the self-governance of homeowners through new technology, but ended with the social stability apparatus's intervention, not only killing neighborhood democracy but also freezing out an inter-community association. The street-level government overseeing the election in question lacked expertise and the power to engage in consistent implementation. Instead, it acted in ad hoc fashion, responding to pressure from different state authorities. The case of the TYJ community and Shenzhen's experiment with the WeChat voting system demonstrates the damaging consequences of fragmented authoritarianism for efforts to implement reforms that would actually facilitate the development of community self-governance.[83]

3.3.2 Fragmentation in Property Legislation and Enforcement

Back in the early 1990s, not many Chinese people owned cars, and parking was not a problem. A rule issued by the city land administration in 1993 had a clear definition of common space, including parking space, and stated clearly that it belonged to homeowners collectively, and thus that developers had no right to sell or rent it.[84] The 2007 Property Law contradicted this local rule by distinguishing between aboveground and underground parking space, giving the latter to the developer.

How should that central-local inconsistency be dealt with? Technically speaking, as a special economic zone Shenzhen City has the authorized legislative power to deviate from national legislation. However, that power is not well-defined.[85] In any case, what matters is enforcement: If the Shenzhen government were able to enforce either the rule or the law, that is, developers' ownership or homeowners' common ownership, it would be able to resolve the dispute. Because it has been unable to do so, disputes over common space are more numerous in Shenzhen than in either Shanghai or Beijing.

On the one hand, the city land administration has not established a registration system allowing developers to register their property rights to parking space with the government. They therefore have to rely on their subsidiary MCs to exercise de facto control over that space. This is a major factor in developers' and MCs' opposition to the establishment of HoAs, as control over parking space is hugely profitable. At the end of the day, what matters is who controls the MC and who controls the parking space. If you have a strong and capable HoC such as the one under the leadership of ZJJ, the homeowners take control; otherwise, the developer and its MC take control. The situation varies across neighborhoods, and parking space in Shenzhen thus remains an unsettled issue with hundreds of thousands of disputes.[86]

In 2014, the Shenzhen land administration tried to resolve the issue by drafting a new ordinance on parking space, which it circulated publicly for comments.[87] In the draft, it stuck to its 1993 approach.[88] Homeowners thus welcomed it, but developers challenged it both in the mass media and through channels connected to the city's top leadership. The developers again made a claim about social stability. The general counsel of one leading developer wrote a public letter protesting against the proposed draft but signed it "a Shenzhen citizen." The letter stated that,

> developers have already transferred their property rights over about 300,000 parking spots in condominium complexes across the city, forming stable property relationships with a total value of over several dozen billion RMB.[89] It would create … chaos to the social order if the department in charge did not recognize and register such property rights.[90]

He also blamed the city land administration for all of the disputes over parking space for failing to allow the registration of property rights to such space.[91]

Because of this opposition from real estate interests, the draft never became an official local ordinance. Disputes over parking space in Shenzhen thus continue. The aforementioned letter writer is probably right that the government is responsible for such disputes, but not only the city land administration.

Instead, it is the fragmented nature of authority, which swings between stability concerns and concerns about homeowners, that is at fault. If the city's top leadership is not prepared to coordinate the different departments and interests in the city, it is unlikely to provide a clear property rights system for parking space. The result is ongoing conflict in residential neighborhoods.

3.4 Shanghai: Coordination

The Shanghai city government perceives an intermediate degree of risk posed by homeowner mobilization and takes it as something it needs not to suppress but to carefully deal with. It has been able to develop its neighborhood governance since the very beginning of its housing reform.[92] The strategy emphasizes creating an institutional infrastructure to ensure various government agencies to obey the law and to support and monitor the development of homeowner self-governance. The Shanghai city government has also formulated a series of action plans to coordinate the various departments and levels of government. In particular, it centralizes the power and resources of neighborhood governance within the street-level government offices while simultaneously effectively monitoring and disciplining the street-level government offices, an approach I call centralized decentralization. It is a capable and supportive state that has enabled the development of self-governance in Shanghai's neighborhoods.

3.4.1 Top-Level Coordination

The major difference between Shanghai and the two other cities under study is that Shanghai has a top-level comprehensive strategy for neighborhood governance. The top leadership of the Shanghai city government takes the government's role in neighborhood governance seriously. Understanding the importance of such governance to the city's development and stability, it has developed a comprehensive governance strategy. Top leadership refers to the leaders of the city government itself rather than the leaders of government departments, which, like their counterparts in other cities, often have different and sometimes mutually conflicting functions and preferences.

The Shanghai city government responded to the passage of the 2007 Property Law by promulgating a three-year action plan to strengthen residential neighborhood management.[93] In 2009, the city government promulgated a decision on strengthening the institutionalization of HoAs.[94] In 2011, the Shanghai city government promulgated the Rules of Residential Real Estate Management, which incorporates the essentials of the aforementioned documents and their practices.[95]

Then, in 2014, under the leadership of Han Zheng, the then party secretary of Shanghai and now First Vice Premier of the State Council and a member of the Politburo Standing Committee of the CCP, the Shanghai city government conducted a "No. 1 Research Investigation" on "Innovating Social Governance and Strengthening Grassroots Government," during which Han chaired five meetings, demonstrating the priority the city government accorded to neighborhood governance.[96] This research investigation resulted in a package of documents on street-level government reform, reform that I define as centralized decentralization and discuss further in the following section. Finally, in 2018, the Shanghai city government formulated another three-year-action plan for "constructing beautiful homes" in residential neighborhoods. According to the plan, by 2020, more than 95 percent of neighborhoods in Shanghai should establish HoAs, with 100 percent of those neighborhoods including party groups.[97]

Under the city's co-governance strategy, the street-level government and its party branch play a leading role in coordinating the different stakeholders in neighborhood governance, not only the various government agencies involved, such as the city housing administration, but also real estate developers, MCs, and HoCs. What needs to be emphasized here is that the street-level party-state's leading role is stakeholder coordination rather than the direct administration of and provision of public services to individual neighborhoods. The co-governance framework actually emphasizes homeowners' self-governance and requires the street-level government to promote, support, and monitor the establishment and operation of HoAs.

The Shanghai city government has even made the percentage of HoAs a major index of societal development and uses it to evaluate the performance of related government agencies.[98] In Shenzhen's fragmented system and Beijing's repressive system, in contrast, as we have seen, homeowners encounter multiple barriers and even veto points on their path to establishing and operating their own associations. A centralized city government in which different departments and levels of authority coordinate with one another makes homeowners' efforts much easier, and that is exactly what Shanghai has.

A key question with a strong government is how to preserve homeowner autonomy. The Shanghai city government is concerned with ensuring that neighborhood democracy does not endanger the party's leadership, which is why it insists on such leadership in the co-governance framework. However, having supported the development of HoAs, and providing the necessary institutional infrastructure for such development to take place, it has to respect homeowner self-governance, albeit with one caveat: that is, that homeowners do not challenge the party's leadership or incur mass incidents/protests that cause social instability.

3.4.2 Centralized Decentralization

Different from Shenzhen, Shanghai has reformed its system of government in the past decade, granting primary power and responsibility to the street-level government offices. The city government has strengthened these offices by giving them more people, money, and power and by clarifying the law so that it is clear that they should play the leading role in neighborhood governance. Accordingly, a given street-level government has a say in all matters pertaining to its jurisdiction.

Even more importantly, the street-level government also holds power over the personnel of other government agencies. In other words, they have the power to evaluate any city government department officials based within those offices, as well as veto power over their promotion. This institutional design forces various government departments to work together with the street-level government in neighborhood governance.

At the same time, the city government monitors and disciplines the street-level government through a uniform information platform, which can be triggered by calling the mayor's hotline, "12345." There are also clear deadlines for resolving any issues raised through the hotline. Trivial matters must be resolved within twenty-four hours.[99] For more complicated matters, the information platform presents a clear timetable and specifies exactly which department is handling the issue. Multiple homeowner activists told me that they find the hotline quite useful in pressuring the street-level government officials to do what they are supposed to. Whenever they call the hotline, they said, street-level officials feel the pressure and accelerate the process.[100]

3.4.3 The Enabling State in Action

Both the interview and survey data collected in this research show the street-level government in Shanghai to be much more supportive of HoAs than their counterparts in Beijing and Shenzhen.[101] In our fieldwork in Shanghai, we also found that quite a few of the city's homeowner activists had become involved in community governance at the invitation of the party secretaries of the RCs of their neighborhoods. Among these were entrepreneurs and city government employees.

This supportive atmosphere results from the city government's co-governance strategy, according to which the street-level government and its party branch are encouraged to nurture "backbone"[102] and "warm-hearted men"[103] in residential communities. As discussed earlier, homeowners' participation in community governance is voluntary and unpaid, which imposes the problem of collective action. Mobilization by street-level party-state officials helps to overcome that problem. Such officials try to identify potential homeowner activists who are both capable of leading the establishment and operation of HoAs and are not opponents of the government.

The following case demonstrates how motivated officials at the street level can coordinate government agencies and social stakeholders to transform an unstable neighborhood into a well-governed community. Homeowners in a middle-class neighborhood were very angry about the poor management services they were receiving. Twenty activists sent a petition letter carrying their finger prints in blood to the party secretary of their RC, who was shocked but responded with a proposal for a meeting. Before that meeting could take place, however, the RC posted a notice calling for a public meeting with homeowners. The activists suspected that the RC had betrayed them because this public meeting seemed to differ slightly from that originally proposed by the party secretary. They thus decided to launch a public protest.[104]

However, the party secretary learned of their plans through party members in the community and contacted various government agencies for help in solving the neighborhood's problems, as well as the anti-riot police to respond to the planned protest. He also contacted the MC to discuss a plan for resolving the issues the homeowner activists had raised and improving the overall level of service. With a plan in place for improving the community's management service, as well as the potential threat of anti-riot police involvement, the party secretary was able to persuade the leading homeowner activist to attend the planned meeting before launching the protest. She accordingly put the protest on hold and attended the meeting with three other activists. An MC representative, the homeowner activists, and members of the street-level government together agreed on a plan to hold a homeowners' meeting and improve neighborhood governance.[105]

With the support of the street-level government, homeowners subsequently elected an HoC and managed to replace the original MC with a new one. To resolve the many problems within the neighborhood, including building maintenance, the newly elected HoC even managed to obtain funding of about RMB 10 million from the city government with the support of the RC.[106] This funding also served to enhance the credibility of the HoC among homeowners. Following the improved physical environment and management service, homeowners no longer had any reason to complain or protest. HoC members also agreed to hold regular joint meetings and discussions with the RC and the MC with respect to important decisions. This co-governance framework ensures that various parties can work together smoothly to respond effectively to homeowners' demand for community goods.

Another example serves to explain why coordination among HoCs, RCs, and various government agencies is so important for the achievement of community self-governance. An HoA in Shanghai passed a resolution to implement new parking rules in the neighborhood. Whether the homeowners on the losing side of those rules would obey them was a big question. To enforce the rules, the HoC chairman and the RC party secretary went to the police station together to make sure that should any conflict over the rules arise, the police would know how to respond. Any inconsistency among these various authorities would have caused confusion among homeowners and endangered community self-governance. Coordination in advance successfully avoided such problems.[107]

Because of the effective co-governance, the Shanghai city government is confident about allowing homeowners to make their own decisions regarding community affairs. One significant difference between Shanghai and the two other cities is that its HoAs are permitted to operate their own maintenance funds in their own bank accounts.[108] In Beijing and Shenzhen, although HoAs theoretically have their own maintenance funds, to actually use those funds they have to apply to the city housing administration. The decision ultimately rests with the housing administration rather than the HoAs. Furthermore, the application process takes a long time, and applications are rarely approved unless maintenance is necessitated by some emergency.[109] The city housing administration's concern is that homeowners might abuse their power in operating the maintenance funds. In Shanghai, however, HoCs are trusted to access and operate those funds as they see fit.

Inter-community cooperation is also in evidence in Shanghai, with the city government providing regular training to homeowners across the city. When such training is found not to be as effective as that provided by private entities such as HB's corporation, the government is actually open to their input. In 2018, the Shanghai Communist Youth League supported the establishment of the Shanghai Association of Young Homeowner Committee Members, the purpose of which is to build a platform for young HoC members to communicate and share information.

How do homeowners view this framework in which the government plays a proactive role? Our research suggests that they consider it an opportunity to govern themselves and engage with the government to achieve their agenda. For example, in the aforementioned case of parking rule enforcement, the HoC chairman involved said:

> If you cannot handle individual violations, there [will] be no rules in the community. Of course you need cooperation with the RC and the MC. As I told the party secretary of the RC, we homeowners' committee [members] can handle any dispute at this stage [if we have your support]. But if conflicts explode [in] the end, it [will] be the RC's [responsibility] to clean up the mess.... The RC needs to believe that our two parties can cooperate to solve the problems. It's his [the party secretary's] responsibility as the party secretary of the RC: if he wants to do his job well, then we need to work together.... The point is to tell him that if we get to enforce our rules and govern our community well, it is good for his job evaluation; [it's] good for everybody.[110]

Similarly, when it came to obtaining government support for establishing the Shanghai Association of Young Homeowner Committee Members, the Shanghai Communist Youth League was responding to the party's call to penetrate society at the grassroots level. However, instead of communist youths penetrating homeowners' committees, the Youth League obtained a list of all homeowner committee members under the age of 35 and then helped the targeted individuals to establish the association. This official endorsement has encouraged the participation of young homeowners in community governance and given the association's members greater leverage in their dealings with both government agencies and MCs.[111]

4

Rule of Law for Democracy

This chapter provides a legal explanation for the different homeowners' association (HoA) rates in Shanghai (94 percent), Shenzhen (41 percent), and Beijing (12 percent). Despite China being a unified regime with national law that is supposed to apply across different parts of the country, the local rules applicable to HoA elections differ across the three cities. Beijing has consistently followed national law, whereas Shenzhen adopted its own legislative rules until the passage of the Civil Code in 2020, at which time local rules gave way to national law, and Shanghai has left the choice to individual neighborhoods, with its courts relying on the idea of autonomy in private law to justify local practices that deviate from national law. Both the national rule adopted in Beijing and the city rule adopted in Shenzhen have imposed significant decision-making costs on the establishment and operation of HoAs. By contrast, the Shanghai approach, that is, allowing homeowners to write their own voting rules into HoA constitutions to reduce decision-making costs and using the courts to safeguard procedures and minority interests, contributes to functioning neighborhood democracy in Shanghai.

This legal explanation supplements the capacity-risk framework I proposed in Chapter 3. Precisely because the Shanghai municipal government is willing to (because of the lower risk of homeowner mobilization to social stability than in Beijing) and able to (because of its highest state capacity of the three cities) develop a coordinated strategy for HoA development, the Shanghai courts, as part of the local state machine, have adopted an approach deviating from the national law to support HoAs. The salient role of the courts in this process also testifies to the legalistic approach that homeowners and the local state have agreed upon in Shanghai.

Yoram Barzel and Tim Sass argue in a seminal paper that developers structure the voting rules of condominium associations to minimize the expected costs of wealth transfer and decision-making.[1] The institutional background is that developers write and record the covenants of condominium associations at their creation and buyers vote by foot. Because each buyer needs to consent to such covenants at her purchase of a condominium, unanimous consent is the foundation of the sacredness of condominium covenants. Chinese condominium associations are distinctive in that their constitutions are written not by developers but by homeowners after they move in.[2] What has troubled Chinese homeowners is their low participation rate. In the Chinese context, high decision-making costs can prevent homeowners from establishing HoAs and electing homeowners' committees (HoCs, an executive body of HoAs), resulting in governance failure, whereas high wealth transfer costs can result in abuses of power by HoCs, leading to neighborhood conflicts and instability.

Take a real-world example: In one Shanghai condominium complex in 2020, there were 1,291 households, of which 703 voted, 417 for the given motion and 278 against, with 8 abstaining.[3] According to the Civil Code passed in 2020, which is concerned about HoC's abuse of power, at least two-thirds of households must participate in a vote.[4] Hence, the aforementioned motion – lacking a two-thirds participation – cannot be passed. However, the condominium association's constitution, which was passed by a two-thirds majority of the 1,291 households, stipulates that the votes of households that receive a ballot but do not vote are considered as having participated and in agreement with the majority opinion of those that voted. Should this stipulation be considered valid, the aforementioned motion would meet the two-thirds participation requirement of the Civil Code and pass with a more than two-thirds majority. Does the Civil Code allow homeowners to choose their own voting rules? Most Chinese legal scholars believe not,[5] but the Shanghai courts have carefully interpreted the Civil Code to allow homeowners to choose their own voting rules to reduce decision costs, and, more than that, institute procedural guardrails to minimize the cost of wealth transfer, or "the tyranny of the majority," using Shanghai judges' words.[6]

Shanghai courts' innovative interpretation of the Civil Code to accommodate homeowners' demand for self-governance proves that law is a dual-direction channel in Shanghai, reflecting and being shaped by both bottom-up demands and top-down concerns. In a way, the courts in Shanghai have become the channel through which homeowners participate and shape institutions that matter to their interests. The Shanghai courts have proved more responsive to homeowners' demand and more adept than the national legislature, the national housing administration, the Supreme People's Court (SPC), local courts in Beijing and Shenzhen, or the legislative and executive branches of the Shanghai municipal government at minimizing the costs of wealth transfer and decision-making. I therefore call this chapter rule of law (courts) for (neighborhood) democracy.

The remainder of the chapter is organized as follows. Section 4.1 discusses the evolution of national rules for homeowner voting and the failure of the SPC and national housing administration to adapt the Civil Code to practices preceding its promulgation. Section 4.2 examines local practices in Beijing and Shenzhen, including judicial practices. Section 4.3 investigates why and how the Shanghai courts endeavor to minimize the costs of wealth transfer and decision-making for condominium governance. Section 4.4 concludes this chapter.

4.1 The Evolution of National Homeowner Voting Rules

The central government has struggled to formulate a voting rule that would minimize the costs of both decision-making and wealth transfer. The first national regulations concerning voting rules were promulgated by the State Council in 2003. Called the Regulations on Real Estate Management ("the 2003 Regulations" hereafter), they copied the rule in Shenzhen requiring more than half of HoA members to participate in a vote and more than half of participating members to agree on a resolution. I call this rule a *simple majority* rule.[7] In 2007, the National People's Congress (NPC) promulgated China's first Property Law, which includes a chapter on condominium governance. The 2007 Property Law takes a stricter approach, requiring an *absolute majority* to pass a resolution in a condominium, meaning that more than half of HoA members need to agree on a resolution for it to pass.[8] Because the Chinese legal system requires lower laws and regulations to be consistent with higher laws, the State Council revised the 2003 Regulations to comply with the 2007 Property Law.[9]

The Ministry of Housing and Construction (MHC), which was in charge of drafting the 2003 Regulations and supervising real estate and management companies (MCs), promulgated Guiding Principles on HoAs and HoCs in 2009 ("the 2009 Guiding Principles" hereafter). Still in effect today, they stipulate that HoA constitutions can determine whether uncast ballots can be counted as votes agreeing with the majority of voting homeowners.[10] Taking silence as agreement with the majority vote significantly reduces decision-making costs. I call this rule a *relative majority* rule. This relative majority rule was first incorporated into the Guiding Principles of HoA Decision-Making promulgated by the Shanghai Department of Housing and Construction (SHDHC) in 2008.[11] The MHC rule was probably copied from Shanghai, as the SHDHC is also subject to MHC leadership, and there was regular communication between local housing administrations and the MHC at the time.

The relative majority rule carries a risk of wealth transfer resulting from a few activists making decisions that benefit themselves at the cost of nonvoting homeowners. Suppose, for example, that in a neighborhood of 1,000 homeowners only three homeowners vote (two vote yes, and one votes no). In theory, the resolution can pass according to the relative majority rule (2 + 997 voting yes; 1 voting no). The key is to ensure that the 997 nonvoting homeowners were informed and had a chance to vote. If so, their silence can be deemed agreement with the majority of homeowners who voted. For that purpose, the 2009 Guiding Principles require sending a ballot to every homeowner in the condominium, with a public notice posted for those who are unreachable.[12]

More importantly, according to the 2009 Guiding Principles, the relative majority rule needs to be incorporated into an HoA constitution to be applied to homeowner decision-making. The 2009 Guiding Principles does not explicitly specify whether the relative majority rule can apply to the passage of an

HoA constitution, but based on the wording that an HoA constitution can determine whether such a rule applies strongly suggests that the constitution itself should be passed by means of the absolute majority rule adopted by the 2007 Property Law. The 2009 Guiding Principles leaves the door open for homeowners to significantly lower the cost of decision-making by successfully adopting a constitution incorporating the relative majority rule at their first homeowners' assembly in accordance with the absolute majority rule of the 2007 Property Law. However, with the exception of those in a few cities, including Shanghai, most local governments and courts refuse to recognize the relative majority rule on the basis that it contradicts the *mandatory* absolute majority rule in the 2007 Property Law that HoAs much comply with and cannot replace with their own rules.[13]

One intention of the PRC's first Civil Code, which was passed by the NPC in 2020, replaced the 2007 Property Law by incorporating a revised version of it, and a milestone in the country's legislative history, was to "properly reduce the voting threshold for matters homeowners need to decide together, particularly the threshold of using building maintenance funding."[14] First of all, it requires at least two-thirds of homeowners to participate in a vote. It then requires the agreement of over half or three-fourths of participating homeowners (the latter percentage reserved for three matters of particular importance: collecting building maintenance funding, rebuilding, and changing the use of common facilities or space or using them for commercial purposes) to pass a resolution.[15] In total, the rule requires only one-third or one-half (for matters of particular importance) of homeowners to agree to pass a resolution, seemingly lowering the voting threshold in comparison with the 2007 Property Law, which requires one-half or two-thirds (for matters of particular importance) of homeowners to pass a resolution.

However, the Civil Code's wording has not achieved the legislators' declared intent to lower homeowners' decision-making costs: A minority of homeowners can defeat a motion by either not participating (ensuring that voting does not satisfy the two-thirds participation requirement) or by participating actively. For example, a member of the NPC suggested that the SPC issues a judicial interpretation of Article 278 of the Civil Code. The NPC member suggested that although the intention of the legislation was to lower the voting threshold, the wording of Article 278 had made it harder to pass a resolution in condominiums. For example, the 2007 Property Law requires a two-thirds absolute majority to pass a resolution for rebuilding, whereas the 2020 Civil Code requires the participation of two-thirds of homeowners and then the agreement of three-fourths of participating homeowners to pass a rebuilding resolution. As Chinese society is aging, the central government has been promoting the installation of elevators in old buildings. Installing elevators constitutes rebuilding and is generally supported by homeowners on higher floors but opposed by those on lower floors because it increases the property value for the former at the expense of all homeowners. The government is in favor of installing elevators. When all homeowners participate in such a decision-making process, the participation rate is higher than the minimum two-thirds required by the Civil Code. Now, however, the agreement of three-fourths of participating homeowners is needed, a more stringent requirement than the 2007 Property Law's two-thirds requirement. The SPC has stated that despite this exceptional case, overall the Civil Code still lowers the voting requirement. It has further stated that it will discuss with the NPCSC how Article 278 should be interpreted,[16] which is not particularly helpful.

The two-thirds participation requirement was intended to increase the participation rate, which is a legitimate concern and of value to democracy.[17] The concern seems to have been that homeowners who did not participate might be unaware of the voting, meaning that the relative majority of participating homeowners could not represent their opinion. There may also have been a practical concern: Homeowners who do not participate might protest and demand a different resolution after voting has taken place, potentially creating instability in the neighborhood concerned. The Chinese government has an interest in minimizing neighborhood conflicts, and requiring a certain participation rate could prevent dissenting homeowners from claiming that a passed resolution does not reflect the majority opinion. The logic is relatively straightforward: If you participate in voting, but lose, you need to accept the majority vote. The challenge is that participation rates have generally been low, and the cost of getting two-thirds of homeowners to vote is high.

With the Civil Code explicitly requiring the participation of at least two-thirds of homeowners in a condominium as a precondition for the passage of any resolution, the question now is whether an HoA constitution can still incorporate the relative majority rule, which takes the silence of nonvoting homeowners as agreement with the majority. The wording of Article 26 of the 2009 Guiding Principles ("whether votes of homeowners who have not participated in a vote can be counted as agreeing with the majority ...") is in direct conflict with the Civil Code's participation requirement ("must have at least two thirds of homeowners participate in voting ..."), whereas the 2007 Property Law leaves some room or ambiguity for the MHC or Shanghai courts to claim that they are not in direct conflict, as it says nothing about participation.

It is possible that there were errors in the legislative drafting process.[18] In any case, the resulting legislation has created confusion in Shanghai and beyond by significantly increasing the cost of decision-making for homeowners. After promulgation of the Civil Code, homeowners petitioned the MHC asking whether homeowners who have been sent a notice to participate in a homeowners' assembly but have not responded can still be counted as participating in the assembly (and their uncast votes therefore deemed to be in agreement with the majority), which was the practice advocated by the 2009 Guiding Principles. The MHC responded that the power to interpret the Civil Code belongs to the NPC Standing Committee (NPCSC) and suggested that the homeowners direct their inquiry to the NPCSC.[19]

4.2 Local Practices in Beijing and Shenzhen

This section examines local practices in Beijing and Shenzhen to lay down a baseline of comparison for the discussion of the Shanghai approach in Section 4.3.

The Beijing municipal government was slow in passing HoA legislation, which did not appear until 2010, three years after the passage of the Property Law, twelve years after corresponding legislation by the Shanghai municipal government, and sixteen years after Shenzhen.[20] The Beijing municipal rules copied the Property Law's HoA rules.[21] Local courts in Beijing have also taken a deferential approach to the municipal administration,[22] which perceives a high risk of homeowner mobilization, and has thus adopted a repressive approach to contain the establishment and operation of HoAs. Different from Shanghai, which recognizes the benefits of using HoAs to relieve itself of the burden of neighborhood governance, the Beijing municipal government is primarily concerned with the risks and challenges brought about by HoAs. In practice, this has meant that frontline government offices often refuse to approve the homeowner practice of writing the relative majority rule into HoA constitutions. When homeowners have challenged such disapproval of neighborhood autonomy in court, the Beijing courts have interpreted the Property Law strictly in support of local governments.[23] Both before and after the passage of the 2020 Civil Code, the Beijing courts have adopted a clear approach of rejecting the incorporation of the relative majority rule in condominium association constitutions based on their reasoning that national rules are mandatory and not subject to change by condominium constitutions.[24]

The first HoA in China was born in Shenzhen, which thus gave birth to the first local legislation on HoAs in China. Shenzhen's local legislation adopted the simple majority rule,[25] which was later copied by the State Council in the 2003 Regulations. It is noteworthy that even after the 2007 Property Law replaced the simple majority rule with the absolute majority rule, which the State Council followed in revising the 2003 Regulations, Shenzhen's local legislation did not follow the national rule, although Shenzhen did revise its local real estate management regulations in 2007.[26] Such intentional insistence on a local rule was very much a function of the legislative autonomy conferred on the government by the city's status as a special economic zone (SEZ).[27] However, the scope of the city's SEZ legislative autonomy is ambiguous, and, in exercising it, it should not contradict national laws; it can only adapt national laws to the local situation. The distinction between contradiction and adaptation is a difficult one and lacks clear criteria. Overall, the Shenzhen courts have stuck to Shenzhen's local simple majority rule. In some cases, the Shenzhen intermediate court has argued that Shenzhen's local legislation does not contradict the Property Law but is only an adaptation.[28] In other cases, the same court has simply stated that the local rule applies within Shenzhen.[29] The Shenzhen courts have also taken the local rule as a mandatory rule that is not subject to modification by HoA constitutions.[30]

As discussed earlier, the 2020 Civil Code incorporates an explicit participation rate requirement that differs from the 2007 Property Law. The Standing Committee of the People's Congress of Shenzhen revised its real estate management regulations in 2019 before the NPC passed the Civil Code but after the NPCSC circulated a draft of the Civil Code for comment, and abolished the simple majority voting rule that had been effective since 1994. The 2019 version of the local regulations simply states that HoA resolutions become effective only if the participation and approval rates satisfy the requirements of national law, thereby relinquishing the city's ambiguous – and controversial – legislative autonomy over the matter for the first time.[31] The Chinese government's efforts to unify laws and regulations across the country and the launch of legality review of local laws and regulations[32] may be the reason. The bottom line is that Shenzhen never received explicit authorization to formulate laws contradictory to national laws. Whatever legislative autonomy it had was therefore controversial, vulnerable, and subject to challenge.

Immediately after this local legislative change, the Shenzhen courts began deciding disputes in accordance with the Civil Code, invalidating resolutions that would have been valid under the old simple majority rule but that were invalid under the Civil Code.[33]

4.3 Rule of Law in Shanghai

In contrast to Beijing and Shenzhen, Shanghai has exhibited considerable respect for neighborhood autonomy, with the Shanghai judicial system in particular serving to defend local practices against national law, including the Civil Code.

That being said, the Shanghai government's approach to handling the conflict between national law and local practices is something of a paradox: On one hand, its local Real Estate Management Regulations, promulgated by the Shanghai People's Congress Standing Committee (i.e., the local legislature), always kept step with the national law, including the 2003 Regulations,[34] the 2007 Property Law,[35] and the 2020 Civil Code.[36]

On the other hand, as mentioned, in 2008, the SHDHC created the relative majority rule in its Guiding Principles of HoA Decision-Making, which was later adopted by the MHC in 2009. Shanghai's Guiding Principles provides that HoA constitutions can determine how to treat ballots that are sent to homeowners but uncast, including considering such ballots as agreeing with the majority of participating voters.[37] HoAs can adopt the relative majority rule by a two-thirds majority in a vote that adheres to the national rule rather than the relative majority rule. Many HoAs in Shanghai have adopted the relative majority rule. The SHDHC's proactive effort to lower decision-making costs for homeowners, which is consistent with the Shanghai municipal government's strategy of supporting homeowner self-governance, was evident in the aforementioned provision.

However, the aforementioned provision is not authoritative enough to legitimize the local practice of the relative majority rule in the face of seemingly contradictory national law, particularly the 2020 Civil Code. The Civil Code has a clear participation rate requirement that seems totally inconsistent with the relative majority rule that treats uncast ballots as votes aligned with the majority of actual votes. Shanghai judges have developed an elaborate method to overcome potential legal conflicts between the Civil Code and HoAs' use of the relative majority rule, thereby ensuring that HoAs can continue to effectively practice the relative majority rule. This is quite remarkable considering that even the SPC, the highest court in China, has refused to take a stance to overcome the conflicts.

More than that, Shanghai courts have defended democratic procedures in ways that protect the interests of minority homeowners, rather than unconditionally endorse HoAs' majority votes that are based on the relative majority rule. In other words, the Shanghai courts have demonstrated remarkable judicial craftsmanship and have not simply taken the side of HoAs. Yes, the Shanghai municipal government wants to support HoAs. And yes, the Shanghai courts are well aware of this point. Nevertheless, the Shanghai courts have managed to strike a balance between supporting HoAs and protecting minority interests from being encroached upon by a relative majority.

Neither other branches of the Shanghai government nor the party organs in Shanghai have been able to adopt such a balanced approach. In this sense, the rule of law, or more specifically, courts in Shanghai, plays a key role in the development of neighborhood democracy.

4.3.1 Judicial Craftsmanship Before the Civil Code

Courts in Shanghai have a tradition of supporting HoAs. As early as 2006, the Shanghai High People's Court issued a reply, which was applicable to all courts in Shanghai, granting HoCs the right to sue the government. While acknowledging that the letters of law were not clear regarding whether or not HoCs can be plaintiffs in administrative litigation, the reply argues that "allowing HoCs to sue administrative agencies on behalf of homeowners will help the people's courts to address cases that might intensify conflicts or cause mass incidents."[38] The underlying rationale for this reply is that judicial resolution of neighborhood disputes involving HoCs can avert a situation in which unorganized homeowners engage in public protests that threaten the stability and legitimacy of the regime.[39]

This is by no means to say that the Shanghai courts unconditionally endorse the development of HoAs. The No. 2 Intermediate Court of Shanghai, which is an appellate court and whose jurisdiction covers half of the city, published a white paper summarizing the findings of its adjudication of neighborhood disputes from 2008 to 2017. In this report, the court emphasized that "homeowners' shallow consciousness of self-governance" left room for HoC members' abuse of power, which could prompt dissenting homeowners to seek a resolution to the problem in court.[40]

Before the passage of the 2020 Civil Code, dissenting homeowners in Shanghai challenged resolutions that HoAs had passed according to the relative majority rule. The homeowners argued that the simple majority rule in Article 76 of the Property Law was mandatory: HoA constitutions could not replace it with a relative majority rule. Shanghai courts often ruled that incorporating a relative majority rule in HoA constitutions is an application of the homeowner self-governance principle and equally applicable to all HoA members, violating no homeowner's interest.[41]

Courts in Shanghai not only have acted in ways that reduce the decision costs of HoAs but also have instituted procedural guardrails ensuring that all homeowners have a right to vote, a right to be elected, and a right to have protections against "the tyranny of the majority." The white paper published by the Shanghai No. 2 Intermediate Court states that HoA constitutions adopt the relative majority rule to solve the problem of insufficient homeowner participation, but without procedural guardrails, homeowners might develop an impression of homeowners' assembly being manipulated by HoCs and MCs that send ballots to homeowners and collect their votes.[42]

The first procedural guardrail required homeowners to incorporate into their HoA constitution the relative majority rule before using it to make decisions. One judicial decision in Shanghai made it clear that, for an HoA to approve the relative majority rule, the HoA would first need to follow the Property Law's absolute majority rule.[43] In one decision that invalidated an HoA's resolution, a Shanghai court elaborated on its reasoning: Although the election committee had made it publicly known that uncast ballots would be treated as votes agreeing with the majority of cast ballots, such a rule imposes a limit on homeowners' right without consent from homeowners or a statutory basis, and therefore is not binding on homeowners. As a result, the voting rule in the Property Law should apply, which made the HoA resolution invalid.[44]

Some judicial decisions in Shanghai revoked homeowner resolutions that HoAs had passed on the basis of the relative majority rule that the HoAs had never electorally incorporated into their constitutions, though the decisions failed to specify which voting rule should govern HoAs' attempt to incorporate the relative majority rule into their constitutions. In one decision, an HoA had incorporated into its constitution the relative majority rule but had specified that this rule did not apply to the election of HoC members or to the selection of MCs. The disputed HoA resolution – which called for removing this exception from the HoA constitution and for selecting a new MC – was passed on the basis of the relative majority rule, with 3,167 uncast ballots deemed to be in agreement with a majority of less than 900 homeowners who had voted. The court revoked this resolution on two bases: (1) homeowners had not voted on the changed constitutional rule before the HoC had applied the rule to the resolution; (2) the HoC in question failed to prove that it had informed homeowners of this change of rule, as the details of this proposed change were not included on the ballot.[45] It is unclear how the court would have adjudicated this matter had the details been on the ballot.

Some Shanghai courts have refrained from requiring that HoAs vote on a proposed relative majority rule before applying it. These court decisions reason that as long as homeowners are informed of the use of the relative majority rule before a vote and are given a fair chance to vote, the relative majority rule is acceptable. The idea is simple: If a homeowner is informed of the consequence of not voting and still does not vote, it will be fair to assume that the homeowner will with the majority vote.[46]

Shanghai courts recognize that the relative majority rule might increase the cost of wealth transfer and have therefore exerted a higher degree of scrutiny in cases where minority interests are at stake. The following are two examples to illustrate the Shanghai courts' strict scrutiny in such cases.

The first case concerned the right to be elected. In its announced election rules, an HoC required that all candidates be under the age of seventy. The reasoning behind this discriminatory rule was that older homeowners would be unable to carry the heavy workload associated with HoCs. The rule was disputed in a court of law, which found that the rule violated senior homeowners' legal rights.[47]

The second case concerned a group of minority property owners whose property in the condominium complex was designed not for residential but commercial use. These commercial spaces in condominiums typically face the street and are rented out by the property owners to small business owners. These owner-landlords do not live in the condominium and constitute a minority group in HoAs. In one condominium, an HoA passed a resolution to charge owners of these commercial spaces a property-management fee that was three times the amount paid by residential property owners. The former fee was challenged in a local court, which revoked the resolution on the basis that the HoA had failed to justify the higher fee.[48] As a comparison, in Shenzhen, where a simple majority rule was mandatory, a local court declined commercial property owners' request to revoke a similar resolution on the basis that the resolution was passed by the majority of HoA members following the voting procedures properly.[49]

The Shanghai courts have limited their application of strict scrutiny to cases where minority interests are at stake, reflecting its careful balancing of the cost of decision-making and wealth transfer. In cases where there is no risk of "the tyranny of the majority," Shanghai courts have demonstrated tolerance of procedural flaws. In one case, a Shanghai court elaborated as follows:

> HoA resolutions are the sphere of homeowners' self-governance, in which the law should not over-intervene. Considering the huge number of homeowners and the variety of their interests, the court should not adopt a rigid rule or require absolute procedural perfection in reviewing HoA resolutions. The purpose of judicial review of HoA resolutions is to prevent the majority of

> homeowners from benefiting themselves at the cost of minority homeowners. The consequences of adjusting parking fees apply uniformly to all homeowners and the plaintiff does not provide evidence to show that his right was violated.[50]

4.3.2 Interpreting the Civil Code

In May 2020, China passed its first Civil Code, which took effect on January 1, 2021. The Civil Code increases the decision-making cost for HoAs by requiring that, for a valid and binding passage of a resolution, more than two-thirds of HoA's members participate in the votes. The purpose of the requirement is to promote participation, not necessarily because of its value to democracy in the Tocquevillian sense but because actual participation might reduce the likelihood that dissenting homeowners would challenge a resolution. In other words, participating dissenting homeowners would be less likely to cause a stir than nonparticipating dissenting homeowners who might claim that they were deprived of the opportunity to vote.

In reality, however, it is very hard, if not impossible, for condominiums in China to satisfy the two-thirds participation requirement. There are various reasons for low participation. As discussed earlier in this book, homeowners face the problem of collective action; free riding is prevalent. It is partly because of the relative majority rule, which by treating nonparticipating homeowners as agreeing with the majority votes significantly lowers HoA's decision-making cost, that most of Shanghai's neighborhoods have functioning HoAs.

The passage of the Civil Code has had a debilitating effect on neighborhood governance in Shanghai.[51] For example, Ms. Gu petitioned the Shanghai municipal government about a failed HoC election. She and her neighbors had spent eight months preparing for an HoC election, but the effort was for nought because of the Civil Code's new rule requiring the participation of at least two-thirds of HoA members. Records of past elections in the neighborhood showed that the voting participation rates had ranged from 25 percent to 50 percent, figures that were far less than the 66.7 percent threshold set by the Civil Code.[52] To replace an underperforming MC, to use the common funding to repair old buildings – all such matters require collective decision-making on the part of homeowners.

With the aging of both condominium buildings and China's population, it has become increasingly urgent for homeowners to collectively agree on how to use their property and resources. One critical issue is the installation of elevators in old buildings. During the annual meeting of the Shanghai Municipal People's Congress in 2021, there were dozens of proposals about which rule the Shanghai Congress should suggest or even mandate for facilitating HoAs' decision-making procedures for the installation of elevators.[53] However, the Shanghai Congress revised its own legislation so that it would comply with the Civil Code's two-thirds participation requirement.[54] The Shanghai Congress provided a platform for its members to submit feedback, but seemed to be incapable of making its own laws that are deviating from the national law. In this sense, it was not responsive to local demands; instead, its priority in the past two decades was to comply with the national law regarding neighborhood governance. The main thing the Shanghai Congress did was to pass proposals from its members to different departments of the Shanghai Municipal Government for a response. Since the executive branch needs to handle the daily business of neighborhood governance, it might be more responsive than the legislative branch to homeowners' demands for clarifications regarding Article 278 of the Civil Code. In the executive branch in Shanghai, the most relevant department is the SHDHC. How did it handle the conflict between the local practice of the relative majority rule and the Civil Code's participation requirement?

The SHDHC's first response was to implement the Civil Code. In the past years, the installation of elevators in old buildings has been a signature project for the Shanghai Municipal Government in its bid "to win the heart of the people" (民心工程). The success of such projects requires that a majority of HoA members consent to the installation of elevators in the given condominium buildings. This fact created an incentive for the SHDHC to lower homeowners' decision-making costs. Before the passage of the Civil Code, the SHDHC relied on the relative majority rule to achieve a majority consent.[55] However, on January 21, 2021, twenty days after the Civil Code took effect, the SHDHC issued a notice not only requiring that HoAs comply with the new rule but also explicitly stating that the old SHDHC rule was inconsistent with the Civil Code.[56] This notice exacerbated long-simmering conflicts between upper-floor homeowners and lower-floor homeowners, as the added value stemming from the installation of elevators benefited the former homeowners more than the latter. With the new rule in place, blocking an initiative to add elevators to old buildings would be much easier for lower-floor homeowners now than previously.

The practical challenges created by the Civil Code brought about a change in tone at the SHDHC, which – five months after the enactment of the Civil Code – subtly indicated that HoA constitutions can include rules governing the definition of participating homeowners in ways that do not contradict laws and regulations.[57] However, the subtlety with which the SHDHC conveyed the change came at the expense of clarity: HoAs can have their own rules only so long as the rules do not contradict laws and regulations, the most important of which can be found in the Civil Code. So, this notice is far from settling the matter caused by the Civil Code. The SHDHC probably preferred to maintain its old practice of the relative majority rule but did not want to risk contradicting the newly effective Civil Code, at least not in its officially issued rules.

There was confusion and inconsistency in local practices across streets and districts in Shanghai after the passage of the Civil Code. On March 22, 2021, a street-level government in Songjiang District of Shanghai replied that the relative majority rule was incorporated into the concerned HoA constitution and therefore the majority decision achieved through applying this rule was valid.[58] On July 24, 2021, the Huangpu District housing administration confirmed a street office's disapproval of an HoA's use of the relative majority rule.[59]

The legality of the relative majority rule became such a thorny problem that the Shanghai municipal authorities needed to confront it after the passage of the Civil Code. They could not simply promulgate rules that contradict the Civil Code. Ultimately, the problem was solved by Shanghai courts, demonstrating the unique role of the judiciary in conciliating the central–local conflicts and making rules for neighborhood democracy. Recently, the SHDHC has been soliciting feedback on its draft of a revision to its Guiding Principles. The latest version has not been officially promulgated but has been based upon Shanghai courts' interpretation of Article 278 of the Civil Code that I will explain further.[60]

Judges in Shanghai are part of a bureaucratic system. Instead of being independent and remote from the daily problems of urban governance, they are embedded in the government and the society and incentivized to provide a solution. Courts and judges are in a unique position to address the challenge to the legality of local practices brought up by the Civil Code, which both the municipal legislative and executive branches have failed to address.

The Shanghai High People's Court, lacking the authority to do so, did not issue its own interpretation of Article 278 of the Civil Code. Instead, it coordinated lower courts in Shanghai to develop jurisprudence that conciliated the conflict between the Civil Code and local practices, to ensure that all courts in Shanghai follow this jurisprudence, and to promote this jurisprudence to the public, particularly homeowners, through producing and circulating videos on social media. The Shanghai judiciary also sought the SPC's recognition of their jurisprudence.

First, immediately after the promulgation of the Civil Code in May 2020 but before it took effect in January 2021, the Xuhui District Court in Shanghai published a video titled "Silence Means that You Will be Represented," which encourages homeowners to vote, emphasizes that the process of distributing ballots needs to be transparent and recorded, and most importantly, warns homeowners that silence means agreeing with the majority of those who have voted. The key presenters in the video were two judges of the Xuhui District Court.[61] At the time of this video's release, the Civil Code, though not yet in effect, had raised serious questions about the validity of Shanghai homeowners' use of the relative majority rule. The two judges in the video therefore did not directly refer to the Civil Code; nevertheless, the video was released strategically to subtly reveal Shanghai courts' preference for the relative majority rule and remind homeowners of its risk. Indeed, one of the social media accounts posting the video was that of the Shanghai High People's Court, indicating that the video was not an unapproved act of a renegade low court in Shanghai.

Of course, the release of the video did not resolve the apparent inconsistency between the civil code and the local practice in Shanghai. Shanghai courts have thus needed to address head-on in judicial acts the legality of the local practice of the relative majority rule. One option for the Shanghai High People's Court was to issue an official interpretation of the Civil Code, which would have given rise to the same problem that beset the SPC: The power to interpret the Civil Code belongs to the NPCSC; courts only have the power to apply, not the power to interpret, the Civil Code. In practice, of course, applying the Civil Code to specific cases inevitably involves interpreting it, and, might provide an acceptable forum to clarify its meaning.

As a general practice not specifically related to the issue discussed here, the Shanghai High People's Court has organized a study group of junior judges to discuss complicated cases. After the passage of the Civil Code, these judges not only discussed the challenge it posed for the local practice in Shanghai but also reached a consensus that the local practice needed to be defended. The only question was how to defend the validity of the local practice against the Civil Code's explicit participation requirement.

The first strategy was that it needed to be done through a decision made by a higher court in the Shanghai judicial system. From high to low, there are three levels of courts in Shanghai: the Shanghai High People's Court, three intermediate people's courts, and sixteen district people's courts, one in each district in Shanghai. Among the intermediate courts, the No. 1 Intermediate People's Court serves as an appellate court for cases decided by seven district courts, and the No. 2 Intermediate People's Court serves as an appellate court for cases decided by the other nine district courts.[62] Most cases end in an appellate court. The No. 2 Intermediate People's Court decided to exercise its "elevated jurisdiction" (提级管辖), meaning that the court would exercise jurisdiction over cases typically destined for courts lower than the court exercising this elevated jurisdiction. The purpose of elevated jurisdiction is to make decisions of wide implications and guiding effects on courts across a jurisdiction of the exercising court.[63]

The second strategy was to seek SPC's recognition of the concerned decision, which was particularly important considering that the decision was essentially to interpret the Civil Code. The SPC holds an annual competition for outstanding judicial decisions. High People's Courts select the best decisions from their own jurisdictions and submit them to the SPC, which, among them, selects the very best decisions.[64] Upon being selected, such judicial decisions do not become guiding cases or gain precedent effect in the country. Nevertheless, being selected as an outstanding decision is a recognition and preempts challenges based on the wrong application of laws. In other words, when the Shanghai High People's Court submitted to the SPC's annual competition the aforementioned "elevated jurisdiction" decision of the Shanghai No. 2 Intermediate People's Court, it was giving the SPC an informal chance to review the decision. The SPC eventually selected this decision as one of the

116 cases granted a second-class award in 2022 (the first-class award went to 20 decisions; in total there were 4,838 decisions submitted for consideration.)[65] The honor bestowed on the Shanghai court's decision does not mean that the SPC officially recognized the Shanghai approach to the relative majority rule as its own approach. As mentioned earlier, the SPC has stated elsewhere that the power to interpret the Civil Code belonged to the NPCSC. Nevertheless, this recognition means that the SPC did not believe that the Shanghai No. 2 Intermediate Court had incorrectly applied the law; if such an incorrect application had come to the attention of the SPC, it would never have granted this decision an award. Moreover, in the eyes of the public such as Shanghai homeowners, the SPC's recognition greatly enhanced the legitimacy of the Shanghai practice of relative majority rule. It is no wonder that multiple social media accounts run by homeowner activists posted the full text of the award-winning decision with highlighted words of "granted the national second-class award for judicial decisions."[66]

The third strategy by which the Shanghai judiciary sought to defend the local practice against Article 278 of the Civil Code was to publicly laud the awarded decision so as to ensure that all the courts in the Shanghai judiciary would note, grasp, and follow the decision in their own proceedings. To this end, the Shanghai No. 2 Intermediate Court publicized on its social media account the full text of the decision. The Shanghai No. 1 Intermediate Court, the other appellate court in Shanghai, quickly followed suit confirming the validity of the relative majority rule incorporated in HoA constitutions.[67] And when handing out awards for the judicial decisions of Shanghai in 2022, the Shanghai High People's Court singled out a decision issued by a district court, which, following the Shanghai No. 2 Intermediate Court, ruled that incorporating the relative majority rule into HoA constitutions does not violate the Civil Code.[68] Such efforts of promotion have helped inform vast swaths of Shanghai homeowners about the local judiciary's approach to the relative majority rule. Moreover, multiple judicial decisions across district courts in Shanghai have followed the approach.[69] In one of these decisions, the court even explicitly stated that "according to settled precedents in Shanghai, the agreed-upon relative majority rule is valid and does not violate Article 278 of the Civil Code."[70] Though China is not a common law jurisdiction and its judicial decisions generally do not have precedent effect. The SPC's effort to create "guiding cases" comes closer of granting such cases precedent effect, but the decision issued by the Shanghai No. 2 Intermediate Court was not selected as a guiding case, legally having no precedent effect.

The last, and most important, was to develop a coherent legal reasoning capable of reconciling the local practice in Shanghai with the letters of the Civil Code. Much of this task fell on the shoulders of Judge Wang, who wrote the "elevated jurisdiction" decision for the Shanghai No. 2 Intermediate Court. A graduate of Peking University Law School, she was herself a homeowner who was personally familiar with HoAs. Indeed, prior to writing this decision, she had presented a training session to homeowners in Shanghai upon the invitation of the Shanghai Youth League, a party organization, and, after the session, had kept in touch with quite a few homeowner activists in Shanghai. These experiences acquainted her with the challenges of establishing and operating HoAs, especially the challenges related to the low participation rates and high decision-making costs in HoAs.

Judge Wang developed a coherent jurisprudence that achieved a workable degree of reconciliation between the local practice in Shanghai and the Civil Code. This reconciliation proceeded according to two steps. First, she stressed the legislative purpose of the Civil Code, which was to lower the threshold of establishing HoAs and to promote homeowner self-governance. Judge Wang reasoned that a binding homeowner resolution requiring the active participation of at least two-thirds of the HoA members would egregiously increase the decision-making cost of homeowners and defeat the clear and explicit legislative purpose of the Civil Code.[71] To back up this argument, she investigated the history of related legislation since 2003 and found no evidence that the Civil Code was intended to reverse previous laws' well-documented support of HoA development.[72]

The second step in Judge Wang's reconciliation strategy was to examine whether a nonparticipating voter's silence can be construed as consent with a majority vote under Chinese private law. Judge Wang cited Article 140 of the Civil Code, which states that silence can serve as consent when there is law, *ex ante* agreements, or customs that sanction such a practice. Specifically, she reasoned that, regarding the case before her, (1) the HoA members had explicitly agreed upon their HoA constitution's relative majority rule before the dispute arose between the two litigating parties; (2) neither party was challenging the overall validity of the HoA constitution; and (3) because it has been a long-time practice of using the relative majority rule to make decisions in the concerned condominium and in Shanghai neighborhoods in general, homeowners in the concerned condominium should already understand that silence translates into tacit acceptance of a majority vote.[73]

Third, Judge Wang inquired in detail whether the adoption of the relative majority rule would violate the rights of nonvoting (i.e., silent) homeowners. She elaborated that homeowners refrained from voting do so because (1) they did not care, (2) they were willing to defer to the majority, or (3) they were not aware of the vote. While Judge Wang reasoned that the last of these three situations was the only one worthy of real concern, according to her, HoAs could satisfactorily address this concern by putting into place procedures to ensure that homeowners were well informed and sufficiently reminded of the consequence of not voting. Judge Wang further addressed the concern that homeowners' assembly would be easily manipulated under the relative majority rule; after all, only 472 of the 1,073 homeowners had voted in the case over which she presided.[74] She elaborated that, if the Civil Code was interpreted as requiring the active participation of at least two-thirds of HoA's members, minority homeowners would find it easier to block resolutions, including those favored by most HoA members.[75] As long as organizers of homeowners' assembly have followed strict procedures for the dissemination of ballots to HoA members, the act of receiving a ballot should count as participation in a vote on the part of the recipient even if the recipient does not actually vote.

Through the aforementioned three steps, Judge Wang succeeded in reconciling the Civil Code with the local practice in Shanghai and achieved a workable balance between reducing homeowners' decision-making costs and preventing "the tyranny of the majority."

The Shanghai case also illustrates the unique advantage that courts hold in addressing conflicts between national law and local practices and in supporting neighborhood democracy.

4.4 Conclusion

In this chapter, I have examined how Shanghai courts have managed to minimize the cost of decision-making and the cost of wealth transfer for homeowners in neighborhood governance. The courts have successfully undertaken the task of reducing conflict between national law and local practice. From a vertical perspective, the Shanghai courts have done better in resolving the conflict between national law and local practice than the SPC that dodged the issue. From a horizontal perspective, the Shanghai courts have done a better job than the Shanghai municipal legislative and executive branches, demonstrating the unique advantages of courts in handling the central-local conflict.

A comparison to Beijing and Shenzhen qualifies my thesis for local judicial craftsmanship: The fact that local courts in Beijing and Shenzhen have not been able to achieve what Shanghai courts have done highlights the importance of the co-governance strategy of the Shanghai municipal government as a background institution, only under which Shanghai judges have been able to play an active role supporting neighborhood democracy.

5

Property

A Political Right, Social Right, or Legal Right?

National law grants local governments the power to "guide and assist" the establishment of homeowners' associations (HoAs),[1] and yet local governments in Beijing, Shanghai, and Shenzhen have exercised that power very differently owing to the differing degrees of risk to social stability posed by homeowner self-governance and varying degrees of state capacity in urban governance. Correspondingly, what property rights homeowners claim and how they claim those rights are a function of the effectiveness, or lack thereof, of the local states and laws in supporting neighborhood self-governance. The homeowners' movements in the three cities differ by both the scope of their property rights claims and the concomitant ways in which they claim those rights.

Beijing homeowners' claims are the broadest, including not only the right to control and manage their neighborhoods but also the political right to organize inter-community associations and to participate in national lawmaking. Their keyword is democracy. Shenzhen homeowners focus on and claim absolute sovereignty within their neighborhoods, challenging national and local laws with their social construction of homeownership and manipulation of inconsistencies across different levels and fragments of laws. Their key word is property rights, broadly defined. Shanghai homeowners' claims are the narrowest. They define and exercise their homeownership rights in accordance with national and local laws, although not necessarily in a passive or deferential manner. Their keyword is law.[2]

Correspondingly, the homeowners' movement in the three cities reflect different local features. The leading homeowners in Beijing are political entrepreneurs, devoting themselves more to systemic change and even Chinese democracy than to the self-governance of their individual neighborhoods. The homeowners' movement in Beijing has witnessed inter-community mobilization, the establishment without governmental approval of a citywide homeowners' organization to fight management companies (MCs), street-level governments, court decisions, and even the city government, and the mobilization of homeowners nationwide to influence the making of national property law.

The leading homeowners in Shenzhen are social entrepreneurs who navigate through the social, legal, and bureaucratic mazes to claim absolute homeownership sovereignty. They make use of the mass media, communicate and sometimes fight with city bureaucrats, send letters to city leaders, and, most significantly, litigate aggressively and frequently in court, including in the Supreme People's Court (SPC). They have also established inter-community associations, with the recognition of the city government, to serve as intermediaries between homeowners and other parties, primarily street-level governments and developers and their MCs, but have made no attempts to unite homeowners to fight the government as their counterparts in Beijing have done.

Finally, the defining characteristic of homeowners in Shanghai is respect for laws and rules. Their motto is "studying rules, understanding rules, mastering rules and making use of them!"[3] Homeowners' demand for an understanding of the law is so high that several homeowner activists actually founded a company, developed a legal database, and organized offline homeowner gatherings to meet that demand. This company now serves as the main platform for citywide homeowners to communicate and share knowledge with one another.

5.1 Beijing: Property as a Political Right

Owing to the arbitrary grassroots governance that is often hostile to homeowner self-governance in Beijing, many homeowners see little use in complying with the law and feel an urgent need to unite homeowners citywide or even nationwide to both fight against repression and promote institutional reform. Politically charged homeowner activists believe that "living changes China"[4] and hope to improve China's political system through what they call "neighborhood revolution."[5] In the following, I detail the experiences of two leading homeowner activists, homeowners' efforts to establish their own citywide organization, and their mobilization of homeowners across the country to influence the making of national property law in 2007.

5.1.1 Leading Activists as Political Entrepreneurs

I was able to interview most of the leading activists in Beijing, as they form a small circle.[6] Democracy was always a keyword in our conversations. In fact, I occasionally had to interrupt them to draw them back to the more mundane details of the daily operation of HoAs in Beijing. In the following, I present the stories of two leading activists to demonstrate the political nature of the homeowners' movement in Beijing.

5.1.1.1 "It Feels Like Being Back in the Square Again!"

The first activist I interviewed was CFS, who claimed to be a veteran of the June 4 Movement in 1989. CFS got involved in neighborhood governance by accident. In 2004, the MC of his neighborhood decided to raise management fee without homeowner approval, and even sent an attorney's letter to homeowners who refused to pay. CFS's neighbors were scared and angry, and he volunteered to talk to the MC. However, the company said that it did not talk to individuals. It would deal only with HoAs because they represented all homeowners. At the same time, however, it also expressed the view that it would be too difficult for this particular neighborhood to set up such an association because it was a large community of 4,500 apartments.

CFS stood at a bus station near his neighborhood holding a poster on which he wrote how many signatures he needed to achieve the target of 2,500 and how many days were left for him to do so. He also asked his neighbors for support, and got together a team of about 30. He stood at the bus station for more than two months without a single day's break. His teammates also spread the news in an online neighborhood forum. His stubbornness and insistence moved his neighbors, and he eventually got all of the signatures he needed.

With those signatures, he proceeded to establish a preparatory committee for election, as required by law. The residents' committee governing his neighborhood did not want CFS and his team to establish an HoA. Hence, the membership of the preparatory committee was key. The residents' committee had previously selected about 300 Olympic volunteers[7] in the neighborhood and now mobilized them to register for the committee. However, CFS and his team managed to get 600 homeowners to sign up:

> It was really encouraging! Our neighbors were really awesome! We had only a small table in the neighborhood square with a small billboard. Neighbors came in and gave us copies of their property rights certificates and signatures [which showed great trust because such copies can be used in property transactions]. To speak the truth, I felt like I was … back in the square [Tiananmen Square] again!
>
> So I arrived at a conclusion naturally: our real estate management regime and homeowners' association system decide that homeowners' *weiquan* (defending their rights) is a community-based, continuous, small-scale, social movement. The current institutional design forces homeowners to initiate campaigns, to mobilize and organize their neighbors, and there have to be leaders and slogans, etc. It has all the elements of a social movement, but it is of a smaller population and less fierce – you can take it as being apolitical but it has all the elements. So back then I thought it was a great enterprise and an effective channel for me to fulfill my political and social ideals.[8] [emphasis added]

The last stage was voting: "I was so impressed by the situation. Several uncles and aunties were crying – they were in their 50s and 60s! They said they had never voted for their own affairs, and finally they had the feeling of voting for themselves and deciding their own affairs."[9]

This was just the beginning of CFS's career as a leading homeowner activist. It would require another paper to cover his whole career. It has not all been smooth sailing. Exactly because he is so political, he has encountered numerous difficulties. However, today he is an expert consultant to dozens of communities in Beijing and nationwide. The sad part of his story is that he was forced out of the community described earlier and no longer chairs his own homeowners' committee (HoC, an executive body of HoAs). He was threatened and even injured by employees of the MC, and after he got married he decided to move away out of fears for his family's safety. Today, he introduces himself as an expert in community governance rather than a *weiquan* expert.[10]

5.1.1.2 "I believe in the Power of Ballots!"

QB's legal career grew together with the rise of homeownership in China.[11] His legal practice in the past three decades has centered on real estate and homeownership.[12] He operates a law firm under his own name, and its main business today is class action suits filed by homeowners.[13] The firm employs about fifty lawyers who get homeowners organized across the country to defend their rights.

QB's weapon is China's election law, according to which voters numbering more than thirty can initiate a process of impeachment against a member of the local people's congress at the urban district level.[14] QB has used this law in Beijing and other Chinese cities to establish HoAs or protect homeowners' property rights. His description was corroborated by a news item on homeowners' attempt to impeach a local people's congress member in the Fengtai district of Beijing.[15] Although the attempt did not succeed, it proved an effective, relatively low-cost strategy for getting homeowners' affairs attended to by high-level officials. QB said:

> Thirty voters? It's easy to find even 300 voters! One neighborhood has at least ... 1,000 voters. If a district chief's membership in the local people's congress is questioned by 300 voters, it would be a big scandal and he might lose his position. For us the cost is low, just signatures plus national ID numbers and contact information. It's not illegal to do that.[16]

The challenge for petitioners in China is that their petitions often get buried in the huge bureaucratic hierarchy and never reach the real decision-makers. QB's weapon does make sense in this regard. However, when I asked him whether it was just an effective way of petitioning,[17] he replied: "It's not petitioning. It's using constitutional means to defend our own civil rights. That's my strategic summary after so many years of practice. Capitalist constitutions can be used – why cannot a socialist constitution be used? The election law under our constitution can also be used!"[18]

QB has run for the local people's congress in Beijing twice, the first time in Chaoyang District in 2003 and the second time in Haidian District in 2006. The first time, the government forced the law firm he worked for at the time to fire him, resulting in his disqualification from standing on the ground that he no longer had any connection with the district. At the time, QB said, he already had the support of thirteen HoAs in Chaoyang District, with more than 20,000 homeowner voters. The second time he ran, the government simply refused to register him as a candidate. QB took his disqualification as indicating the power of the ballot box: "They were so scared that they had to fire me. You have to understand ... how scared they were [of the power of the ballot box]!"[19]

QB took homeowners as voters and China's election law seriously. He said the law provided a basis for both his own and homeowners' safety. When I asked him whether he had really believed in the law then, he admitted:

> No, it was organizational force. Your safety is not that you act according to law, but also that you have the force to claim your rights according to law. If you don't get organized, you have no force.... Only when both parties have force can we sit at the table to negotiate. Nobody talks to you when the difference in force is so huge.[20]

QB has never been arrested but he has been monitored. He currently cannot practice law in Beijing because the Beijing Bar Association refuses to conduct an annual review of his membership.[21] He still goes to his office and leads his law firm, but technically speaking he does not handle any cases. It is his team that does so.

Neither QB nor CFS is alone. Every homeowner activist in Beijing instructed me on the important meaning of their movement for democracy in China, although some saw that meaning as more implicit than others. The political nature of the movement will become clearer in the next two sections about Beijing, but, to conclude this section, not only QB, but also a couple of other leading activists in Beijing have run for local people's congresses. As one of the other activists who did so commented in an interview: "I'm not interested in getting elected but [in] teaching people how to deal with their property rights and practice democracy. What does 'living changes China' mean? This is what it means."[22]

5.1.2 Inter-Community Mobilization and Association

Homeowners in Beijing started the process of founding an inter-community association of homeowners at a fairly early stage,[23] with the initiative to create such an association being raised as early as 2006. The chairmen of four HoCs held a meeting on June 25, 2006, after which they sent a joint letter to HoAs across the city that read in part as follows: "Homeowners and HoAs are often isolated and have no support.... There is also a need to create a home for HoAs in Beijing or even all over the country, to build a foundation for social stability and social harmony. Such an organization should be an association of HoAs."[24]

It is unsurprising that the homeowners of Beijing would want to create an inter-community association. Such an association of HoAs could play multiple roles, the two most important being (1) to provide a platform for the exchange of information and knowledge and act as an intermediary between the government and homeowners and (2) to represent homeowners in the city and even across the country as an independent power, thereby reforming the current government structure. The drafters of the former letter chose to emphasize the second role.

Setting up any organization in China requires approval from and registration with the government. On August 29, 2006, thirty two HoAs sent a request as joint applicants to the Beijing city housing administration.[25] Around the same time, the founders of this proposed inter-community association, primarily the four drafters of the letter, decided to "do all they can to strengthen communications among HoAs and provide free support and help to communities that need help." They visited three to four neighborhoods each month to guide them through the process of establishing an HoA.[26]

They even held the first annual meeting of HoAs on January 21, 2007. On the advice of their lawyers, however, they avoided using the name Beijing Association of Homeowners' Associations (BJHC) because doing so would be illegal without approval. Instead they used the name Application Committee for BJHC. HoCs' members and representatives from 103 communities, 30 academics, 10 lawyers, and 29 members of the news media attended this first annual meeting of Beijing homeowners.[27] The BJHC held annual meetings until 2017 despite never obtaining approval from the Beijing city government. I analyze the Beijing city government's attitude to the proposed association in Table A.2 in Appendix II.

The MLY HoA is one of the thirty two joint sponsors of the BJHC.[28] The first HoC in MLY, after being elected, decided to sue the developer and its affiliated MC over multiple issues involving real estate management and property rights to common space and facilities. In response, the MC sued the homeowners for not paying their management fee. The homeowners lost the suit in the first-instance court.[29]

However, the appellate court reversed the lower court's decision, ordering a reduction in the management fee on the basis that the MC had committed fraud in calculating its operating costs. That decision did not end the case, however. The MC applied to reopen the case with a supportive experts' opinion from law professors in Beijing and a supportive letter from the Beijing Real Estate Management Association, and the appellate court granted their application.

In response, the BJHC issued a public letter calling for support for the MLY homeowners. The letter read in part:

> Please protect the victory of MLY because it is our joint victory! Please support MLY's actions because its destiny will be our common destiny. Please voice your support for MLY, because it is supporting you yourselves! The court should maintain its decision as it is to protect the majority of people's interests! Let's join hands together, work together, defend our rights together, and construct our beautiful homes together!

Under this public pressure, the appellate court confirmed its original decision in the retrial.[30]

The MC then created an emergency in the MLY neighborhood by abandoning it immediately. Without security guards or cleaning staff, the neighborhood filled with garbage and descended into chaos. The situation divided MLY homeowners, with some accusing the activists of having created the conflict against their neighbors' interests simply to become famous.[31]

Faced with this situation, the BJHC organized a meeting calling for the "mutual cooperation of Beijing homeowners," and sent a joint letter to the government requesting that it take action to disqualify the MC and issuing the following warning: "For social stability, the government should make a resolution as fast as possible!"[32] A deputy mayor of the Beijing city government responded publicly, and the government forced the MC to return to the neighborhood to maintain its operations until another MC selected by the MLY HoA could take over.[33]

The power of inter-community mobilization in this instance is clear, with the joint force of real estate interests and government authority being forced to compromise. The Beijing homeowners' movement achieved its peak through the nationwide mobilization of homeowners in the making of China's first property law in 2007, which I discuss in the following section.

5.1.3 Lobbying in the Making of the 2007 Property Law

Lobbying in the making of the 2007 Property Law was an unprecedented example of civic participation led by an independent organization in the legislative history of the PRC. The BJHC had always been more interested in institution-building than individual neighborhood governance. The 2007 Property Law is the first basic law pertaining to property rights in China, and lays out the rights that the country's homeowners enjoy and specifies how they can govern their communities in its Chapter 6.[34] It is a foundational law on homeowners' rights. The Chinese legislature, that is, the NPC, adopted an "open-door" legislative strategy, inviting citizens to submit their opinions on the draft law, which underwent seven reviews by the NPC Standing Committee before the NPC vote.[35] It is thus clear that the macro-political environment in that decade left space for civic participation. However, the participation of the BJHC, an unregistered, unapproved nongovernmental organization (NGO), was still exceptional.

The BJHC publicized a proposal on the revision of the draft property law in the annual meeting of Beijing homeowners in January 2007 and sent the proposal to HoAs nationwide.[36] On February 11, 2007, it organized multiple news conferences called "Joint signature action to improve chapter six of the draft property law and further protect homeowners' rights" in cities across the country. In these conferences, homeowners released a uniform version of the proposal and called for action. In the Beijing conference that was held in the MLY neighborhood, one HoC chairman said during a speech:

> We used half of our life savings as a mortgage in purchasing an apartment. Now, we are getting together from all across the country ... forming a community with mutually connected interests. We are all on the same boat[, but that boat is the] Titanic. We have the same identity as homeowners and the same destiny. In the context of China, property rights are not only property rights, but also human rights.... Therefore, every homeowner should care about our common interest, cherish our rights, and participate enthusiastically.[37]

Signatures were initially sent to the BJHC in two ways: through a website, which collected only 1,800 signatures before being shut down by the government not long after the aforementioned news conference, and on paper via the postal service or via email. The BJHC eventually collected 14,186 individual signatures and 66 collective signatures in the form of HoAs, representing 167,825 citizens, and publicly sent its proposal together with all of these signatures to the national legislature.[38]

There is no way to prove the causality between the BJHC's lobbying and the subsequent revision of the disputed chapter. However, the substantive revisions of the draft were consistent with its proposal.[39] Though the government never officially recognized the BJHC's participation in the making of the property law, and never even acknowledged receipt of its proposal,[40] both its founders and homeowners' communities felt that they had made a major contribution to the legislation.[41] In the words of one homeowner: "Defending our rights is democracy; democracy is a way, a power; neighborhood business is our common business."[42]

In summary, leading homeowners' activists such as CFS and QB and leading homeowners' organizations such as the BJHC have adopted property rights as a cause for political mobilization and neighborhood governance as an experimental site for democracy. We now turn to a discussion of the situation in Shenzhen.

5.2 Shenzhen: Property as a Social Right

Shenzhen is the birthplace of China's market economy, and thus also of the country's real estate development and management industries.[43] Homeowners in Shenzhen established the first HoAs in China[44] and are famous nationwide for their rights consciousness.[45] Owing to the fragmented nature of authoritarian governance in Shenzhen, the city's homeowners focus on and claim absolute sovereignty within their neighborhoods, challenging national and local laws with their manipulation of inconsistencies across different levels and fragments of laws.[46] They cite local regulations against national law in some cases, whereas cite national law against local regulations in other cases, as explained in the two cases further.

They consider the law to be a milder, more feasible instrument for fulfilling their rights than public protests. Although they use law and litigation a lot, their claims to absolute homeowner sovereignty within their neighborhoods are not confined by law or local regulations. Their pursuit of absolute homeowner sovereignty includes two specific aspects. The first concerns whether the city government can impose regulations on homeowners' management rights, for example, requiring expert participation in selecting MCs,[47] and the second whether homeowners have absolute control over the common space and structures in their neighborhoods. Two leading homeowners in the city built their careers as activists through their contestation of each.

Homeowners in Shenzhen also regularly communicate with one another, learn from one another, and share expertise and information with one other. There are leading homeowner activists who are widely known and influential in Shenzhen, but they are not as enthusiastic about the "big idea" of democracy as their counterparts in Beijing, and neither are they interested in mobilizing homeowners for a political movement. Instead, leading homeowner activists have managed to obtain approval from the city government to establish citywide homeowners' organizations, which in return play an intermediary role between homeowners and other parties including government and market entities.

In the following section, I investigate experiences of two leading activists and inter-community cooperation in the city.

5.2.1 Leading Activists as Social Entrepreneurs

Shenzhen is the other center of China's homeowners' movement, boasting quite a few nationally famed homeowners, including ZJJ, who was reported as the No. 1 Homeowner by the national media for his creative use of law in defending homeowners' right to govern their own neighborhoods, and FGZ, who litigated twenty one cases within eleven years to take back common space and a building in his neighborhood from a developer, successfully bringing the last case to the SPC, unprecedented in Chinese homeowners' movement.

5.2.1.1 Defending Rights According to Law?

ZJJ was stuck in his building's elevator when it plummeted from the twenty-fifth floor to the fifth floor, a common experience to his neighbors, and agreed to run for the HoC after finding that he had no way to sell up his apartment.[48] He bought his first apartment in Shenzhen in 1998 after working in the city for a decade. He was one of the best known among his neighbors because he had appeared in the local TV news on behalf of his employer, a state-owned telecoms company, from time to time.

After ZJJ's election, he and his neighbors negotiated with the developer to solve various problems, particularly replacing the elevators, but the negotiations failed. In response, ZJJ's neighbors planned to protest in front of the Shenzhen city government building, as many other homeowners in the city were doing at the time, causing the government considerable headache.

However, ZJJ thought of another way: defending homeowners' rights according to law. In his view, protests would not solve their problems. This was right after "rule of law" had been written into China's constitution in 1999.[49] ZJJ invited a government official and three lawyers to the community to teach his neighbors related laws and regulations. They then brought a class action suit against the developer,[50] won their case, which was then widely reported nationwide as signaling a new way of defending homeowners' rights, a "moderate and rational way" welcomed by both homeowners and the government as opposed to social protests and conflicts.[51]

ZJJ next moved to replace the MC and came into direct confrontation with the city housing administration, which insisted that based on a local regulation,[52] the power to select MCs belonged to experts in the city housing administration's database. The HoA of ZJJ's condominium building selected a new MC through a majority vote without participation of the experts, which was declared invalid by the city housing administration. ZJJ argued that homeowners' property rights and contract rights were protected by both the constitution and law, which should prevail over local regulations. In response, the city housing administration issued a decision relieving ZJJ of his position as the HoC chairman. But ZJJ's neighbors re-elected him to the same position.

The ongoing drama caught nationwide media attention. He was applauded as a pioneer in defending homeowners' property rights by China Central Television (CCTV), which commended him for "blazing a way of defending rights according to law with both passion and reason."[53] A senior official in the MoC called the city housing administration to express his concern. As a result, the administration made no further moves to enforce its decision, but it never formally revoked it.[54]

The battle gained ZJJ his reputation as China's No. 1 Homeowner, the title of a report on him published in *China Reform*, an influential national magazine.[55] In the past fifteen years, he has meticulously leveraged his fame and interpreted laws to achieve his community governance goals, and has had two unprecedented achievements: (1) taking control of the parking space in his neighborhood and (2) obtaining a certificate of the organizational code for his HoC.

In the case of property rights over parking space, ZJJ studied the original construction plan and the building permit and determined that the parking space had not been counted in calculating the floor area ratio of the neighborhood, which meant that the developer had not paid for it. Therefore, it had been transferred to homeowners together with the land use rights to the neighborhood.[56]

This was an expanded interpretation of condominium owners' joint ownership, and a smart claim, and one that ZJJ still insists upon today, although the 2007 Property Law actually states that the parking space in original building plans should be decided by agreement, thereby acknowledging developers' right to it.[57] ZJJ's claim was made in 2006, however. The developer could not devise a more reasonable argument than ZJJ's and was unable to use illegal means to deal with him because of the national media coverage. Hence ZJJ was able to take control of the parking space for the neighborhood, bringing in several million RMB per year.

However, this cash flow created another problem: In the absence of its own bank account, the HoA had to deposit the money into the MC's account, a major inconvenience when there was a change in MC.[58] ZJJ needed the government to issue an organizational code to the HoA, which it needed to open a bank account in Shenzhen, and again found a law to suit his purposes. The Organizational Code Regulation contained a list of entities eligible for organizational codes, a list that did not include HoAs.[59]

However, ZJJ argued that one particular clause that ended with a section saying "other organizations established according to law"[60] meant that HoAs should be included in the list. The city government objected, and ZJJ requested that they contact Beijing for instructions. They did so immediately in ZJJ's presence. The person reached in Beijing said that he knew ZJJ from the CCTV report and asked to speak to him directly. ZJJ made the aforementioned argument during the phone conversation. The person in Beijing told the Shenzhen official that, as a place of market reform, Shenzhen should give ZJJ's suggestion a try, with his community serving as an experimental site. The HoA got an organization code as a result.[61] After receiving the code, ZJJ even managed to register the parking space under the HoA's name.

With both a property rights certificate for the parking space and an organizational code, ZJJ's HoA had the full legal capacity to manage the neighborhood. ZJJ is still active and regularly gives advice to homeowners in Shenzhen and nationwide. He has also maintained a good relationship with government officials.

Although ZJJ had tried to run for election to the local people's congress, he told me in a recent interview that "I don't think people's congress membership is that meaningful. I often send materials to them (i.e., government officials) and ... influence them. They often exchange ideas with me. That is to say, we have already made huge efforts, though the result is uncertain."[62] It is clear that, unlike his counterparts in Beijing, ZJJ has not been particularly interested in larger-scale political reform.

5.2.1.2 Twenty-One Suits within Eleven Years!

FGZ's involvement in the homeowners' movement was also coincidental. He was an engineer in a European company before his retirement and bought an apartment in a central area of Shenzhen in 1988. In the following decade, the developer continued to control the neighborhood after homeowners moved in. It built another two-floor building within the neighborhood boundaries, converted empty space on the ground floor into studios, many of which were leased to prostitutes, and announced plans to build a shopping mall on the neighborhood green space. FGZ's then college-age daughter was even once harassed by visitors looking for sex services in the neighborhood.[63]

In 2000, FGZ drafted a petition letter about the need to defend the green space in his neighborhood, solicited signatures from dozens of his neighbors, and sent it to the mayor of Shenzhen. Much to the surprise of his neighbors, albeit not to FGZ, the mayor responded and halted the construction on the neighborhood green space. FGZ chose the timing deliberately because the Shenzhen city government had recently publicly committed itself to building a city of "bluer sky, greener land, clearer water."[64] Hence, a rights claim asking for the preservation of green space in a central area of the city was likely to draw the mayor's attention.

In 2002, the Shenzhen city government started enforcing laws against illegal buildings and structures. FGZ capitalized on the momentum of such enforcement to sue the Land and Urban Planning Agency for not enforcing such laws in his neighborhood. During the litigation, he contacted the local media to widely publicize illegal structures and businesses in the neighborhood. Under the combined legal and media pressure, the agency demolished all illegal structures within the neighborhood and therefore eliminated all related businesses.

This was a good start, but what made FGZ famous and caused him to be named a leading homeowner in Shenzhen were the twenty one lawsuits he filed within eleven years, the last of which ended up before the SPC, a step unprecedented in the Chinese homeowners' movement.[65] FGZ and his fellow homeowners claim collective rights to a two-floor building within the boundaries of their condominium complex, which the developer built after the homeowners had moved in but with governmental approval of changing the original building plan. They argued that the 2007 Property Law gave homeowners common property rights to everything within the boundaries of the condominium complex but not individually owned, which is not true as our discussion about parking space has revealed.[66] In response, the developer argued that (1) the 2007 Property Law does not apply since the building in dispute was built before 2007;[67] (2) a local regulation which Shenzhen promulgated in 1994 grants property rights to the builder.[68]

On November 11, 2002, the HoC of which FGZ was the chairman sued the developer and the MC for compensation and the return of the two-floor building at the Shenzhen Intermediate People's Court (hereinafter "the Shenzhen Court"), which rejected the case on the basis that the HoC had no property rights to the disputed real estate and therefore lacked direct interests and standing.[69] The HoC appealed to the Guangdong High People's Court, which on December 23, 2003 revoked the Shenzhen Court's decision and requested that it retry the case.[70] It duly did so, and dismissed all of the HoC's claims on October 20, 2004. The HoC again appealed to the Guangdong High People's Court, which on December 30, 2006, again revoked the Shenzhen Court's decision and ordered a retrial.[71]

In this second retrial, the Shenzhen Court confirmed that the HoC was qualified to lodge the litigation. However, it decided that the authority to decide how to deal with the rental income from the illegal studios lay with the city land administration and, further, that the two-story building did not belong to the homeowners as it was independent and separate from other parts of the neighborhood.[72] The HoC appealed yet again. In its final decision on July 6, 2011, the Guangdong High People's Court supported the HoC's claim for compensation but not its claim to the building on the ground that the homeowners had not paid for its construction.[73]

The HoC applied to the SPC for judicial supervision. Technically, litigants are entitled to only two instance trials in China, with the SPC having discretion over whether to reopen a case. The SPC not only decided to reopen the case but also to adjudicate it itself (instead of sending it back to Guangdong). This procedural decision captured nationwide media attention and was viewed as a milestone.[74] The substantive decision that the SPC rendered on November 17, 2013, however, explicitly rejected the HoC's claim that land use rights within the neighborhood boundaries had been transferred from the developer to homeowners on the basis that the developer had obtained approval from and paid the government for the right to use the land beneath the building,[75] consistent with the local regulation Shenzhen promulgated in 1994.[76] The implication was therefore that the government and the developer still had the power to decide on land use in the neighborhood even after the apartments had been sold to homeowners.[77] Overall, it was the process rather than the result that mattered most to FGZ.[78]

Despite multiple litigations involving city government agencies, FGZ has managed to maintain a good relationship with the city government overall,[79] and explicitly stated his disapproval of defending homeowners' rights through public protests: "Don't make the government deem you a ticking time bomb! Only with a good relationship with the government can we get support for HoAs' existence and operation; otherwise we cannot move an inch and might even be blocked, which is worse!"[80] In 2009, FGZ was even elected director of the RC, the official authority governing his neighborhood and two others nearby.

With his rising fame, numerous homeowners began calling him for advice but he remained cautious during such communication. He said that he initially communicated only by phone individually, emphasizing that he never sought to "unite homeowners."[81] He knew what the city government feared most, and he did not want to destroy the mutual trust he had built up with the city government. However, as discussed further, he actually ended up establishing the most influential citywide organization of homeowners in Shenzhen.

In summary, the leading homeowner activists in Shenzhen have a strong consciousness of property rights and want to control their own living space, which they believe they are entitled to do because they have paid for it. They see themselves as having an implicit contract with the government. They take law as a more mild and feasible instrument for them to fulfill their rights and to defend their home than public protests. They are good at manipulating the inconsistencies of different levels of laws and regulations, and mobilizing social and political resources, to define and claim their property rights as broadly as possible.

5.2.2 Inter-Community Cooperation

On June 26, 2012, leading homeowners in Shenzhen, including FGZ and ZJJ, the *Shenzhen Housing and Real Estate Magazine* (hereinafter "the Magazine"), and the Shenzhen University Institute of Social Management Innovation jointly launched the Shenzhen Homeowners' Forum in FGZ's neighborhood, which since then has been held about every one or two months.[82] In the first forum, participants discussed the case of FGZ's neighborhood governance and its applicability to other neighborhoods.[83] The forum's goal is to "bridge the gap between homeowners and MCs, between homeowners and government agencies, between individual homeowners and their HoCs."[84] Its official statement promises that,

> across the gap we will build bridges and communicate to survive and develop; we will voice our well-intended and rational voice to promote ... virtuous interactions between individual homeowners and their HoCs, between homeowners and real estate companies, and between homeowners and government agencies. We believe that in between the gap as far as we're good at communication and insist and persist, we'll promote the formation of social consensus and push MCs to innovate and reform, to push forward social fairness and justice, and to push our era forward![85]

The forum's two slogans are "Making a dialogue is the most beautiful gesture of life"[86] and "Participation is power."[87] Its founders also emphasize "four hearts": "homeowners' heart to be comforted; MCs' heart to be secure; RCs' heart to be together; the government's heart to feel assured."[88] In contrast to similar ventures in Beijing, which seek to replace the government as the entity in charge of homeowners, the Shenzhen Homeowners' Forum is intended as a platform for homeowners to share information and an intermediary among various stakeholders.

Thanks to coverage in the Magazine and other news media,[89] the Shenzhen Homeowners' Forum has become increasingly influential. Homeowners from communities across the city, as well as MC employees, scholars, local people's congress members, and government officials, attended this forum regularly. Two Shenzhen city leaders also attended the forum once.[90]

The forum's guiding philosophy of serving as a bridge with rather than leading a social movement against the government also contributed to the establishment of citywide organizations of homeowners. The first such organization, the Shenzhen Southern China Center of Harmonious Community Development, which was approved by the Shenzhen Department of Civic Affairs and supported by the Guangdong Province Department of Civic Affairs, was established in November 2015. One of the founders of the Shenzhen Homeowners' Forum delivered a speech at the launch ceremony in which he asked "What is the difference between ruling and governance?... Governance involves [many] more entities beyond government agencies.... The source of governance can be law, but can also be [a] social contract.... Between us there is a social contract, and let's do our business according to it."[91]

The following year, on March 6, 2016, the Shenzhen Center of Promoting Transparent and Harmonious Communities (SZHC) was officially launched with government approval at the Shenzhen Civic Center, which is also home to the city government. FGZ has been the center's general secretary. His two deputies were YZM, a young man who was also the chair of his own HoC and wrote a column for the Magazine on homeowners' movement before joining the SZHC, and another HoC chair who was also a member of the city people's congress.[92]

Various government agencies, including the mayor's office and the news media, sent official delegates to attend the opening ceremony,[93] and a senior official from the city housing administration spoke highly of the SZHC in his public congratulatory speech. He claimed that he was an early supporter of and participant in the Shenzhen Homeowners' Forum and stated that the general trend was to establish a framework of self-governance by homeowners, professional service delivery by MCs, and governmental supervision.[94]

The SZHC has successfully played an intermediary role to conciliate conflicts between homeowners and MCs in the city, one that has proved to be more effective than government conciliation, as the following example shows.

One community in Shenzhen decided to organize a public protest against its MC. The government learned of its intention before the planned protest and sent officials and people's congress members to the community to negotiate. However, the community's homeowners did not trust them, and thus one of the government officials called on FGZ.

FGZ went to the neighborhood and analyzed the situation together with the homeowners. He urged them not to convert a civic issue into a political one. Once they protested publicly, he explained, it would become a matter for the government's stability maintenance apparatus instead of the housing administration, which would only complicate their situation. The homeowners then asked FGZ whether he could guarantee that the MC would solve their problem. He said that he could offer no such guarantee but that he would talk to the company. The homeowners and the company eventually reached an agreement, and protest and conflict were avoided. It seems that such a satisfactory conclusion was possible only because FGZ was an influential homeowner activist with credibility on both sides.[95]

5.3 Shanghai: Property as a Legal Right

Homeowners in Shanghai are in many ways the opposite of homeowners in Beijing. One homeowner activist in Shanghai told me:

> I had contact with CFS and SKX in Beijing at the beginning, but we do not really pee in the same pot. Our ways of doing things are different.... Those people [homeowner activists in Beijing and Shenzhen] are nonsense: they see everything [in the neighborhood] as homeowners' [property].... They do not study laws and regulations; just want to fight; and get a group of people [to fight].

> Sometimes we use that way [fighting], but only when we have to … and you cannot use that way too often.… What's our pursuit? For example, how to organize a homeowners' meeting, procedurally how to make it strict, or how to make information transparent in a community, we pursue these details … these are what our homeowners are concerned about.[96]

Homeowners in Shanghai take law seriously. They define and claim their property rights in accordance with the law. Homeowners in Beijing and Shenzhen also claim to take the law seriously. The difference lies in the distance between homeowners' claims and the original intention of national and/or local legislation. What differs Shanghai from Beijing and Shenzhen is a basic consensus among different stakeholders on the applicability and meaning of laws and regulations in the community governance arena.

In Shanghai, homeowners seem to be much more obedient and mild-mannered than their counterparts in Beijing and Shenzhen. They are in some sense invisible or, in the words of a leading Shanghai-based sociologist, "quite passive."[97] An observer will find no evidence of inter-community mobilization or organization, but he or she will see active online groups of homeowners and regular offline gatherings of homeowners across the city, with homeowner activists sharing their experience of and expertise in community governance. Although this does not look like a social movement, these rule-based, obedient homeowners have been successful in taking control over the governance of their neighborhoods.

In the following paragraphs, I first discuss the scope of homeowners' rights in Shanghai, and then examine how they exercise and defend self-governance by law. Finally, I address how the demand for legal knowledge leads to inter-community cooperation in Shanghai.

5.3.1 Common Property Rights as Defined by Law

What does "common property rights" mean? Homeowners in both Beijing and Shenzhen claim absolute control over the space within the boundaries of their communities, including all public facilities and aboveground and underground parking space. However, the 2007 Property Law has specifically stipulated that property rights over public facilities and aboveground parking space belong to homeowners, but underground parking space to developers.[98] In addition, it is unclear in law whether a developer and/or the government can alter an original building plan to build more facilities or structures. In FGZ's case, we saw that he fought very hard against government rezoning but failed.

When homeowners in Shanghai found themselves in a similar situation, they not only chose not to fight the city government's rezoning; they actually deferred to it. The situation was this. European-Style Flower Capital is a residential condominium complex of 1,538 apartments that were valued at an average price of RMB 57,000 (US\$8,430)/m^2 in 2018. In the original sales contract, the developer promised to build an elderly service center and a clubhouse but instead constructed a building for the RC and a commercial building, respectively. Some homeowners in the complex were angry at first and wanted to claim ownership of both buildings.

After members of the HoC checked the government registration and discovered that the developer had all of the documents it needed for the rezoning and that the current buildings also had clear registered titles, they gave up their claims. The HoC deputy chair pointed out that the only name she saw on the real estate certificate was that of the MC: "You want me to take it back?! Is it possible?!"[99] Although some of her neighbors may have felt disgruntled, that was the end of the story. This could be taken as evidence of Shanghai homeowners' law-abiding approach serving to limit their property rights. However, a few other cases show otherwise.

Under national law, developers are required to provide real estate management facilities, and homeowners hold common property rights to those facilities.[100] In Beijing and Shenzhen, many HoAs do not have their own offices, whereas in Shanghai quite a large percentage do.[101] The following case shows how one HoC in Shanghai claimed its right to an office. Overseas-Style Garden is a condominium complex of 1,620 apartments with an average price of around RMB 82,000 (US$12,125)/m^2 in 2018. Its HoC sued the developer for not providing an office as required by law. The developer lost in both first- and second-instance litigation and was ordered to provide the HoC with RMB 2.4 million in compensation, and the HoC also went to court for enforcement of that order.[102] The case demonstrates that homeowners in Shanghai do actively defend their property rights in accordance with the law.

The most contested component of the common space in China's condominium complexes is underground parking space, which national law grants to developers.[103] In the past two decades, the country's car ownership rate has skyrocketed, leading to a shortage of parking space in cities. A single parking space in central Shanghai can sell for as much as RMB 0.5 million–1 million.[104] Unlike their counterparts in Beijing and Shenzhen, Shanghai homeowners do not claim property rights contrary to the law, which they deem to be pretty clear.

That does not mean, however, that they have never tried to exert control or influence over the parking space within their communities. Although they recognize that they do not have property rights to the underground parking space in their complexes, they claim management rights over the entire neighborhood, which means that a developer needs the cooperation of the HoC to operate underground parking areas. One HoC chair explained the situation as follows.

> Yes, he [the developer] has parking spots. But whether he can sell his parking spots and how to sell [them] – all these issues need to be solved through the real estate management company. Now we [the homeowners' committee] have control over the management company, and if we do not allow outside people to come in, you are finished. If a developer does not understand his situation and

> becomes our opponent, we have various procedures to follow.... Once we disagree, you can do nothing with your parking spots.[105]

5.3.2 Self-Governance by Law

In the management of their neighborhoods, HoCs in Shanghai resort to the law as a self-preservation strategy. First, they stick to the law and emphasize transparency and procedure in their election and operation. Second, in regulating homeowners' behavior within the community, they also resort to the law, which they view as a rational and effective means of governance. Third, they defend their autonomy and challenge the party's leadership via the law.

Community elections can be messy affairs, as is well documented in village elections in rural China.[106] In urban China, they can be even more complicated, as residents of condominium complexes were strangers to one another before they moved in. Further, resident mobility can be high, and, unlike in rural China, there are no lineage connections. How can a credible election be run in communities of homeowners with diverse backgrounds and opinions? How can the losing party be made to accept the election result?[107] Shanghai homeowners' solution is transparency. They video-record the entire election process and make the results traceable by voters. In one case, a homeowner challenged an election result, claiming that she had not voted. The election committee was able to find the signed ballot associated with her apartment, showing that her husband had voted. Once the results of the investigation were publicized, the rumor of election manipulation disappeared.[108]

Another problem is the potential abuse of power by HoCs. How can such abuse be avoided? How can homeowners be convinced that HoC members have not abused their power? One HoC member answered as follows:

> What's the most important thing when homeowners are questioning your integrity? It should be following the rules, which is the first thing you should do to protect yourself. If you have procedural problems and get all [of your] decisions overturned, you [will] not even be able to protect yourself; what else can you do for the community? Community stability requires everybody to follow rules.

He gave an example. His committee had originally agreed to limit its budget to RMB 1,000 per year, which proved to be too low to run the neighborhood effectively. What did the committee members do? They called for another homeowners' meeting to revise the budget instead of overspending.[109]

HoCs in Shanghai are also adept at using laws to regulate homeowners' behavior. Parking on common ground is a prevalent problem,[110] and homeowners thus need a management mechanism to decide who can park where and when. Many communities in Shanghai have passed rules about parking on common ground that may differ from prior practices. In one case, a homeowner had occupied two parking spaces for a long time but the HoA passed a new rule stipulating that each apartment was entitled to only one aboveground space. Instead of engaging in a face-to-face debate with the homeowner, the HoC decided to send him an attorney's letter explaining that the association's resolution was binding. As a result, the homeowner accepted the loss of his former *de facto* possession of the additional space. As the committee chair explained to us, "When you put everything on paper, it cannot be too rude or ridiculous. Face-to-face debate often devolves into name-calling. Sending an attorney's letter to the other party is a more rational way to resolve disputes and leaves him a way to back down."[111]

Being law-abiding is not the same as obedience to the authorities. Shanghai HoCs have not been shy about pursuing administrative litigation against the government.[112] For example, on February 24, 2014, the party branch within the community of LQF, who had chaired his community's HoC since 2010, reported to the street-level government that it would call a homeowners' assembly to elect a new HoC because five of the HoC's seven members had resigned. LQF did not dispute that an election was necessary, but he argued in court that the Party branch did not have the power to call for a homeowners' assembly. He was technically correct, as the law says nothing about the Party's role in communities, although the Shanghai city government had established party branches in all residential communities and relies on them in governance.

LQF's dispute was a neighborhood matter, but it was also a direct challenge to the Party's leadership, and thus politically sensitive. The court did not avoid the issue but adjudicated that there was nothing wrong with a party branch *reporting* what was going on in the community, implicitly acknowledging LQF's argument that the party branch did not have the power to call for a meeting without overturning the government's decision.[113] This case testifies perfectly to one slogan of Shanghai homeowners: "We do not worship authority. We respect laws and procedures, and are in awe of rules!"[114]

5.3.3 Entrepreneurship in Law

Shanghai homeowners accord the law such an important place in self-governance that there is huge demand for legal knowledge. To meet that demand, one homeowner activist founded an online platform to collect all of the laws, regulations, and rules pertaining to HoAs and developed an app for homeowners' use. He also founded an online/WeChat group in which homeowners from Shanghai and elsewhere in the country discuss various legal and operational issues involved in establishing and running HoCs. The group also regularly organizes offline meetings in which homeowners share their experiences and expertise. These meetings constitute the main inter-community forum of homeowners in Shanghai, which lacks any citywide association of HoAs such as those in Beijing and Shenzhen.

The aforementioned app is called *mass ants* to emphasize how numerous homeowners are and their potential to change the society. Instead of having any ambitious political agenda to bring together several million homeowners (like his counterparts in Beijing) or social agenda to bridge various stakeholders (like his counterparts in Shenzhen), HB, the founder of the online platform and mass ants app, who is also an HoC chair, simply wants to build a great enterprise. HB, who is young and runs his own IT company, believes in the development of HOA's in China, which he sees as having huge business potential. He even asked me to join him because, he said, "this is huge!"[115] In the following paragraphs, I investigate HB's history from a neighborhood activist to providing a platform for citywide homeowners to communicate, to highlight the role of law and the style of inter-community cooperation in Shanghai.

HB's neighborhood is a condominium complex of 772 apartments that sold at an average price of RMB 50,000/m^2 in 2018. His participation was accidental. He needed people to play badminton with, and so organized an online badminton group in his community. In the beginning, he took care of everything, including booking badminton courts, providing equipment, and arranging transportation. People only had to join. Over time, increasing numbers of his neighbors joined his informal badminton club.[116] He then made use of the group to organize a protest against a nearby factory that was polluting the air[117] and to demand that the government enforce zoning laws against an illegal structure in the neighborhood.[118] HB's mobilization and organization ability made him an important person in his neighborhood, a point he explicitly acknowledged: "Your organization and mobilization ability is the reason that other people respect you. If an HoC has no basic mobilization ability, why would the government respect you?"[119] However, the mobilization to which he refers is restricted within neighborhood boundaries, and must proceed in legal, orderly fashion.

In the case of the protest against the polluting factory, HB organized a group of thirty people to drive their cars to and circle the factory at midnight, a time at which they would not cause a disturbance to public order. Also, once they were at the factory, they informed the police to enforce laws against the factory's illegal emission instead of private enforcement.[120] In the case of the illegal structure, he organized a group of about 100 people to watch as it was erected on the roof of a building and informed the government enforcement agency of their plans in advance. The enforcement agency, which was worried about social stability given the size of the crowd, was forced to send enforcement officials to demolish the illegal structure.[121] In both cases, HB's organization and mobilization of homeowners put considerable pressure on the government, but as no boundaries were crossed, the government had no excuse to suppress their activities.

As a result of HB's role in establishing the badminton club and organizing the two protests, he became the person with whom the government chose to deal in helping the community to establish an HoA. The RC even took part in HB's online group to better understand the dynamics of the community.[122] An HoA was eventually established and an HoC as the executive body was elected in 2016 with HB as the chair, a position he has held ever since. A recent success was changing the neighborhood's MC against the government's will.[123]

HB mastered the art of homeowner activism within the boundary of law through the aforementioned neighborhood participation: He know what the laws are and how to use them, sometimes together with a well-controlled demonstration of homeowner mobilization. He began sharing his expertise on *Zhihu*, a popular Chinese Q&A website,[124] and many homeowners began contacting him online for suggestions. When the number of questions grew too large to reply to individually, HB established the aforementioned WeChat group for homeowners to discuss various issues with one another, and later developed the mass ants app.[125] HB and the deputy chair of his HoC are the majority shareholders in the company that owns the app, and the chairs or deputy chairs of four other HoCs have become minority shareholders.[126]

As noted earlier, HB has also organized multiple offline homeowners' meetings in Shanghai. The topics discussed are generally very practical, such as how to operate a community maintenance fund, how to organize a homeowners' meeting, how to select an MC, and how to make use of new media in community governance.[127] HB is also active in the WeChat group he operates and maintains, leading discussions and enforcing rules aimed at ensuring high-quality conversations. One rule is that members cannot post anything unrelated to homeownership, including political rumors and advertising.[128]

HB regularly reiterates in group chats that the group's purpose is "better communities and [a better] living environment and … the preservation and improvement of [our] assets."[129] HB's app and the online and offline activities he has organized have brought homeowners living in different communities across Shanghai together. However, such inter-community connections are limited to the sharing of information, knowledge, expertise, and experience. They in no way constitute an organization of homeowners. HB is simply a service provider. He has shown no interest in organizing or mobilizing homeowners across the city. His ambition is limited to developing a stable community governance regime that protects homeowners' assets, an ambition shared by most homeowners in Shanghai.

Of course, as an entrepreneur, HB also wants to make a fortune from the city's urban transformation through the digitalization of homeownership laws and regulations. The law plays a central role in his plans:

> Many problems with current HoCs [stem from not] being … professional: they do not understand how to get things done, and they like to fight. Actually, with the use of laws and regulations, we can make … society more harmonious. Do not intensify conflicts – there is an effective way – it is just that homeowners do not know how to do it legally yet.[130]

Part III
Benefits and Risks

6

The Origin of Self-governed Communities in Authoritarian Cities

Social scientists have long emphasized the importance of social norms and communities to development[1] and democracy,[2] but these theories beg a prior question: Where do communities come from? The classic examples in the literature all take communities as a given: New England settlers with the same religion,[3] merchants of the same ethnic groups,[4] professionals of the same industries,[5] villages, and towns with decades of history and family relationships dating back several generations.[6] It was in this spirit that Tocqueville commented, "it is man who establishes kingdoms and creates republics; the town seems to come directly from the hands of God."[7] New England towns in Tocqueville's writing were essentially self-governed local communities. Such communities, he went on, "escape human effort so to speak," are "rarely created," and "arise by itself."[8]

In the context of liberal democracy, particularly in America, scholars have challenged this inherited notion of civic engagement, recognizing that communities "constitute sites of political engagement and contestation,"[9] making the case for "bringing the state back in" and assessing its restrictive and constitutive roles in the development of civic communities and organizations through public welfare programs,[10] by providing public and institutional infrastructure,[11] and even via training activists and nurturing civic spirits in the midst of state-sponsored political campaigns.[12] Influences such as these have had both positive and negative consequences for democracy, the latter of which were exemplified in the relationship between the Trump presidency and right-wing civic extremism.[13]

Self-governed local communities would appear least likely to develop and prosper in authoritarian regimes, which are considered to be hostile to the development of autonomous civic organizations and often play neighbors and groups against one another.[14] What's more, cross-country data bolster this notion of authoritarianism working against civic communities, revealing that "statism" constrains individual associational activity of all types, particularly social movement associations.[15] China seems to be no exception, in that its civic organizations are suppressed, eliminated, marginalized, or assimilated.[16] The only chance for their survival in China, if any, is said to be the fragmentation of the authoritarian state.[17]

This conventional wisdom, however, is challenged by the apparent durability and prevalence of homeowners' associations (HoAs) in China, an authoritarian country that is instinctively suspicious of civic associations and whose government apparatus closely monitors and controls their development. This research examines the origin of Chinese HoAs, investigating the factors contributing to their successful establishment and, as a consequence, exploring the origin of self-governed communities in China's urban neighborhoods.

Based on a unique dataset of questionnaire survey about Chinese homeowners, I found that democratized neighborhoods have enjoyed better governing outcomes than their non-democratized counterparts, while also showing that the local government played a helping hand in establishing HoAs and thereby afforded neighborhoods mechanisms for self-governance. I also found that homeowner activists in democratized neighborhoods developed greater trust in the local government and deemed local officials both more supportive of neighborhood self-governance and less likely to collude with real estate management companies (MCs) and developers than was the case within non-democratized neighborhoods.

Section 6.1 examines the theory about state and self-governed communities. Section 6.2 introduces my survey design. Section 6.3 presents qualitative evidence about the government's helping hand in supporting self-governed communities. Section 6.4 conducts a quantitative analysis of survey data. Section 6.5 concludes this chapter.

6.1 Theory about State and Self-governed Communities

There are two prevailing views regarding the relationship between communities and the state. The first view holds that communities are an alternative to the state and can either check the abuse of state power[18] or supplement the state in terms of governance or provision of services.[19] This view often assumes communities are exogenous – a kind of gift from history and culture – or it considers them to be formed through frequent and repeated interactions. Raghuram Rajan, former IMF chief economist and former head of India's central bank, recently devoted an entire book to examining how markets and the state leave the community behind and arguing that "a real community pulls itself up."[20] Tocqueville commented that the continuous action of laws and of mores, circumstances, and above all time succeed in the consolidation of local self-governed communities.[21] Robert Putnam's study of civic communities in Italy tracing their roots to the medieval period,[22] as well as his study of the collapse and revival of American community, consider frequent and repeated civic interactions the key to community formation.[23] But how are communities to be reinvigorated if only communities can pull themselves up? International development agencies such as the World Bank have engaged in community building worldwide, with an unsatisfactory if not disastrous record.[24]

The second view rejects the notion that communities are natural[25] and argues that communities can be an instrument of political control, particularly in non-democratic states. The intimate relationship between mass organizations and the state in the rise of fascism in Italy and Germany[26] and in today's authoritarian regimes, sustains the notion that states can engineer community formation and thus exercise additional indirect political control through such communities. Mattingly, for his part, found that Chinese local governments expropriated land and implemented the one-child policy by co-opting village community elites.[27] But while these studies reveal the pernicious potential of the state, they do not address whether there is a general role the government can play in a bottom-up effort to form communities – an effort that does not implicate cultivating civic organizations as a pretext for infiltration and containment of democratic practices.

The prior instrumentalist view of communities fails to differentiate civic organizations according to their internal governance mechanisms, particularly with regard to whether the internal governance of a civic organization is democratic or authoritarian. This emphasis on the internal governance of civic organizations is essential, in that Tocqueville takes democratically governed associations based on equal citizenship to be a kind of free school of democracy whereby the habit and mind of democracy are nurtured. Considering this original function of civic associations in light of contemporary theoretical suppositions, we might argue that democratically governed civic associations promote democracy, whereas hierarchically structured civic associations, whether due to their reliance on external funding or authority or because of their embeddedness in traditional hierarchical society, can be a convenient tool of authoritarian control.

China scholars have taken villagers' committees in rural China[28] and residents' committees (RCs) in urban China,[29] which are the lowest end of the party-state bureaucracy and govern one to several neighborhoods, as typical mechanism of political control; they have also addressed the symbiotic relationship between non-government organizations (NGOs) and local government agencies in China.[30] Homeowners in China have been studied, with most research focusing on urban activism in the context of contentious politics.[31] None of the earlier research have examined the internal governance of HoAs in China. Read recognized the democratic potential of homeowner self-organization in China about two decades ago,[32] and, more recently, Tomba's award-winning book emphasized how the growth of a property-owning middle class resulted from social engineering and challenged the normative assumption that the middle class could push China toward democratization.[33] Tomba's book touches upon but does not focus on HoAs.

Both Read and Tomba were prescient in pointing to the lasting shadow of the state in China's modern urban residential neighborhoods,[34] but now is the time for an updated and systematic investigation of the relationship between the local government and homeowners in urban China, particularly regarding the role of the government in urban China's ongoing neighborhood democratization, a process in which homeowners wrest control over their neighborhoods from MCs through establishing self-governed HoAs.

To clarify, bringing the state back in is not a new idea.[35] My study merely builds on this established notion by focusing on the origin of communities in authoritarian regimes, an important but neglected realm within the literature on civic engagement. More specifically, I wonder how the state can be – and has been – involved in transforming a neighborhood of strangers into a self-governed community. To my knowledge, work of this sort has not yet been pursued, as scholars have largely failed to consider the implications of extant theories within an authoritarian context.

I argue that authoritarian regimes' efforts to foster communities go beyond simple social and political control, narrowly defined in the existing literature as reducing or eliminating potential challenges to authoritarian rule. Instead, such efforts can be motivated by a broad concern about effective governance, which is a basis of legitimacy for any regime, democratic or authoritarian. Self-governed communities pose a dilemma for an authoritarian regime. On the one hand, these regimes have traditionally opposed mediating institutions that rival them; on the other hand, self-governed communities can relieve the regime of the burden of governance, which, if handled poorly, could undermine regime legitimacy.[36] The need for social control in daily and grassroots politics can be less salient than satisfying citizens' demand for effective governance and a certain degree of voice in such governance. An authoritarian regime seeking public approval and broader legitimacy might enable and even encourage the development of civic associations – building institutional infrastructure, including a capable and clean bureaucracy, to help individual citizens overcome the collective action problem encountered while forming such communities. In return, individual citizens may develop a greater degree of political trust owing to the community autonomy and effective governance they have realized and on which they now rely.

6.2 Survey Design

My target population was homeowner activists in neighborhoods undergoing or having been recently democratized. Within each of the three megacities, it is difficult to find a significant number of activists by drawing a random sample from the urban population. Even if neighborhoods with an HoA were identifiable based on government information, which is often quite decentralized and fragmented, it would be nearly impossible to find all the neighborhoods in the process of establishing such an association. That said, activists in the same city often communicate with one another via private groups in social media, mainly WeChat, the most popular social app in China with over one billion users. Thus, I deployed these groups of homeowner activists to contact respondents. I disseminated the link for the web-based survey questionnaire in the WeChat groups and encouraged activists to forward it to their own neighborhood group. Such a respondent-driven sampling technique based on social media enabled us to evaluate homeowner activists' perceptions of the institutions related to homeownership with a larger dataset than that afforded by interviews alone.[37]

Compared to traditional chain-referral sampling, my method mitigated biases by reducing dependence on respondents. Snowball sampling has been used commonly to survey hard-to-reach populations, such as undocumented workers and post-disaster service workers.[38] The risk of this technique, however, is that only a cluster within a targeted population might end up being sampled due to the limited range of respondents' social networks. But the WeChat group of a neighborhood can contain members with either strong or weak ties. My approach meant that a homeowner in such a group could access my survey questionnaire through the link posted by another group member, even if the two of them happened to be complete strangers in reality. Since the penetration rate of WeChat is close to 95 percent in the three megacities, I was able to reach a diverse sample of the target population. Still, to maximize the diversity within my sample, I interviewed extensively and started with a dozen initial seeds in the sampling process.

Another major advantage of my method is that a web survey can guarantee respondents' anonymity and privacy. When not in the presence of interviewers, respondents may be less inclined to fear retaliation, may reduce preference falsification, and may increase the response rate regarding sensitive items, especially those touching on topics related to political trust, government-business collusion, and so on.

But a web survey also presents certain methodological problems, one of which is the lack of control over recruitment. Self-selected respondents may submit their answers multiple times, by mistake, or with the intention of skewing results. To discourage respondents from submitting multiple observations, I offered no financial compensation for their participation. In addition, and based on the IP address for the response, I dropped duplicate observations (a total of thirty six) from my database.

Since my sampling method was neither probabilistic nor random, there can be systemic, unobserved differences between homeowners in neighborhoods trying to establish an HoA and those not engaged in such an effort. We recognize these potential differences, but the purpose of my study was to evaluate the local government's role in the process of neighborhood democratization. If a neighborhood had not been active in this regard, having no problem with the MC, then the homeowners would not have enough experience with the government's performance. Another potential coverage error owes to the variation within a neighborhood. Some homeowners, of course, may not belong to the WeChat group of their neighborhoods; still, however, there is a good reason to believe such individuals would also be less interested in self-governance and thus not much different from ordinary homeowners in my sample.

To adjust for coverage and response error in my non-probabilistic sample, and to reduce sample imbalance on covariates and avoid model dependency, I employed the entropy balancing method, which balances the marginal distribution of covariates between the treated group and the control counterfactual after weighting.[39]

6.3 The Government's Helping Hand: Qualitative Evidence

Local governments vary in their attitudes and approaches to neighborhood democratization. As the conventional wisdom on authoritarianism goes, its government can repress civic and democratic communities, creating obstacles at each stage of neighborhood democratization, out of both concern for the "trouble" or shock to the status quo brought by homeowner activists and collusion with MCs.

Cutting the other way, repeated interactions between local officials and homeowner activists may result in some degree of trust and a reciprocal relationship whereby local officials support self-governance in exchange for homeowners' support for the party-state and adherence to legal strictures. If frontline party cadres can develop a long-term reciprocal relationship with homeowners, these officials can affect a cooperative relationship with homeowner activists, helping overcome the collective action problem and supporting neighborhood self-governance in exchange for homeowners acting as "good citizens,"[40] who adhere to legal boundaries, do not make trouble by street protests, and accept the party's authority.[41]

In my fieldwork, I found that some homeowner activists had become involved in community building at the invitation of the RC party secretaries of their neighborhoods. In some cases, frontline party cadres worked with homeowner activists whom they did not initially accept, wary as they were that the popular support of these activists might make these individuals difficult to control, but eventually determined that their cooperation would be essential to resolving neighborhood governance problems. In return, such "prickly" activists also realized they needed government support in neighborhood self-governance and trusted the government more than they had at the beginning, following repeated interactions and cooperation that encouraged the enhancement of neighborhood management and services.

"Old Bull" is a private entrepreneur and was initially excluded from the HoC despite earning the highest number of votes among candidates in a preliminary election. Under pressure from homeowners, the street-level government put him on the list of substitutes. Once the election results were publicized, a formal candidate resigned voluntarily and Old Bull ended up on the HoC, to the surprise of the street-level government, which accepted the result reluctantly and eventually cooperated with this new committee member. By standing on the side of the HoC in a situation rife with physical conflict, the street-level government helped enforce parking rules promulgated by the HoA by standing on the side of the HoC and arrested residents who engaged in usury, a practice that Old Bull and his HoC had tried without success to eliminate from their neighborhood. With the support of the government, Old Bull replaced the preliminary MC with a new one, and since that point, the neighborhood has held regular gatherings during festivals to promote communication among neighbors. A symbol of this achievement of neighborhood governance was that the fountain in the central place of the neighborhood finally started working, much to the delight of Old Bull and his neighbors.[42]

Old Bull now believes firmly in cooperating with the government. In his view, "they really wanted to solve the problems for us and were willing to put in the effort." And as he added,

> We need to see that government officials wanted to have some governance achievements (政绩) and we [needed to know we] can cooperate with them on such things. In many cases, their purpose of having some achievements is overlapping with the enhancement of neighborhood management and provides opportunities for us to defend our interests. If we can make ourselves better in a positive way, I believe that many government agencies are willing to support us.[43]

Also consider the case of "Bean's mom," who led a group of twenty activists to protest the poor management services in their neighborhood. They sent a petition letter to the RC party secretary depicting activists' fingerprints in blood and even planned to go on a demonstration beyond their neighborhood. In response, the party secretary contacted the MC to discuss a plan to address the activists' concerns about neighborhood management. With the RC's support, homeowners subsequently elected an HoC and replaced the original MC with a new one. To resolve the many problems within the neighborhood, including building maintenance, the newly elected HoC, of which Bean's mom was a deputy chairperson, with the support of the RC, obtained funding from the city government, funding that enhanced the credibility of the HoC among homeowners. Through long-term communications and repeated interactions, Bean's mom has come to believe that the party secretary shared the same goal of improving neighborhood services and solving problems in neighborhood governance.[44]

6.4 Quantitative Analysis

To test my theory more rigorously, I designed a survey to examine the impact of HoAs on neighborhood governance and homeowner activists' political trust, and the relationship between government behaviors and homeowner activists' political trust. Specifically, I looked at survey data to test the following hypotheses:

H1: Homeowner activists in neighborhoods that have established HoAs are more likely to report effective governance, ceteris paribus.

H2: Homeowner activists in neighborhoods that have established HoAs have more trust in the local government than do activists in neighborhoods that have not, ceteris paribus.

H3a: Political trust is positively correlated with the government' presumptive support for the HoA, as perceived by homeowner activists, ceteris paribus.

H3b: Political trust is negatively correlated with the government's presumptive collusion with MCs, as perceived by homeowner activists, ceteris paribus.

6.4.1 Key Variables

I designed several variables related to the outcomes of self-governance at both neighborhood and individual level. *Developer-affiliated Management* distinguishes developer-affiliated companies from others dominated by homeowners. *Community Activity* measures the frequency of community activities such as recreational events or holiday parties. *Democratic Value* measures whether homeowners accepted collective decisions that worked against their own preferences. *Community Identity* is a scale variable that reflects the degree to which respondents see themselves as members of the community.

Participating homeowners were surveyed on their degree of trust in various government agencies, from the central level to the street level, although our primary focus was on the street level because it is here where homeowners have the greatest degree of interaction. To gauge robustness, we also measured political trust by using an index – calculating an average score, individually – oriented toward local government agencies, including street-level offices, police departments, district housing departments, district petition offices, and district governments. My rationale for this alternative approach was that homeowner activists may petition to the district government and police when the street office failed to resolve their problems.

I assessed homeowners' activism by asking respondents about their self-identified role within the neighborhood, with options such as *ordinary homeowner*, *enthusiastic homeowner*, *rights-protection activists*, *member of preparatory committee*, *member of HoC*, or chairperson of HoC. Based on the response to this question, we constructed a dummy variable, *Activist*, that took the value of 0 if the respondent reported participating in no neighborhood governance activity (ordinary homeowners) and 1 otherwise. Descriptive analysis revealed that homeowner activists in China differ from nonactivists in many respects.[45] In my sample, 61 percent self-identified as homeowner activists, with roughly 62 percent of these activists reporting ten to twenty hours or more per week invested in neighborhood affairs. By contrast, nearly all nonactivists reported between zero and ten hours of community work per week.[46] Most notably, I found homeowner activists have lower levels of trust toward the street government (not the central government) than do nonactivists, while also holding a stronger belief in democratic decision-making, and having more leisure time to volunteer in neighborhood governance when compared to nonactivists. Based on these data, we contend that activists are the middle class and have not been coopted by local authorities.

I measured the presence of HoA with a dummy variable, *Association,* which takes the value of 1 if a respondent's neighborhood has established the HoA and elected the HoC. In the questionnaire, we asked respondents to report the specific stage of their HoA establishment, so we could evaluate the relative robustness of the associations. Individual-level variables, neighborhood-level variables, and city dummies were fully balanced across respondents living in the neighborhood with HoAs and without them. Individual-level variables include *activist, age, gender, vocation* (e.g., working in the public sector or not), *working hours, level of education,* and *duration of residence in the neighborhood.* Neighborhood-level characteristics include *neighborhood size* (number of households), *age of buildings, average housing price,* and three dummy variables indicating whether there were any petitions, physical conflicts, or administrative litigation that occurred during the process of HoA establishment, HoC re-election, or MC replacement. The analysis below relies on the balanced samples.[47]

6.4.2 Results

Is community self-governance effective? In the first three columns of Table 6.1, I regress the presence of an HoA on governance outcomes at the neighborhood level. A negative correlation in Column 1 offers strong evidence for the

Table 6.1 HoAs and community governance

	Developer-affiliated management (1)	Community activities (2)	Democratic value (3)	Community identity (4)
Homeowners' association	−0.80***	0.12**	0.38*	0.07*
	(0.14)	(0.04)	(0.16)	(0.03)
Activist			0.50*	0.09**
			(0.16)	(0.03)
Observation	834	786	813	813

Note: Models 1 and 3 report the coefficients from logistic regression. Models 2 and 4 report the coefficients from OLS regression.
$^*p < 0.05$, $^{**}p < 0.01$, $^{***}p < 0.001$ (two-tailed test).

enabling effect of HoAs: that is, democratized neighborhoods have a greater chance of replacing the early MC affiliated to the developer. That is to say, homeowners organized under the HoA are more likely to overcome collective action problems and to protect their property rights against fraudulent or incompetent developers and MCs than are those who remain disorganized. Column 2 shows that respondents in neighborhoods with an HoA are more likely to have community activities.

At the individual level, I demonstrate, in Column 3, that organized residents were more likely to comply with democratic decisions than were their counterparts in neighborhoods without an HoA. In addition, activists showed greater respect for democratic principles than did ordinary homeowners.[48] Column 4 reveals that respondents in neighborhoods with an established HoA reported a higher degree of community identity than those without an association. These results, taken together, suggest that HoAs have effectively strengthened homeowner self-governance and control over their neighborhoods, fostered community interactions, cultivated support for democratic values, and generated a sense of community belongingness among residents.

To test H2, I regressed trust in the street government on HoA. Table 6.2 displays the results of the ordinary least square analysis. As we expected, Column 1 shows that, as a neighborhood became democratized, homeowners' trust in the street-level government increased by 0.65 units or roughly 24 percent of the standard deviation. The result was statistically significant at 0.01 level. In Column 2, the model with additional controls of homeowners' activism and trust in the central and city government generated a more statistically

Table 6.2 HoAs, activism, and political trust

	DEV: Trust in street-level government		
	(1)	(2)	(3)
Homeowners' association	0.65***	0.65***	0.13
	(0.19)	(0.15)	(0.26)
Activist		−0.53***	−0.91***
		(0.16)	(0.22)
Association × activist			0.76*
			(0.31)
Trust in central government		−0.24***	−0.24***
		(0.05)	(0.05)
Trust in city government		0.91***	0.92***
		(0.05)	(0.05)
R^2	0.01	0.44	0.45
Observation	813	813	813

Note: The models report the coefficients from OLS regression.
*$p < 0.05$, ** $p < 0.01$, *** $p < 0.001$ (two-tailed test).

significant coefficient estimate for HoA. In Column 3, I included the interaction term of HoA and activism in regression. The coefficient estimate of the interaction term is positive and statistically significant at 0.05 level – meaning that, once a neighborhood established its HoA (i.e., became democratized), activists' trust in the street office increased on average by 0.76 units. This result is consistent with my hypothesis that activists in democratized neighborhoods trusted the local government more than their counterparts did in neighborhoods without HoAs.

Figure 6.1 illustrates the marginal effect of an HoA, with covariates held at the means. In neighborhoods without an HoA, activists had significantly lower trust in the street government than did nonactivists; but as we moved from neighborhoods without HoAs to democratized neighborhoods with HoAs, activists' trust in the street government nearly paralleled that of nonactivists. This finding suggests activists tend to build stronger trust in the local government due to their experience working with supportive local officials.

To test H3a and H3b (or the mechanism of political trust), we asked homeowners to evaluate the street-level government's support for the HoA, *Government support*, as well as its degree of collusion with MCs, *Government collusion*, on a scale from 1 to 10. I then regressed the two variables on HoAs in separate models. In the first two columns of Table 6.3, I show that homeowners in democratized neighborhoods were more likely to agree that the street-level government supported the establishment of an HoA and were less likely to agree that the street-level government colluded with MCs than were homeowners in non-democratized neighborhoods. These results are statistically

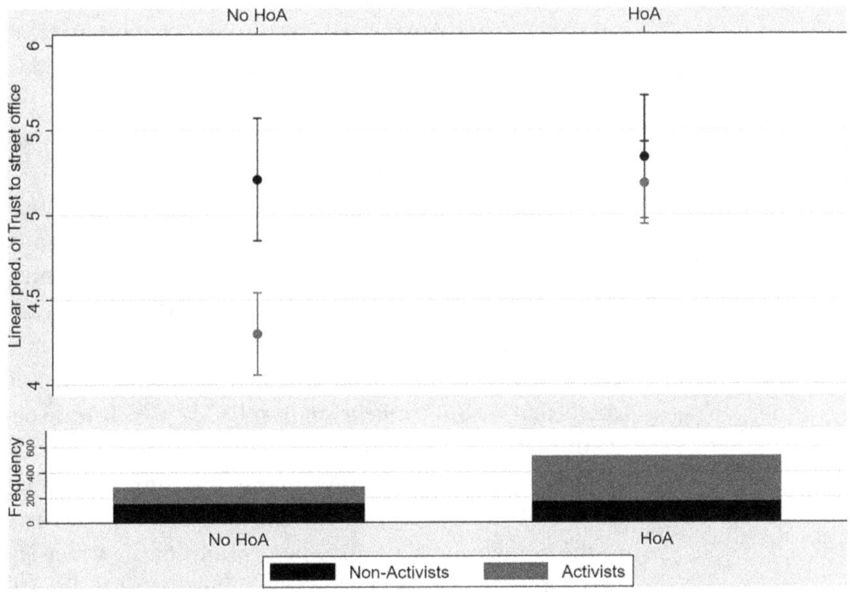

Figure 6.1 Marginal effect of homeowners' association on political trust

Table 6.3 Mechanism of political trust

	Government support	Government collusion	Trust in street government	
	(1)	(2)	(3)	(4)
Homeowners' association	0.64**	−0.88***	0.14	−0.04
	(0.21)	(0.18)	(0.23)	(0.24)
Activist	−1.06***	0.27	−0.41*	−0.73***
	(0.23)	(0.20)	(0.20)	(0.20)
Association × activist			0.44	0.57*
			(0.28)	(0.29)
Government support			0.32***	
			(0.02)	
Government collusion				−0.33***
				(0.03)
Trust in central government	−0.24**	0.21**	−0.16***	−0.17***
	(0.08)	(0.07)	(0.05)	(0.05)
Trust in city government	0.74***	−0.51***	0.67***	0.75***
	(0.08)	(0.07)	(0.05)	(0.05)
R2	0.19	0.13	0.57	0.54
Observation	813	813	813	813

Note: The models report the coefficients from OLS regression.
$^{*}p < 0.05$, $^{**}p < 0.01$, $^{***}p < 0.001$ (two-tailed test).

significant and substantively meaningful: When an HoA was established, the predicted value of perceived government support increased by 0.71 units (about 21 percent of the standard deviation), and the predicted value of perceived government collusion decreased by 0.86 units (about 31 percent of the standard deviation). This evidence suggests the local government plays an important role in establishing HoAs.

The next question is: Does this positive perception of local government translate into greater political trust? In the final two columns of Table 6.3, I show the results of mediation analyses. Column 3 adds the variable *Government support* to the main model (Model 3 in Table 6.3). The coefficient of the interaction term between an HoA and activism dropped in value and even surrendered statistical significance. Such a reduction was absorbed by the coefficient of *Government support* (0.32), which was statistically significant at 0.001 level. Similar patterns exist in Column 4, where the coefficient estimate of *Government collusion* (−0.33) was also significant. That is to say, the positive impact of an HoA on political trust among activists can be partially attributed to the homeowners' positive perceptions of the street-level government. I further estimate that 35 percent of activists' trust in the street-level government can be explained by their perception of government support for HoAs.[49]

6.4.3 Robustness and Alternative Explanations

I considered important alternative explanations for these results. If social trust were the basis of community, for example, I would expect to find that activists in democratized neighborhoods presented a stronger belief in their neighbors' participation in self-governance and greater trust in their neighbors than did activists in non-democratized neighborhoods. In the survey, I asked respondents how many neighbors they believed would be willing to serve the neighborhood (*Attitude to neighbors*), and roughly 35 percent said most neighbors would be willing to do so. We then asked respondents how much they trust their neighbors on a scale from 0 to 10, and the average value was slightly above 7. This is a measure of community-wide *generalized trust* that does not depend on whether one knows one's neighbors.[50] Finally, to measure the prevalence of strong social ties, I asked participants how many friends they had in the neighborhood with whom they were in regular contact.[51] This can be construed a measure of *particularized trust*, referring to trust in those with whom one has a personal relationship.[52]

As shown in Column 1 of Table 6.4, the interaction term of homeowners' association and activism does not have a statistically significant coefficient, meaning activists in democratized neighborhoods do not evince a stronger belief in their neighbors than their peers in non-democratized neighborhoods.

When regressing generalized trust in an HoA and activism in Column 2, I show that activists in democratized neighborhoods have an even lower level of trust in their neighbors than do activists in neighborhoods without HoAs, with a statistical significance at the 0.05 level. In the process of forming an HoA, activists may be discouraged by passive or self-interested neighbors and may, as a consequence, view them in a more negative light.

Table 6.4 HoAs, activism, and social trust

	Attitude to neighbors (1)	Trust in neighbors (2)	Number of friends (3)
Homeowners' association	0.28*	0.47	−0.13
	(0.13)	(0.24)	(0.14)
Activist	−0.23*	0.66**	0.90***
	(0.11)	(0.21)	(0.12)
Association × activist	−0.20	−0.60*	0.25
	(0.16)	(0.29)	(0.17)
R2	0.03	0.01	0.15
Observation	812	813	812

Note: The models report the coefficients from OLS regression.
*$p < 0.05$, ** $p < 0.01$, *** $p < 0.001$ (two-tailed test).

As for nonactivists, the establishment of an HoA does not impact their generalized trust in neighbors. This finding is consistent with our theoretical expectation. In Column 3 of Table 6.4, we demonstrated no correlation between particularized trust in neighbors and the establishment of an HoA. Thus, the establishment of an HoA was not linked to strengthened social trust among homeowner activists; rather, such activists seem to develop a more negative view of their neighbors than do ordinary homeowners, who are, presumably, free riders.

In addition, I rerun the main model using an alternative measure of political trust (Table 6.2), homeowners' activism (Table 6.3), and homeowners' association (Table 6.4), respectively. It turns out that my main finding does not change much.

Because activists differ from their inactive neighbors in many respects mentioned earlier, one may wonder whether the observed effect of HoAs on political trust was driven by systematic differences at the individual and neighborhood levels. For example, activists tended to be elderly women, who had been living in the same neighborhood for years – a situational characteristic that could have inclined them to show more trust in the local government. To address this concern, in my regressions, I included interaction terms between association and certain key variables correlated with homeowners' activism such as age, gender, democratic value, and so on. As shown in Table A.3 in Appendix II, including these additional interactions did not substantially change my central findings. Finally, in the interest of external validity, I further surveyed approximately 800 homeowners from other cities using the same chain-referral, social media-oriented sampling technique and reached a result consistent with my previous finding and as reported in Table A.10 in the Appendix II.

6.5 Conclusion

This chapter demonstrates that the party-state has much to gain by supporting neighborhood democratization in its urban neighborhoods and that an authoritarian regime may honestly cultivate self-governed communities in the interest of more effective governance and greater political legitimacy.

7

Neighborhood Governance during China's COVID Lockdowns

This chapter examines the benefits of homeowner self-governance to the party-state in the context of China's COVID lockdowns, and, more importantly, the risk of the party-state's dependence on homeowners and the latter's capacity to shape key party-state policies in the same context.

The party-state in China cites the Wuhan lockdown as a prime example of its strength.[1] Early literature on China's fight against COVID has generally embraced the idea of a strong, authoritarian state.[2] Critics of the party-state paint an image of an entity armed with limitless resources, dominating society, and causing widespread violations of individual rights.[3] The recent Shanghai lockdown seems the clearest example, showcasing how an omnipotent state can overpower society and misuse its authority.[4]

Based on fieldwork across multiple Chinese cities, with a primary focus on Wuhan and Shanghai, this chapter offers a grassroots-level perspective. It delves into how the Chinese state and society tackle COVID lockdowns, highlighting the role of homeowners' associations (HoAs), and the interactions between HoAs and residents' committees (RCs), the lowest tier of the party-state's bureaucratic hierarchy, in urban China's neighborhoods.

When the state enters a neighborhood to enforce lockdown orders, it steps into a territory legally under the collective control of Chinese homeowners. For the party-state, this "neighborhood front" is as vital as "the hospital front" in its battle against the pandemic.[5] For homeowners, these neighborhoods are spaces where safety, liberty, and property rights hold tangible significance.[6] The question arises: Who holds sway in these communities, the homeowners or the party-state's local agents?

My fieldwork uncovers significant limitations in the Chinese state's capacity to enforce COVID lockdowns and underscores the pivotal role Chinese homeowners and their associations played during these lockdowns. The lockdowns were executed not through the coercive might of the state but through the voluntary cooperation of Chinese homeowners. By late 2022, faced with the highly infectious COVID variant Omicron, numerous Chinese homeowners reassessed the costs and benefits of lockdowns.[7] Many began to resist government overreaches, frequently challenging the legal standing of both frontline governmental agents and specific lockdown measures. As an increasing number of Chinese homeowners began to oppose, withdrawing their support and resorting to legal resistance, the stringent lockdowns eventually dissipated.[8] Lacking the requisite manpower and financial resources to enforce lockdowns on such a vast scale, the party-state capitulated within days as resistance transitioned from neighborhoods to broader public spaces.[9] In essence, while hundreds of millions of Chinese homeowners initially collaborated with the party-state, enforcing its lockdown measures, they also played a decisive role in terminating those policies through their collective legal resistance. Contrary to the prevailing belief of the party-state's dominance, these COVID lockdown episodes in China reveal a reliance on homeowner collaboration for governance and a willingness to yield when homeowners advocate change.

Paradoxically, cooperation serves as a mechanism of resistance and a method to augment societal power during China's COVID lockdowns. I call this Chinese approach "cooperating to resist" (CtR).

This chapter is structured as follows. Section 7.1 examines various limitations in the party-state's enforcement of COVID lockdown measures. Section 7.2 examines the mechanisms and outcomes of homeowners' cooperation with the party-state during lockdowns, underscoring the indispensability of this collaboration in the fight against COVID. Section 7.3 probes into the resistance by Chinese homeowners against overreaching lockdown measures, emphasizing their use of legal narratives to safeguard their freedom and property rights. Section 7.4 clarifies the concept of CtR and distinguishes it from related theories such as cooptation, "rightful resistance," and "weapons of the weak." Section 7.5 concludes the chapter.

7.1 The Limits of the Almighty State

During COVID lockdowns, RC party secretaries and workers struggled to ensure citizens remained at home, got tested, and received essential services like food and medical treatment when necessary. Some scholars have argued that the party-state's neighborhood organizations were strengthened and empowered during the COVID-19 pandemic to carry out these tasks.[10] However, the reality is quite different; neighborhood organizations were neither institutionally nor financially strengthened during the pandemic.[11] Instead, they were tasked with enforcing often excessive lockdown policies, being pushed to their limits and, in some cases, suffering from exhaustion or death from continuous overwork.[12] Many of them left their posts halfway through the crisis.[13]

The party-state encountered significant limitations in enforcing lockdowns due to the illegibility of neighborhoods,[14] even with the assistance of technology, as well as limited human and financial resources, and distorted incentives among its agents. Additionally, the fragmentation of the party-state as an organization added to these challenges.

7.1.1 Illegibility

One might find it amusing to suggest that neighborhoods in Chinese megacities are illegible to the all-powerful party-state. Equipped with technologies such as a health code system, which purportedly tracks citizens in their every step of moving, and grid managers dispatched by the party-state to penetrate neighborhoods, how could these neighborhoods be considered illegible? However, my fieldwork reveals that the fear of the almighty party-state is somewhat exaggerated. While instances of excessive control have indeed occurred, their effectiveness is limited. China's efforts to transform urban areas into well planned and fully legible "gardens," using James Scott's well-known metaphor,[15] have encountered resistance from citizens and the state's own limitations in terms of human, financial, and organizational resources.

7.1.1.1 The Health Code System

The health code system, widely discussed online and feared as a tool of government control that would plunge Chinese citizens into a real-world version of "1984,"[16] has proven to be less effective than anticipated and has generated significant criticism without achieving its goal of effective monitoring.[17] In simple terms, Chinese citizens are required to install an app on their smartphones to report their COVID-related health information: red indicates a positive COVID test result, yellow signifies close contact with an infected individual, and green indicates no known COVID-related issues.[18] The color may change depending on factors like travel to "high-risk" areas or the completion of required COVID tests.[19] It's important to note that this app is not uniform nationwide; different provinces and cities have developed their own apps for COVID control, creating additional barriers for cross-regional travel.[20]

To be clear, the health code app can indeed locate and track citizens, but with certain caveats. First, it is not always accurate, with cases reported where individuals were missing from the government's app. In one instance in Wuhan, hundreds of residents were waiting in line for regular COVID tests, and one individual with a red code was found among them. When the health worker conducting the tests noticed this, they left the person aside and proceeded to test the next individual. Subsequently, the person with the red code disappeared when nobody was paying attention. This incident led to the entire neighborhood being locked down, and the RCs struggled to identify the individual in question. Ultimately, it was unclear whether the person even lived in that neighborhood.[21]

To exacerbate matters, citizens developed techniques to manipulate the app and change their code color as they see fit. Some of these techniques were advanced, involving hacking the system, while others were rudimentary, with citizens who tested negative sharing or selling copies of their health code to others in need. In certain places in Wuhan, such as university campuses, this even became a small-scale trade, particularly among young students who were more creative and rebellious. In one university, campus printing stores became hubs where these health code copies were bought and sold.[22]

Second, even when the app functions correctly, its tracking does not always align with reality. For example, the app may indicate that Citizen A has come into close contact with infected Citizen B, which is technically accurate as A and B were within 5 m of each other. However, the reality is that A and B were in separate cars on a highway and had a momentary "close contact" when their vehicles were parallel to each other with closed windows. Does this mean that A is now at risk of COVID exposure and should have their code changed from green to yellow? Common sense would suggest otherwise, but under the health code system, the answer is yes. Another example involves a Wuhan resident who went grocery shopping, and three days later, it was discovered that someone else who had visited the same grocery store tested positive for COVID. The resident was subsequently ordered to undergo a seven-day quarantine.[23] The criteria for tracking in such cases remained unclear, as other neighbors who had visited the store at the same time were not subject to quarantine.[24] These cases, referred to as "close contact in time and space" (时空伴随) by Chinese media, underscore the gap between technology and reality.[25]

One can argue that the issue with the health code system is its overreach, and there is nothing wrong with overreaching as more control is what the party-state wants. I disagree, as this overreach doesn't serve the government's goal of COVID control effectively and instead results in widespread anger and resistance, harming both the legitimacy of COVID control measures and the government itself. For instance, the Wuhan resident mentioned earlier cooperated with authorities for the initial seven-day quarantine, even though she was certain she was not infected. However, when the government insisted on another week of quarantine, she became furious and even threatened to commit suicide if forced to comply. She described the health code system as chaotic and absurd.[26]

Last, the health code system is plagued by bureaucratic confusion. One would expect that technology provides preliminary information, and government bureaucrats can decide, based on additional on-the-ground facts, whether the information is accurate and whether to rely on it. However, the reality is quite the opposite: technology controls people, including bureaucrats, rather than the other way around. Nobody knows who has the final authority over the health code color. While citizens theoretically have the option to apply via RCs to correct errors in the app that result in an incorrect color, in practice, RC party secretaries and other frontline government workers have found their applications bounced between different government departments.[27] While they were tasked with implementing lockdown orders, they had no control over the health code system.[28] The root cause of this chaos lies in the involvement of multiple government departments in COVID control, each with its own information channel or platform and no means to access or verify one another's information.[29] Additionally, there was a lack of trust in frontline government workers at the neighborhood level.[30] These factors combined to make it exceedingly difficult to correct technological errors in the health code system.

7.1.1.2 Urban Grid Management

The party-state recognized that it could not rely solely on technology for governance and thus created a system called grid management to enhance its effectiveness in collecting information and delivering services. The idea behind grid management was to divide each city into standard grids consisting of 300–500 households, acknowledging that Chinese neighborhoods were too large to govern effectively.[31] However, the party-state lacked the necessary human and financial resources to make this system work effectively. Grid managers often lacked incentives and expertise to carry out the complex tasks required to make neighborhoods legible and governable, often exacerbating conflicts within neighborhoods.[32]

Many grid managers were part time, mostly retirees. These retiree grid managers received a modest communication fee as compensation, typically around RMB 100 (US$13) per month. Their tasks include collecting and reporting information from each household and serving as a communication channel between RCs and residents. However, they themselves did not have access to government information and are not well connected with or particularly popular among their neighbors.[33] When tasked with enforcing unpopular government policies, such as COVID lockdowns in late 2022, their lack of authority became a significant issue.[34] They were unable to take a hardline approach with citizens, and those who attempted to do so often intensified conflicts, eroding government legitimacy.[35] The workload imposed on them far exceeded the compensation they received. Moreover, during the pandemic, the elderly, who were particularly vulnerable, made up a significant portion of the government's grid managers, many of whom resigned.[36] Consequently, in multiple neighborhoods I investigated in Wuhan, residents complained that they could not reach their grid managers.[37]

Each RC often employed a few full-time grid managers, typically college graduates specializing in social work.[38] These individuals were more dedicated and professional grid managers but were considered outsiders in the neighborhoods.[39] They are required to gain a detailed understanding of the neighborhood such as the exact number of residents in each apartment. Such a job often requires visiting residents' homes and faces resistance in the form of silence (residents refusing to open their doors) or even threats (such as putting a knife at the door as a sign of resistance to a COVID test).[40] They were expected to organize COVID tests for hundreds of residents in their grids. Their monthly salaries typically ranged from RMB 3,000–4,000 (US$400–540).[41] When these grid managers walked into a neighborhood, they often found that whatever map they had been given did not match the landscape on the ground. One young grid manager shared with us that she was brought to tears when she realized that the map did not match the neighborhood layout, and she needed to coordinate a COVID test for the entire neighborhood the following morning. Eventually, she resigned, as did many other full-time grid managers during the pandemic.[42]

Grid managers spent most of their time collecting information as different government departments requested them to collect all sorts of information, sometimes repetitively, showing the lack of coordination among these government departments. Ironically, despite the availability of health codes and other surveillance technologies, many government agencies still relied on grid managers to visit households and collect information through paperwork and handwritten reports.[43] It is evident that grid managers had little capacity to address citizens' demands. When citizens under lockdown relied on these grid managers for food and had no alternative options, some individuals died from starvation or illness.[44]

7.1.2 Limited Resources

In my previous discussion of grid managers' workload and compensation, I touched upon the issue of limited resources. To provide a more comprehensive understanding of the party-state's organization at the neighborhood level, let's take a neighborhood in Shenzhen I visited as an example. In this neighborhood, the RC governs an area of 0.6 km^2, encompassing three intracity villages, nine condominium compounds, and two office buildings, with a total resident population of 42,400.[45] The government employs seven workers for this neighborhood who have regular employment contracts with the government (在编人员), including the RC party secretary.[46] The RC also has a budget that allows for the hiring of thirty-five grid managers. However, due to the low compensation discussed earlier, 60 percent of these grid managers resigned during the pandemic.[47]

RC party secretaries, serving as the leaders of the party-state at the neighborhood level, received better compensation and were less likely to resign. In Shenzhen, their monthly salaries ranged from RMB 7,000–8,000, roughly equivalent to the pay of skilled factory workers. Being a party secretary comes with institutional prestige and benefits; nevertheless, RMB 7,000–8,000 was a meager salary that party secretaries frequently complained.[48] The increased workload during the lockdowns exacerbated this dissatisfaction. For example, party secretary Liu in Shenzhen reported that he could only manage four to five hours of sleep each day during the several months of COVID lockdown.[49] He received a bonus of RMB 2,000–3,000 for the extra work he put in during the lockdown period.[50] The risk of overwork was palpable, with one neighborhood party secretary known to our interviewee succumbing to overwork, aggravated by existing health issues. Such cases were not uncommon, as media reports and official government narratives highlighted the sacrifices made by frontline government employees during COVID lockdowns as heroic acts in service to the party and the people.[51]

Incentivizing frontline government employees required both positive and negative measures. In the Nanshan District of Shenzhen, two party secretaries of the street-level government, which supervises the work of RCs, were dismissed during COVID lockdowns for failing to fulfill their duties.[52] In the Futian District of Shenzhen, more party secretaries faced disciplinary action.[53] However, these disciplinary measures had limited impact on grid managers who were already inclined to resign and did not receive sufficient benefits from the party-state to match their workload.

As a consequence of the labor shortage, the RC in the Shenzhen neighborhood mentioned earlier allocated most of its resources and attention to controlling the three intracity villages.[54] These villages were populated by migrant workers who had fewer attachments to any community and were more vulnerable to the economic hardships resulting from lockdowns. Consequently, they were more likely to resist violently and attempt to escape.[55] Residential condominium compounds were left to self-management, a topic I will delve into further in Section 7.2.

To compensate for the shortage of frontline government employees, the party-state implemented two measures. First, party members were required to "sink into urban neighborhoods" (党员下沉).[56] The idea was to utilize the manpower of the 90 million Chinese Communist Party (CCP) members, who typically exhibit a higher degree of loyalty and incentive to work for the party-state.[57] CCP members were tasked with various responsibilities in urban neighborhoods, including aiding in lockdown policies such as COVID testing and entry control, as well as service delivery, from trash collection to food distribution.[58] However, this approach encountered challenges, as it was hard to evaluate such party-members volunteering work outside their ordinary jobs. Complaints were common in cities like Shanghai, Wuhan, and Shenzhen, with some CCP members merely taking pictures of their supposed tasks, sending these pictures to their supervisors, and not effectively completing the work. For instance, in Wuhan, a group of CCP members failed to distribute 2,000 eggs despite eight hours of work due to distractions like chatting and taking photos.[59] Moreover, as most of these CCP members came from government agencies and state-owned enterprises, they were accustomed to giving orders rather than providing services, often imposing restrictions on homeowners' actions instead of facilitating them. For instance, they were often preoccupied with collecting information on homeowners' purchases rather than procuring food for them. This approach created considerable frustration among homeowners who were tirelessly seeking sustenance for themselves and their neighbors, while CCP members demanded detailed logistics and financial information and dictated what should or should not be purchased.[60]

The second measure, typically employed during emergent COVID outbreaks, involved outsourcing control to market entities, such as private security companies. However, this outsourcing approach had two significant problems. First, these private companies did not consistently deliver high-quality service. In times of surging demand, some of these companies resorted to hiring individuals who did not adhere to established rules and norms. These individuals, often referred to as "thugs," not only tarnished the government's legitimacy through their appearance but also proved challenging to direct when tasked with specific missions by the street-level government that had hired them.[61] In certain cases, these individuals even demanded higher payments, citing excuses such as not being aware that they needed to wear the requisite white protective suits (大白), which posed significant discomfort during hot summer days.[62] Second, these outsourcing arrangements were costly, far exceeding the expenses associated with paying the government's own employees. As one-off contracts, the government had to pay RMB 680–1,000 per person per day.[63] While local governments were initially willing to do so due to the urgency of COVID outbreaks and the goal of achieving zero COVID, these ongoing outbreaks placed local governments under increasing financial strain. Consequently, they began to default on payments to these private companies, which, in turn, resorted to various means to seek compensation.[64] The sight of individuals wearing white protective suits and demanding compensation on social media platforms became a significant source of embarrassment and damaged the party-state's legitimacy.[65]

Overall, the relentless pursuit of zero COVID placed an overwhelming burden on the party-state. Even in relatively affluent local governments like Shanghai and Shenzhen, the limitations of their human and financial resources became apparent. According to a party secretary in Shenzhen, the most aggressive COVID control measures cost RMB 20 million per confirmed COVID case. Such measures involved testing entire neighborhoods with several thousand households and relocating residents of the affected building and surrounding buildings to hotel rooms.[66] While I lack specific details regarding the party secretary's estimate, RMB 20 million does not go far when considering that only 1,000 residents might need to be quarantined in hotel rooms for one week. This leaves approximately RMB 2,000 for each resident, without accounting for additional lockdown-related expenses. (A budget hotel room in a Chinese city like Wuhan typically costs about RMB 300.) The outcome of this relentless pursuit of zero COVID was that local governments found themselves financially depleted, struggling to compensate COVID testing companies, and forced to reduce government employees' salaries, not only in economically challenged cities but also in prosperous ones like Shenzhen.[67]

7.1.3 Distorted Incentives and Fragmented Organization

Within China's top-down pursuit of zero COVID, local officials face tremendous pressure to prevent COVID outbreaks and exhibit extreme risk aversion. Consequently, it is easier to impose lockdowns on neighborhoods or entire cities than to lift them. Officials who make the decision to lift lockdowns would be held accountable if subsequent COVID outbreaks occurred. However, it is the street-level government and RC employees who grapple with daily turmoil, threats of unrest, and the various challenges associated with lockdowns. Given the fragility of the zero-COVID target, officials were essentially testing the system's limits, evaluating how much pressure it could endure without sparking full-scale unrest. When sparks of unrest did emerge, the system often responded with negotiations, wherein the government requested more patience and renewed promises regarding when lockdowns would be lifted. Unfortunately, this process eroded much of the government's credibility due to unfulfilled promises.

RC party secretaries faced direct pressure from residents and endeavored to pacify them by proposing better solutions to the problems residents encountered. However, resolving such issues during a lockdown necessitated coordination with multiple other departments. For instance, elderly individuals often required regular medical treatment, which RC party secretaries sought to facilitate by allowing them to leave the lockdown area for treatment.[68] Nevertheless, hospitals frequently declined to admit patients from neighborhoods under lockdown, fearing that a single COVID case could lead to their own lockdown.[69] Tragically, people lost their lives due to hospitals' aversion to the risk of COVID lockdowns.[70]

Adding to the complexity, the party-state grappled with the perennial issue of fragmentation.[71] As discussed in my previous section on illegibility, various government departments maintained their sources of information and platforms, impeding the free flow of information across departments. Simultaneously, they relied on neighborhood workers to collect and report information, effectively making this task the primary responsibility of these workers.[72] Another manifestation of fragmentation was the lack of coordination among different functional and territorial authorities. Each authority issued its own travel permits, which were not necessarily recognized by each other, resulting in segmented "warzones" within Chinese cities.[73] In one instance, a grid manager was halted on her way back after distributing food to her colleagues as she did not acquire a new form of permit the street-level government had just ordered.[74] The grid manager had to call a leader within the street-level government to gain access. When the system operated with such rigidity and relied on personal phone calls, the burden on each government employee became considerable.

7.2 Cooperation

When the Chinese government decided to enforce lockdowns, whether in a building, neighborhood, city block, or, in its most extreme form, an entire city, it faced two primary challenges: (1) ensuring compliance with lockdown orders, ensuring citizens stayed within their apartments or neighborhoods, and

(2) providing essential services, particularly food, to those under lockdown. Additionally, the Chinese government organized regular and frequent testing in these areas, which incurred substantial human and financial costs. In tandem with this, COVID-positive patients were relocated from neighborhoods to quarantine centers. These aspects were interconnected; the more effectively basic needs such as food were met, the more likely citizens were to comply with lockdown policies.

The party-state encountered significant challenges in fulfilling both functions. In neighborhoods where homeowners could self-govern, the government was relieved of the responsibility to enforce lockdown orders and provide services. The government prioritized neighborhoods lacking such self-governing capacity, such as aged neighborhoods where elders concentrated and intracity villages where migrant workers lived.[75] Even in these neighborhoods, the government was, at best, able to provide food that met only the most basic needs. For instance, during my visit to Wuhan, one interviewee complained of losing 7.5 kg of weight during the COVID lockdown.[76] In another neighborhood, one interviewee reported witnessing the government provide free food on only one occasion, while another interviewee stated that there were multiple such instances, yet the government still couldn't adequately meet residents' basic needs.[77] In a third neighborhood under investigation, an interviewee mentioned that the government distributed food a total of three times, leaving her and her neighbors to fend for themselves. By comparison, she organized group shopping events ten times during the seventy-six-day lockdown in Wuhan, involving sourcing food, arranging transportation, and distributing goods to hundreds of households in the neighborhood.[78] The role of the RC, according to one interviewee, was primarily "comforting"[79] or, in the words of another resident, "doing everything except being helpful."[80]

Emerging from where the authoritarian state often fell short, mutual help and cooperation among homeowners facilitated both the implementation of lockdown orders and the provision of vital services required for their survival during lockdowns.

7.2.1 How to Cooperate?

Homeowners and their associations provided food, aided in implementing COVID tests and lockdowns, and became an integral component of China's COVID control system. Among the three pivotal tasks – lockdown, COVID testing, and food delivery – HoAs prioritized food delivery, followed by COVID testing, and least of all, lockdowns. Further, I detail their involvement in these areas.

Food Supply: This task encompassed sourcing food, organizing group shopping within neighborhoods, and navigating the COVID control system to ensure the transportation and distribution of food. Leveraging homeowners' diverse social networks was crucial. In communities with several thousand households, there were usually homeowners familiar with a supplier due to familial ties, professional backgrounds, or past interactions. For instance, one neighborhood depended on a milk supplier to provide everything from vegetables to meat during the pandemic.[81] On another occasion, a homeowner bridged a connection between farmers from his native village outside Wuhan and his neighbors.[82] With transportation permits – sometimes acquired through bribes – a covert market for these permits emerged in Shanghai in 2022, offering a workaround to the strict COVID control system.[83]

Homeowner activists who had led their neighbors fighting against developers and management companies before the pandemic became "food captains."[84] Their connections established before the pandemic, both within and across neighborhoods, now became source of information and credibility.[85] In Wuhan, an online group of over fifty HoA chairpersons was used to share food supply and demand information.[86] In Shanghai, food captains had various online groups where they can exchange information.[87] Such online groups of HoA chairpersons and food captains became the backbones of an, technically speaking, informal economy that supplied food to countless residents in Wuhan, Shanghai, and beyond during the prolonged lockdowns from 2020 to 2022.

In some cases, bags of potatoes and cabbages had to be transferred over barbed wire barriers set up by RC workers. Distributing massive quantities of food required an extensive volunteer system. This system operated on the principle of reciprocity:[88] Each household needed to buy food and a wife would feel ashamed about ordering food from the neighborhood captains if her husband had never volunteered for food distribution in the neighborhood.[89] There was informal and invisible mental accounting every household was keeping and plenty of compliments and complaints to be issued as currencies of punishment and award to sustain the system.[90] Surely there were disputes and quarrels, and the judicial authorities[91] even issued documents to regulate "group shopping," but overall nobody disputed the fact that it was food captains that supplied most of the food to citizens under the prolonged lockdowns.[92]

Lockdown Measures: HoAs implemented these with flexibility absent in RCs. While exiting one's home during busy hours was discouraged, late-night dog walks were tolerated by HoAs.[93] The more rigid RC workers, concerned with their liabilities, lacked the manpower to maintain consistent surveillance, making reliance on HoAs for lockdown adherence necessary.[94]

Lockdowns by HoAs gained compliance because they utilized peer pressure. A monitoring and reporting mechanism evolved where neighbors held each other accountable. It was not even HoC members but someone's neighbor who would stop this someone from breaking lockdown orders. This was motivated by the shared desire to curb the virus spread and avoid extended lockdowns. A neighbor who broke lockdown orders and put the entire neighborhood at risk would face lots of scolding, critiques, and reputational costs, and would think twice before doing such a thing.[95] In a neighborhood where one and one's family live, such reputational mechanism worked quite effectively.[96]

Support for lockdown measures hinged on the collective belief in the virus's peril and the government's handling. Over time, as these measures became unpopular, many HoAs distanced themselves, focusing more on services than on lockdown enforcement.[97]

COVID Testing: The sheer scale and efficiency of China's mass COVID tests astounded many.[98] While the state's mobilization capacity was significant, the collaboration of homeowners and their associations was indispensable. The government, in most cases, was able to send health workers to neighborhoods to conduct the test, whereas, organizing hundreds of thousands of residents in each neighborhood to participate in regular, sometimes, daily, tests, was mostly done by homeowner volunteers and their associations.[99] In neighborhoods with active HoAs or homeowner volunteer groups, COVID tests were organized in a much more efficient way than those without.[100] In Kangcheng, the biggest residential neighborhood in Shanghai with over 90,000 residents, homeowner leaders were able to mobilize over 100 volunteers to organize COVID testing within twenty-four hours of receiving a notice from the RC party secretary.[101] Toward 2022's end in Wuhan, with dwindling financial resources due to repeated large-scale testing, there was a shift toward neighborhood self-tests. Some HoAs took the initiative, training homeowners to administer tests within their communities.[102]

However, as the pandemic waned, skepticism arose. Homeowners questioned the continued presence of COVID positive cases in long-locked-down areas, suspecting potential falsification of results by testing companies for profit.[103] Some neighborhoods resisted tests conducted by companies sent by the government and opted for self-conducted tests, a phenomenon I delve deeper into in Section 7.3.

7.2.2 Consequences and the Party-State's Reactions

What were the consequences of HoAs stepping in and cooperating with the government to implement COVID lockdowns, organize COVID tests, and provide food to citizens under lockdowns? Such cooperation supported the government in fulfilling its goals and prevented the system from collapsing. In this sense, this collaboration was crucial to China's successful implementation of its COVID lockdowns. This is why the Chinese government tolerated such large-scale civic mobilization, actively engaged with homeowner civic groups, and often took credit for their contributions. Homeowners generally did not mind the government taking credit as long as they were able to maintain their lifestyles and businesses.

In the Three Peace Neighborhood in Wuhan, the government did not provide support "for even one second"[104] as the RC was newly established in December 2019, overseeing seven neighborhoods of over 20,000 residents.[105]

When asked about the RC party secretary, the HoA chairwoman responded, "How could he take care of us? He had no manpower. We did everything by ourselves."[106] In 2022, toward the end of the pandemic, a party branch was established in the neighborhood. Consequently, the Three Peace Neighborhood was recognized as a model of party-led grassroots governance in Hubei province.[107] A leader from the Wuhan CCP personnel department advised the HoA chairwoman not to "overemphasize" the role of the HoA, thereby not overshadowing the CCP's contribution.[108] The HoA chairwoman recognized this hint. In her interviews with us, she added that the RC party secretary worked tirelessly during COVID, noting that "our neighborhood was the one he didn't have to worry about since we took good care of ourselves."[109]

In the Three Birds Neighborhood, where food captains needed to carry bags of potatoes and vegetables over barbed wires erected by RC workers, the RC eventually took over group shopping from food captains at the end of the pandemic when the government finally came around and prioritized "guaranteeing food supply" (保供). The RC then issued an award to the leading captain who started the whole process of group shopping in the neighborhood. By issuing such an award, the RC was able to count this leading food captain as one of its volunteers in fulfilling its task of "guaranteeing food supply" in its report to the upper-level government.[110]

In the ProsperityChina Neighborhood, the RC party secretary, having been around for ten years and deeply embedded in the community, effectively mobilized civic groups for COVID control. There were thirty-three civic groups (including music, dance, sports, etc.) in this neighborhood of 12,429 residents. The RC party secretary had only seventeen direct workers, yet he managed to mobilize 235 volunteers to implement lockdown orders and provide food and other essential services during the lockdowns. President Xi Jinping praised the ProsperityChina Neighborhood for its success in COVID prevention during his 2020 visit to Wuhan.[111] The official narrative emphasizes the CCP leadership and how the party secretary led the people fight a war against COVID to success. It is true that the state can implement its goal much more effectively with the cooperation of a vibrant society than without, but it is not the case that the CCP led or dominated the society. As the RC party secretary acknowledged, he and his workers were able to tap into the resources and energies of these organic and vibrant groups as he had focused on embedding the state in the society.[112] It is a case that demonstrates the vital role the society played during China's fight against COVID and a right approach the CCP should take in handling its relationship with the society.[113]

Furthermore, by demonstrating their utility in governance, autonomous civic groups can influence and shape the government's policies, even to a certain extent curbing the government's potential abuse of power. I will delve into the topic of civic organizations resisting government overreach in the next section. However, I'd like to highlight how, by being insiders, organizations like HoAs can subtly mold local government policies.

In 2022, in Zhengzhou, fatigued local government officials, weary from the relentless pursuit of zero COVID, sought suggestions during a closed-door meeting attended by a prominent homeowner activist. This homeowner advised the government leader that: (1) they didn't legally have the authority to lock down the city or neighborhoods; and (2) if the aim was to keep COVID cases low, then simply limiting the number of tests could be effective – fewer tests meant fewer confirmed cases.[114] This suggestion was swiftly adopted by the city leadership.[115] This is not an example of bold defiance but illustrates the subtle influence on governmental policies. The homeowner activist was in a position to offer such advice because he was not a government employee, yet was not an adversary, having been invited to the forum to provide insights. This unique insider–outsider status is key to the existence of civic organizations in China, impacting their potential to shape and resist government policies, a topic I'll address in the subsequent section.

7.3 Legal Resistance

Toward the end of China's COVID lockdowns, widespread resistance and conflicts arose in urban neighborhoods in Shanghai, Wuhan, Shenzhen, Zhengzhou, and other cities. Homeowners from various backgrounds, including lawyers, entrepreneurs, and housewives, initiated challenges. The State Council's promulgation of the "Twenty Guiding Principles of COVID Prevention" (hereinafter referred to as the "Twenty Guiding Principles") on November 11, 2022, further bolstered this resistance by publicizing a split within the central party-state regarding COVID policy.[116] The widespread neighborhood resistance across various Chinese cities ultimately led to the end of China's COVID lockdowns.[117] The protest on Urumqi Road in Shanghai, which captured significant international media attention,[118] exemplified and culminated the broad neighborhood resistance. As one participant of the Urumqi Road protest remarked, protesting on the street was his second experience with such resistance; his first involvement was in his neighborhood, protesting a COVID lockdown.[119]

Adjacent to Urumqi Road, the TalentsGathering Neighborhood, a relatively upscale one in Shanghai with lawyers and entrepreneurs on its HoC, was the first to end its lockdown through protests.[120] As early as May 23, 2022, homeowners in this neighborhood began protesting against COVID lockdowns. They argued that, according to standards set by the Shanghai city government, their neighborhood was at low risk for COVID spread and, thus, residents should be free to move.[121] Earlier, when government contract workers arrived to erect barricades for the lockdown, homeowners insisted they provide evidence of legal authorization for such actions. Confronted by homeowner opposition, these workers were compelled to leave without completing their task.[122]

A hallmark of such neighborhood resistance was homeowners emphasizing their indispensable role in China's fight against COVID and questioning the legal basis for lockdowns. Chinese homeowners called for transparency, respect for their property rights, and the freedom to work. Carefully, they conveyed their intention was not to challenge the party-state or even the entire COVID control system, but merely the unjustified lockdown measures. They grounded their resistance in solidarity and legality, asserting that local officials lacked a proper legal basis or formal authority to enforce lockdowns.

On the ground, police generally refrained from using their legal coercive powers to back such measures. While they were present during mass conflicts, their actual use of legal coercive power was restrained. "Being present to maintain order" was how the police's role was often described when homeowners defied questionable COVID lockdown protocols. RC workers primarily used persuasion and negotiation to appease frustrated citizens. Only rarely did the police formally exercise their enforcement powers, such as arresting non-infected citizens demanding the removal of strict lockdown barriers or protocols.

In this section, I will explore the nature and narratives of homeowners' legal resistance, the limitations of state coercion in response, and the source of homeowner power stemming from their symbiotic relationship with the state.

7.3.1 Illegality, Not Unconstitutionality, as a Reason for Resistance

Chinese homeowners frequently referred to the problematic legality of COVID lockdown measures in their resistance. However, they stopped short of publicly challenging the legitimacy of the entire COVID control system or critiquing its constitutional validity during their routine resistance and protests, despite the questionable constitutionality of China's COVID lockdowns.[123] To them, the constitutionality of the broader COVID control system was outside the purview of homeowners and was not a point of contention in daily neighborhood governance. Nonetheless, when the government relied on entities without the required legal qualifications, including the street-level government and RCs, to enforce lockdown orders, it is hard to guarantee the legality of their enforcement.

Compounding the issue, city and district governments, to elude liabilities, often refrained from producing written directives or official documents to validate neighborhood lockdowns in 2022. The COVID control approach became outcome driven rather than rule based, undermining the rule of law that China endeavored to establish over the past four decades, even contradicting President Xi Jinping's advocacy for law-based governance.[124]

In a viral video, two homeowners challenged an RC worker attempting to seal a building due to its questionable legality.

> Look at this seal – it doesn't even have a date. When a court seals a property, it clearly states the start and end dates. Do you have that? You can't just seal a building on a whim ... If someone tried sealing your house with this, would you allow it? Show us the official document issued by the district or city government.[125]

The worker presented his ID in response, to which a homeowner remarked, "Ah? You think you can seal this building with that? As a government worker, you must understand the law. You need to follow reason and law, not just obey order blindly."[126]

In 2022, in a Wuhan neighborhood, homeowners collaborated with the RC's lockdown decision, marshaling eighty volunteers for order maintenance and food distribution. However, they rejected the new RC party secretary's decision to bring external security guards, breaching the understanding they had with his predecessor. The HoC chairman, a bridge between the RC and homeowners, informed the RC party secretary, "We can handle our issues and safeguard our entrances; we don't need outsiders."[127] The situation eventually escalated, leading to over 200 homeowners gathering and dismantling the barricades established by the RC. When the urban district government dispatched a deputy director for negotiations, the homeowners pointed to the State Council's Twenty Guiding Principles, emphasizing its warning against over-prevention.[128]

Another notable instance of legal resistance occurred in Beijing's Chaoyang District. On November 23, 2022, a neighborhood was placed under "temporary control" by the Chaoyang District for three days. Residents complied but became restless when the restriction wasn't lifted as promised. A leading homeowner, who was also a lawyer, mobilized his neighbors to protest and reminded them that "all exercise of public power must have a clear legal authorization": Since the official order of the Chaoyang District was only for a three-day lockdown, the neighborhood's RC had no legal basis to stop residents from leaving the neighborhood anymore.[129] Offering his legal services for free in case of any arrests, the lawyer's efforts bore fruit, with residents regaining their freedom by noon on November 26. Solidarity among homeowners and a clear legal stance were pivotal.[130]

In Shenzhen, proposals began to circulate among homeowner activists in November 2022 about how to resist the government's unreasonable COVID control policies.[131] Several factors particularly incensed homeowners: (1) Adults were forced to relocate to quarantine centers, leaving children, who were unable to fend for themselves, alone at home.[132] (2) Positive cases persisted even after nearly two months of lockdown. This led to suspicions that the only source of infection might be the COVID tests themselves, raising concerns about possible data fabrication by profit-driven testing companies.[133] (3) Extreme lockdown measures, such as blocking building exits with barricades, had tragic consequences, exemplified by incidents like the one in Urumqi, Xinjiang.[134] In response, an HoA in Nanshan district of Shenzhen adopted two courses of action: (1) The HoA arranged secondary COVID tests for all members who previously tested positive, effectively checking the accuracy of the government's tests. (2) The HoA issued a letter to its members, urging them to resist "unreasonable COVID control measures."[135] The letter prominently quoted the State Council's Twenty Principles, underscoring the importance of adhering to the law during pandemic prevention efforts.[136] It's vital to understand that this was a formal letter issued by an HoA, constituting a publicly defiant collective action organized by an entity legally recognized by the government.[137] Eventually, this letter made its way to online homeowner groups in other neighborhoods and cities, including Shanghai, achieving its intended reach and impact.[138]

7.3.2 The Limit of State Coercion

Interestingly, police, the core of China's stability-maintaining system and law enforcement system, rarely enforced COVID lockdown orders and played the role of mostly "observers."[139] The police were there to maintain order, but as far as the order was not broken and there were no physical conflicts, they made no arrests, not even stopping homeowners from breaking down the barricades. Homeowners in cities like Beijing,[140] Wuhan,[141] Zhengzhou,[142] Foshan,[143] and Shanghai[144] took efforts to remove barricades without being arrested.

The closest instance I found in my fieldwork concerning police enforcement during COVID lockdowns occurred in Shanghai. After a five-hour negotiation between a homeowner wishing to leave and RC workers urging him to stay, a police officer interjected, saying, "I can still keep you for 19 hours. Would you prefer to continue here or at the police station?"[145] While this threat underscores the coercive undertones of China's COVID lockdowns – a point this chapter acknowledges – it also highlights the restraint shown by the police, especially given the murky legal grounds of many lockdowns. In this case, the police tacitly recognized the maximum detention time (twenty-four hours) and the unlikelihood of any legal repercussions for the homeowner.[146]

The "typical cases" publicized by national legal authorities substantiate the preceding observation of police self-restraint: People did get arrested for violent attacks on government workers enforcing lockdown orders, but only when violence was involved.[147]

Two reasons account for this police self-restraint. First, police authorities were reluctant to enforce lockdowns without official authorization from a legally qualified entity. Second, homeowners frequently recorded and broadcasted their actions. The risk of nationwide media exposure also influenced police behavior.[148]

Generally speaking, Chinese police often find their hands tied when handling the so-called "conflicts among the people" (人民内部矛盾) initiated by the regime's insiders, neither directly challenging the party's authority nor breaking the law, and even safer, based on rights recognized by the party-state, such as the right to work and the right to property. Take another example: In Shanghai, on November 28, 2022, homeowners called police to stop RC workers from locking down the neighborhood. In the presence of two parties of the conflict (homeowners demanding freedom and RC workers intending a lockdown), a homeowner asked specifically what the police would do if the

RC workers assaulted or detained him, the police responded that such workers would face assault charges.[149]

Remarkably, the party-state exercised significant self-restraint, even when confronted with organized challenges to its COVID control measures, as long as these challenges were legally grounded and posed by homeowners generally compliant with the regime. Consider the letter from the Shenzhen HoA calling for resistance against unreasonable COVID measures. Its widespread circulation swiftly caught the party-state's attention. On the very day of its release, a deputy secretary of the CCP Nanshan District Political and Legal Committee visited the HoC chairman.[150] Surprisingly, the only request was to retract the letter; no punitive actions were suggested. This was because the letter neither violated the law nor posed a direct challenge to the CCP's authority.[151] The retraction, which was less formal and appeared hastily written,[152] was rightly interpreted by many as a coerced move.[153] Despite the public's interpretation, the government had no basis for action, as the HoA had complied with every request.[154]

The Shenzhen incident illustrates the authoritarian state's limited capacity to manage dissenters who are also regime collaborators. When these collaborators adhere to the rules and exhibit cooperative gestures, the state finds it challenging to exert coercion.

7.3.3 The Source of Homeowner Power: Dependence, Not Independence

Homeowners' legal resistance proved effective because they were not only insiders but also the backbone of the regime, having consistently shown their cooperation. When they began to withdraw or even merely threatened to withdraw their cooperation, the regime found itself compelled to acquiesce. The party-state was well aware of this dynamic. In his 2023 New Year TV speech, just a few weeks after widespread protests led to the end of China's COVID lockdowns, President Xi Jinping noted, "it is common to hold different opinions regarding the same issue."[155]

Understanding their critical role in China's COVID response, homeowners smoothly transitioned from being volunteers aiding the government in implementing COVID policies to champions defending their neighbors and their own rights against excessive COVID control measures. Protesting the government's order to seal a building, one homeowner in Shanghai, standing between the building to be sealed and the government worker attempting to seal it, said in a tired voice, "during this period we were working very hard for COVID prevention, but we were disgusted by such an action. Isn't that our law superior to your leader's will? Do you follow your leader or the law?"[156] This homeowner continued, "it is not that we do not cooperate, but as a volunteer we cannot do such a thing, right? … What kind of a person would I be (if I did this)? How would I face my neighbors? We would like to quit!"[157]

In another instance in Shanghai, a homeowner questioned an RC party secretary about the exact number of COVID cases and the expected duration of the lockdown. When informed that this data was only shared with party members in the neighborhood, the homeowner retorted, "how many volunteers are in this neighborhood? Can your party-member volunteers meet the needs of 5,000 households for food distribution? Can you even guarantee that those volunteers guarding the east gate are party members?! Can you?! How could you share the information only with party-member volunteers?"[158] This homeowner continued, "as a resident I have my right to information and my right to monitor. How could it be possible that COVID cases have become more and more while we all have stayed at home?"[159]

In China's urban neighborhoods, the authoritarian state has struggled to govern alone, both in ordinary times and during crises like the pandemic. To achieve effective governance, it requires societal collaboration.[160] This outcome, which even the party-state acknowledges as "co-governance," emerges from a balance of interests and negotiations between the government and homeowners, as well as the broader citizenry. Both the government and its citizens cooperate and contend with each other in the co-production of social order. Neither side achieves its complete goals, often feeling "forced" to compromise. An authoritarian state must strike a balance in this co-governance: between a society reluctant to cooperate, driving up the cost of governance, and a society willing and able to govern itself that might challenge authoritarian rule. Given that homeowners offer an indispensable service to this system, it's logical for the state to concede certain points to prevent widespread disruption.

The overall picture is that when homeowners, cooperators of the government, protested by law, the government needed to give in. Dependence brought to power. Neither the government nor homeowners were free from the constraints imposed on them by each other. Facing homeowners' united and legal resistance, the authoritarian state has limited ways of responses, particularly since its use of naked violence is quite limited to respond to such challenges.

7.4 CtR: A New Paradigm of State-Society Relationship

How is cooperation a way of resistance? Cooperation fosters interdependence between the state and society in China, embedding the society within the Chinese state's fabric. This interdependence and integration, as opposed to independence and separation, lend power, strength, and resilience to Chinese society within an authoritarian regime. Integration brings the Chinese society into the Chinese state. According to Michael Walzer, outsiders are rarely successful when they criticize a system and an effective dissent must be "a little to the side, but not outside" of the system he challenges.[161] Regular cooperation generates trust, prevents the authoritarian state from marginalizing the society, and gives the civic groups such as HoAs the knowledge and connections they need to work the system. "People are represented by the decisions they make and the institutions they build, not by the politicians they elect."[162] Chinese homeowners' power to resist and constrain the authoritarian state comes from their cooperation and participation in neighborhood governance.

CtR is much more active and progressive than James Scott's "weapon of the weak"[163] and "everyday resistance"[164] which are passive evasion of law and order as reflected in their typical forms such as foot-dragging, dissimulation, desertion, false compliance, feigned ignorance, and sabotage.[165] There might be some overlap here, such as the Shenzhen HoC chairman's "hidden transcript" in the badly formatted second public letter, but there have been regular public and direct resistance and protests, too.[166] Such resistance and protests are often based on law, looking for safety and power from law. Different from civic groups in liberal democracies such as the United States, Chinese homeowners need to get inside the system through cooperation first to gain the power to dissent and disagree. Cooperation also makes CtR more than "rightful resistance," which Lianjiang Li and Kevin O'Brien have used to describe Chinese peasants' resistance to state taxation in the late 1990s and early 2000s.[167] Chinese peasants' rightful resistance is easier to dismiss as the regime does not depend upon them as much as it depends on homeowners.

Being an insider of the authoritarian regime sounds very much like being co-opted. A few political scientists have recently rediscovered the new continent, finding that, contradictory to what Acemoglu and Robinson write about China, the party-state does not govern by itself alone. Using the party-state's own words, the ability to unite and mobilize the people is a key to the success of both the Chinese revolution and governance. President Xi Jinping has called the party to learn from the Fengqiao Experience (枫桥经验), in which police relied on neighborhood monitoring and reporting to find "counter-revolutionaries" in the 1950s.[168] Recently, Daniel Mattingly, a Yale political scientist, has argued that the party-state was able to use intermediaries such as village elders to exercise political control over the society.[169] Lynette Ong, a Toronto political scientist, examines how the Chinese state engages nonstate actors to coerce and mobilize the masses for state pursuits.[170] She calls this "outsourcing repression."[171]

Wasn't the Chinese state outsourcing repressing to HoAs in its fight against COVID? Weren't the HoAs being co-opted? Such a critique is right about the overlapping interest of the state and the society. In cooperation, the society is partly doing the state's bidding, but it neglects that the society is also doing its own bidding, being independent and autonomous, serving its own interests against the common enemy, that is, the pandemic, and bending the state to its will ultimately. The state might think it is using the society, but exactly because of this, the society is able to resist the state encroachment through cooperation. All that being said, I need to prove that Chinese society has its own autonomy and independence; I will explain in detail further how property comes into play.

CtR does not sound as heroic as civil disobedience or nonviolent noncooperation. We all want to see the weak and the oppressed stand up to the strong and the oppressor. But we tend to forget that the success of civil disobedience and nonviolent noncooperation relies as much on noncooperation and disobedience as on cooperation and obedience before such social movements. One reason for the success of India's noncooperation movement was the participation of the middle class: When thousands of students left their government-controlled colleges and universities, teachers resigned from government schools, lawyers gave up their legal practices and left the government court to join the movement, and consumers boycotted the import of foreign cloth, the effects of their actions on the economy were huge and the colonial government eventually was forced to give in.[172] The noncooperation was effective because cooperation of the Indian middle class had been essential to the colonial rule and economy before the movement.

To qualify the CtR thesis, I do not argue that cooperation always leads to successful resistance but simply to call our attention to the link between cooperation and resistance and understand the mutual dependence and embeddedness of the state and the society in an authoritarian regime.

7.5 Conclusion

This chapter, anchored in fieldwork across multiple Chinese cities with Wuhan and Shanghai as the primary focus, offers a bottom-up perspective on China's COVID-19 lockdowns between 2020 and 2022. The interplay between Chinese homeowners and the party-state manifests in a concept I've termed "cooperating to resist" (CtR), presenting a fresh paradigm of the state–society relationship. Initially, homeowners adeptly cooperated with the party-state to tackle the mutual challenge of the pandemic. Yet, they also skillfully resisted overbearing lockdowns, which culminated in their abrupt ending, contrary to the top leadership's original plans. This resilience exhibited by homeowners stems from their collaborative dynamic and interdependence with the party-state.

8

Contesting Party Leadership

General Secretary of the Chinese Communist Party (CCP or simply "the party" hereinafter) Xi Jinping famously declared that "the party leads everything."[1] At the end of his first term, in 2017, he added to the party's charter that "party leadership is the most fundamental characteristic and biggest advantage of socialism with Chinese characteristics."[2] The next year, in addition to removing presidential term limits from China's constitution, he had a pared-down version of the preceding statement appended to Article One: "party leadership is the most fundamental characteristic of socialism with Chinese characteristics."[3] Scholars have examined the party-state's efforts to incorporate party leadership into charters of state-owned enterprises,[4] raising questions of whether party committees would and should play a direct role in corporate governance, the establishment of party units in non-government organizations (NGOs),[5] and Chinese branches of such transnational corporations as Walmart.[6] It seems, indeed, that "the party leads everything." It is therefore somewhat incongruous that Chinese homeowners have been able to resist the party's effort to penetrate homeowners' associations (HoAs). Though successful in sanctioning its leadership in Article One of China's Constitution, the party has failed to establish full party control over HoAs in the face of considerable homeowner resistance, much of which has been in the form of legal action. This chapter explains how and why this failure has occurred.

8.1 The Party-State's Plan of Complete Control and the Challenge to Its Legality

General Secretary Xi Jinping has declared the need for China to strengthen party leadership at every level of society. It is no surprise, then, that the party finally set its sights on urban neighborhoods. A national strategy began to form in 2017, when, for the first time since the country's market-oriented reforms got underway in 1978, the CCP Central Committee and the State Council jointly promulgated a plan for neighborhood governance.[7] This plan recognizes that neighborhoods are the basic units of social governance and that the basic principle of neighborhood governance is party leadership.[8] In 2019, the Office of the CCP Central Committee promulgated an opinion on improving party-building at the urban grassroots level, with the specific stipulation that party organizations should be established in HoAs.[9] In 2021, the Central Committee and the State Council again commented on grassroots-level governance in yet another jointly promulgated plan[10]: It emphasized the point that improving neighborhood governance is a foundational project for the modernization of China's governance.[11] Such improvements would require that party leadership over various NGOs – including HoAs – be strengthened at the grassroots level, and one way to achieve this aim would be to ensure that party-approved talent leads grassroots efforts related to these organizations.[12] In 2022, the party's organization department issued measures to improve party leadership at the urban grassroots level. The measures specifically mention the need to increase the percentage of party members in homeowner committees (HoCs), which are the elected executive bodies of HoAs.[13] Earlier, in 2020, this requirement of party membership in HoCs had been explicitly articulated in a document jointly issued by the Ministry of Housing and Construction and other party-state organs.[14] It is this policy – the establishment of quotas granting party members privileged access to HoCs – that has been challenged by homeowners in various ways.

The party faces a major challenge to the legality of the preceding plan for two reasons. First, if the party imposes such constraints directly without legislative or administrative channels, citizens have no obligations to comply with such constraints. Legally speaking, party documents are binding only on party members and thus cannot be straightforwardly applied to citizens who are not party members, a majority of whom constitute China's homeowners. To make it worse, many party documents circulate only to party cadres and sometimes only among cadres above a certain level. As a result, ordinary citizens might not be aware of the existence of a certain party document, not to mention complying with it. Homeowners' response to party documents is to evade them since they do not create a legally binding obligation and cannot be legally enforced, as has happened in Beijing and Shanghai.

Second, Chinese homeowners' right to self-governance is protected by the Property Law and the Civil Code. The party has not yet added party leadership to the prior laws. This explains, why, even for the aforementioned party documents, which are not subject to legality review, their issuers at the central level have used words such as "encourage" and "in general" to avoid creating a mandatory requirement and inconsistency between party policy and law. On the other hand, if a local party-state chooses to implement the preceding plan through legislative or administrative documents, such documents will risk contradicting the earlier laws and being invalidated in citizen-initiated legality review. As a result, some local governments, like that in Shenzhen, although have promulgated administrative documents to implement the party's plan, have adopted a soft approach and avoided making the requirement mandatory, similar to that of the aforementioned central party-state documents.

In cases where local governments have created a mandatory requirement in legislative or administrative documents, homeowners' response has been to petition to a higher authority to exert pressure on the issuer, which may "clarify" that the petitioned document has not imposed a legal obligation and is therefore not binding on homeowners, as it has occurred in Hefei, the capital city of Anhui province in central China. If the government insists that such documents have created a legally binding obligation, homeowners can file with a higher authority to review the legality of the documents and often succeed in forcing the government to revise or even invalidate them, as has happened in Yinchuan of Ningxia autonomous region in northwestern China and Huizhou of Guangdong province in southeastern China.

Resisting homeowners typically proceed with considerable tact. They have zeroed in on specific and concrete legal issues, with much of the criticism pointing to an alleged inconsistency between a local policy and the aforementioned national laws and central party-state documents, which have avoided creating a mandatory requirement on paper, while embracing – and vowing allegiance to – the party and its leadership. This diplomatic balancing act is an old maneuver illustrated by a slogan attributable to rebelling lords in the early Han Dynasty: "Kill Chao Cuo to clear the wings of the Emperor." The lords knew that it was the emperor who wanted to stifle their autonomy and limit their power, but rather than blame him, they blamed one of his chief advisors, Chao Cuo, who was essentially an executor of the emperor's agenda.

These homeowners also argue that party control over HoAs is impractical for two reasons: (1) there is an insufficient number of party members in HoAs who have time, incentive, or the required expertise to be on HoCs; (2) party control would exacerbate, not alleviate, social instability and other problems in urban neighborhoods.

In an authoritarian regime, homeowners' efforts to resist party-state policies that encroach upon their legal rights can contribute to the development of democracy in at least three ways.[15] First, the resistance can help develop a culture of civic engagement with even the party-state on equal footage and as citizens, rather than subjects whose rights can be taken away at the whim of the regime. Through collectively launched petitions and requests for legality review, homeowners can compel the party-state at the local level to address legitimate concerns and adjust policies accordingly. Second, the resistance often involves the mobilization of a large pool of homeowners both within and across neighborhoods, which strengthens the bonding among homeowners. Third, the collective resistance also increases the visibility and weight of HoAs and HoCs in the eyes of both ordinary homeowners and the party-state and serves to announce and defend neighborhood democracy against party-state intrusion. It is noteworthy that petitions and requests for legality review are more effective when filed in the name of HoCs than individual homeowners.

8.2 Evasion

In Beijing, Shanghai, and Shenzhen, party-state directives concerning party-member quotas for HoCs are "soft requirements" rather than "hard" ones, that is, the directives only encourage HoCs to meet the stipulated quota and specify neither strict consequences nor strict remedies in cases where the HoC fails to meet the stipulated quota.[16] Homeowners' response to such directives have been to evade them as there is no legal enforcement.

In Beijing and Shanghai, it is the local party's organization department that issues these soft requirements, in compliance with central-party policy, to strengthen party leadership at the grassroots level in urban neighborhoods. As a result, the requirement is not as widely circulated as, say, a local regulation would be as the latter needs to be issued to the public. In Shanghai, the party's organization department circulated the document with a party-member quota for HoCs only to party cadres at or above street-level government,[17] which means that party members at the neighborhood level, which is one level below but directly deal with homeowners, are not entitled to access it. In Beijing, a similar document was addressed to organization departments of various municipal party-state institutions[18] instead of homeowners whose right to self-governance is threatened by the party-member quota requirement.

As a result, homeowners might pretend that they are not aware of the existence of such documents to subtly challenge their authority and effect. For example, on the Beijing municipal government's website, a homeowner asked whether or not the requirement actually existed, as she could not find it in written form in any of the local property-management regulations.[19] Of course this homeowner must be shown the document – the question was her way to say that the party's requirement had no legal basis. She went on to pose a central question: Does the requirement [if it exists] mean that an HoC cannot be established if it lacks the participation of party members? The Beijing Housing and Urban-Rural Construction Commission replied that the quota requirement (i.e., 50 percent of HoC members must be party members) was, in principle, not mandatory. Interestingly, however, the reply dodged the question of whether there can be HoCs that fail to satisfy the 50-percent quota. The commission was clearly in a bind: If it had declared that HoCs could exist without meeting the quota, the commission would have jeopardized the central party's goal of increasing party control over HoCs; on the other hand, the commission must have been well aware that, had it made the quota requirement a hard one, the policy would have risked violating the Civil Code.

As a matter of practicality, the party-state in its plans to strengthen its governance of urban neighborhoods is trying to achieve two goals: shift the burden of governance and service delivery to homeowners themselves, and control HoAs by ensuring that a substantial percentage of HoC homeowner members are also party members serving to prevent potential challenges to the party's leadership. To achieve the first goal, the party-state must promote homeowner participation in neighborhood governance. However, participation is problematic. For example, homeowners are busy with vocational, family, and personal responsibilities. Many party-member homeowners, in particular, are political and economic elites whose institutional and corporate duties leave neither time nor incentive to take on the sometimes risky responsibilities that accompany HoC membership and that yield few if any tangible benefits. As for homeowners who do not belong to the party, some of them are activists willing to fight for their neighborhoods' interests. To allow these individuals, an influential position in HoCs would entail its own risks for the party. The result is that, in Beijing, different street-level governments have different policies dependent upon the availability of party members in the neighborhood and the resistance from non-party-member homeowners.[20]

In Shanghai, the situation is similar to that in Beijing. One homeowner leader confided, "The policy is just advice; it is not enforceable."[21] Another Shanghai homeowner activist – one who happened to be a party member – admitted that "this policy is enforced where it can be enforced, and not enforced in face of strong homeowner opposition."[22]

In Shenzhen, it is the municipal housing bureau that issued a document to implement the party-member quota requirement. However, it has adopted a soft approach rather than a mandatory requirement to avoid contradicting the Civil Code. Multiple homeowner activists told me personally that it is impossible for the party-state to enforce such a policy uniformly and fully. These same homeowners also confirmed that many HoCs fall far short of the required quota for party members and, in some cases, lack even a single party member.[23] In Shenzhen, one party secretary of a residents' committee (RC) which is in charge of implementing the quota requirement complained about the recruitment problem: "Where would I find these party members to participate in HoCs? Even I wanted to quit (from the RC)!"[24]

Given the contradiction between the quota requirement and the Civil Code, city governments in Beijing, Shanghai, and Shenzhen alike have adopted a soft approach. In response, homeowners subtly evade the quota rather than openly denounce it, saving face for both sides.

8.3 Collective Petition

When evasion of the quota requirement is neither possible nor satisfactory, homeowners may resort to petitioning. The act of petitioning evokes a humble approach to achieving a goal: on bended knee, a subject entreats a ruler to grant a favor that only the ruler can grant.[25] "So conceived, the petition seems to presume a form of abasement, the supplicant rendered as subject, every aspiration converted into a meek request whose fulfillment is a matter of the ruler's whim."[26] This conceived image of petitioning was very much the reality in pre-modern China. However, several elements make homeowners' petitioning more democratic than is oftentimes assumed. The first element is that this petitioning is based on *mobilization and collective action* – in other words, on requests made not by a single "subject" but by a group of "citizens." Collective petitioning commonly takes the form of a signature list, demonstrating the will of hundreds or thousands of citizens. The second element contributing to the democratic nature of petitioning is that petitioners are essentially holding a particular officeholder accountable for resolving their problems by *directing their claim to this officeholder*. In many cases, this person is the highest-ranking official (e.g., a governor) in an administrative jurisdiction (e.g., a province). By putting a high official under an unwanted spotlight, petitioners politely – yet with some degree of underlying force – request a substantive government response to their concerns.[27] But why would petitioners direct their concerns to a high-profile government leader rather than to a specific bureaucratic agency responsible for the matter at hand? As Hannah Arendt wrote, the anonymous rule of the bureaucrat is more despotic and fearsome than the visible rule of a dictator because no one can speak with or petition this "nobody."[28] By directing their claims to a specific high-profile government official, Chinese homeowners find a way both to overcome the tyranny of the Chinese bureaucratic rule and to hold government accountable. The third element is that petitioners frame their petitioning in the language of *law and rights*. In other words, petitioners express the belief that they, as citizens, are entitled to a solution that is a matter not of the ruler's whim but of a just legal foundation. It is worthwhile to note that petitioners often entangle their rights claims with the regime's interests, essentially arguing that, by protecting the petitioners' legal rights, the regime is serving its own interests.

In the case of the party-member quota for HoC members, homeowners have collectively petitioned the local government when it treated the quota requirement as a "hard" requirement. Precisely this type of scenario came to a head in Hefei, the capital city of Anhui province in central China: There, the municipal housing administration issued a document requiring that half of the members of each newly established HoC be party members.[29]

Homeowner activists in Hefei tried to communicate individually with the municipal housing administration but got no positive response or sometimes no response at all. There are two likely reasons for this disappointing outcome. The first one is the faceless bureaucratic rule, without naming a specific bureaucrat, no bureaucrat takes responsibility in responding to homeowners' calls. The second likely reason, and one cited by government bureaucrats in Hefei, is that individual complaints might not reflect the will of the several million homeowners in a city.[30] The government of Hefei has also argued, in very much a similar train of thought, that a policy cannot be changed just because one or two homeowners have complained about it.

An informal association known as the Hefei Homeowners' Forum has been in place in the city since early 2010, and Hefei's homeowner activists have established online groups facilitating convenient daily communication and mobilization.[31] Thus, after the disappointing responses and nonresponses from the municipal bureaucracy regarding the complaints made by individual homeowners about the hard quota requirement, a leader of the homeowner movement in Hefei turned to several online homeowner groups, where he advocated a strategy of collective petitioning. It did not take too much persuasion to convince the members of the online groups to embrace the idea of a petition, as the mandatory quota was, in many instances, threatening the existence of HoCs which were not able to meet the requirement. Soon, fifteen HoCs representing 100,000 homeowners in Hefei signed an officially sealed letter petitioning the local government to reconsider the quota. A leader of this collective petition was aware that such action in China involves risk but felt that other considerations made the risk tolerable. Commenting on the wisdom of *collective* petitions, the leader argued, "Individuals are powerless; you need to show organizational strength."[32] The leader added, "We're not going to take to the streets or block roads; we're just sending a letter to our government's leaders. What can they do to me for that?"[33]

To overcome the tyranny of the faceless municipal and provincial bureaucracies, the petition signed by the fifteen HoCs was addressed to the governor of Anhui Province. On the main government website for Anhui Province, there is a page called "The Governor's Mailbox" (省长信箱). Thus, in addition to mailing hard copies of the official petition to the government, homeowners also submitted the petition online through the online portal. The wording of the petition is noticeably civil, starting with a polite salutation to the addressee: "Dear Governor Li Guoying." It is important to note that the salutation is addressed not simply to the title of a government leader (i.e., "Dear Governor") but to the title followed by the individual's family name and given name (i.e., "Dear Governor Li Guoying") – a subtle tactic that pinned down the specific official for whom the contents of the petition were intended.[34] In stark contrast to the disappointing responses and nonresponses from the municipal housing administration, the petition delivered to the governor got a response within one week. Though it was the municipal housing administration that responded (a fact that did not surprise the petitioning homeowners), the logical consensus was that the governor's office must have been behind the housing administration's quick response.[35]

Much of this petition invoked the legal rights of homeowners, but it also appealed to the government's core interests. The title of the petition summarized the dilemma: "Should HoC members be elected by homeowners or sent by the party?" At the very start of the petition, the signatories praised the party for having established and pursued the basic principle of "governance according to law" (依法执政). The petition then argued that the new hard requirement attributable to the municipal housing administration (not the party) violated provincial and national laws and regulations governing property management. The petition ended with the claim that the inflexible requirement violated the party-state's pursuit of the "governing according to law" principle. Neither the content nor the tone of the petition suggests a meek supplication whose fulfillment is a matter of the ruler's whim; rather, the petition laid out in a civil yet confident tone a legal argument to which the government – the petition argued – is legally obligated to respond. The petition also detailed the specific challenges that the local requirement would impose on homeowners, including the sheer impossibility of all the HoCs being able to satisfy the quota requirement and the very real possibility of local party cadres' abuse of power. Both of these problems, according to the petition, would undermine the legitimacy and the interests of the party state. The petition even surmised that, if they were to intervene in neighborhood affairs, local party units would encounter insurmountable difficulties and would thus be better off leaving these time-consuming and laborious tasks to the homeowners themselves.[36]

After responding to the petition, the Hefei municipal housing administration organized a meeting with several of the petitioning homeowners. At the meeting, the municipal representatives clarified that the government had no intention of mandating the quota: it was a flexible requirement – a suggested goal – not a hard-and-fast requirement. In fact, the director of the administration attended the meeting and left his phone number with homeowners, telling them that they could call him if they came across any problem understanding or interpreting local policy in the future.[37] The administration also officially replied to homeowners' petition on the webpage of "The Governor's Mailbox." The online reply contained the same clarifications and was publicly accessible to website visitors.[38] A local newspaper reported this interaction between homeowners and the government,[39] including the latter's clarifying response, making it widely known and generally applicable to all HoCs in Hefei.

8.4 Legality Review

The success of the petition requires collective action, involving homeowners across multiple neighborhoods. When such collective action is not feasible, homeowners in different parts of China have succeeded in invalidating the local government's party-member quota requirement through legality review. They grabbed the momentum of China's ongoing campaign to build a system capable of reviewing the legality of local legislative and administrative documents. In this section of the chapter, I demonstrate how individual citizens can harness the party-state's "rule of law" campaign in ways that effectively counter its encroachment on individual rights.

Local governments in China have long embraced the practice of promulgating an endless stream of technical, jargony documents meant to further the governments' various agendas. This surfeit of documents – many of which contradict one another, national laws, and the constitution – has become a threat to China's "rule of law." The documents can be grouped into two categories. The first category is local legislation, including laws passed by local people's congresses and administrative rules passed by local governments. Reviewing the legality of the first category of documents falls under the jurisdiction of people's congresses that operate at or above the level at which the local government operates. The second category concerns local non-legislative administrative documents (规范性文件), such as those issued by departments of local governments. Reviewing the legality of these documents falls under the jurisdiction of the departments of justice that, as with the first category, operate at or above the level at which the document issuer operates.

Legality review is new in China. Though the CCP Central Committee in 2013 put establishing a system of legality review on the party-state's agenda,[40] it was not until 2018 that both the Department of Justice (DoJ) and the National People's Congress Standing Committee (NPCSC) made it tops on their agenda. The State Council, of which the DoJ is a part, promulgated two foundational documents to promote the review of the legality of administrative documents in 2018.[41] The State Council required that all administrative departments across China establish mechanisms for reviewing the legality of administrative documents by 2019.[42] Relatedly, in 2018, the State Council restructured its departments, resulting in a strengthened DoJ. The newly constituted DoJ quickly prioritized the implementation of legality review.[43]

About this same time, the NPCSC started to strengthen its power of review regarding the legality (including the constitutionality) of laws, regulations, and rules. In December 2017, the NPCSC for the first time promulgated a report on the progress of developing a system of legality review, and this action, in itself, reflected the seriousness with which the NPCSC intended to exercise its power of legality review in the near future.[44] In 2018, the NPCSC required that all local people's congresses establish a platform for citizens to file applications for legality review. An NPCSC official explained that "any individual citizen could initiate the legality review procedure of the supreme power organ of the country [i.e., the NPC] by filing an application."[45] On December 4, 2019, China's Constitution Day, the NPCSC's own platform of accepting citizens' applications for a legality review went online. Although the NPCSC established a system to handle these citizen applications for legality reviews, there is no reason to assume that all citizens understood either the system itself or the difference between the two types of legality review. The NPCSC explicitly stipulated that the people's congresses at various levels upon receiving misfiled applications should first transfer them to the DoJ at the same level and then follow up on the DoJ's handling of them.[46]

In this section, I examine two cases of citizen-initiated legality review: one initiated by a homeowner who was also a well-connected party member in Yinchuan, a city in northwestern China's autonomous region of Ningxia; the other initiated by a homeowner who was a total outsider to the party-state in Huizhou, a city in Guangdong Province. Both of these individuals succeeded in abolishing the party-member requirement in their respective municipalities. The Huizhou case was more significant in the sense that it led to the abolishment of local quota-related regulations entirely. In the Yinchuan case, the local regulations just reverted to the central party-state's phrasing, which treated the quota requirement as a nonbinding form of encouragement.

Lao Ma in Yinchuan worked in the party organization department of a state-owned energy company. He was thus quite familiar with the policies and practices of party organization and had even taught himself some rudimentary aspects of law. Interestingly, he had former classmates and relatives occupying senior positions in the local government. In 2018, he bought a condominium and tried to establishing an HoA in the condominium complex. He quickly discovered that the local HoC quota requirement, issued by Yinchuan's municipal housing administration, was a formidable obstacle to his goal. Lao Ma requested that the municipal DoJ reviews the legality of the administration's quota document. Lao Ma chose legality review based on his previous experience in *weiquan* ("rights defense") to overcome other barriers to establish an HoA in his neighborhood which gave him two lessons: first, petitioning was ineffective, as no government body was obligated to respond to a petition; and second, applying for administrative review and pursuing litigation were effective because such formal procedures require a formal reply from the related authorities.[47] Undertaking a formal legal procedure is also relatively safe for homeowner activists, as either repeated petitioning or petitioning based on inaccurate assertions might lead the public security bureau to charge the given petitioner with the offense commonly referred to as "picking a quarrel" (寻衅滋事).

Lao Ma was aware of the nationwide campaign to promote legality reviews of administrative documents, so he filed an application for such a review with the local DoJ. Within a month, the local DoJ responded positively, stating that it had already sent suggested corrections to the local housing administration.[48] Subsequently, the local housing administration changed its regulation from "at least half of the members of each HoC must be party members" to "each HoC is encouraged to have party members among its membership."[49]

During our interview, Lao Ma emphasized that he had been a party member for fifteen years, but that the idea of "party leadership in neighborhood governance" was, in his view, nonsense. He had come to this conclusion for two reasons: first, party members at the grassroots level were incapable of leading neighborhood governance as they were accountable only to their upper-level party authorities and often abused their power; second, instituting a party-leadership in HoCs would further weaken the accountability of neighborhood governance as local homeowners cannot sue the party for perceived malfeasance.[50]

The process of legality review for Wei in Huizhou was more complicated than in the aforementioned case but also resulted in a more significant victory for homeowners in the city. Wei, who had not attended college, was an insurance salesman working for a private company. As with Lao Ma in Yinchuan, Wei had bought a condominium, which was his most valuable asset. He was well aware that quality real-estate management contributes significantly to the value of condominiums. In a private interview with me, Wei conveyed his belief that the party quota requirement violated homeowners' private rights, specifically their freedom to choose their own HoC members. He illustrated the problem with an analogy: "when I go to a wet market, I can decide whether to buy pork or beef; if [the party-state] requires me to buy pork, that will be a violation of my rights and interests."[51]

The Huizhou municipal housing administration was quite aggressive in implementing the party-state's quota policy of promoting party leadership in neighborhood governance. On September 3, 2021, the housing administration issued Document No. 141 jointly with not only the local political and legal committee of the party but also twelve other related government departments. The document stated that party members had to constitute at least 60 percent of HoC membership – a figure that was 10 percentage points greater than that in other cities. The document went on to stipulate that the quota was binding on all newly established HoCs and that existing HoCs needed to satisfy this requirement by holding new membership elections in which positions in the HoC would be reserved exclusively for party members.[52] On October 9 of the same year, the housing administration issued Document No. 158, this time jointly with the local organization department of the party to reiterate the specific requirements for the quota.[53] While Document No. 141 was addressed to related government departments, Document No. 158 was addressed to related party units.

In attempting to establish an HoA in his neighborhood and in serving as an HoC chairman, Wei acquired considerable experience harnessing the law to negotiate with and resist the government. When government officials asked his neighborhood to hold new HoC membership elections in which positions in the HoC would be reserved exclusively for party members, he responded – in his capacity as the HoC chairman – by demanding that the officials issue a formal statement requiring the prior-mentioned elections so that he could challenge the requirement in court. The government officials, aware such a formal move on their part would put them at risk of an embarrassing legal defeat, retreated from their previously strident demands and ultimately left his HoC alone.[54]

Wei also socialized with some of Huizhou's homeowner activists. In the course of these interactions, he learned that several local HoCs had stopped operating out of deference to Document No. 141. He realized that the members of these HoCs were not as good at handling government pressure as he had been. He thus decided to take further action: He would force the Huizhou government to officially invalidate the document. In his initial efforts to achieve this end, he petitioned and then complained to various government agencies, but never received a timely or satisfactory reply.[55]

At the time, there was considerable media coverage in China regarding the government's new campaign to promote the new system of legality review. Wei followed this media coverage and learned, in particular, that the Guangdong Provincial People's Congress Standing Committee (Guangdong PCSC) held high hopes for the system. Wei decided to give the system a try, and on May 30,

2022, he filed an application for a legality review not under his own name but under the name of his HoC. On July 10, 2022, the Huizhou Municipal DoJ called him to discuss the matter. It turned out that Document No. 141 did not fall under the jurisdiction of the Guangdong PCSC because the document was administrative in nature, not legislative.[56] The Guangdong PCSC transferred the case to the Huizhou PCSC, which in turn transferred it to the Huizhou DoJ. All three governmental bodies took Wei's application for legality review seriously, particularly after they learned that Wei had a record of exhausting available legal channels in his previous efforts on behalf of his HoA. In other words, officials knew that Wei was not a person who could be easily persuaded or intimidated to give up his pursuit of homeowner self-governance.

A technical difficulty in this particular case of legality review was that the document in question had been issued by both the Huizhou housing administration and by the local political and legal committee of the party.[57] A DoJ's power of review regarding the legality of official documents extended only to government departments, not party organs. Nevertheless, upon the insistence of Wei and under pressure from the Guangdong PCSC, local DoJ officials managed to persuade the municipal housing administration to abolish Document No. 141 as a hard requirement of party membership is indeed violating the Civil Code and not authorized explicitly by the central party-state. Consequently, the housing administration formally abolished Document No. 141 on August 15, 2022.[58] To be clear, we should understand that the PCSC and the housing administration, rather than seek to weaken the central party-state, were simply struggling to ensure legal consistency, which is the purpose of the legality-review system. When a determined citizen points out a legal inconsistency in a party-state matter, the government bodies responsible for ensuring the legality of local laws, regulations, and rules have little choice: they must reestablish legal consistency.

However, we should also bear in mind that the government's formalistic approach to ensuring legal consistency often needs a push from citizens before the bureaucratic wheels start turning. Thus, the Huizhou housing administration continued to implement the requirement spelled out in Document No. 158, which, as we will soon see, faced a fate similar to that of Document No. 141. Wei himself was unaware of Document No. 158 until the housing administration, having abolished Document No. 141, attempted to implement the party-member requirement in Document No. 158.

To make it worse, on September 26, 2022, the housing administration initiated a formal investigation of Wei, focusing on his eligibility to be an HoC chairman.[59] The housing administration's excuse for this investigation was that Wei's name was not on the housing-ownership certificate for his place of residence. Instead, the certificate was under his wife's name. The formal investigation notice was sent to Wei's HoC and was most likely meant to be a threat in retaliation for his activism concerning neighborhood governance.

However, as unyielding as ever, Wei was not intimidated. On October 4, 2022, he filed another application with the Guangdong PCSC, this time requesting a review of the legality of Document No. 158. And this time, a deputy director of the Huizhou PCSC held a meeting with Wei and fourteen other Huizhou-based HoC chairpersons in Wei's neighborhood, during which the deputy director acknowledged the illegality of Document No. 158.[60] As with Document No. 141, the PCSC could not formally abolish Document No. 158 as such an action would fall outside the PCSC's jurisdiction.[61] On November 8, 2022, the Huizhou housing administration and the Huizhou party's organization department – that is, the two joint issuers of Document No. 158 – issued a supplemental document in which the wording for the 60-percent quota now clarified that HoCs should "try to have 60 percent of their membership be party members."[62] This considerably softened tone immediately transformed the hard requirement into a soft one, that is, into mere encouragement. In other cities such as Shenzhen (also in Guangdong Province), the wording of the requirement has had a similarly encouraging (not mandatory) tone. The supplemental document with the softened tone represented an effort by Huizhou authorities to rescue their document from the likely ominous consequences of a legality review. However, not all authorities were convinced that such a baleful outcome was on the horizon. For example, on one occasion during this long ordeal, Wei had a meeting with an official of the Huizhou housing administration who expressed doubt that Wei could succeed in abolishing Document No. 158. Without missing a beat, Wei responded in his typically resolute way: "You'd better abolish the document yourself, and save me the trouble of going through the Guangdong PCSC."[63] On March 6, 2023, the Huizhou housing administration and the party's organization department issued an official notice to abolish both Document No. 158 and its supplemental document. The official notice states that related party-state units should refer directly to the central and provincial party-state laws and policies regarding the promotion of party membership in HoCs.[64]

Wei's case was the most significant victory that Chinese homeowners had won in fighting against the party-state's effort to exert party control over HoCs. The various joint issuers of Document No. 141 and Document No. 158 comprised fifteen party-state bodies, including powerful party organs such as the organization department and the political and legal committee. These various party-state bodies were ultimately forced to abolish their own previous officially issued documents because of Wei's tenacious and insistent efforts to call for a review of the legality of the documents. The earlier described events showcase how an ordinary Chinese homeowner can protect his right to self-governance by leveraging the Chinese party-state's campaign to build a formalistic rule-by-law system.

8.5 Conclusion

From evasion to collective petitions to legality reviews, homeowners in China have exhibited increasingly direct resistance to the party's efforts to infiltrate HoAs. The surprising finding presented in this chapter is that the more direct and the more legalistic such resistance is, the more substantive the results can be in favor of the activists. There is space even in today's increasingly authoritarian China for homeowners to defend their right to self-governance from party infiltration. The success of these defensive efforts is not necessarily a loss for the party-state. As all the prior-cited interviewees emphasized, they did not oppose party leadership in general. What they opposed is the impracticality of letting grassroots party cadres dominate or even run homeowner organizations. The interviewees and many like-minded homeowners in China want a reasonable degree of autonomy in their neighborhood-based and property-based self-governance. Moreover, they want this form of self-governance to thrive alongside party leadership, but only so long as the party does not engage in an overreach of power.

9

Associations beyond Neighborhoods and Property

This book is about neighborhood democratization, not democratization in general, which is a much more complicated and larger topic. Nevertheless, I would like to discuss the implications of homeowners' associations (HoAs) beyond neighborhoods and property. Homeowners in China do go beyond their neighborhoods and demand the right to participate in broader urban governance and the right of HoAs to associate with other HoAs citywide and even nationwide. Moreover, some homeowner activists even demand democratization in other arenas that are not directly related to property rights.

In their examination of civil society organizations in historical Prussia, Richard Brooks and Timothy W. Guinnane differentiate the right to associate and the right of associations and reveal how the Prussian state failed to maintain the boundary between apolitical associations such as business organizations and political civil society groups.[1] In a similar spirit, this chapter examines homeowners' associational activities beyond neighborhoods and property and the Chinese party-state's failure in containing such activities within neighborhoods and to property-related issues. There is one caveat: Homeowners do not always conduct associational activities beyond neighborhood and property through HoAs, but even in such cases, the democratic practices of HoAs serve as the start and catalyst.

More specifically, I divide homeowners' associational activities along two dimensions: physical boundaries of neighborhoods and virtual boundaries of property rights as an arena. The following two-by-two Table 9.1 reveals four categories of associational activities: one category (the "in/in" category) refers to associational activities that stay squarely within the physical boundaries of neighborhoods and the virtual boundaries of property rights; the other three categories refer to associational activities that push beyond these boundaries.

The Chinese state is grudgingly willing to accommodate associational activities beyond the physical boundaries of neighborhoods but within the virtual boundaries of property rights. By contrast, the state is quite hostile to associational activities beyond the virtual boundaries of property rights and in more political arenas. Therefore, it has been easier for homeowners to cross the physical boundaries than the virtual boundaries. Nevertheless, not a few Chinese homeowners have successfully executed the latter move, even if sometimes

Table 9.1 Four categories of associational activities

Property Rights \ Neighborhoods	In	Out
In	HoAs	Not in my Backyard ("NIMBY"); Association of HoAs
Out	Residents' Committees ("RCs")	Local People's Congresses; The Beijing Bar Association

their efforts were curtailed by the state. Whether successful or not, these democratic practices are inherently invaluable.

Sections 9.1 and 9.2 examine homeowners' associational activities that cross the physical boundaries of neighborhoods, focusing on homeowner mobilization in municipal governance in the form of NIMBYism ("not in my backyard") and cross-neighborhood associations of HoAs, respectively. Section 9.3 presents cases in which homeowners cross the virtual boundaries of property rights and exercise their freedom of association in residents' committees (RCs), a form of "grassroots mass autonomous organization" sanctioned by the Chinese constitution but controlled by the party-state to govern urban neighborhoods, in running for local people's congresses, and in pushing forward real elections (instead of fake elections orchestrated by the party-state) of the board of the Beijing Bar Association. Section 9.4 concludes this chapter.

9.1 Mobilization beyond Neighborhoods

As Lee Fennell has most vividly illustrated, the value of real property is impacted not only by factors inside property boundaries but also by factors beyond such boundaries, which gives homeowners incentives to participate in municipal governance.[2] NIMBYism ("not in my backyard") is the most famous example of such homeowner activism in the US context. Scholars have written about NIMBYism in China, but few have noted the role of HoAs in this movement.[3] The involvement of HoAs both reduces the cost of organizing homeowners and promotes rational and constructive conversations between homeowners and local governments, increasing the chance of compromise (from both sides) and decreasing the chance of direct conflicts.

In Beijing in 2017, six HoAs, representing thousands of homeowners in the city, worked together to shelve a light-rail project valued at RMB 10 billion. The HoAs accomplished this feat by skillfully wielding a considerable assortment of financial, human, information, and organizational resources. Among the six HoAs were rich ones, which offered financial support to the poor ones, many members of which were retirees willing to petition the government daily. Also, the funding provided by rich homeowners enabled HoAs to hire a group of lawyers who focused on procedural irregularities of the project's environmental impact evaluation (EIE). The government was obligated to collect public feedback in its EIE and conducted this task somewhat duplicitously, posting a "call for feedback" flyer in a seldom-visited part of one of the neighborhoods concerned. The location of the flyer almost guaranteed that the flyer would attract little public attention, and at the same time, the government agency responsible for posting the flyer planned to take a photo of it as evidence that the agency had fulfilled its duty to collect public feedback. Unfortunately for the agency, a homeowner found the flyer and reported it to the HoAs concerned, which then circulated the flyer's information in a successful bid to mobilize homeowner resistance to the light-rail project.[4]

We cannot take homeowner mobilization for granted. It was the status of homeowners' committees (HoCs, executive bodies of HoAs) that lent credibility to organizers of this resistance, who were HoC members, enabling the latter to collect signatures from over 80 percent of homeowner members of the six HoAs. On one hand, these HoA leaders sent the signed petitions to leading figures in the Beijing municipal government and promised to take further collective action if the government did not abandon the light-rail project. HoA leaders backed up this verbal pressure by carrying out daily group visits to the relevant municipal government office. The credibility of the threat further forced the government to face the legal challenges HoAs have posed with the assistance of lawyers paid for with donations from rich homeowners in these HoAs. Eventually, the Beijing municipal government canceled the plan to build the light rail.[5]

This chapter offers no comprehensive evaluation of the pros and cons of this project nor normative judgment of whether this project should have been built or not. The sole purpose is to demonstrate the role of HoAs in this process and how they became more or less equal counterparts to the municipal government with the strength of organization, different from the conventional view of a society dominated by the state. This case from Beijing is not the only one in which Chinese homeowners forced a local government to cancel projects of significant economic or infrastructural value.[6]

The second case I would like to discuss took place in Shenzhen and resulted in a win-win situation for homeowners and the municipal government. In 2003, the Shenzhen municipal government publicized a plan to build an underground tunnel as part of the Shenzhen–Hong Kong Expressway. The announcement triggered a two-year-long process of homeowners' protests and negotiations with the municipal government regarding the design of the project. The central concern voiced by the homeowners was that the underground tunnel might create hazardous or noxious gas emissions in the neighboring residential communities. Though most of the tunnel was underground, the government's original plan included a 361-m stretch that would not be entirely enclosed and that would thus lead to the direct emission of gas into about ten nearby neighborhoods.

Similar to the preceding case of the activist Beijing homeowners, the Shenzhen HoAs obtained a formidable mix of financial, human, and informational capital that they then harnessed for the purpose of bargaining on a strong footing with the government. In this effort, the HoA activists deployed multiple strategies, including street protests, petitions, media campaigns, and seeking administrative review of the government's design of the tunnel. On one occasion, the HoAs organized a peaceful rally of 4,000 homeowners. In a not-so-veiled threat, they had submitted to the municipal public security bureau a request for a demonstration permit, which they knew would not be issued.[7] The rally was thus unapproved but tolerated, and it demonstrated that the tunnel project was an issue that lots of homeowners were deeply concerned about and willing to take actions.

Despite these aggressive tactics, the HoA activists displayed a remarkable capacity to negotiate with the government in a professional way and within the legal framework. Two of the HoAs authorized two homeowners who were environmental protection experts to conduct an EIE of their own. The homeowner experts concluded that the gas emissions from the proposed project would fail to comply with national standards. These HoAs managed to pressure the author of the government's EIE report to examine the homeowner experts' report in a public meeting and to admit that the two homeowner experts had made no technical mistakes. Nevertheless, the government refused to accept all the findings of the homeowners' expert report. In response, the homeowners sent their report to well-respected experts who served in the Department of Environmental Engineering at Tsinghua University and who confirmed the validity of the homeowners' report.

Seemingly unfazed at these successive rebuttals by the homeowners, the Shenzhen municipal government refused to give in. The homeowners displayed the same steadfastness: They mobilized members of the local people's congress to question the project, solicited widespread media coverage across mainland China and Hong Kong, and petitioned the Guangdong Provincial Environment Protection Bureau and the National Environmental Protection Bureau to review the Shenzhen municipal bureau of environmental protection's EIE report.

Eventually, the pressure proved too much: The Shenzhen municipal government changed the design of the tunnel. The homeowners' activism had delayed the entire project for two years, and the price tag for the government's new tunnel design was RMB 1 billion more than the original quote. But the change of design guaranteed that the neighborhoods would remain high-end residential and commercial areas. Also of note is the fact that, in the end, the local government was awarded a national prize honoring governance innovation for its demonstrated willingness to negotiate and to change the course of its policy. The outcome of this case has generally been considered a win-win situation for all the parties involved.[8]

9.2 Associations beyond Neighborhoods

In my comparison of Beijing, Shanghai, and Shenzhen, I have given a detailed ethnographic account of how homeowners from various neighborhoods have connected with one another, shared information and knowledge, and in some cases, collaboratively mobilized to fight for their property rights. Here, I would like to go beyond these three cities to discuss as a general matter why homeowners want to build up cross-neighborhood and even cross-city associations, what such associations look like nationwide, and the government's responses to them.

To be clear, the degree of formalization of such associations varies and correlates with the government's tolerance or support for them. Some are highly formal independent legal entities, whereas others are loose networks that, for example, organize regular homeowner events but have no recognized legal status as an association. As of 2024, I have been able to count a total of forty formal and informal associations across all of China, from south to north, and from small to big cities.

9.2.1 Homeowners' Demand for Associations of HoAs

Across neighborhoods in urban China, homeowners share the goal of self-governance and face common obstacles including all the logistical hurdles associated with collective action, the natural territorial opposition of powerful management companies, and government checks on potentially disruptive grassroots organizations. In their efforts to establish HoAs and to strengthen their neighborhood-based self-governance, homeowners across China face largely the same legal system: On one hand, it grants homeowners the right to establish HoAs, but on the other hand does not clarify their legal status. Hence, the law is quite indeterminate as to whether HoAs can, for example, have their own bank accounts, file lawsuits, and join other associations. Moreover, Chinese law sometimes leaves the scope of common property rights unspecified: For example, do these rights cover facilities such as parking spaces, which, though built by developers in conjunction with a residential complex, have not been transferred to specific homeowners. To address all of these issues effectively, homeowner activists must first learn how to mobilize their neighbors and deal with developers, courts, banks, and the government. Common challenges generate a need for mutual learning and mutual support.

There have been continuous efforts to establish cross-neighborhood associations in the most developed areas of China, including the Yangtze River Delta area such as Shanghai, Zhejiang, and Jiangsu, the Pearl River Delta area, that is, Guangdong, and the Beijing–Tianjin area. These locations should come as little surprise given that their real estate markets were some of the earliest and most developed in China. However, in less developed provinces such as Hubei,[9] Henan,[10] Anhui,[11] and Sichuan,[12] and even in smaller cities in these provinces, such as Yichang,[13] there have been attempts – including some successful ones – to establish associations of HoAs.

Central China's Henan province in the city of Zhengzhou was the site of an interesting effort to establish a citywide association of HoAs. A major trigger of this effort was a document issued by the Zhengzhou municipal bureau of housing and construction. The document seemed to run counter to national law by declaring that HoAs needed to obtain approval from rather than register with the local government as stipulated by national law. This move granted the local government much more power than national law seemed to allow. FCJ, a homeowner activist in Zhengzhou, believing that this new municipal rule could sound the death knell for many HoAs, sought to mobilize the city's homeowners against the restrictive move.[14] Other homeowner activists in Zhengzhou shared this concern, and one such individual, MYL, put it this way: "I was feeling so angry and powerless.... It was so hard to fight alone; then, I thought, if we were united, the government wouldn't be able to ignore us anymore. That's how the association was formed."[15] Together FCJ and MYL established a citywide association of HoAs in Zhengzhou and even attempted to establish a province-wide association that failed.

The vast territory of China also provides ample space for homeowner activists to experiment with neighborhood governance or even to escape a particularly repressive local government for a more liberal one. SKX, a homeowner activist based in Beijing, ran unsuccessfully for election to a local people's congress,[16] and then gave talks to homeowner meetings around China, partly to sell his idea of a "homeowner trust," a mechanism that, in his view, would significantly reduce decision-making costs for homeowners.[17] A founder of the Application Committee for Beijing Association of Homeowners' Associations (BJHC), CB, traveled around China to mobilize homeowners nationwide after the Beijing municipal government had prohibited the BJHC from holding events in the city. Similarly, YZM, a leader of the Shenzhen Center of Promoting Transparent and Harmonious Communities (SZHC), moved to Wuhan, after the Shenzhen municipal government had barred him from operating within the city's limits. In Zhengzhou, after the city's national security authority investigated his pursuit of disruptive political reforms, FCJ found himself banished from the citywide homeowner platform that he had cofounded – not one to give up, however, he shifted his focus to share ideas with homeowners in other cities.[18]

On a national level, YH, who is a professor at a top university in China, has led a research center focusing on HoAs and neighborhood governance, which has the distinction of being the longest-enduring platform for HoAs across China. The center has sponsored events across the country in a mission that YH has described as "sowing the seeds of homeowner self-governance": These events include the publication of a neighborhood-governance periodical, conflict-mediation meetings for competing homeowners, and annual conferences at which homeowners can share information and experiences with one another.[19]

Multiple homeowner activists across far-flung Chinese cities have told me that YH is the "big sister" and an invaluable leader in the nationwide community of homeowner activists, and has supported the development of cross-neighborhood organizations in their respective cities,[20] including the first officially approved provincial-level association of HoAs in China. For local homeowner activists, having the endorsement of a homeowner leader such as YH can endow them with credibility and social capital that will stand them in good stead as they interact with both homeowners and local governments.[21] Needless to say, YH's affiliation with a top Chinese university has also proved helpful.

The center has survived governmental scrutiny for two main reasons. First, the organization is university-affiliated and is officially a research center rather than an NGO, which would have been subject to potentially repressive government oversight. Second, YH has carefully focused on issues closely related to neighborhood governance and has thus avoided issues of a more political and controversial nature. For example, in past years, YH focused narrowly – yet uncontroversially and effectively – on neighborhood garbage recycling. In fact, the recycling agenda had been initiated and promoted by the Chinese central government. For YH, who is aware of possibly detrimental entanglements, her center's survival and growth are the top priority.

9.2.2 Government Demand for Associations of HoAs

As discussed elsewhere in this book, local governments need to strike a balance between their demand for effective neighborhood governance and their desire to control homeowner mobilization. Improvements in neighborhood self-governance can, for example, relieve the government of the burden of maintaining social stability by reducing conflicts between neighbors, and thus by, reducing the need for police intervention.[22] When a government's demand for effective neighborhood self-governance is more urgent than the government's demand for control of homeowner mobilization, the government will likely extend official recognition not only to individual HoAs but indeed also to an association of HoAs. A citywide or even province-wide association of HoAs has the potential both to facilitate homeowner self-governance and to confine homeowner mobilization to neighborhood issues. Such "confined neighborhood democratization," if fully achieved, enables the government to "have its cake and eat it too."

Associations of HoAs can also yield valuable information that the government bureaucracies do not have or fail to deliver to government decision-makers.[23] A mayor in the city of Huai'an in Jiangsu Province began paying attention to the issue of neighborhood governance only after he had been bitten by a dog in his own neighborhood. When he called for a meeting with street-level government officials to discuss neighborhood governance, everyone told him how well their neighborhoods were governed. The mayor eventually contacted a homeowner activist for a more accurate evaluation of the situation of neighborhood governance in the city. Being pushed by the mayor, elements of the Huai'an municipal government expanded its local regulation to *require* the establishment of an association of HoAs. This was the first time a local government had ever instituted such a requirement.[24] To overcome their bureaucratic systems' informational failure, local governments across China regularly invite leaders of associations of HoAs, whether formally registered or not, to participate in local law-making.

So far, the Shanghai municipal government seemed to strike a balance between utilizing and controlling associations of HoAs. The city, which is one of China's four municipal administrative regions akin to a province, is the site of two associations of HoAs: Mass Ants, which is registered as a for-profit corporation, and the Shanghai Association of Young Homeowner Committee Members, under the leadership of the Shanghai Communist Youth League. Neither can be counted as an officially registered association of HoAs. The former, which can have HoAs as its customers but not as its members, is driven by profit-making and is thus also less likely to get politically motivated than a non-profit association of HoAs. As for the latter, it is sponsored by – and hence well under the control of – the party-state.

I have collected and examined all publicly available data on associations of HoAs in China, including both news reports and a database of registered entities in China. My data reveal that there are five province-level associations of HoAs, eight city-level associations of HoAs, ten county-level associations of HoAs, and nineteen street-level associations of HoAs. Among the many news reports that I collected, quite a few concerned the attempts to establish associations of HoAs. I analyzed these particular reports with other data in order to determine whether or not the associations had in fact been officially established. Overall, I found that the lower the level of such an association, such as at the street level, the more likely the association would be to have an official status. Indeed, at the street level, I found no news reports about failed attempts to establish such associations; rather, multiple street-level governments have actively supported the establishment of the associations. It becomes less so moving up to the county level: 16.7 percent of reported attempts to establish associations of HoAs failed. This figure grew to 77.8 percent at the city level. Whether to gain an official status as an association of HoAs depends on the local government's demand for effective neighborhood governance and its view of the threat posed by such an association to social stability.

Across China from south to north, and from big to small cities, either homeowners or the government, or both homeowners and the government, have demanded homeowner self-governance in the form not only of HoAs but also of cross-neighborhood associations (i.e., associations of HoAs).

A few local governments, from the provincial level to the street level, have recognized cross-neighborhood associations, particularly in those places where government demands for HoAs have become urgent. At the province level, only two associations have received government approval to have HoAs as members: the Tianjin Metropolitan Association of HoAs,[25] which was founded in 2013 and has been inactive since 2015, and the Hainan Provincial Association of HoAs, which was founded in 2018, and, as of 2024, is still active.[26]

The establishment of the Hainan Provincial Association of HoAs illustrates the government demand for the association of HoAs.[27] Since the 1980s, Hainan has undergone multiple real-estate boom-and-bust cycles involving the sale of millions of condominiums mostly to buyers from outside Hainan. A high percentage of these buyers, as their primary residence is elsewhere, reside in Hainan Province only a few months during the year, mostly in the winter for vocational reasons. The Hainan government has a name for neighborhoods hosting large numbers of part-time homeowners: "neighborhoods of migratory birds." The cost of decision-making in such neighborhoods is particularly high, as these "migratory birds" are reluctant to pay management fees or vote for the motion to use maintenance funding to do necessary repairs. Homeowners who live year-round in the neighborhoods complain about mismanagement and deterioration of buildings.

All in all, the Hainan provincial government needs homeowners, whether they reside in their homes all the time or not at all, to make their own decisions, pay their dues, and spend their own funding, to maintain their neighborhoods. The government has tried other ways too, including sending judges to neighborhoods to resolve the explosively increasing number of disputes stemming from chronic mismanagement. Nevertheless, there is a general understanding that well-functioning HoAs would probably be the most effective means of averting and resolving such disputes and relieving the government of the burden. The Hainan provincial government's need for self-governance in "neighborhoods of migratory birds" has become so urgent that perhaps nowhere in China does a government's demand for effective self-governance so markedly surpass official concern about possibly disruptive homeowner mobilization. A province-wide association of HoAs specializing in promoting the establishment of HoAs has the efficiency of scale and has been established officially with the approval from the Hainan provincial government.[28]

Two failed efforts to officially register province-level associations of HoAs merit our attention. The first failed effort centered on the BJHC whose application for approval was never acknowledged by the Beijing municipal government and which has been barred from operating in Beijing due to its confrontational and political approach since 2018.[29] The other failed effort took place in Henan. Inspired by the official approval of establishing a provincial association of HoAs in Hainan, homeowner activists including FCJ and MYL submitted an application to establish such an organization in Henan Province, far to the north of Hainan province. Interestingly, rather than transmit an official reply to these homeowners, the Henan provincial government communicated with them through private channels:

> There is no chance that the [Henan] government can approve a provincial association of HoAs. Henan is different from Hainan, where neighborhoods are full of migrant-bird residents who pose no threat to social stability. Henan has over 100 million people in total, and residents in the province's big cities such as Zhengzhou are permanent residents. A province-wide association with so many members would have the capacity to overturn the sky.[30]

The Guangdong provincial government has allowed the registration of a non-governmental organization, the Guangdong Province South China Harmonious Community Development Center,[31] which is led by an HoC chairman in Guangzhou, the capital city of Guangdong, and operates across the province. It is important to clarify that, as this center is legally an NGO, though it is allowed to operate across Guangdong province, its role is closer to that of YH's research center and limited to holding events and sharing sessions than that of the Hainan Provincial Association of HoAs which can have HoAs as its members.

Beijing and Guangdong are among those locations where homeowners are most active in pursuit of self-governance, yet governments there have barred the official establishment of province-wide associations of HoAs. Hainan faces the opposite problem: insufficient homeowner participation. But the government there has allowed the registration of what is currently China's only active and official province-wide association of HoAs. This comparison demonstrates the curious push and pull between the party-state's need for homeowner self-governance and the party-state's abiding fear of potentially disruptive cross-neighborhood homeowner mobilization.

Overall, governmental recognition and support for cross-neighborhood associations is still the exception rather than the rule, showing that the party-state always keeps a wary eye on the development of independent organizations. The lesson here, however, is that, even against the backdrop of China's generally repressive party-state, there is space for the growth of independent homeowner organizations when the party-state's demand for such organizations overrides its concerns about the potentially disruptive threats posed by these organizations.

9.3 Associations beyond Property

In China, associational activities whose focus extends beyond residential property are much harder to proceed than associational activities whose focus, though they extend beyond a neighborhood's boundaries, restricts themselves to the arena of residential property. From the government's perspective, the utility of both HoAs and associations of HoAs is neighborhood governance. Once an association sets its sights on issues that go beyond neighborhood governance, the association, whether it intends to or not, poses a clear challenge to the party-state without offering it any guaranteed benefits. The state's tolerance and limited support of homeowner activism is built upon the assumption that homeowners want to preserve the value of their property and to improve the neighborhood governance. Homeowners have taken notice of the state's assumption and, to avoid conflict, have generally followed this compartmentalized approach to homeowner self-governance. Nevertheless, this diplomatic approach belies homeowners' understanding that a successfully run HoA has something akin to "the power of the ballot" and is thus a force that homeowners can apply to the structural barriers weighing down on homeowner rights and other rights.

In this section, I will discuss three examples in which activists who were HoC members or participated in homeowner self-governance through other ways went beyond the arena of residential property in an attempt to effect change in other areas of Chinese society and politics. In the first example, homeowners "meddled" in the prearranged elections of the RCs, the constitutionally sanctioned but rarely implemented form of resident self-governance. Homeowners got motivated to care about RC elections because of the difficulties they had in dealing with RCs in their efforts to establish and run their HoAs. Since RCs represent state power in the neighborhood and wield both political and legal power in HoA affairs, disgruntled homeowners sometimes mobilize to vote out a widely disliked RC director or to create so much trouble and noise that the RC director will compromise with the homeowners. When homeowners meddle with an RC election, they are essentially meddling with the local government. Such disruptions have occurred from time to time owing to jurisdictional overlap between RCs and HoAs, the two of which frequently compete with each other for control over residential neighborhoods.

Once homeowners make the leap from economic rights (the right to elect HoC members) to political rights (the right to elect RC members), a natural question presents itself: What would stop homeowners from seeking political participation on a larger scale? The answer hinges on the degree to which such political participation would threaten the party-state. Homeowners would have to read into their specific context and determine what is allowed and what is prohibited. In a more relaxed political climate, homeowner activists might sense that they can push previously untested boundaries in a bid to see how the party-state would respond. In a more repressive climate, homeowners would likely be risk averse and stay within the confines that the party-state has delineated.

In other words, some non-property-related political participation is an inevitable part of homeowners' action to protect their property rights whereas others might be a remote extension and more connected by ideas and ideals rather than pragmatic needs. In the second example, based on their initial success in running for HoCs, multiple homeowner activists tried to run for local people's congresses which inspired and contributed to China's "new citizen movement." In the third example, homeowner-lawyer activists, inspired by their success in homeowner mobilization and funded by their revenue from providing legal services to HoAs, launched a remarkable campaign to mobilize members of the Beijing Bar Association to exercise their "power of the ballot" to replace the orchestrated, fake elections of the Board of the Beijing Bar Association with real elections.

As I argue throughout this book, the extent to which the party-state tolerates homeowners' associational activities is a function of two things: the extent to which the activities satisfy the pragmatic needs of the party-state and the extent to which the activities threaten the power of the party-state. Homeowners whose associational activities threaten the power of the party-state without meeting the pragmatic needs of the party-state face repression. Not surprisingly, the party-state was forced to live with the reality that homeowners meddling with RC elections and even to compromise in some cases; to the opposite the party-state did not hesitate to use coercive power and repression against attempts to democratize other sections of the society, such as the Beijing Bar Association; in-between is homeowners' run for local people's congresses – the party-state would not allow them to succeed but neither would it exert coercive power as it did in the case of preventing democratization of the Beijing Bar Association.

The cases of running for local people's congress and campaigning for the direct election of the Board of the Beijing Bar Association happened before 2008 when the political climate was more relaxed; participating in RC elections has been happening from the early 2000s until today – after the COVID lockdowns, there has been a renewed interest in participating in RC elections in Shanghai as more homeowners have understood the importance of these grassroots-level RCs to their daily life through their experiences during the lockdowns.

9.3.1 Democratizing RCs

It is not a big leap from running in an HoC election to "meddling in" an RC election. I use the word "meddling" because the government often prearranges RC elections. In them, residents are issued ballots listing several officially designated candidates, each of whom will be "elected" without any campaign or fanfare, thus leaving most residents in the dark as to who these candidates are. In many RC elections, the local government designates the RC party secretary, which is a party position and not membership in the RC, to be a candidate for the position of RC director, thus all but guaranteeing that the party secretary can wield the constitutionally sanctioned power of an RC director and the constitutionality of the party leadership in urban neighborhoods.

This party-state plan for controlling RCs becomes problematic when RCs get deeply involved in divisive neighborhood affairs that inevitably result in losers and winners in a single neighborhood. As discussed, RCs play a substantial role in HoA elections. For example, RC directors chair election committees that can screen HoC candidates. Homeowners who are on the losing side of an election often have incentives to create trouble for an RC party secretary. One way to create trouble is to disrupt or even derail an official plan to get the RC party secretary elected to be an RC director. A controversial election giving rise to publicly voiced recriminations would look bad for the party-state which might respond by blaming the party secretary and relocating him or her to another neighborhood. Homeowners who engage in such disruptive behavior do so not necessarily out of a noble intention to advance democracy but out of self-interest. Indeed, self-interest is often at the heart of homeowners' democratizing efforts targeting RC operations.

This was certainly the case in 2018, when a newly appointed RC party secretary in the Shanghai neighborhood of the Spanish Garden sided with a group of young homeowners who intended to fire a management company supported by a group of old party-member homeowners. These old party members saw themselves as "loyalists" in the neighborhood, and part of this loyalty took the form of support for the RC party secretary. However, their preference for the controversial management company superseded their responsibility as party members. When the local government designated the RC party secretary to be an official candidate for the position of RC director, the group of old party members quickly helped register residents to vote and then slyly encouraged these newly registered voters not to vote, resulting in a stillborn election, as less than half of the registered voters ended up voting.[32]

Because of this "political incident," the local government removed the RC party secretary from his position, because that he was not officially elected to be the RC director and that he was not able to take control of the neighborhood.[33] And rather than directly punish the old party members for their controversial manipulation of the election, the local government sent an investigative team to mediate a reconciliation among the various opposing groups of homeowners.[34] In other words, the party-state in this particular case viewed the homeowners' actions not as a challenge to the party-state's leadership, but as a failure of frontline party cadres to solve neighborhood governance problems.

In sum, homeowners have learned to meddle with RC elections in ways that successfully exert pressure on grassroots party-state bureaucrats. The result of this trend in Shanghai is that its municipal government often requires HoA elections and RC elections to be held at different times so as to minimize the possibility of mutual inferences stemming from the elections.[35]

9.3.2 Running for Local People's Congresses

What are the connections between HoAs and running for local people's congresses? The connection between the two is based on both pragmatism and idealism. At the pragmatic level, homeowners seek support from local people's congress members. For example, homeowners can channel their opposition to a particular urban infrastructure project through a local people's congress member, as we have seen in the earlier Shenzhen case. Moreover, gaining official recognition has been a common strategy adopted by homeowner activists to increase their social and political capital and leverage in their dealing with grassroots government officials. Being a member of a local people's congress would suit this goal. Moreover, running for local people's congress can be based on a homeowner activist's ideal of democratic governance. Maowen Du, a 64-year-old retired medical doctor and homeowner in Beijing's Huilongguan neighborhood ran for a local people's congress in 2003. His campaign statement, which was posted in the neighborhood, explained his reason for running:

> Would you believe that a 64-year-old retired doctor wants to run for a seat in the Changping District People's Congress? Well, it's true. My experiences and the realities on the ground have convinced me that every citizen has a democratic right to participate in people's congress elections.... I'm running in an election for a seat in the local people's congress because I'm a homeowner and I love this neighborhood that brings me both happiness and pain. I understand the hardships of us homeowners and am willing to endeavor to protect every homeowner's legal rights and interests.... If elected, I'll be a new type of people's congress member and work vociferously for neighborhood self-governance and the legal rights and interests of all homeowners.[36]

Dr. Du was part of a movement in which Beijing activists around 2003 began running for local people's congresses. Two activists who initiated this movement were homeowner activists: QB, whom I discuss at the end of this chapter, was a high-powered lawyer specializing in the grassroots organizing of homeowners; and, SKX was an HoC chairman who had earned a nationwide reputation as an expert in neighborhood governance. In fact, SKX set up his own campaign office and rented an SUV displaying, in large print, the slogan "Please cross out all candidates on the list and fill in the blank with my name: SKX." Neither SKX nor QB garnered a winning number of votes, but as SKX confessed to me in 2018, the key was not to get elected, but to publicly let everyone know that rights on paper need to be exercised if they are to have substance – a lesson that many homeowners had already learned from their participation in HoA elections and operations.[37]

The most enthusiastic support for the "local people's congress" movement came from Beijing's Haidian District, where top Chinese universities have created a residential population consisting, in part, of idealistic students and professors. Ultimately, out of 420 members of the Haidian District People's Congress in 2003, 10 had independently campaigned for their seat rather than rely on an official designation from the Haidian District Government.[38] The democratic activist Xu Zhiyong, who later became a dissident for helping to organize the nationwide civil rights movement known as "the New Citizens' Movement," was one of these local congress members. In fact, he had already helped democratize his neighborhood through various activities, including a successful campaign that got him elected to be an HoC chairman.[39]

In sum, China in 2003 offered glimmers of hope for democratic activists, many of whom were homeowner activists. It marked the beginning of Hu Jintao's presidency, which initially signaled an interest in moving China toward democracy and the rule of law.[40] Since then, of course, the political climate in China has grown repressive: Xu Zhiyong is now in prison. But as late as 2019, Xu Zhiyong still publicly advocated for citizens to run for district-level people's congresses as a way of practicing democracy.[41] It is fair to say that Chinese homeowners' self-governance movement was one of the foundations of Xu Zhiyong's New Citizens' Movement, which is now closely monitored and frequently repressed and by the party-state.

9.3.3 Democratizing the Beijing Bar Association

The Beijing Bar Association (BBA) had over 20,000 members back in 2009. A lawyer needed to pay RMB 2,500, which was about 10 percent of an entry-level lawyer's annual income in 2009, for a membership in the BBA to practice law in Beijing. Though the 20,000 lawyer members were supposed to elect a board of the BBA, the decision-making body of the association, before 2009 the board elections had been prearranged and 90 percent of the members had not had a chance to participate in the elections.[42]

QB, as mentioned earlier, was a leading lawyer specializing in grassroots organizing of homeowners in Beijing. Encouraged by his own success in organizing homeowners to exercise "the power of the ballot," he hatched a plan to help Beijing lawyers to exercise their "power of the ballot." Officially there were two steps to elect a board member. The first step was for lawyer members to elect about 200 representatives to attend the annual meeting of lawyers' representatives. The second step was for these lawyers' representatives to elect a board, including the president and vice presidents of the BBA.

QB's first step was to mobilize and organize lawyers to elect their own representatives against the officially designated ones. This first step, according to QB, was not much different from mobilizing and organizing homeowners to elect their own HoCs. QB and his team members had organized HoC elections in dozens of neighborhoods in Beijing and even summarized essential tips for a successful campaign in a handbook that was handily applicable to their campaign to democratizing the BBA. QB persuaded Ms. Ma, a member of his team who had practiced her skills of public speech in organizing HoC elections, to run for an election to be a lawyers' representative.[43]

QB was running not only Ms. Ma's but also dozens of other candidates' campaigns. His law firm became the headquarters of these independent candidates' running for the congress of the Beijing lawyers' representatives. Thanks to his success in law practice related to homeowner rights and housing-related disputes, QB had enough funding to support the operation, which cost him about RMB 300,000 in 2009.

QB and these independent candidates were successful in this first step and many of them, including Ms. Ma, succeeded in beating officially designated members and becoming a lawyer's representative to attend the annual meeting to elect a board of the BBA.[44]

Their next and second step was to nominate several of their own to the board of the BBA. This requires on-the-site coordination and campaign during the annual meeting of the Beijing lawyers' representatives. QB, who was the mastermind of this coup, did not run himself and therefore was not a lawyers' representative. His plan was to campaign for these independent candidates on the site and coordinate their strategies, including whom to nominate. This second step eventually failed as the Central Political and Legal Committee of the Chinese Communist Party could not allow the democratization of the BBA to happen and directly intervened. On the day of the meeting of the Beijing lawyers' representatives, hundreds of militarized police guarded the venue of the meeting, walling off QB and his peers from entering the venue to mobilize. The Committee even blocked all communication signals (i.e., cellular phones and the internet) from and to the venue of the meeting. Inside the venue, the Committee and the Beijing Bureau of Legal Affairs, the latter of which oversaw the BBA, required all lawyers' representatives to accept and elect candidates officially designated by them. Without effective coordination from QB and being intimidated by the presence of militarized police, those independent lawyers' representatives were not able to elect any of their own to the BBA board. Afterward, the BBA disbarred QB and two other organizers of this campaign.[45] In an effort to pacify its rank-and-file members, the BBA eventually reduced its annual membership fee.

Nevertheless, this attempt by QB and his peers to democratize the BBA deserves to be regarded as a milestone of China's democratization movement. Although the 2009 effort to democratize the BBA was certainly not an extension solely of the homeowner self-governance movement, the deep involvement of QB and Ms. Ma demonstrates how democratization in one area of society can spill over into another area, at least when the overall political climate allows. It takes practice to make democracy work, and in China, there is perhaps no safer ground on which to engage in this practice than urban neighborhoods.

9.4 Conclusion

In this chapter, I have examined why and how homeowners mobilize beyond both the physical boundaries of their neighborhoods and the virtual boundaries of neighborhood governance to participate in broader or far-removed physical and political space, and I have examined the governmental response to these types of association and mobilization. This chapter strikes home the idea that China's homeowner self-governance movement has provided an environment in which millions of homeowners can practice democracy in ways that lay a foundation for civic participation in other areas of society such as municipal infrastructure projects, running for local people's congresses, and reforms in the legal profession. The party-state's ideal is to have the benefits of neighborhood democratization and confine it to property and neighborhood issues. Homeowners might toe the line as a strategy of survival. In the long run, what matters are the growth of independent associations and the practice of democratic and organizational skills, which can contribute to larger-scale democratization in China when the political climate allows.

Conclusion

Democracy in China?

Is the term "authoritarian commons" an oxymoron? No, it is not. It highlights the tension and interaction between homeowners and the authoritarian state. Total party-state control risks eroding party-state legitimacy simply through incompetence, whereas delegating service delivery to independent-minded middle-class residents can endanger party-state control. In the face of bottom-up demand for neighborhood self-governance, the authoritarian state legalizes homeowners' associations (HoAs) but reserves political and legal means to control the development of HoAs. Neighborhood self-governance may increase homeowners' trust in the party-state, as both quantitative and qualitative data in this book have demonstrated. However, it does not mean that homeowners and their associations always cooperate with the party-state. Instead, their cooperation is a way to resist and preserve their material property interests and pursuit of democracy.

The answer to the question of whether liberal commons can emerge in an authoritarian regime is local and as follows: The authoritarian commons feature multiple equilibria that depend on local states' institutional infrastructural power and the degree of risk that homeowner self-governance poses to the authoritarian rule. A local state with strong infrastructural power, including the judicial capacity to balance different interests in neighborhood governance, and an intermediate degree of risk can make the institutional reforms to accommodate grassroots democracy.[1]

Can homeowners tell us anything about democracy in China? To answer, please allow me to quote Tocqueville again:

> You draw a man out of himself with difficulty in order to interest him in the destiny of the entire state, because he poorly understands the influence that the destiny of the state can exercise on his fate. But if it is necessary to have a road pass by the end of his property, he will see at first glance that there is a connection between this small public affair and his greatest private affairs, and he will discover, without anyone showing him, the close bond that here unites particular interest to general interest.[2]

Overall homeowners appear to represent the best chance of democratizing urban governance in China. A major advancement for Chinese citizens over the past four decades of market reform has been the establishment of private property rights.[3] Transitioning from an economy devoid of private housing prior to the 1980s, China now boasts one of the wildest and pricey urban real estate markets globally. Approximately one-third of China's economy is anchored to the real estate sector. This is the economic foundation for the mutual dependence of the Chinese state and its homeowner society.

As a result, HoAs have been a rare form through which Chinese citizens get associated and have real elections recognized by law and respected by the government, which makes homeowners a more promising group than, for example, workers.[4] This legal right to associate gives an organizational basis for Chinese homeowners to develop an autonomous civic space that is outside the governmental control. As Michael Mann writes, the masses do not revolt because they are organizationally outflanked.[5] Chinese homeowners gain organizational strength through their legally recognized right to associate in their neighborhoods. Homeownership enables Chinese citizens to govern themselves in their own neighborhoods. To an extent, this is a direct competition with and challenge to the state sovereignty. But as the state needs homeowners' cooperation among themselves and with the state to better govern urban neighborhoods, it needs to live with this inconvenient reality in which it concedes some power to HoAs.

Homeownership also distinguishes HoAs from other civic groups in China. Much scholarly attention has been devoted to non-government organizations (NGOs) in China, which are the usual subject of studies on civil society in China. However, these NGOs often lack independent resources, and predominantly depend on foreign or government funding, with their agendas largely shaped by these funders.[6] Property rights, specifically, homeownership, gives Chinese citizens both their own source of wealth and their own agenda, which is primarily about the preservation of their home value, an *apolitical* pursuit the party-state recognizes and respects.

This book focuses on democracy within neighborhoods, which is significant in itself: Can you imagine any other context in urban China in which hundreds of people could gather and vote to determine their own affairs? Even just learning how to decide issues together through the mechanism of "one person, one vote" instead of appealing to the authorities is of tremendous value in transforming subjects of an authoritarian regime into citizens of a future democracy.

More than that, homeowners' democratization efforts have gone beyond their condominiums and even the arena of property rights and real estate management. The party-state's efforts to contain neighborhood democratization within the physical boundaries of condominiums and the virtual boundaries of neighborhood governance have not always succeeded. My examination of the cross-neighborhood and nationwide mobilization and association of homeowners reveals the potential of hundreds of millions of Chinese homeowners to act as an independent political power in both city and national politics.

Nevertheless, the party-state has not given up its plan to "have the cake and eat it too." Homeowners are willing, often at ease, to kowtow to the party's leadership, but when the party's penetration efforts encroach upon their right to self-governance, they have not been reluctant to evade, petition, and even directly fight back through law. It is still quite unlikely, even given China's strengthening control over society and economy in the past decade, that the party-state would take homeowners' legal rights to associate and to self-governance back, unless it is willing to remove the market economy as a foundation of its governance. The reason is simple: The party-state relies on homeowners for informational, financial, and human resources to govern, not the other way around. With the worsening financial situation of the party-state, I do not see an immediate future that the party-state can afford to hire more people to directly administer condominium complexes. Such attempts even in the better years have failed.

What's the implication of neighborhood democratization on China's future? As demonstrated in this book, scale matters, particularly for democracy. So, here is a total speculation. From a comparative perspective, authoritarian states with a high capacity of governance facing an intermediate degree of risk to its rule successfully steered the democratic transition in South Korea[7] and Taiwan.[8] As evidence of high state capacity in both regimes, democratization took place after a long-period prosperity under the leadership of a strong and capable dictator, Park Chung Hee in South Korea[9] and Chiang Ching-kuo in Taiwan,[10] respectively. In comparison, weak state capacity often accompanies the failure of democratization.[11] What we can extrapolate from this research is that democratization requires strong state capacity, including well-functioning courts to balance the cost of collective decision-making and the cost of wealth redistribution.

This book has also left a few related issues unaddressed. First, how will the downturn of the Chinese economy impact the development of HoAs? The party-state has tried to reduce its reliance on real estate for economic development with limited success and the real estate sector is facing a great degree of uncertainty. Several factors have made neighborhood governance an even more salient problem than before. The first one is that with the slowing down of real estate development, many developers have become more reliant on their real estate management businesses. Second, the aging of apartments and the deterioration of neighborhoods have become an urgent problem after three decades of rapid real estate development, which requires action and payment from homeowners to address. Third, Chinese local governments are running out of money and become less likely than before to directly intervene in neighborhood governance. In other words, they rely more than before on homeowners to govern their own neighborhoods. Overall, I predict that (1) conflicts in urban China's neighborhoods will intensify as time goes by; (2) the party-state will become more attentive to the development of HoAs and try to "have the cake and eat it too," with efforts to increase support and strengthen control; and (3) with the coordination from the top of the party-state, there will be more convergence of local practices, though regional divergence is likely to last to the predictable future.

Second, would technology solve the informational insufficiency of the party-state? I am not sure, but this book provides some clue: During China's COVID lockdowns when the party-state machine was at full speed, it relied on foot soldiers (i.e., urban grid managers) to collect information that was often inaccurate and repetitive. Technology seems to not be able to overcome some fundamental shortages of the party-state as an organization, particularly the fragmentation and conflicts of its various units, not to mention the prevalent principal–agent problem.

The third issue this book has left unaddressed is the potential exclusionary effect of the homeowners' movement.[12] As I have written elsewhere, the alliance of bureaucratic and real estate interests still dominates urban politics in China, and although the rise of homeowners has provided a counterbalance to such dominance, it has done so to only a limited degree.[13] The problem with NIMBYism ("Not in My Backyard") in the United States is the overwhelming influence that homeowners exert in urban and suburban politics. The situation in China is still pretty much the opposite, and therefore the rise of homeowners may render the system more balanced and more democratic owing to the input and participation of millions of homeowners. However, the exclusionary effect does exist, as even in China homeowners have an advantage over property-less tenants.[14] Nevertheless, granting homeowners self-governance power does not necessarily conflict with proposals to empower other societal groups and classes. As it happens, fighting for their rights helps Chinese middle-class homeowners understand the struggles that other less privileged groups of the Chinese society have been facing against the same regime. Eventually, "the challenge for the modern community is to get more of the good while minimizing the bad."[15]

Last but not least is the agency or accountability problem of homeowner self-governance. Homeowners' committees (HoCs), the executive body of HoAs, are in charge of the daily operation of HoAs. Are members of HoCs angels? No. Might they abuse their power? Yes. Can they be corrupt and prone to bribery by management companies or captured by the party-state? Yes. Do they engage in factional conflicts? Yes. Nevertheless, a few factors make HoC members more accountable than the party-state's bureaucrats. First, their legitimacy comes from homeowner elections, and they are subject to elections upon the completion of each term, which is usually three to five years. HoC members who have abused their power or been corrupt risk not being re-elected. Elective pressure keeps them from abusing their power and alienating their constituents. Second, they and their family members are subject to neighborhood pressure and reputational sanctions. Third, their work is subject to the daily and decentralized monitoring of homeowners who together hold expertise related to various aspects of condominium management and governance, such as price of a particular construction material needed for building maintenance. Moreover, there is often an oppositional faction in a neighborhood which keeps a close eye on the behaviors of HoC members.

To conclude, urban neighborhoods with indivisible condominium ownership and a size similar to that of Tocqueville's New England towns have been and will continue to be a great school of democracy in China.[16]

Appendix I: Summary of Research Methods

This study combines archival research, a questionnaire survey, and two rounds of ethnographic research: one from 2018 to 2019, and the other in 2023. In Chapter 6, I have discussed how, where, and from whom I conducted the questionnaire survey. Here, I would like to give more information about my ethnographic and archival research.

Given my concerns about the representativeness of my sample, I employed various strategies to counteract potential sample bias. One primary method involved collecting and corroborating information from multiple sources with diverse backgrounds. For instance, triangulation is a routine method I employed: If homeowners, residential committee workers, and management company employees (who often hold opposing views in neighborhood disputes) concur on a disputed neighborhood issue, I deem that issue verified, even though their interpretations might differ.

I also gained access to the archives of both individual HoAs and citywide homeowner organizations and was therefore able to verify the information obtained in the interviews with documentary evidence, including meeting minutes and photos collected by both those organizations and leading homeowner activists over the past two decades.

Additionally, I was mindful of the geographic and socio-economic characteristics of the neighborhoods I studied. I aimed to encompass neighborhoods both proximate to city centers (which are typically upscale, inhabited by legal, financial, and other professionals, and affluent entrepreneurs) and those more distant and economically challenged.

The first round of ethnographic research focuses on three Chinese megacities: the capital Beijing, with a population of 21.5 million; Shanghai, the country's economic powerhouse, with a population of 24.3 million; and Shenzhen, the heart of the country's market economy, with a population of 13.4 million. I selected these three cities as my research sites for the following reasons. First, they are the most economically developed, having witnessed the rapid growth of the middle class and homeownership levels in the past two decades. If we are interested in understanding interactions between the middle class and the state in China, the country's most important megacities serve as ideal field sites.

Second, the three cities demonstrate different styles of urban governance and are subject to different political and social constraints, and therefore enable us to observe different dynamics of homeowner–state interactions.

I have been able to identify all of the major citywide homeowner organizations and platforms in the three megacities and have carried out in-depth interviews with their leaders. The less significant homeowner activists I interviewed fell into one of two groups. Members of the first group were affiliated with citywide homeowner organizations and were usually introduced to me by those organizations' leaders. The second group comprised homeowner activists who were not affiliated with such organizations. I arranged interviews with them in a variety of ways, including referrals from scholars in the field and sometimes just cold-calling them after obtaining their contact information.

These interviews, including at least one interview with each of the homeowner organization leaders, lasted from one to four hours. I also asked the interviewees, scholars, and government officials whose work is related to the homeowner arena for a list of names of other potentially significant interviewees and continued to update the list until no new names were identified. I also compared my list with the lists of leading neighborhood governance experts/homeowner activists published in the mass media, which confirmed that I had managed to interview most of the leading homeowner activists with a known nationwide or citywide impact.

I have also visited many urban neighborhoods, with interviews conducted in some of them, and participated in meetings of both individual neighborhoods and homeowner activists from across a single city or even the entire country, as well as the conferences on neighborhood governance organized by the three city governments. These participatory observations afforded me opportunities to verify the information gleaned from individual interviews, to deepen my understanding of the diversity of, and nuisance caused by, activist groups in the three cities, and to observe activists' interactions with ordinary homeowners, real estate managers, and government officials.

The second round of ethnographic research focuses on neighborhood governance during China's COVID lockdowns, and the impact of China's new Civil Code and party-building efforts in its urban neighborhoods. Most of these interviews took place offline between January and July 2023. My fieldwork on COVID-19 lockdowns primarily targeted Wuhan and Shanghai. These cities witnessed major citywide lockdowns at the beginning and end of China's COVID-19 prevention and control measures, respectively.

Constraints in time and resources meant I couldn't study all Chinese cities in depth even after two rounds of ethnographic research across six years. However, I did ensure a diverse range in my interviews, covering both large and small, coastal and inland, and northern and southern cities. Beyond Beijing, Shanghai, Shenzhen, and Wuhan, my study ranged from conducting seven interviews in Zhengzhou (a major inland city with a population

Table A.1 Interviews by city and interviewee identity

City \ Interviewee Identity	Homeowner interviews	Interviews with government employees	Interviews with employees of real estate management companies	Interviews with legal professionals	No. of interviews
Shanghai	85	7	1	1	94
Wuhan	27	9	2	0	38
Shenzhen	27	5	2	4	38
Beijing	21	4	3	4	32
Zhengzhou	6	1	2	0	9
Yichang	2	1	0	0	3
Hefei	2	0	0	0	2
Hangzhou	1	0	0	0	1
Xi'an	1	0	0	0	1
Yinchuan	1	0	0	0	1
Changsha	1	0	0	0	1
Foshan	0	1	0	0	1
Huai'an	1	0	0	0	1
Haikou	1	0	0	0	1
Huizhou	1	0	0	0	1
Total =	177	28	10	9	224

exceeding 12 million) to one in Yinchuan of Ningxia in northwestern China. While these interviews are far from being representative, they reinforce my observation from cities I have investigated in depth.

Table A.1 provides information about the number of interviews I conducted in each city and categorized according to interviewee identities. I have identified each interview with a serial number and keep a list of interviews with their serial numbers and detailed information such as location, time, and interview identity. I have also recorded interviews where they were allowed and transcribed these interviews, totaling 1.8 million Chinese words.

Appendix II: Survey Data and Analysis

A.1 Summary Statistics

Table A.2 Summary statistics

	Count	Mean	SD	Min	Max
Homeowners' association	841	0.65	0.48	0	1
Activist	841	0.61	0.49	0	1
Community hours	831	1.42	0.91	1	5
Developer-affiliated management company	841	0.42	0.49	0	1
Management fee raise	808	0.40	0.49	0	1
Community activity	791	2.01	0.62	1	3
Democratic value	841	0.72	0.45	0	1
Community identity	841	9.00	2.03	0	10
Trust in central government	841	7.55	2.50	1	10
Trust in local governments	841	5.55	2.33	1	10
Trust in street office	841	4.95	2.74	1	10
Government support	841	5.35	3.37	0	10
Government collusion	841	7.26	2.76	0	10
Neighbors' participation	838	2.84	1.05	1	4
Number of friends	838	3.04	1.23	1	5
Trust in neighbors	841	7.29	1.96	0	10
City: Beijing	841	0.28	0.45	0	1
City: Shanghai	841	0.41	0.49	0	1
City: Shenzhen	841	0.32	0.47	0	1
Duration of residence	839	4.04	1.13	1	6
Age	841	3.03	1.04	1	5
Female	841	0.51	0.50	0	1
Education	840	3.64	0.99	1	5
Working hours	826	3.51	1.48	1	5
Public sector	832	0.56	0.50	0	1
Building age	840	3.65	0.82	1	5
Neighborhood size	841	3.73	1.49	1	8
Average housing price	841	6.69	2.28	1	12
Petition	841	0.62	0.49	0	1
Litigation	841	0.17	0.38	0	1
Violence	834	0.37	0.48	0	1

Table A.3 Unbalanced sample between activists and nonactivists

	Nonactivists		Activists		T-test
	Mean	SD	Mean	SD	***P***
Trust in central government	7.59	2.42	7.54	2.56	0.78
Trust in street office	5.27	2.67	4.71	2.78	0.00**
Democratic value	0.67	0.47	0.75	0.43	0.01**
Community hours	1.02	0.20	1.67	1.09	0.00***
Homeowners' association	0.52	0.50	0.73	0.44	0.00***
City: Beijing	0.27	0.44	0.28	0.45	0.59
City: Shanghai	0.48	0.50	0.36	0.48	0.00***
City: Shenzhen	0.25	0.43	0.36	0.48	0.00***
Duration of residence	3.70	1.21	4.27	1.02	0.00***
Age	2.75	0.98	3.22	1.04	0.00***
Woman	0.56	0.50	0.48	0.50	0.04*
Education	3.71	1.02	3.60	0.98	0.13
Working hours	3.63	1.48	3.44	1.47	0.06
Public sector	0.58	0.49	0.55	0.50	0.43
Building age	3.54	0.88	3.73	0.77	0.00**
Neighborhood size	3.69	1.59	3.76	1.43	0.51
Housing price	6.49	2.34	6.81	2.23	0.05
Petition	0.48	0.50	0.71	0.46	0.00***
Litigation	0.08	0.27	0.23	0.42	0.00***
Violence	0.28	0.45	0.43	0.50	0.00***
Observations	324		517		841

Note: Table shows results of comparison between the homeowner activists and nonactivists.
* $p < 0.05$, ** $p < 0.01$, *** $p < 0.001$ (two-tailed test).

Table A.4 Balanced sample between neighborhoods with and without an HoA

	HoA (treatment)		No HoA (control)		No HoA (weighted control)	
	Mean	SD	Mean	SD	Mean	SD
Trust in central government	7.71	2.39	7.27	2.69	7.70	2.56
Trust in city government	7.08	2.49	6.50	2.62	7.07	2.47
Activist	0.69	0.46	0.47	0.50	0.69	0.46
City: Beijing	0.24	0.43	0.33	0.47	0.25	0.43
City: Shanghai	0.44	0.50	0.34	0.48	0.44	0.50
City: Shenzhen	0.31	0.46	0.32	0.47	0.31	0.46
Building age	3.67	0.78	3.63	0.90	3.66	0.86
Neighborhood size	3.68	1.39	3.83	1.67	3.67	1.63
Housing price	6.72	2.31	6.62	2.23	6.70	2.11

Table A.4 (cont.)

	HoA (treatment)		No HoA (control)		No HoA (weighted control)	
	Mean	SD	Mean	SD	Mean	SD
Petition	0.66	0.47	0.54	0.50	0.65	0.48
Litigation	0.17	0.38	0.17	0.37	0.17	0.38
Violence	0.40	0.49	0.33	0.47	0.39	0.49
Duration of residence	4.14	1.08	3.88	1.21	4.13	1.11
Age	3.10	1.04	2.93	1.03	3.07	0.99
Female	0.49	0.50	0.55	0.50	0.48	0.50
Education	3.61	0.96	3.71	1.06	3.62	1.06
Working hours	3.53	1.47	3.48	1.48	3.55	1.47
Public sector	0.54	0.50	0.61	0.49	0.54	0.50
Observations	547		294		284	

Note: Table shows results of entropy balancing across homeowners in the neighborhoods with an HoA (treatment) and without an HoA (control). Treatment group has 547 observations; unweighted control group has 294; and the sum of the control weights is 284.

A.2 Additional Robustness

Table A.5 Alternative measure of political trust

	DEV: Trust in local government		
	(1)	(2)	(3)
Homeowners' association	0.35*	0.35***	−0.00
	(0.17)	(0.11)	(0.19)
Activist		−0.49***	−0.75***
		(0.11)	(0.16)
Association × activist			0.51*
			(0.23)
Trust in central government		−0.15***	−0.15***
		(0.04)	(0.04)
Trust in city government		0.86***	0.87***
		(0.04)	(0.04)
R^2	0.01	0.61	0.61
Observation	811	811	811

Note: The models report the coefficients from OLS regression; the specification is based on Model 3 of Table 6.2 in Chapter 6.
* $p < 0.05$, ** $p < 0.01$, *** $p < 0.001$ (two-tailed test).

Table A.6 Alternative measure of homeowner activism

	Trust in street government			Trust in local government		
	(1)	(2)	(3)	(4)	(5)	(6)
Association	0.61**	0.61***	0.27	0.33*	0.33**	0.14
	(0.20)	(0.15)	(0.17)	(0.17)	(0.11)	(0.13)
Activist		−0.43*	−1.06***		−0.45***	−0.80***
		(0.17)	(0.24)		(0.12)	(0.17)
Association × activist			1.27***			0.70**
			(0.33)			(0.25)
Trust in central government		−0.22***	−0.23***		−0.14***	−0.15***
		(0.05)	(0.05)		(0.04)	(0.04)
Trust in city government		0.89***	0.91***		0.85***	0.85***
		(0.05)	(0.05)		(0.04)	(0.04)
R^2	0.01	0.43	0.44	0.00	0.59	0.59
Observation	812	812	812	812	812	812

Note: The models report the coefficients from OLS regression; the specification is based on Model 3 of Table 6.2 in Chapter 6.
* $p < 0.05$, ** $p < 0.01$, *** $p < 0.001$ (two-tailed test).

Table A.7 Alternative measure of HoA

	Trust in street government			Trust in local government		
	(1)	(2)	(3)	(4)	(5)	(6)
Association (registered)	0.63**	0.63***	0.13	0.35*	0.35**	−0.02
	(0.19)	(0.15)	(0.27)	(0.17)	(0.11)	(0.19)
Activist		−0.49**	−0.85***		−0.46***	−0.73***
		(0.16)	(0.23)		(0.12)	(0.16)
Association × activist			0.72*			0.54*
			(0.32)			(0.23)
Trust in central government		−0.25***	−0.25***		−0.14***	−0.14***
		(0.06)	(0.06)		(0.04)	(0.04)
Trust in city government		0.91***	0.91***		0.84***	0.84***
		(0.06)	(0.06)		(0.04)	(0.04)
R^2	0.01	0.41	0.42	0.01	0.58	0.59
Observation	813	813	813	813	813	813

Note: The models report the coefficients from OLS regression; the specification is based on Model 3 of Table 6.2 in Chapter 6.
* $p < 0.05$, ** $p < 0.01$, *** $p < 0.001$ (two-tailed test).

Table A.8 Mediation analysis

	DEV: Trust in street government	
	(1) Government support as Mediator	(2) Government collusion as Mediator
ACME	0.31***	0.25***
	(0.09)	(0.07)
Total effect	0.84***	0.84***
	(0.18)	(0.19)
% of total effect mediated	34.94%***	29.39%***

Note: The table reports the results from mediation analysis. ACME standards for average causal mediation effect. The mediation models control for respondents' city, age, gender, education, vocation, working hours, duration of residence, age of building, neighborhood size, and average housing price as well as whether there was any petition, physical conflict, and administrative litigation occurred in the neighborhood.

* $p < 0.05$, ** $p < 0.01$, *** $p < 0.001$ (two-tailed test).

Table A.9 Controlling confounders to activist

	DEV: Trust in street government			
	(1)	(2)	(3)	(4)
Association	0.53	0.58	0.47	−0.11
	(0.35)	(0.63)	(0.49)	(0.21)
Activist	−1.00***	−0.92***	−0.76***	−0.53***
	(0.22)	(0.23)	(0.16)	(0.16)
Association × activist	0.83**	0.91**	0.62**	0.49*
	(0.31)	(0.32)	(0.23)	(0.22)
Association × democratic	−0.65			
	(0.34)			
Association × residence		−0.21		
		(0.15)		
Association × age		0.08		
		(0.16)		
Association × woman		−0.03		
		(0.29)		
Association × building age			−0.16	
			(0.13)	
Association × petition				0.18
				(0.23)
Association × litigation				−0.14
				(0.29)
Association × violence				0.00
				(0.23)

Table A.9 (cont.)

	DEV: Trust in street government			
	(1)	(2)	(3)	(4)
Trust in central government	−0.22***	−0.22***	−0.14***	−0.10**
	(0.05)	(0.05)	(0.04)	(0.04)
Trust in city government	0.90***	0.89***	0.85***	0.78***
	(0.05)	(0.05)	(0.04)	(0.04)
R^2	0.45	0.46	0.61	0.64
Observation	813	813	813	813

Note: The models report the coefficients from OLS regression. All the main effects of the interaction terms are included in the regressions. The specification is based on Model 3 of Table 6.2 in Chapter 6.
* $p < 0.05$, ** $p < 0.01$, *** $p < 0.001$ (two-tailed test).

Table A.10 Extended sample

	DEV: Trust in street-level government		
	(1)	(2)	(3)
Homeowners' association	0.48***	0.48***	0.11
	(0.14)	(0.11)	(0.21)
Activist		−0.55***	−0.80***
		(0.12)	(0.17)
Association × activist			0.51*
			(0.24)
Trust in central government		−0.17***	−0.17***
		(0.03)	(0.03)
Trust in city government		0.80***	0.81***
		(0.03)	(0.03)
R^2	0.01	0.42	0.42
Observation	1594	1594	1594

Note: The models report the coefficients from OLS regression. The sample includes observations from the three megacities, as well as other cities in China.
* $p < 0.05$, ** $p < 0.01$, *** $p < 0.001$ (two-tailed test).

Notes

Introduction

1. Morris Cohen, *Property and Sovereignty*, 13 CORNELL L.Q. 9 (1927). For recent interpretations and rebuttals, *see* Thomas W. Merrill, *Property and Sovereignty, Information and Audience*, 18 THEORETICAL INQ. L. 417 (2017); Larissa Katz, *Governing Through Owners: How and Why Formal Private Property Rights Enhance State Power*, 160 U. PA. L. REV. 2029 (2011).
2. Merrill, *id*. For a significant exception, *see* ELINOR OSTROM, GOVERNING THE COMMONS: THE EVOLUTION OF INSTITUTIONS FOR COLLECTIVE ACTION 103–142 (1990) (municipalities and private companies used court orders, elections, and public hearings to impose constraints on themselves).
3. ALEXIS DE TOCQUEVILLE, DEMOCRACY IN AMERICA 101–102 (James T. Schleifer trans., 2010).
4. *See, e.g.*, Amanda Taub, *The Unsexy Truth about Why the Arab Spring Failed*, VOX (January 27, 2016), www.vox.com/2016/1/27/10845114/arab-spring-failure; ANNE APPLEBAUM, IRON CURTAIN: THE CRUSHING OF EASTERN EUROPE 1944–1956 (2012).
5. *See, e.g.*, JESSICA C. TEETS, CIVIL SOCIETY UNDER AUTHORITARIANISM: THE CHINA MODEL (2014); Kang Xiaoguang (康晓光) & Han Heng (韩恒), 分类控制：当前中国大陆国家与社会关系研究 [*The System of Differential Controls: A Study of the State-Society Relationship in Contemporary China*], 《社会学研究》 [SOCIOLOGICAL RESEARCH], no. 6, 73 (2005). As the famous economist Raghuram Rajan writes, "… healthy communities are essential for sustaining vibrant market democracies. This is perhaps why authoritarian movements like fascism and communism try to replace community consciousness with nationalist or proletarian consciousness." RAGHURAM RAJAN, THE THIRD PILLAR: HOW MARKETS AND THE STATE LEAVE THE COMMUNITY BEHIND xvii (2019).
6. For the definition of fragmented authoritarianism, *See* Kenneth G. Lieberthal, *Introduction: The Fragmented Authoritarianism Model and Its Limitations, in* BUREAUCRACY, POLITICS, AND DECISION MAKING IN POST-MAO CHINA 1, 1–30 (Kenneth G. Lieberthal & David M. Lampton eds., 1992); Andrew Mertha, *Fragmented Authoritarianism 2.0: Political Pluralization in the Chinese Policy Process*, 2009 CHINA Q. 995 (2009). For the development of civil society in China, *see* Anthony J. Spires, *Contingent Symbiosis and Civil Society in an Authoritarian State: Understanding the Survival of China's Grassroots NGOs*, 117 AM. J. SOCIOL. 1 (2011); Jessica C. Teets, *Let Many Civil Societies Bloom: The Rise of Consultative Authoritarianism in China*, 213 CHINA Q. 19 (2013).

7. Chinese Academy of Social Sciences (中国社会科学院), 《当代中国调查报告丛书：中国社会和谐稳定跟踪调查研究》 [Contemporary China Investigation Report Series: A Follow-up Survey of Harmony and Stability of Chinese Society] (2013) (showing China's homeownership rate in 2013 to be 93.5%); Kan Feng (阚枫), 社科院：我国家庭住房自有率达 93.5% [*Chinese Academy of Social Sciences: The Homeownership Rate in Our Country reached 93.5%*], China News (December 25, 2013), http://sh.house.163.com/13/1225/19/9GVDJ2IL00073SDJ.html.
8. Interview No. BJ-HO-080318-3.
9. Interview No. SZ-HO-xxxx18*-18.
10. "Incomplete statistics showed that more than 400 million people of China's nearly 1.4-billion population have become middle-income earners, said He Lifeng, director of the National Development and Reform Commission (NDRC), adding that the figure is still on a fast rise." Bai Yang, *China Creates World's Largest Middle Class*, People's daily (March 14, 2018), http://en.people.cn/n3/2018/0314/c90000-9437028.html. This number is close to that in the Global Wealth Report issued by Credit Suisse in December 2018, which says that 35 percent of the global middle class (1.1 billion) are Chinese. *See* Credit Suisse Research Institute, *Global Wealth Pyramid: Decreased Base*, Credit Suisse (December 1, 2018), www.credit-suisse.com/corporate/en/articles/news-and-expertise/global-wealth-pyramid-decreased-base-201801.html. For a definition and percentage of the middle class in China, *see* Zhang Yuan et al., *The Rise of The Middle Class in The People's Republic of China* (ADB Economics Working Paper Series No. 247, 2011); CSIS, *How Well-Off Is China's Middle Class?*, Global Trade Magazine (June 13, 2017), www.globaltrademag.com/global-trade-daily/commentary/well-off-chinas-middle-class ("Chinese households keep a greater proportion of their wealth in their home. China has an above average home ownership rate of 87%."); Wade Shephard, *How People in China Afford Their Outrageously Expensive Homes*, Forbes (May 30, 2016, 04:41 PM), www.forbes.com/sites/wadeshepard/2016/03/30/how-people-in-china-afford-their-outrageously-expensive-homes/#a760332a3ce5; Rebecca Seales, *The Country Where 70% of Millennials Are Homeowners*, BBC News (April 6, 2017), www.bbc.com/news/world-39512599. ("While young people around the world are struggling to get on the property ladder, an HSBC study found that 70% of Chinese millennials have achieved the milestone.")
11. Wuquan Fa (物权法) [Property Law] (promulgated by Nat'l People's Cong., March 16, 2007, effective October 1, 2007) art. 70 (Chinalawinfo). Common property includes hallways, elevators, common ground, water towers, roads, parking lots, etc. For a discussion of China's urban property regime, *see* Donald Clarke, *China's Stealth Urban Land Revolution*, 62 Am. J. Comp. L. 323 (2014).
12. For various definitions of urban commons, *see, e.g.*, Sheila R. Foster, *Collective Action and the Urban Commons*, 87 Notre Dame L. Rev. 57 (2011); Sheila R. Foster & Christian Iaione, *The City as a Commons*, 34 Yale L. & Pol'y Rev. 281 (2015); Nicole Stelle Garnett, *Managing the Urban Commons*, 160 U. Pa. L. Rev. 1995 (2011).
13. *See, e.g.*, Gerald E. Frug, *The City as a Legal Concept*, 93 Harv. L. Rev. 1057 (1980).
14. *See, e.g.*, Jill L. Tao & Barbara C. McCabe, *Where a Hollow State Casts No Shadow: Homeowner Associations in Local Governments*, 42 Am. Rev. Pub. Admin. 678 (2012).

15. *See, e.g.*, Robert C. Ellickson, *Cities and Homeowners Associations*, 130 U. Pa. L. Rev. 1519 (1982); Robert C. Ellickson, *New Institutions for Old Neighborhoods*, 48 Duke L.J. 75 (1998); Robert Henry Nelson, Private Neighborhoods and the Transformation of Local Government (2005); Robert Henry Nelson, *Privatizing the Neighborhood: A Proposal to Replace Zoning with Private Collective Property Rights to Existing Neighborhoods*, 7 Geo. Mason L. Rev. 827 (1998).
16. *See e.g.*, 物业纠纷渐成"城市病" 业主知情权未受到重视 (Real estate management disputes become an urban illness, homeowners' right to information neglected), http://finance.people.com.cn/n1/2017/0510/c1004-29264711.html (last visited December 29, 2020); All the three city governments mentioned frequent real estate management disputes as a reason for revising local regulations in the corresponding legislative reports. *See* Report on the Legislative Affairs of the Draft Bill of Beijing City Real Estate Management Regulation [关于《北京市物业管理条例（草案）》立法工作情况的汇报], November 8, 2019, on file with author; 关于《深圳经济特区物业管理条例（修订草案）》的说明 [Illustration on Shenzhen Special Economic Zone Property Management Administrative Regulation (Revised Draft)], March 19, 2018, on file with author; Huang Yongping (黄永平), 关于《上海市住宅物业管理规定 修正案（草案）》的说明, 上海人大 (Shanghai Municipal People's Congress)(March 1, 2019), www.spcsc.sh.cn/n8347/n8407/n5742/u1ai185842.html (last visited December 30, 2020).
17. Xiao Youmei (肖幼美), *Property Co-Management Model From Shenzhen to the Whole Country* (物业共管模式从深圳走向全国), Shenzhen Evening News (深圳晚报) (November 20, 2015), www.szzx.gov.cn/content/2015-11/20/content_12503879.htm.; Xiang Yun (向云), *The Birth of the First Homeowners' Association in Mainland China* (中国内地第一个业主委员会诞生始末), 《中国物业管理》[China Property Management], no. 5, 2011; Beijing Department of Housing Management, 关于业主委员会几个问题的探讨 [*Discussion on Several Issues of Owner's Committee*],《中国房地产》[China's Real Estate], no. 10, 1999; Qi Qi (齐颀), 运作不规范 权益难保障——本市业主委员会建立和运行情况透视 [*Irregular Operation, Difficult to Protect Rights and Interests – The Establishment and Operation of Homeowners' Committee in Shanghai*], 《上海人大月刊》[Shanghai People's Congress Monthly Journal], no. 9, 1999, 16–17.
18. *See* Josiah Ober, Demopolis: Democracy Before Liberalism in Theory and Practice (2017).
19. CCP Central Committee Office (中共中央办公厅), On Strengthening and Improving Urban Grassroots Party Construction (关于加强和改进城市基层党的建设工作的意见), November 8, 2019, www.gov.cn/zhengce/2019-05/08/content_5389836.htm.
20. Huang Yongping (黄永平), 关于《上海市住宅物业管理规定 修正案（草案）》的说明, 上海人大 (Shanghai Municipal People's Congress)(March 1, 2019), www.spcsc.sh.cn/n8347/n8407/n5742/u1ai185842.html.
21. *Illustration on Shenzhen Special Economic Zone Property Management Administrative Regulation (Revised Draft), supra* note 16.
22. *Report on the Legislative Affairs of the Draft Bill of Beijing City Real Estate Management Regulation, supra* note 16.
23. Property Law, *supra* note 11, Art 75; Civil Code, art 277.

24. Rajan, *supra* note 5, at 267.
25. David Stasavage, The Decline and Rise of Democracy: A Global History from Antiquity to Today 6 (2020). "Early democracy emerged when rulers needed consent and cooperation from their people because they could not govern on their own."
26. *Id.*

1 Defining the Authoritarian Commons

1. Douglass C. North, Institutions, Institutional Change and Economic Performance (1990).
2. To the author's knowledge, nobody has used this term "authoritarian commons" before. The closest concept is "illiberal commons," coined by Monica Eppinger in a recent paper. She proposes thinking of the illiberal commons in two ways: One is a resource or social space used by liberal subjects who do not enjoy a robust right to exit; the other is a space or resource held by illiberal subjects. The latter is closer to *authoritarian commons* than the former. However, Eppinger does not elaborate on how space or resource by illiberal subjects is governed and not to say the dynamic interactions between the illiberal state and its subjects. *See* Monica Eppinger, *Cold-War Commons: Tragedy, Critique, and the Future of the Illiberal Problem Space*, 19 Theoretical Inquiries in Law 457, 488 (2018). In the Chinese context, though study on the interactions between authoritarianism and civil society in China has been burgeoning, there has been not much discussion on self-governance and the control over space, which the term "authoritarian commons" highlights. Urban planning and geography scholars have studied space control in China but have not connected their research with authoritarianism. *See, e.g.*, You-Tien Hsing, The Great Urban Transformation: Politics of Land and Property in China (2010). There are two existent research studies that have touched upon the contest over space between the authoritarian state and self-governed communities without using the term "authoritarian commons": Ya-Wen Lei, The contentious public sphere: Law, media, and authoritarian rule in China (2019) (Lei shows how the Chinese state and citizens contest over public space (internet and mass media) for their respective goals.); Shitong Qiao, *Fragmented Laws, Contingent Choices: The Tragicomedy of the Village Commons in China*, 29 Duke J. Comp. & Int'l L. 235 (2018). (Qiao investigates the contest over land in intracity villages between the local government and village communities and the role of law in such a contest.)
3. Hanoch Dagan & Michael A. Heller, *The Liberal Commons*, 110 Yale L.J. 549, 581–582 (2000).
4. *Id.*, at 566.
5. In a recent essay, Monica Eppinger also criticizes that "western commons scholarship does not routinely reflect on its own epistemological background." *See* Eppinger, *Cold-War Commons*.
6. *See* Robert C. Ellickson, *Cities and Homeowners Associations*, 130 U. Pa. L. Rev. 1519 (1982); Gerald E. Frug, *Cities and Homeowners Associations: A Reply*, 130 U. Pa. L. Rev. 1589 (1981). *See also* Robert C. Ellickson, *New Institutions for Old Neighborhoods*, 48 Duke L.J. 75 (1998); Clayton P. Gillette, *Courts, Covenants, and*

Communities, 61 U. Chi. L. Rev. 1375 (1994); Gregory S. Alexander, *Dilemmas of Group Autonomy: Residential Associations and Community*, 75 Cornell L. Rev. 1 (1989).

7. *See, e.g.*, David J. Kennedy, *Residential Associations as State Actors: Regulating the Impact of Gated Communities on Nonmembers*, 105 Yale L.J. 761 (1995).
8. Mark Tushnet, *Authoritarian Constitutionalism*, 100 Cornell L. Rev. 391, 448 (2014).
9. Daron Acemoglu & James A. Robinson, Why Nations Fail: The Origins of Power, Prosperity and Poverty (2013); Shitong Qiao, *Rights-Weakening Federalism*, 102 Minn. L. Rev. 1671 (2017). (Chinese local governments expropriate resources, mainly land, from less productive sectors, such as agriculture, and distribute them to more productive industrial sectors.)
10. *See, e.g.*, Frank Upham, *The Paradoxical Roles of Property Rights in Growth and Development*, 8 Law & Dev. Rev. 253, 264 (2015); Frank K. Upham, The great property fallacy: Theory, Reality, and Growth in Developing Countries (2018). (Explaining how economic growth depends on the right to destroy.) Qiao, *Rights-Weakening Federalism*, 102; Yue Hou, The Private Sector in Public Office: Selective Property Rights in China (2019). (This book argues that a system of selective property rights is key to understanding the private sector growth in the absence of the rule of law.)
11. *See* Roderick M. Hills, Jr. & Shitong Qiao, *Voice and Exit as Accountability Mechanisms: Can Foot-Voting Be Made Safe for the Chinese Communist Party*, 48 Colum. Hum. Rts. L. Rev. 158, 162–171 (2016). (Exploring how decentralized governance might be consistent with the Chinese Communist Party's idea of "democratic centralism.")
12. *See, e.g.*, Jeremy Waldron, *Montesquieu's Place in the Rule-of-Law Tradition*, unpublished manuscript, on file with the author.
13. Taisu Zhang & Tom Ginsburg, *China's Turn Toward Law*, 59 Va. J. Int'l L. 306 (2019); Mary E. Gallagher, Authoritarian Legality in China: Law, Workers, and the State (2017); Hualing Fu & Weitseng Chen, *Authoritarian Legality, The Rule of Law, and Democracy*, in Authoritarian Legality in Asia: Formation, Development and Transition (2020).
14. Douglass C. North & Barry R. Weingast, *Constitutions and Commitment: The Evolution of Institutions Governing Public Choice in Seventeenth-Century England*, 49 J. Econ. Hist. 803 (1989); North, *supra* note 1.
15. Yoram Barzel, A Theory of the State: Economic Rights, Legal Rights, and the Scope of the State (2002); Yoram Barzel, Economic analysis of property rights (1997).
16. I take Tom Merrill's recent essay on sovereignty and property as a signal to depart from the mainstream economic analysis of property law that he has cofounded with Henry Smith. Merrill, *supra* note 1. For the mainstream economic analysis of property law, *see, e.g.*, Thomas W. Merrill & Henry E. Smith, *The Property/Contract Interface*, 101 Colum. L. Rev. 773 (2001); Thomas W. Merrill & Henry E. Smith, *Optimal Standardization in the Law of Property: The* Numerus Clausus *Principle*, 110 Yale L. R. 1 (2000); Henry E. Smith, *Property as the Law of Things*, 125 Harv. L. R. 1691 (2012); Lee Anne Fennell, *The Problem of Resource Access*, 126 Harv. L. Rev. 1472 (2012). Of course, progressive property law scholars have devoted considerable

effort to the political dimension of property rights. *See* Joseph William Singer, *Property as the Law of Democracy*, 63 DUKE L. J. 1287 (2013); Gregory S. Alexander et al., *A Statement of Progressive Property*, 94 CORNELL L. REV. 743 (2008); Ezra Rosser, *The Ambition and Transformative Potential of Progressive Property*, 101 CAL. L. REV. 107 (2013). Frank Upham's recent book, *The Great Property Fallacy*, investigates in-depth interactions between politics and property rights using comparative and historical data, particularly in its chapter on Japanese land reform. UPHAM, THE GREAT PROPERTY FALLACY, *supra* note 10.

17. One example is Michael Heller's decision to focus on the anticommons as a property form rather than on the political origin of this property form, which constitutes a trade-off between generalizability and depth. Michael A. Heller, *The Tragedy of the Anticommons: Property in the Transition from Marx to Markets*, 111 HARV. L. REV. 621 (1998).
18. Katrina Miriam Wyman, *Problematic Private Property: The Case of New York Taxicab Medallions*, 30 YALE J. ON REG. 125 (2013).
19. Roderick M. Hills, Jr. & David Schleicher, *Planning an Affordable City*, 101 IOWA L. REV. 91, 96 (2015). Roderick M. Hills, Jr. & David Schleicher, *Building Coalitions Out of Thin Air: Transferable Development Rights and "Constituency Effects" in Land Use Law*, 12 J. LEGAL ANALYSIS 79 (2020).
20. Roger B. Myerson, Village Communities and Global Development https://home.uchicago.edu/~rmyerson/research/villages.pdf. (Economic development depends on political leadership to provide essential public goods and services, and trusted leaders may be found in local politics. Modern economic growth began in nations where local leadership was regularly integrated into national politics.)
21. Ronald J. Gilson & Curtis J. Milhaupt, *Economically Benevolent Dictators: Lessons for Developing Democracies*, 59 AM. J. COMP. L. 227 (2011); YUEN YUEN ANG, HOW CHINA ESCAPED THE POVERTY TRAP (2016). (Successful development is a coevolutionary process in which markets and governments mutually adapt); JOE STUDWELL, HOW ASIA WORKS: SUCCESS AND FAILURE IN THE WORLD'S MOST DYNAMIC REGION (2013). (Economic development in Korea and Taiwan took off before democratization with strong government intervention.)
22. *Id.*
23. *Id.*
24. ACEMOGLU & ROBINSON, WHY NATIONS FAIL, *supra* note 9; DARON ACEMOGLU & JAMES A. ROBINSON, THE NARROW CORRIDOR: STATES, SOCIETIES, AND THE FATE OF LIBERTY 201–236 (2019).
25. From a comparative perspective, the successful democratization of Taiwan and South Korea under a strong and capable dictatorship indicates that it is not necessarily a self-defeating mission.
26. Art. 70, Property Law. Common property includes hallways, elevators, common ground, water towers, roads, and parking lots.
27. For the definition of urban commons, *see, e.g.*, Sheila R. Foster, *Collective Action and the Urban Commons*, 87 NOTRE DAME L. REV. 57 (2011); Sheila R. Foster & Christian Iaione, *The City as a Commons*, 34 YALE L. & POL'Y REV. 281 (2015); Nicole Stelle Garnett, *Managing the Urban Commons*, 160 U. PA. L. REV. 1995 (2011).
28. Dagan & Heller, *supra* note 3, at 552.

29. Garrett Hardin, *The Tragedy of the Commons*, 162 SCIENCE 1243 (1968); open-access commons does not always end up with tragedy. *See, e.g.*, Carol Rose, *The Comedy of the Commons: Custom, Commerce, and Inherently Public Property*, 53 U. CHI. L. REV. 711 (1986).
30. ELINOR OSTROM, GOVERNING THE COMMONS: THE EVOLUTION OF INSTITUTIONS FOR COLLECTIVE ACTION 30 (1990).
31. Carol M. Rose, *The Several Futures of Property: Of Cyberspace and Folk Tales, Emission Trades and Ecosystems*, 83 MINN. L. REV. 129, 155 (1998).
32. For early literature on polycentric governance in the urban context, *see* Vincent Ostrom, Charles M. Tiebout & Robert Warren, *The Organization of Government in Metropolitan Areas: A Theoretical Inquiry*, 55 AM. POLIT. SCI. REV. 831 (1961). Recently, there has been increased interest in urban commons among legal scholars, led by Sheila Foster and others. *See* Foster, *supra* note 27; Garnett, *supra* note 27; Foster & Iaione, *supra* note 27.
33. *See, e.g.*, Interview No. SZ-HO-082018-5, Interview No. SH-HO-062618-5.
34. Interview No. SZ-LA-111918-2.
35. *See* SZ-HO-092118-13 and *Beijing Business Newspaper*, 北京将拆分 82个超大社区 [*Beijing Plans to Divide Super Neighborhood Blocks*], SINA (Jan. 16, 2020), https://tech.sina.com.cn/roll/2020-01-16/doc-iihnzhha2719090.shtml.
36. *See, e.g.*, Interview No. SZ-HO-xxxx18*-18, Interview No. SH-HO-062918-8.
37. Interview No. BJ-HO-080218-2; Interview No. SZ-HO-xxxx18*-18; Interview No. SH-HO-042319-24.
38. Sina, 大妈小区内占地跳广场舞：贴条阻停车 有住户被逼搬家 [*Grannies Did Square-Dancing in the Community: Sticking a Strip to Stop Parking, Some Residents Were Forced to Move*], FENGHUANG NET (Nov. 19, 2013), http://news.ifeng.com/society/2/detail_2013_11/19/31359376_0.shtml; Fazhi Daily Newspaper, 芜湖一男童被狗咬伤后狂犬病发作身亡 [*A Boy in Wuhu City Was Bitten by a Dog and Died from Rabies*], XINHUA NET (Aug. 7, 2018), www.xinhuanet.com/2018-08/07/c_1123233767.htm.
39. WU YING, 《社区何以可能：芳雅家园的邻里生活》 [HOW THE COMMUNITY IS POSSIBLE: A POSSIBLE ANALYSIS OF A COMMERCIAL RESIDENTIAL ENCLAVE'S NEIGHBORING] (2015).
40. Chen Youhong (陈幽泓), "小区宪法"是社会契约中最基本最重要的规定 [*Neighborhood Constitution Is the Most Fundamental Regulation in Social Contract*], 6 《和谐社区通讯》 (2012). This is consistent with Epstein's take on covenants as mini-constitutions. *See* Richard A. Epstein, *Covenants and Constitutions*, 73 CORNELL L. REV. 906 (1988).
41. Art. 75 of Property Law; 物业管理条例 [Ordinance on Real Estate Management] (Promulgated by the State Council, June 8, 2003), Art. 21, 22, 23; Art. 17 of the Guiding Rules of Homeowners' Associations and Homeowners' Committees (业主大会和业主委员会指导规则) (promulgated by Ministry of Housing and Urban-Rural Development, 2009), www.mohurd.gov.cn/wjfb/200912/t20091216_198111.html.
42. Art. 76 of Property Law; Art. 278 of Civil Code. 4.
43. *See* Chapter 4.
44. *See* Chapter 3, Section 3.2 (the case of Sunshine Manhattan).
45. *See* Chapter 3, Section 3.3.1 (the TYJ case).

46. *See* Chapter 2, Section 2.1, for details of RCs.
47. Benjamin Read noticed the democratic potential of Chinese HoAs as early as 2003, but recently Luigi Tomba's award-winning book emphasizes how the growth of a property-owning middle class is the result of a process of social engineering and challenges the normative assumption that the middle class could push China toward democratization. Both Read and Tomba are prescient in pointing to the lasting shadow of the state in China's modern urban residential neighborhoods. However, we need an updated and systematic investigation of HoAs to renew this debate. Luigi Tomba, The Government Next Door: Neighborhood Politics in Urban China (2014); Benjamin L. Reed, *Democratizing the Neighborhood? New Private Housing and Homeowner Self-Organization in Urban China*, 49 China J. 31 (2003).
48. Interview No. BJ-HO-080318-3.
49. Robert D. Putnam, Bowling Alone: The Collapse and Revival of American Community (2001); Robert D. Putnam, Making Democracy Work: Civic Traditions in Modern Italy (1993); Francis Fukuyama, Trust: The Social Virtues and The Creation of Prosperity (1996); Janos Kornai, Bo Rothstein, & Susan Rose-Ackerman, Creating Social Trust in Post-Socialist Transition (2004); Janos Kornai & Susan Rose-Ackerman, Building A Trustworthy State in Post-Socialist Transition (2004). On the other hand, it is quite common that authoritarian and fascist regimes draw organizational resources from civic associations. *See, e.g.*, Dylan Riley, *Civic Associations and Authoritarian Regimes in Interwar Europe: Italy and Spain in Comparative Perspective*, 70 Am. Sociological Rev. 288 (2005); Daniel C. Mattingly. The Art of Political Control in China (2019). The key is to examine whether such associations are voluntary and democratically governed or structured hierarchically and controlled by the top-down authoritarian regime. For how HoAs situate in this debate, *see* Chapter 6 of this book.
50. *See, e.g.*, Monica Martinez-Bravo et al. *The Rise and Fall of Local Elections in China: Theory and Empirical Evidence on the Autocrat's Trade-off*. No. w24032. National Bureau of Economic Research, 2017; Baogang He, Rural democracy in China: The Role of Village Elections (2007).
51. Based on a study of the Ukrainian land reform, Monica Eppinger argues that "the relationships between property and democracy are not always mutually felicitous." Her case study features the problem of oligarchy in the farming industry, which does not exist in my study. *See* Monica Eppinger, *Property and Political Community: Democracy, Oligarchy, and the Case of Ukraine*, 47 Geo. Wash. Int'l L. Rev. 825 (2015).
52. Read, *Democratizing the Neighborhood?*, *supra* note 47.
53. *See* Chapter 6 for a detailed analysis of my survey data.

2 Neighborhood Democratization

1. 三里屯街道 [Sanlitun Street], 行政区划网 [Administrative Division Website], www.xzqh.org/html/show/bj/132.html.
2. 民治街道 [Minzhi Street], 行政区划网 [Administrative Division Website], www.xzqh.org/html/show/gd/37514.html.

3. In China, developers purchase large plots of land from the city government, which issues the land use rights certificates and approves the development plan. Developers obtain the grand land use rights and housing ownership certificate after construction. After a developer sells apartments to individual purchasers, this grand certificate is replaced by certificates issued to individual apartments, which certifies both individual apartment ownership and common property rights to the land in the neighborhood.
4. 城市居民委员会组织条例 [Organic Regulation of the Urban Residents Committee] (promulgated by Standing Committee of National People's Congress, December 31, 1954, abolished January 1, 1990); 城市居民委员会组织法 [Organic Law of the Urban Residents Committee] (promulgated by Standing Committee of National People's Congress, January 1, 1990).
5. 中华人民共和国宪法 [The PRC Constitution Law] (amended by National People's Congress, March 11, 2018); 中华人民共和国城市居民委员会组织法 [Organic Law of the PRC Urban Residents Committee] (promulgated by Standing Committee of National People's Congress, December 26, 1989).
6. *See, e.g.*, Bing Guan & Yongshun Cai, *Interests and Political Participation in Urban China: The Case of Residents' Committee Elections*, 15 The China Review 95 (2015).
7. *Id.*
8. Guo Ying (郭莹) & Wu Aimin (吴爱民), 我国城市居民自治分析 [*An Analysis of Self-Governance of City Residents in Our Country*], 《四川行政学院学报》 [Journal of Sichuan Administration Institute] (May 15, 2014, 04:37 PM), https://chn-oversea-cnki-net.proxy.lib.duke.edu/KCMS/detail/detail.aspx?dbcode=CJFD&dbname=CJFD2012&filename=SXZB201206006&uniplatform=OVERSEA&v=2vI-mbxUsaSPQv3y-84-IDdk6sx2pt06V_AWNXhuQZXYbKKNnqt0DbKGKBjdk6nO.
9. *See, e.g.*, Interview No. BJ-HO-100618-10; SZ-HO-091118-11.
10. Albert O. Hirschman, Exit, Voice and Loyalty: Responses to Decline in Firms, Organizations and States (1970).
11. The exit option is difficult in practice for several reasons. First, relocation costs can be substantial. Second, for most homeowners, their home is their primary investment. Hence, its subjective value is high, and the decision to relocate is not made lightly. Third, for middle-class families with strong preferences concerning their living environment, there are not many suitable location options. They want a home that is within reasonable commuting distance of work and good schools if there is a school-age child in the household. Fourth, in addition to a good living environment, that is, one consistent with middle-class preferences and tastes, the new home needs to be affordable. Considering all of these factors, remaining in one's current home is often the best option. Furthermore, households would not even have to consider moving if their neighborhood were run as promised in their contract with the real estate developer. My survey of several hundred homeowners in Beijing, Shenzhen, and Shanghai revealed that less than 1 percent of them consider relocation as their first choice of remedy. About 20 percent and 60 percent, respectively, cited filing a complaint with the MC and firing the MC via their HoAs as their first remedy choice in the event of poor service.
12. Interview No. BJ-HO-042318-1; SZ-HO-091118-11; SH-HO-081819-35.

13. 物业管理条例 [Regulations on Real Estate Management] (promulgated by State Council, June 8, 2003, amended March 19, 2018) art. 39 (ChinaLawInfo).
14. Cynthia Estlund, Working together: How Workplace Bonds Strengthen a Diverse Democracy 5 (2003).
15. Art. 8 of the Guiding Rules of Homeowners' Associations and Homeowners' Committees (业主大会和业主委员会指导规则) (promulgated by Ministry of Housing and Urban-Rural Development, 2009).
16. *See, e.g.*, Art. 10 of the Beijing Guiding Rules of Homeowners' Associations and Homeowners' Committees (北京市住宅区业主大会和业主委员会指导规则 京建发〔2010〕739 号) (promulgated by Beijing Department of Housing and Urban-Rural Development, 2010).
17. *See, e.g.*, Arts. 11 and 13 of the Beijing Guiding Rules of Homeowners' Associations and Homeowners' Committees, *id.*
18. *See, e.g.*, Art. 26 of the Beijing Guiding Rules of Homeowners' Associations and Homeowners' Committees, *id.*
19. Zeng Jianhua (曾建华), 金湖新村业主委员会有起诉的权利吗? [*Does the Homeowners' Association of Jinhu New Village Have the Right to Sue?*], 《现代物业》[Modern Property Management], no. 3, 2005, 34–41; Liu Changsen (刘长森), 论业主委员会的性质及法律地位 [*On the Nature and Legal Status of Homeowners' Association*], 《中国房地产》[China's Real Estate], no. 5, 2002, 28–31; Chen Wen (陈雯), 论业主委员会的法律地位及制度完善 [*On the Legal Status and System Perfection of the Homeowners' Association*], 《政法学刊》[Journal of Political Science and Law], no. 5, 2003, 41–43.
20. Supreme People's Court, Reply on the Case Concerning Whether the Homeowners' Association of Jinhu New Village Has the Qualifications to Be the Subject of Civil Proceedings (最高人民法院关于金湖新村业主委员会是否具备民事诉讼主体资格请示一案的复函) (民立他字第 46 号), August 20, 2003.
21. *See, e.g.*, Interview No. SH-HO-062818-6.
22. *See, e.g.*, Interview No, SH-HO-062818-7.
23. Chen Youhong (陈幽泓), 社区治理的多元视角：理论与实践 [Dynamic Perspective of Social Governance: Theory and Practice] (2009).
24. Mass Ants, www.mocking-j.com/#/ (last visited March 17, 2019).
25. Conversations on the WeChat Group "National Work Group of Homeowners," February 19, 2019. Homeowners can be compensated by reputational benefits, which contribute partly to overcoming the collective action problem. *See, e.g.*, Henry F. Lyle & Eric A. Smith, *The Reputational and Social Network Benefits of Prosociality in an Andean Community*, 111 Proc. Natl. Acad. Sci. U.S.A. 4820 (2014). 201318372. On the other hand, the gradual involvement of homeowner activists is consistent with Ostrom's argument that institutional change involves many small steps that have low initial costs and that the investment in institutional change is not made in a single step. Elinor Ostrom, Governing the Commons: The Evolution of Institutions for Collective Action 137(2009).
26. Shi Yuntong (史云桐), 有产者的抗争与社会的生产——B市业主维权的类型研究 [The Fight of Property Owners and the Production of the Society – A Study on Different Types of City B Homeowners' Defending Their Rights] (June 2008) (unpublished Ph.D. dissertation, Tsinghua University) (on file with author), at 31.
27. *Id.*

28. Ranjay Gulati, Franz Wohlgezogen, and Pavel Zhelyazkov, *The Two Facets of Collaboration: Cooperation and Coordination in Strategic Alliances*, 6 Acad. of Mgm't Annals 531 (2012).
29. *Id.*, at 532.
30. Richard McAdams, The Expressive Powers of Law: Theories and Limits 24 (2015).
31. *Id.*
32. Interview No. SH-HO-062918-8, 11.
33. *See* Chapter 5, Section 5.2.
34. A dictatorship such as that in North Korea can rely on the support of the military and elite party cadres to remain in power. The party-state in China, in contrast, has built an economy that is more or less based on property rights and market transactions, and that gains its legitimacy from its ability to satisfy the people's pursuit of economic well-being and social welfare. Homeowner is a common identity for China's urban middle class, including both regime insiders, such as party-state employees and outsiders who are essential to economic development such as private entrepreneurs and their employees. Owning an apartment is a very real Chinese dream: Even among migrant workers, whom we cannot count as part of China's middle class, the ultimate plan is to make enough money to purchase an apartment in the town nearest to their village, and many of them have fulfilled that plan. Furthermore, Chinese men are often expected to purchase an apartment before getting married. The support or at least tacit acquiescence of homeowners is therefore essential to the party-state's survival. One reason that the Chinese government dare not burst the real estate bubble is arguably its concern over potential protests by millions of homeowners.
35. *See, e.g.*, Tao Xu (许涛), 全国"有产者"联合起来?——全国业主委员会联合组织调查 [*United Nationwide Property Owners? Investigation of Associations of Homeowners' Committees*],《住宅与房地产》[Residential Property and Real Estate], no. 1, 2007; Shi, *supra* note 26, at 2.
36. People's Bank of China, 2019 年中国城镇居民家庭资产负债情况调查报告 [*Survey Report on Household Assets and Liabilities of Chinese Urban Residents in 2019*],《中国金融》[China Finance] (April 24, 2020).
37. In my fieldwork, the conflict between homeowners and the government over whether the latter can control roads and use space within neighborhoods for municipal facilities is a common problem. *See, e.g.*, BJ-HO-112517-12, SZ-HO-092118-13, SZ-HO-071318-4, SH-HO-061119-29. For news reports, *see, e.g.*, Har Ye Kan, Ann Forsyth, & Peter Rowe, *Redesigning China's Superblock Neighbourhoods: Policies, Opportunities and Challenges*, 22 J. Urb. Design 757 (2017); *The Era of Compulsory Garbage Sorting Begins*, China Daily (June 24, 2019), www.chinadaily.com.cn/a/201906/24/WS5d10650ba3103dbf14329e23.html.
38. *See, e.g.*, Kerry Allen, *Shanghai Rubbish Rules: New Law Sends Chinese City into Frenzy*, BBC News (July 4, 2019), www.bbc.com/news/world-asia-china-48847062.
39. Lee Fennell, The Unbounded Home: Property Values Beyond Property Lines 2 (2009); Stephanie M. Stern, *Residential Protectionism and the Legal Mythology of Home*, 107 Mich. L. Rev. 1093 (2008); Stephanie M. Stern, *Reassessing the Citizen Virtues of Homeownership*, 111 Colum. L. Rev. 890 (2011). In the United States, homeowners have been a powerful group hindering urban

development, drawing much criticism. As Wendell Pritchett and I have argued elsewhere, Chinese and US cities face the opposite situations: too much homeowner participation in urban governance in the United States and still too little in China. *See* Wendell Pritchett & Shitong Qiao, *Exclusionary Megacities*, 91 S. CAL. L. REV. 467 (2018).

40. Pritchett & Qiao, *id.*, at 514. Among the cases that came up in my interviews are homeowner protests against the construction of garbage disposal sites (Interview No. SZ-HO-071318-4) and public transit facilities (Interview No. BJ-HO-082918-9) near their homes over concerns about noise and odor. Also, Beijing homeowners stopped the city government from building a light rail in the eastern part of the city, a multi-billion RMB project (*see* Interview No. BJ-HO-080218-2). *See also Environmental Protest in China: Volatile Atmosphere*, THE ECONOMIST (April 4, 2014), www.economist.com/analects/2014/04/04/volatile-atmosphere (last visited December 31, 2020).
41. *See* Chapter 9, Section 9.3 for a more detailed discussion.
42. Interview No. BJ-HO-080318-3.
43. Interview No. BJ-HO-080318-3.
44. 关于深化城镇住房制度改革的决定 [Deepening the Reform of the Urban Housing System] (promulgated by the State Council, July 18, 1994) (国发[1994]43 号).
45. 关于进一步深化城镇住房制度改革、加快住房建设的通知 [Notice on Further Deepening the Reform of the Urban Housing System and Speeding Up Housing Construction] (Promulgated by the State Council, July 3, 1998) (国发〔1998〕23 号).
46. 中共中央关于制定国民经济和社会发展第十个五年计划的建议 [Proposal of the Central Committee of the Communist Party of China on Formulating the Tenth Five-Year Plan for National Economic and Social Development] (Promulgated by the Central Committee, October 11, 2000); 国民经济和社会发展第十个五年计划城镇化发展重点专项规划 [The Tenth Five-Year Plan for the National Economic and Social Development Key Special Plan for Urbanization Development] (Promulgated by the State Planning Commission, August 7, 2001).
47. Lin Guoqiang (林国强), 业主委员会的性质地位与权利义务 [The Nature, Status, Rights and Obligations of Homeowners' Associations], 《中国房地产》 [CHINA'S REAL ESTATE], no. 11, 1996, 40–42; Beijing Department of Housing Management, *Guanyu Yeweihui Jige Wenti de Tantao* (关于业主委员会几个问题的探讨) [*Discussion on Several Issues of Owner's Committee*], ZHONGGUO FANGDICHAN (中国房地产)[CHINA'S REAL ESTATE], no.10, 1999.
48. 建设部关于宣传、贯彻《物业管理条例》的通知 [Notice of the Ministry of Construction on the Promotion and Implementation of the *Property Management Regulations*] (Promulgated on June 12, 2003) (建住房[2003]122 号).
49. Regulations on Real Estate Management, *supra* note 13.
50. 物业管理条例释义 [INTERPRETATION OF THE ORDINANCE ON REAL ESTATE MANAGEMENT] 48–50 (2003); Sun Xianzhong (孙宪忠), 如何处理《物业管理条例》中的业主委员会和社区立法中的居民委员会之间关系 [On How to Deal with the Relationship Between Homeowners' Associations Defined in the Property Management Regulation and Residents Committee in the Community Legislation], 《中国物业管理》 [CHINA REAL ESTATE MANAGEMENT], no. 2, 2003, 19.
51. INTERPRETATION OF THE REAL ESTATE REGULATION, *id.*, at 48–50; Article 111 of the PRC Constitution (Promulgated by National People's Congress, December 4, 1982, amended on March 15, 1999).

52. Michael Mann, *The Autonomous Power of the State: Its Origins, Mechanisms and Results*, 25 Eur. J. Sociology 185 (1984).
53. *Id.*, at 198.
54. Interpretation of the Ordinance on Real Estate Management, *supra* note 50, at 48–50.
55. Tang Yanwen (汤艳文), 不完全契约形态:转型社会的社区治理结构——以上海康健地区业主委员会的发展为例 [*Incomplete Contract Form: The Community Governance Structure of a Transitional Society – Taking the Development of the Owners Committee of Shanghai Kangjian District as an Example*], 《上海行政学院学报》 [Journal of Shanghai Administration Institute], no. 2, 2004, 68–78, at 74.
56. Article 19 of Regulations on Real Estate Management, *supra* note 13.
57. Article 20 of Regulations on Real Estate Management, *id.*
58. 物权法 [Property Law] (promulgated by Nat'l People's Cong., March 16, 2007, effective October 1, 2007), Chapter 6.
59. Gong Xiantian, *A Property Law (Draft) that Violates the Constitution and Basic Principles of Socialism*, http://links.org.au/node/221 (last visited March 11, 2021); Shitong Qiao, *The Evolution of Property Law in China: Stick by Stick?*, in Private Law in China and Taiwan: Economic and Legal Analysis (Yun-chien Chang et al., ed., Cambridge University Press 2017), 182–211.
60. *See, e.g.*, Su Yongtong (苏永通), 物权立法历程：从未如此曲折从未如此坚定 [The Legislative History of Property Law], 《南方周末》 [Southern Weekly], available at http://finance.people.com.cn/GB/1045/5500798.html (last visited August 1, 2020).
61. For discussions of the rights of civic organizations by legal scholars, see Roderick M. Hills Jr, *The Constitutional Rights of Private Governments*, 78 NYUL Rev. 144 (2003); Richard Brooks & Timothy W. Guinnane, *The Right to Associate and the Rights of Associations: Civil-Society Organizations in Prussia, 1794–1908*, in Organizations, Civil Society, and the Roots of Development 291–329 (2017).
62. Regulations on Real Estate Management, *supra* note 13, art. 12.
63. Art. 76 of Property Law, *supra* note 58.
64. *See* Chapter 4.
65. 中华人民共和国民法典[The PRC Civil Code](promulgated by National People's Congress, May 28, 2020), art. 278.

3 The Three Styles of Authoritarianism

1. Huang Yongping (黄永平), 关于《上海市住宅物业管理规定 修正案（草案）》的说明, 上海人大 (Shanghai Municipal People's Congress) (March 1, 2019), www.spcsc.sh.cn/n8347/n8407/n5742/u1ai185842.html (on file with the author).
2. 关于《深圳经济特区物业管理条例（修订草案）》的说明 [Illustration on Shenzhen Special Economic Zone Property Management Administrative Regulation (Revised Draft)], March 19, 2018, on file with the author.
3. Report on the Legislative Affairs of the Draft Bill of Beijing City Real Estate Management Regulation [关于《北京市物业管理条例（草案）》立法工作情况的汇报], November 8, 2019, on file with the author.
4. *See* Chapter 5.
5. *Id.*

6. BJ-HO-080618-6; for publicly available reports and academic writing on this matter, *see, e.g.*, Feng Wang & Terry L. Cooper, *Chinese Homeowners' Associations: A School of Democracy*, PA TIMES, February 2008, at 4; Li Fan (李凡), 深圳人大代表选举事件及其对中国基层人大选举改革的意义 [*The Election of Representatives of Shenzhen People's Congress and Its Impact on the Reform of China's Grassroots Election of People's Congresses*] *in* 《民主选举：中国的民主治理理论与实践》 [CHINA'S DEMOCRACY MANAGEMENT: THEORY AND PRACTICE] 159 (Yan Jian (闫健) & Yu Keping (俞可平) eds., 2013).
7. *See* Chapter 5.
8. *See* Susan S. Silbey, *The Sociological Citizen: Pragmatic and Relational Regulation in Law and Organizations*, 5 REGUL. GOV. 1 (2011).
9. Lewis A. Kornhauser, *Governance Structures, Legal Systems, and the Concept of Law*, 79 CHI.-KENT L. REV. 355, 362 (2004).
10. "We know that life does not fit into neat little boxes. There always are variations of every process." JULIET CORBIN & ANSELM STRAUSS, BASICS OF QUALITATIVE RESEARCH: TECHNIQUES AND PROCEDURES FOR DEVELOPING GROUNDED THEORY 160 (3d ed. 2008). The categorization here represents what Weber would call "ideal types" or the dominant pattern in the three cities. For more detailed discussion on how sociologists deal with the messiness of reality and theory, *see* MICHAEL MANN, THE SOURCES OF SOCIAL POWER: A HISTORY OF POWER FROM THE BEGINNING TO AD 1760 4 (2012).
11. Michael Mann, *The Autonomous Power of the State: Its Origins, Mechanisms and Results*, 25 EUR. J. SOCIOLOGY 185, 191 (1984). (Mann uses the term "infrastructural co-ordination" in "Figure 1: Two dimensions of state power.")
12. *Id.*, at 188.
13. Mann, *supra* note 10, 113 (2012).
14. RONALD COASE & NING WANG, HOW CHINA BECAME CAPITALIST (2012). (Using Shenzhen as an example of "marginal revolution.")
15. Ya-Wen Lei, *Freeing the Press: How Field Environment Explains Critical News Reporting in China*, 122 AM. J. SOCIOL. 1 (2016).
16. CYNTHIA ESTLUND. A NEW DEAL FOR CHINA'S WORKERS? (2017).
17. For a comprehensive review of different approaches, *see* Hillel Soifer, *State Infrastructural Power: Approaches to Conceptualization and Measurement*, 43 STUD. IN COMP. INT'L DEV. 231 (2008). *See* also FRANCIS FUKUYAMA, POLITICAL ORDER AND POLITICAL DECAY: FROM THE INDUSTRIAL REVOLUTION TO THE GLOBALIZATION OF DEMOCRACY 59 (2014); Mann, *supra* note 10; BO ROTHSTEIN, THE QUALITY OF GOVERNMENT: CORRUPTION, SOCIAL TRUST, AND INEQUALITY IN INTERNATIONAL PERSPECTIVE (2011); Rafael La Porta et al. *The Quality of Government*, 15 J. LAW. ECON. ORGAN. 222 (1999); Cullen S Hendrix, *Measuring State Capacity: Theoretical and Empirical Implications for the Study of Civil Conflict*, 47 J. PEACE RES. 273 (2010); Jonathan K. Hanson, *Democracy and State Capacity: Complements or Substitutes?*, 50 STUD. COMP. INT. DEV. 304 (2015); Jessica Fortin, *Is There a Necessary Condition for Democracy? The Role of State Capacity in Postcommunist Countries*, 45 COMP. POLIT. STUD. 903 (2012).
18. Nicholas Pedriana & Robin Stryker, *The Strength of a Weak Agency: Enforcement of Title VII of the 1964 Civil Rights Act and the Expansion of State Capacity, 1965–1971*, 110 AM. J. SOCIOL. 709 (2004).

19. Francis Fukuyama, Political Order and Political Decay: From the Industrial Revolution to The Globalization of Democracy 61, 552 (2014). ("Good procedures, capacity, outputs, and bureaucratic autonomy are thus all possible ways of defining where a state lies on the vertical axis of Figure 4.") According to Fukuyama, Weber's criteria include that each office has a defined sphere of competence and that officials are subject to strict discipline and control.
20. *Id.*
21. Hanna Bäck & Axel Hadenius, *Democracy and State Capacity: Exploring a J-Shaped Relationship*, 21 Governance 1, 3 (2008).
22. 2020 年北京市行政区划 [2020 Beijing Administrative Division], www.xzqh.org/html/show/bj/38085.html (last visited December 30, 2020).
23. 2019 年北京市常住人口2153.6万人 [Beijing has a population of 21.5 million in 2019], www.gov.cn/xinwen/2020-03/02/content_5485861.htm#:~:text=%E6%95%B0%E6%8D%AE%E6%98%BE%E7%A4%BA%EF%BC%8C2019%E5%B9%B4%E5%8C%97%E4%BA%AC,%E4%B8%8A%E5%B9%B4%E6%9C%AB%E5%87%8F%E5%B0%911%E4%BA%BA%E3%80%82 (last visited December 30, 2020).
24. 2019 年全市一般公共预算收入 5817.1 亿元 [The City's Revenue is 581.7 Billion RMB in 2019], http://czj.beijing.gov.cn/ztlm/ztjsjf/xcdt/202004/t20200424_1881266.html (last visited December 30, 2020).
25. "十三五"时期首都社区建设与治理创新调研报告 [Report on the Capital City's Social Development and Innovation during the Thirteenth Five-Year Period], on file with author.
26. *Id.*
27. 2020 年上海市行政区划 [2020 Shanghai Administrative Division], www.xzqh.org/html/show/sh/38093.html (last visited December 30, 2020).
28. *Id.*
29. 上海市 2019年一般公共预算收支情况 [Shanghai's General Revenue and Expense in 2019], www.czj.sh.gov.cn/zys_8908/czsj_9054/dfczsz/202001/t20200120_181886.shtml (last visited December 30, 2020).
30. 2020 Shanghai Administrative Division, *supra* note 31.
31. *Id.*
32. 深圳市统计局 (Shenzhen Statistics Bureau), 深圳市 2019 年国民经济和社会发展统计公报 (Shenzhen 2019 Report of National Economic and Social Development Statistics), http://tjj.sz.gov.cn/gkmlpt/content/7/7294/post_7294649.html#4222 (last visited December 30, 2020).
33. *Id.*
34. *Id.*
35. 行政区划信息概况 [General Administrative Information], http://mzj.sz.gov.cn/ydmh/xxgk/ydmh/content/post_2929660.html (last visited December 30, 2020).
36. *Id.*
37. *Id.*
38. *Id.*
39. *Id.*
40. 中华人民共和国地方各级人民代表大会和地方各级人民政府组织法 [Organization Law of the People's Republic of China for Local People's Congresses at All Levels and Local People's Governments at All Levels] (amended by Standing Committee of the National People's Congress, August 29, 2015); 地方各级人民政

府机构设置和编制管理条例 [Regulation on the Organization Establishment and Staffing Administration of Local People's Governments at All Levels] (promulgated by National People's Congress, March 15, 2000).

41. *See,* e.g., Alberto Alesina & Paola Giuliano, *Culture and Institutions*, 53 Journal of Economic Literature 898 (2015).
42. Tianjian Shi, Political Participation in Beijing (1997).
43. *See,* e.g., 人民日报点赞上海的规则意识：像"文化磁极"形成独特吸引力 [People's Daily on the Sense of Rule in Shanghai], www.thepaper.cn/newsDetail_forward_1697122 (last visited March 10, 2021).
44. Shitong Qiao, Chinese Small Property: The Co-Evolution of Law and Social Norms (2017).
45. *See e.g.* Avner Greif, *Cultural Beliefs and the Organization of Society: A Historical and Theoretical Reflection on Collectivist and Individualist Societies*, 102 Journal of Political Economy 912 (1994).
46. *See* Chapter 6.
47. *See,* e.g., Human Rights Watch, World Report 2019: China (2019); U.S. Department of State, Country Reports on Human Rights Practices for 2018: China (2019).
48. *See* Interview No. BJ-GO-053118-1; Chen Peng (陈鹏), 国家-市场-社会三维视野下的业委会研究 – 以B市商品房社区为例 [*A Study on Homeowners' Committees from the Perspective of Nation, Market and Society – Based on a Case of Commodity Housing Community in City B*], 10《公共管理学报》 [Journal of Public Management] 75, 2013.
49. Interview No. BJ-GO-053118-1.
50. Interview No. SZ-HO-071318-4.
51. Interview No. BJ-HO-042318-1.
52. Interview No. SZ-HO-071318-4.
53. Interview No. BJ-HO-112517-12.
54. Jinghua Shibao (京华时报), 西安：开发商和物业雇凶打死业主负责人被判死刑 [*Xi'an: Real Estate Developers and Real Estate Management Company Hired People to Beat Homeowners till Death, and Were Sentenced to Death*], Sohu News (December 18, 2010), http://news.sohu.com/20101218/n278370674.shtml.
55. Interview No. BJ-HO-080218-2.
56. *See, e.g.*, Interview No. BJ-HO-080618-7, at 8.
57. Chen Peng (陈鹏), 国家-市场-社会三维视野下的业委会研究 – 以B市商品房社区为例 [*A Study on Homeowners' Committees from the Perspective of Nation, Market and Society – Based on a Case of Commodity Housing Community in City B*], 10 《公共管理学报》 [Journal of Public Management] 84, 2013.
58. *Id.*
59. *See, e.g.*, Yao Baiwan (姚白莞), 中国物业战争史 [*The History of the War Against Property Management Company in China*], November 5, 2020, https://k.sina.cn/article_5979719281_1646b467101900dpb6.html?from=history (last visited December 3, 2020).
60. US scholars have debated the issue of how much autonomy homeowners' associations should have in creating their own charters. *See,* e.g., Clayton P. Gillette, *Courts, Covenants, and Communities*, 61 U. Chi. L. Rev. 1375(1994); Richard A. Epstein, *Covenants and Constitutions*, 73 Cornell L. Rev. 906(1987).; Richard C. Schragger, *The Limits of Localism*, 100 Mich. L. Rev. 371, 388 (2001).

61. Interview No. BJ-HO-082918-9; SZ-HO-070918-19.
62. *See* Section 5.1.2 in Chapter 5 for details.
63. *See,* e.g., Timothy Hildebrandt, *The Political Economy of Social Organization Registration in China*, 208 China Q. 970(2011).
64. Shi Yuntong (史云桐), 有产者的抗争与社会的生产——B市业主维权的类型研究 [The Fight of Property Owners and the Production of the Society – A Study on Different Types of City B Homeowners' Defending Their Rights] (June, 2008) (unpublished Ph.D. dissertation, Tsinghua University) (on file with author), at 100.
65. Liu Yuewen (刘月雯), 社会的嬗变 – 以B市一个业主联合组织为例 [The Social Change: A Case of Homeowner United Association in City B] (2010) (unpublished Master thesis, Tsinghua University) (on file with author).
66. *Id.*, at Chapter 4.
67. Interview No. BJ-HO-080318-3.
68. Interview No. SZ-GO-110718-1.
69. Interview No. SZ-GO-110718-1.
70. Interview No. SZ-R E-102418-3.
71. Zhang Wei (张玮), 深圳拟修订物业管理条例, 聚焦业委会等问题 [*Shenzhen is Planning to Amend the Regulation of Real Estate Management to Focus on the Problems such as HoAs*], South China Daily (May 31, 2018), http://sz.southcn.com/content/2018-05/31/content_182075969.htm.
72. 深圳桃源居的真相 [*The Truth of Shenzhen Taoyuan Homes*], TYJ 315 (April 20, 2011), https://web.archive.org/web/20150404164328/www.szhgh.com/Article/news/society/122.html.
73. CIW Team, *WeChat Year in Review 2018*, China Internet Watch (January 14, 2019), www.chinainternetwatch.com/28056/wechat-2018.
74. For general discussions on the uncertainty of using technology in rule-making process, *see* Stuart Benjamin, *Evaluating E-Rulemaking: Public Participation and Political Institutions*, 55 Duke L. J. 893 (2005).
75. 深圳经济特区物业管理条例 [Regulations of the Shenzhen Special Economic Zone on Realty Management] (promulgated by Standing Comm. Shenzhen People's Cong., October 17, 2007, effective January 1, 2008) art. 14, 17 and 30 (Chinalawinfo).
76. 桃源居党员反映"深透社"民间组织涉嫌违法犯罪 [*Party Members from Taoyuan Homes Reported That SZHC NGO Was Suspected of Committing Crimes*] (on file with the author).
77. SZHC, 关于"桃源公益"造谣传谣报警处理的公开声明 [*Public Statement that SZHC reported to the Police for Taoyuan Public Service's Making and Spreading Rumors*] (January 18, 2017) (on file with the author).
78. SZHC, 桃源居业委会选举工作冲刺会议 [*Election Sprint Planning Meeting by Homeowners' Committee of Taoyuan Homes*] (November 15, 2016) (on file with the author).
79. Interview No. SZ-HO-070418-3.
80. SZCPTHC, *Guanyu Taoyuan Gongyi Zaoyao Chuanyao Baojing Chuli de Gongkai Shengming* (关于"桃源公益"造谣传谣报警处理的公开声明) [*Public Statement that SZCPTHC reported to the police for Taoyuan Public Service's making and spreading rumors*] (Jan. 18, 2017) (on file with author).; Also五万人小区桃源居业委选举投票被无赖折磨, 迟迟不公布 [*Rascals Delay Revealing The*

Election Result of Homeowners' Committee of Taoyuan Homes, A Community of 50,000 People], OEEEE (January 18, 2017), http://baoliao.oeeee.com/index/show/id/144485/p/2.html.

81. 深圳经济特区物业管理条例 [Regulations of the Shenzhen Special Economic Zone on Realty Management] (promulgated by Standing Committee of the Shenzhen People's Congress, October 17, 2007, effective January 1, 2008) art. 14, 17 and 30 (Chinalawinfo).
82. Shenzhen Political and Legal Committee, 关于严查政治谣言、支持深透社组建党支部 [*In Re-investigating Political Rumors and Supporting the Establishment of Party Branch in SZCPHTC*] (on file with author).
83. Another example of this kind is the city housing administration's experiment of granting HoAs legal organizational status, without support from the Department of Civic Affairs, the experiment has been limited to a small percentage of communities. Interview No. SZ-HO-091118-10, Interview No. SZ-HO-092118-12.
84. 深圳经济特区房地产转让条例 [Regulations of Shenzhen Special Economic Zone on Transfer of Real Estate] (promulgated by Standing Committee of Shenzhen People's Congress, July 24, 1993, effective October 1, 1993, revised June 30, 1999) art. 13 (Chinalawinfo).
85. Wang Chengyi (王成义), 深圳特区立法权：历史、学理和实践 [*An Analysis on the Delegated Legislative Power in Shenzhen Special Economic Zone: History, Theory and Practice*], 4 《地方立法研究》 [LOCAL LEGISLATION JOURNAL], no. 1, 1, 2019.
86. Interview No. SZ-LA-111918-2.
87. 深圳市房地产开发项目停车位建设及处分管理办法(征求意见稿) [Regulation on Shenzhen Real Estate Developing Plan Parking Space Construction and Management (Draft for Public Consultation)] (promulgated by the Shenzhen City Department of Land and Urban Planning, December 2, 2014), www.sz.gov.cn/cn/xxgk/zfxxgj/tzgg/201412/t20141202_2720846.htm.
88. *Id.*
89. Homeowners who can see the value of parking space and do not know much about the law are often willing to pay for a fixed parking spot. *E.g.*, Interview No. SZ-HO-082018-5, Interview No. SZ-HO-090118-8.
90. Yan Xueming (颜雪明), 深圳市规土委，你眼中还有物权法吗? [*Shenzhen City Department of Land and Urban Planning, Do You Respect the Property Law?*], SINA SIFA (April 28, 2016), http://finance.sina.com.cn/sf/news/2016-04-28/155528738.html.
91. *Id.*
92. 上海市居住物业管理条例 [Regulations of Shanghai Municipality on Residential Property Management] (promulgated by Shanghai People's Congress, June 9, 1997, effective July 1, 1997, abolished April 1, 2004) (Chinalawinfo) (stipulating that neighborhood governance relied on homeowners' self-governance, MCs' professional service, as well as governments' supervision and coordination).
93. 上海市加强住宅小区综合管理三年行动计划（2007—2009年） [Three-Year Action Plan (2007–2009) of Shanghai Municipality for Enhancing the Comprehensive Administration of Residential Quarters] (promulgated by Shanghai Housing, Land, and Resources Administration, June 5, 2007, effective June 5, 2007) (Chinalawinfo).

94. 关于加强本市住宅小区业主大会、业主委员会规范化建设的若干意见 [The Opinions on Enhancing the Normalization Construction of Owner Conventions and Owner Committees of Residential Areas in This Municipality] (promulgated by Shanghai Municipal Housing Guarantee and Houses Administration, November 16, 2009, effective November 16, 2009) (Chinalawinfo).
95. 上海市住宅物业管理规定 [Provisions of Shanghai Municipality on Residential Property Management] (promulgated by Standing Committee of Shanghai People's Congress, December 23, 2010, effective April 1, 2011) (Chinalawinfo).
96. 社会治理的上海一号课题是怎么做的 [*How was a Shanghai No. 1 Research Investigation on Social Governance Launched?*], 5《领导决策信息》 [Information for Deciders Magazine] 26, 26–27, 2015.
97. 上海市住宅小区建设"美丽家园"三年行动计划 (2018–2020) [Shanghai Three-Year-Action-Plan of "Constructing Beautiful Homes" in Residential Neighborhoods] (promulgated by the Shanghai City Government, February 8, 2018), www.shanghai.gov.cn/nw2/nw2314/nw2319/nw12344/u26aw55185.html.
98. 上海市社会治理"十三五"规划 [Shanghai's 13th Five-Year Plan on Social Governance] (promulgated by Shanghai Party Committee Office and Shanghai City Government Office, December 24, 2016) (on file with the author).
99. Zang Ming (臧鸣), 12345 市民热线建立大数据分析合作机制 [*12345, Citizen's Hot Line, Has Established the Cooperative Mechanism of Big-Data Analysis*], The Paper (April 18, 2017), www.thepaper.cn/newsDetail_forward_1664046.
100. *See, e.g.*, Interview No. SH-GO-022118-1, Interview No. SH-HO-062618-4, Interview No. SH-HO-062918-8.
101. For survey data, *see* Chapter 6.
102. Shanghai Three-Year-Action-Plan of "Constructing Beautiful Homes," *supra* note 97.
103. *Id.*
104. Interview No. SH-HO-062818-6.
105. *Id.*
106. *Id.*
107. Interview No. SH-HO-062618-4.
108. 商品住宅维修资金业务办理指南 [Guideline on Managing Commodity Housing Maintenance Funding] (promulgated by Shanghai Real Estate Management Administrative Centre and Shanghai Housing Maintenance Funding Centre, October, 2009) (on file with author).
109. 关于印发《北京市住宅专项维修资金使用审核标准》的通知 [Notice on Beijing Municipal Audit Standards of Using Housing Maintenance Funding] (promulgated by Beijing Housing and urban-rural development Committee January 7, 2013), http://gwsq.bjchy.gov.cn/fgfiles/zjglbf.html;jsessionid=C38F864AEBAE7F21E9145FEFBEDF7B50; 深圳市人民政府关于印发深圳市物业专项维修资金管理规定的通知 [Shenzhen City Government's Notice on Rules of Shenzhen Housing Maintenance Funding Management] (promulgated by Shenzhen City Government September 10, 2010), www.sz.gov.cn/zfgb/2010/gb714/content/post_4968277.html.
110. Interview No. SH-HWM-062418-2.
111. Interview No. SH-HO-062918-8.

4 Rule of Law for Democracy

1. Yoram Barzel & Tim R. Sass, *The Allocation of Resources by Voting*, 105 Q. J. Econ. 745 (1990).
2. Developers need to draft a temporary management covenant, which is to be replaced by a covenant approved by a majority of homeowners after they move in.
3. 谢湘华与上海市闵行区未明园业主委员会(第五届)业主撤销权纠纷民事一审案件民事判决书 (2021) 沪 0112 民初 32511 号 [Xie Xianghua v. Shanghai Minhang Weimingyuan HoC, Shanghai Minhang District People's Court Civil Case First-instance Trial No. 32511 (2021)].
4. Civil Code of the People's Republic of China, adopted at the Third Session of the Thirteenth National People's Congress on May 28, 2020, art. 278, www.npc.gov.cn/englishnpc/c23934/202012/f627aa3a4651475db936899d69419d1e/files/47c16489e186437eab3244495cb47d66.pdf (hereinafter "Civil Code").
5. Yulou Li (李玉楼) & Yanlin Liu (刘岍琳), 如何理解"三分之二以上参与"：民法典"考验"业委会 [How to Understand "More than Two-Thirds Participation": A "Test" of HoCs by the Civil Code], 《南方周末》 [*Southern Weekly*], June 4, 2021, www.infzm.com/contents/207485?source=124&source_1=260056.
6. 王晓梅 (Xiaomei Wang) & 顾嘉旻 (Jiamin Gu),《民法典》视域下业主未实际投票行为的法效果认定 [Recognition of the Legal Effects of Owners' Non-Actual Voting Behavior Under the Civil Code], 《至正研究》 [*Zhizheng Research*] (January 16, 2023), https://mp.weixin.qq.com/s/KrA_JQIk9_p7jVfLSxaC2w.
7. 物业管理条例 [Regulation on Real Estate Management] (promulgated by the State Council, June 8, 2003), art. 12.
8. 物权法 [Property Law] (promulgated by National People's Congress, March 16, 2007, effective October 1, 2007), art. 76.
9. 物业管理条例 [Regulation on Realty Management] (promulgated by the State Council, June 8, 2003, amended August 26, 2007), art. 12.
10. 业主大会和业主委员会指导规则 [Guiding Rules of Homeowners' Associations and Homeowners' Committees] (promulgated by the Ministry of Housing and Urban-Rural Development, 2009), art. 26.
11. 业主大会议事规则(沪房地资物[2008]389 号) [Homeowners General Assembly Meeting Rules] (promulgated by Shanghai Municipal Housing and Land Resources Administration on June 25, 2008), art. 10.
12. Guiding Rules of Homeowners' Associations and Homeowners' Committees, *supra* note 9, arts. 22 and 26.
13. *See* Section 4.2.
14. 关于《中华人民共和国民法典（草案）》的说明 [Explanation of the Draft of the Civil Code of the People's Republic of China], May 22, 2020, www.gov.cn/xinwen/2020-05/22/content_5513931.htm#1.
15. Civil Code, *supra* note 4, art. 278.
16. 最高人民法院对十三届全国人大五次会议第7017号建议的答复 [The SPC's Response to Suggestion No. 7017 of the Fifth Session of the 13th National People's Congress], July 28, 2022, https://tyjrswj.beijing.gov.cn/fwzl/jxfw/202302/t20230206_2912283.html.
17. Li & Liu, *supra* note 5.
18. The Civil Code copied half of Taiwan's corresponding rule, but failed to copy the other half, which lowers the voting requirement in the case of a failed first vote with insufficient participation. *See* Li & Liu, *supra* note 5.

19. 政府咨询 [Administrative Consultation], Ministry of Housing and Urban-Rural Development, Question raised by Liao Qiubin (廖秋彬) (December 30, 2020), www.mohurd.gov.cn/interaction/consult/query.
20. 北京市物业管理办法 [Beijing Municipal Real Estate Management Regulations] (promulgated by Beijing Municipal Government on April 6, 2010, effective on October 1, 2010).
21. Beijing Municipal Real Estate Management Regulations, *id*., art. 11.
22. 北京市高级人民法院关于印发《北京市高级人民法院关于审理物业管理纠纷案件的意见(试行)》的通知（京高法发[2003]389号）[The Notice of the Beijing High People's Court on Issuing the "Opinions on the Trial of Property Management Dispute Cases by the Beijing High People's Court (Trial)" (2003) (No. 389)].
23. 北京市石景山区西引力小区业主委员会与北京市石景山区人民政府八角街道办事处等其他再审审查与审判监督行政裁定书，北京市第一中级人民法院行政裁定书(2020)京01行申5号 [Xiyinli HoC v. Bajiao Street Office of Shijingshan District Government, Beijing First Intermediate People's Court, Xingshen No. 5 (2020)].
24. 北京市朝阳区吉利家园小区业主委员会与北京市朝阳区人民政府太阳宫地区办事处其他二审行政判决书北京市第三中级人民法院行政判决书 (2014) 三中行终字第 1379 号 [Jilijiayuan HoC v. the Taiyanggong District Office of the Chaoyang District People's Government, Beijing Third Intermediate People's Court, Xingzhong No. 1379 (2014)]; 北京市朝阳区慧忠北里三塔楼小区业主委员会诉北京市朝阳区人民政府大屯街道办事处，北京市高级人民法院行政裁定书(2023)京行申1648 号[Santalou HoC v. Datun Street Office of Chaoyang District People's Government, Beijing High People's Court Xingcai No. 1648 (2023)].
25. 深圳经济特区物业管理条例 [Shenzhen Special Economic Zone Property Management Regulations] (promulgated by the First People's Congress of Shenzhen on June 18, 1994), art. 10, 12.
26. 深圳经济特区物业管理条例 [Shenzhen Special Economic Zone Property Management Regulation] (promulgated by the Standing Committee of the Fourth People's Congress of Shenzhen on September 25, 2007), art. 17.
27. 中华人民共和国立法法 [Legislation Law of the People's Republic of China] (promulgated by National People's Congress on March 15, 2000, effective on July 1, 2000), art. 81.
28. 深圳市罗湖区中航凯特公寓第二届业主委员会等与叶其亮物业服务合同纠纷上诉案,广东省深圳市中级人民法院民事判决书(2017)粤03 民终 1037 号 [Kate Condominium HoC v. Ye Qiliang et al, Shenzhen Intermediate People's Court, Minzhong No. 1037 (2017)].
29. 何冰、深圳碧桂园盛孚物业服务有限公司业主撤销权纠纷民事二审民事判决书广东省深圳市中级人民法院民事判决书(2021)粤03民终2750号 [He Bing v. Shenzhen Country Garden Shengfu Property Service Co., Ltd., Shenzhen Intermediate People's Court, Minzhong No. 2750 (2021)]; 深圳市龙华区玉华花园小区第三届业主委员会、梁逊策业主撤销权纠纷二审民事判决书，广东省深圳市中级人民法院民事判决书(2019)粤03民终31830号 [The third HoC of Yuhua Garden Community in Longhua District, Shenzhen v. Liang Xunce, Guangdong Shenzhen Intermediate People's Court, Minzhong No. 31830 (2019)].
30. 深圳市宝安区泰华豪园第三届业主委员会诉深圳泰华物业管理有限公司物业管理合同纠纷案，广东省深圳市宝安区人民法院 (2016)粤0306民初2241号 [The Third HoC of Taihua Haoyuan Community in Bao'an District, Shenzhen v.

Shenzhen Taihua Property Management Co., Ltd., Guangdong Shenzhen Bao'an District People's Court, Minchu No. 2241(2016)]; 深圳市宝安区泰华豪园第三届业主委员会与郭超勇业主撤销权纠纷上诉案，广东省深圳市中级人民法院(2016)粤03民终11216号 [The third HoC of Taihua Haoyuan Community in Bao'an District, Shenzhen v. Guo Chaoyong, Guangdong Shenzhen Intermediate People's Court, Minzhong No. 11216 (2016)].

31. 深圳经济特区物业管理条例 [Shenzhen Special Economic Zone Property Management Regulations] (promulgated by Standing Committee of the People's Congress on August 29, 2019, effective on March 1, 2020), art. 30.
32. *See* Chapter 8, Section 8.4 for a more detailed discussion on legality review.
33. 欧阳志斌、深圳市世外桃源物业管理有限公司物业服务合同纠纷民事二审民事判决书 (2021)粤03民终7275号 [Ouyang Zhibin v. Shenzhen Shiwai Taoyuan Property Management Co., Ltd., Guangdong Shenzhen Intermediate People's Court, Minzhong No. 7275 (2021)].
34. 上海市住宅物业管理规定 [Shanghai Residential Property Management Regulations] (promulgated by the Standing Committee of the 12th People's Congress of Shanghai on August 19, 2004), art. 11.
35. 上海市住宅物业管理规定 [Shanghai Residential Property Management Regulations] (promulgated by the Standing Committee of the 12th People's Congress of Shanghai on August 19, 2004, amended by the Standing Committee of the 13th People's Congress of Shanghai on December 23, 2010), art. 17; 上海市住宅物业管理规定 [Shanghai Residential Property Management Regulations] (promulgated by the Standing Committee of the 12th People's Congress of Shanghai on August 19, 2004, amended by the Standing Committee of the 15th People's Congress of Shanghai on November 22, 2018), art. 18.
36. 上海市住宅物业管理规定 [Shanghai Residential Property Management Regulations] (promulgated by the Standing Committee of the 12th People's Congress of Shanghai on August 19, 2004, amended by the Standing Committee of the 15th People's Congress of Shanghai on October 28, 2022), art. 18.
37. Homeowners General Assembly Meeting Rules, Article 10, *supra* note 11.
38. 上海市高级人民法院关于业主委员会行政诉讼主体资格问题的解答(2006年7月24日) [Shanghai High People's Court's Explanation regarding the Qualification of HoCs in Administrative Litigation (July 24, 2006)].
39. *See* the story of ZJJ and the government's encouragement of the idea of "defending rights according to law" in Chapter 9 of this book.
40. 2008–2017年涉业主委员会案件审判白皮书 [White Paper on the Judicial Adjudication of Cases Involving HoC from 2008 to 2017], 163 (July 15, 2019), www.163.com/dy/article/EK546R5H0514C18R.html.
41. 郑重与上海市闵行区丽华公寓小区业主委员会等业主撤销权纠纷，上海市闵行区人民法院民事判决书(2022)沪0112民初27268号 [Zheng Zhong v. Lihua Apartment Complex HoC in Minhang District, Shanghai, Minhang District People's Court in Shanghai, Minchu No. 27268 (2022)].
42. White Paper on the Judicial Adjudication, *supra* note 37.
43. 包燕谷等与上海市闵行区银桥花园业主委员会（第二届）等业主撤销权纠纷一审民事判决书，上海市闵行区人民法院民事判决书 (2021)沪0112民初45367号 [Bao Yangu and Others v. The Second Yinqiao Garden HoC in Minhang District, Shanghai, and Others, Shanghai Minhang District People's Court, Minchu No. 45367 (2021)].

44. *Id.*
45. 上海市浦东新区艺泰安邦业主委员会与徐伟芬业主撤销权纠纷二审案件二审民事判决书，上海市第一中级人民法院民事判决书 (2020)沪01民终7473号 [Yitai Anbang HoC in Pudong, Shanghai v. Xu Weifen, Shanghai First Intermediate People's Court, Minzhong No. 7473 (2020)].
46. 上海骏丰嘉房地产开发有限公司业主撤销权纠纷二审民事判决书 上海市第二中级人民法院民事判决书 (2020)沪02民终3424号 [Shanghai Junfeng Jia Real Estate Development Co., Ltd. v. HoA of Junfeng Jiastian and Jiafenghui, Jiading District, Shanghai, Shanghai Second Intermediate People's Court, Minzhong, Minzhong No. 3424 (2020)].
47. 罗媚媚等与上海市浦东新区大华锦绣华城14街区业主委员会业主撤销权纠纷二审案件二审民事判决书 上海市第一中级人民法院 （2020）沪01民终11488号 [Luo Meimei and others v. HoC of Block 14, Dahua Jinxiu Huacheng in Pudong, Shanghai, Shanghai First Intermediate People's Court, Minzhong No. 11488 (2020)].
48. 上海伟栋房地产开发有限公司与上海市松江区久阳文华府邸小区业主大会业主撤销权纠纷案 上海市松江区人民法院民事判决书(2015)松民三(民)初字第1014号 [Shanghai Weidong Real Estate Development Co., Ltd. v. HoA of Jiuyang Wenhua Fudi Community in Songjiang District, Shanghai, Shanghai Songjiang District People's Court, Minchu No. 1014 (2015)].
49. 马丽敏、深圳市罗湖区港逸豪庭第一届业主委员会业主撤销权纠纷二审民事判决书广东省深圳市中级人民法院民事判决书(2018)粤03民终12106号 [Ma Limin v. the First HoC of Gangyi Haoting Community in Luohu District, Shenzhen, Guangdong Shenzhen Intermediate People's Court, Minzhong No. 12106 (2018)].
50. 董光亮等与上海市普陀区名都花园业主委员会业主撤销权纠纷一审民事判决书 上海市普陀区人民法院民事判决书 (2021)沪0107民初11293号 [Dong Guangliang and others v. HoC of Mingdu Garden Community in Putuo District, Shanghai, Shanghai Putuo District People's Court, Minchu No. 11293 (2021)].
51. 汤啸天 (Xiaotian Tang), 法院审级职能改革应注意的几个问题 [Several Issues to Pay Attention to in the Jurisdictional Reform], 《澎湃新闻》 [*The Paper*] (March 10, 2023), www.thepaper.cn/newsDetail_forward_22185880.
52. 上观新闻 [Shanghai Observer], 上海不少小区遭遇尴尬！7成居民不投票、3次业委会选举不成功…小区换届改选咋办? [Many neighborhoods in Shanghai are facing an awkward situation! With 70 percent of residents not voting and three unsuccessful attempts at HoC elections, what should be done for the neighborhood's re-election and transition?] (October 15, 2021), https://mp.weixin.qq.com/s?__biz=MjM5ODI2NDMwMw==&mid=2652932440&idx=1&sn=39903606bdfbf1690ff88834fa66521b&chksm=bd1945d88a6ecccecd86b71d1db27d9d84f38a91e1a1da69dbc7ffc275028b497d5e05769ced&scene=27.
53. 中国经济网 [China Economic Network], 2021年"两会"期间，上海市房管局共收到了20件加装电梯方面的代表委员的建议提案 [During the "Two Sessions" in 2021, the Shanghai Municipal Housing Administration received a total of 20 proposals and suggestions from representatives and delegates regarding the installation of elevators] (May 25, 2021), http://m.ce.cn/fa/gd/202105/25/t20210525_36585651.shtml.
54. Shanghai Residential Property Management Regulations, *supra* note 34, art. 18.
55. 关于进一步做好本市既有多层住宅加装电梯工作的若干意见（沪建房管联〔2019〕749号）[Several Opinions on Further Improving the Installation of

Elevators in Existing Multistory Residential Buildings in This City] (Document No. 749, issued by the SHDHC et al., November 22, 2019).

56. 上海市关于调整本市既有多层住宅加装电梯业主表决比例的通知 [Notice from the Shanghai Municipal Government Regarding the Adjustment of the Voting Ratio of Owners in Existing Multistory Residential Buildings for Elevator Installation] (promulgated by the SHDHC, December 31, 2020), https://zjw.sh.gov.cn/fwgl/20210104/5d4c3520e32143bd8d77ec2a2ca9182d.html.
57. 关于印发《关于进一步贯彻实施〈上海市住宅物业管理规定〉的若干意见》的通知 [Notice on Issuing Several Opinions on Further Implementing the Shanghai Residential Property Management Regulations] (promulgated by the SHDHC, May 18, 2021), www.shqp.gov.cn/xiay/xyzwgk/sqgl/20221105/1039182.html.
58. 松江区东明花苑加装电梯表决程序违规表决结果不符合政府文件规定 [Irregular Voting Procedure and Non-Compliance of the Voting Results for Elevator Installation in Dongming Huayuan, Songjiang District, Contrary to Government Document Regulations] (March 22, 2021), 中共上海市松江区委人民政府网上信访/建议征集受理中心 [Online Petition/Suggestion Collection and Acceptance Center of the CPC Songjiang District Committee and People's Government of Shanghai] (April 6, 2021), https://qxf.sh.gov.cn/310117/reply.setDetailInit.do?id=7D2C2109C54B4EAA8D42502B03449E30.
59. 请求上海市住房管理局对小区业主表决的有效性的认定 [Petitioning the SHDHC to Confirm the Validity of Homeowner Resolution], July 24, 2021, https://qxf.sh.gov.cn/310101/reply.setDetailInit.do?id=ED986967B3E34DA38D073797472E6DF6.
60. 上海市城市管理精细化工作推进领导小组办公室 [Office of the Leading Group for Advancing Urban Management Precision Work in Shanghai], 关于印发《业主大会议事规则》示范文本的通知（座谈会征求意见版）[Notice on Issuing the Model Text of "Rules for HoA Decision-Making" (Draft for Comments)] (October. 25, 2023), on file with the author.
61. 徐汇法院 [Xuhui Court], 业主:不要再沉默 [Homeowner, Don't Stay Silent Anymore] 业委会资讯[HoC Information] (August 28, 2020), https://mp.weixin.qq.com/s/VsZsFHHaHOoQksNS8FEOsQ.
62. The No. 3 Intermediate Court is a special court whose jurisdictions include first-instance cases in which the Shanghai municipal government and its departments are defendants.
63. Lin, *supra* note 48.
64. 全国法院系统2022年度优秀案例分析评选获奖名单 [List of Award Winners for the 2022 National Court System Outstanding Case Analysis Selection], 搜狐(Sohu) (December 31, 2022), www.sohu.com/a/623233609_117927.
65. *Ibid.*
66. 众蚁社区 [Ant Community], 关于业主未实际投票行为（"视为参与""视为同意"等条款）的法效果认定｜全国二等奖判例 [Legal Effect Determination of Owners' Non-Participation in Actual Voting Behavior ("Deemed to Participate," "Deemed to Agree," and Similar Clauses) | National Second Prize Case] (January 30, 2023), https://mp.weixin.qq.com/s/zBpid3S0RzmFhB9nCIhHUw.
67. 刘彦成与上海市闵行区高兴花园二至四街坊业主委员会（第三届）业主撤销权纠纷民事二审案件民事判决书 上海市第一中级人民法院判决（2021）

沪01民终16424号 [Liu Yancheng v. HoC of the Second to Fourth Neighborhoods of Xingxing Garden, Minhang District, Shanghai (Third Session), Shanghai First Intermediate People's Court, Min Zhong No. 16424 (2021)].

68. 陈亮等诉上海市闵行区锦绣江南陶然居业主委员会（第五届）业主撤销权纠纷案 上海市闵行区人民法院民事判决书(2021)沪0112民初22494号[Chen Liang and others v. HoC (Fifth Session) of Jinxiu Jiangnan Taoranju Community in Minhang District, Shanghai Minhang District People's Court, Minchu No. 22494 (2021)]. In 上海市高级人民法院发布2022年度精品案例、优秀裁判文书、示范庭审 [SHANGHAI HIGH PEOPLE'S COURT RELEASES OUTSTANDING CASES, EXCELLENT JUDGMENTS, AND MODEL COURT HEARINGS FOR THE YEAR 2022] (February 22, 2023), www.pkulaw.com/pal/a3ecfd5d734f711dbdca0cc56db94e21821a889e9841e072bdfb.html.

69. 上海豪都房地产开发经营有限公司与上海市青浦区徐泾镇捷克住宅小区业主大会等业主撤销权纠纷民事一审案件民事判决书 上海市闵行区人民法院民事判决书 (2021)沪0112民初22494号 [Shanghai Haodu Real Estate Development and Operation Co., Ltd. v. HoA of Czech Residential Community in Xujing Town, Qingpu District, Shanghai, Shanghai Minhang District People's Court, Minchu No. 22494 (2021)]; 谢湘华与上海市闵行区未明园业主委员会(第五届)业主撤销权纠纷民事一审案件民事判决书 上海市闵行区人民法院民事判决书 2021) 沪0112民初32511号 [Xie Xianghua v. HoC (Fifth Session) of Weimingyuan Community in Minhang District, Shanghai, Shanghai Minhang District People's Court, Minchu No. 32511 (2021)]; 上海豪都房地产开发经营有限公司与上海市青浦区徐泾镇捷克住宅小区业主大会等业主撤销权纠纷民事一审案件民事判决书，上海市青浦区人民法院(2022)沪0118民初4870号 [Shanghai Haodu Real Estate Development and Operation Co., Ltd. v. HoA of Czech Residential Community in Xujing Town, Qingpu District, Shanghai, Shanghai Qingpu District People's Court, Minchu No. 4870 (2022)]; 郭文利等与上海市松江区山的院子花园业主大会业主撤销权纠纷一审民事判决书，上海市松江区人民法院(2021)沪0117民初16661号 [Guo Wenli and others v. HoA of Shandeyuan Garden in Songjiang District, Shanghai, Shanghai Songjiang District People's Court, Minchu No. 16661 (2021)].

70. Minchu No. 4870 (2022), *id.*
71. Wang & Gu, *supra* note 6.
72. *Id.*
73. *Id.*
74. *Id.*
75. *Id.*

5 Property: A Political Right, Social Right, or Legal Right?

1. 物权法 [Property Law] (promulgated by Nat'l People's Cong., March 16, 2007, effective October 1, 2007), Art 75; 中华人民共和国民法典[The PRC Civil Code] (promulgated by Nat'l People's Cong., May 28, 2020), art. 277.
2. Yoram Barzel famously distinguished between economic rights and legal rights: "[E]conomic rights reflect individuals' ability to consume or exchange commodities. These rights may exist in the absence of legal rights, though the latter tend to enhance the former. Legal rights are rights delineated by the state." Yoram Barzel, A Theory of the State: Economic Rights, Legal Rights, and

THE SCOPE OF THE STATE 6 (2002). My categorization is consistent with his, but add the political dimension of property rights to it. Social rights and political rights in my categorization can be viewed as further refinement of his economic rights.

3. Interview No. SH-HO-062918-8.
4. Xia Jun (夏骏), 《居住改变中国》 [RESIDENCE CHANGES CHINA] (2006).
5. *See, e.g.*, Fan Baihua (樊百华), 物业管理革命与城市民主[*The Revolution of Real Estate Management and Urban Democracy*], BEIJING SPRING (July 14, 2003), http://beijingspring.com/bj2/2003/280/2003714150622.htm; Lao Niu (老牛), 革命尚未成功, 业委会重任在肩 [*Revolution is yet to succeed, homeowners' committee has a heavy obligation to fulfill*], WECHAT OFFICIAL ACCOUNT TONGJI CHENGSHI YAZHU (June 29, 2017), https://mp.weixin.qq.com/s?__biz=MzIwNzYwMDY3Mw%3D%3D&mid=2247483859&idx=1&sn=47f2b288605c9e92f2abdd0404699576&scene=45#wechat_redirect.
6. Interview No. BJ-HO-102818-11; Interview No. BJ-HO-xxxx18-14; Interview No. BJ-HO-080318-3; Interview No. BJ-HO-042318-1; Interview No. BJ-HO-080618-6; Interview No. BJ-HO-xxxx18-15.
7. In the preparation for the 2008 Olympics, the Beijing city government mobilized 1.7 million volunteers, including 1 million from local neighborhoods, to help with social management and assistance during the Game. These volunteers were at the command of the government. *See* Ge Weiying (葛维樱) & Wang Mofu (王墨馥), 170万志愿者：北京奥运的基石 [*1.7 Million Volunteers: The Basis of Beijing Olympic Games*], 《三联生活周刊》 [SANLIAN LIFEWEEK] (August 28, 2008), http://news.sina.com.cn/c/2008-08-28/105516189155.shtml; Carol Hung, *For Beijing's Olympic Volunteers, The Rules are Many,* THE CHRISTIAN SCIENCE MONITOR (July 17, 2008), www.csmonitor.com/World/Asia-Pacific/2008/0717/p04s01-woap.html.
8. Interview No. BJ-HO-042318-1.
9. *Id.*
10. *Id.*
11. Li Yihui (李颐晖), 秦兵围绕业主"办案"近20年 [*Qing Bing Who Has Spent Nearly 20 Years in Dealing with Homeowner-Related Legal Cases*], THE BEIJING NEWS (November 11, 2016), http://news.ifeng.com/a/20161111/50239309_0.shtml.
12. *Id.*
13. Interview No. BJ-LA-102818-1.
14. 全国人民代表大会和地方各级人民代表大会选举法(2015修正) [Election Law for the National People's Congress and Local People's Congresses at All Levels (2015 Amendment)] (promulgated by the Standing Committee of National People's Congress, August 29, 2015) art. 44 (Chinalawinfo).
15. Tang Shuquan (唐述权), 北京一社区居民欲罢免选区人大代表的来龙去脉 [*The Story that Residents from a Beijing Condominium Complex Wanted to Remove a Representative of Local People's Congress from the Post*], XINHUASHE (December 9, 2004), www1.people.com.cn/GB/shizheng/14562/3044674.html.
16. Interview No. BJ-LA-102818-1.
17. For the prevalence of petitioning in China, *see, e.g.*, Zhang Taisu. *Why the Chinese Public Prefer Administrative Petitioning over Litigation*, 3 SOCIOL. STUD. 139 (2009).
18. Interview No. BJ-LA-102818-1.
19. *Id.*
20. *Id.*

21. The reason was that he had attempted to mobilize lawyers in Beijing to elect their own leaders, disturbing the Beijing Lawyers' Association's sham election. Interview with QB, January 2019.
22. Miao Wei (苗炜), 舒可心的竞选表演 [The Campaign of Shu Kexin], 《三联生活周刊》 [SANLIAN LIFEWEEK] (December 04, 2003), www.lifeweek.com.cn/2003/1204/7251.shtml.
23. For existing research on the inter-community mobilization of homeowners in Beijing, *see* Aurore Merle, *Homeowners of Beijing, Unite! The Construction of a Collective Mobilisation,* CHINA PERSPECT., no. 2, 7, 2014.
24. Shi Yuntong (史云桐), 有产者的抗争与社会的生产——B市业主维权的类型研究 [The Fight of Property Owners and the Production of the Society – A Study on Different Types of City B Homeowners' Defending Their Rights] (June, 2008) (unpublished Ph.D. dissertation, Tsinghua University) (on file with author), at 92.
25. *Id.*, at 93.
26. *Id.*
27. *Id.*, at 91.
28. Interview No. BJ-HO-080318-3; BJ-LA-102818-1.
29. Shi, *supra* note 24, at 94.
30. *Id.*, at 95.
31. *Id.*, at 96.
32. *Id.*, at 98.
33. Chen Youhong (陈幽泓) et al., 民事纠纷中的"社会总动员"——美丽园冲突解决与秩序重构的启示 [Social Mobilisaiton in Civil Disputes – Lessons from Beijing Meili Garden about Conflict Resolution and Order Restructure] (2007) (unpublished manuscript) (on file with author); Shi, *supra* note 24, at 98.
34. 全国人民代表大会常务委员会法制工作委员会民法室 [Standing Committee of National People's Congress Legal Work Committee Civil Law], 《物权法立法背景与观点全集》 [Collections of PRC Property Law Legislative Background and Opinions] 367–391 (2007).
35. Mao Lei (毛 磊) & Du Wenjuan (杜文娟), 物权法草案已趋成熟 [*The Draft of the PRC Property Law Is About to Complete*], RENMINWANG (December 31, 2006), http://paper.people.com.cn/rmrb/html/2006-12/31/content_12171182.htm.
36. Shi, *supra* note 24, at 102–103.
37. Shi, *supra* note 24, at 104.
38. 北京市业主委员会协会申办委员会 [BJHC], 万人上书：要求完善物权法第六章更好地保护业主权益修改建筑物区分所有权部分条款 [Ten-Thousand People Petition: Requirements for Improving Chapter Six of Property Law], March 5, 2007, on file with the author.
39. The BJHC's proposal included three suggestions: (1) all common areas and facilities should be jointly owned by homeowners instead of being owned and transferred by developers; (2) in deciding the total area of space eligible for votes, it should be the total area of individual apartments rather than the total area of the neighborhood; and (3) HOA's should be registered as NGOs and should be given standing in court and in arbitration tribunals. The final draft of the property law included adjustments in line with two of these suggestions. First, in addition to roads, green space, and real estate management facilities, all other common space and facilities would also belong to homeowners collectively. Because it kept underground

parking space under developers' ownership, it did not go as far as homeowners would have liked. Nevertheless, the revision achieved significant progress, as the previous disputed draft wording had stipulated that only "roads, green space and real estate management facilities" belong to homeowners collectively. Second, the final draft added wording to the effect that individual homeowners could sue to revoke decisions made by HOAs. It thus granted HOAs standing in court in an indirect manner: If an entity can be sued, it should be able to sue. Interview No. BJ-HO-080318-3.

40. *Id.*
41. Chen Bing, 关于"要求《物权法》保护业主权益——公民联署行动"之回顾与思索 [*Reflection on a Joint Petition of Citizens that Asked the PRC Property Law to Protect Homeowners' Rights*], Yangguan Zhongguo Yezhu Lianmeng (September 14, 2012), http://blog.sina.com.cn/s/blog_a57481790101cg01.html (last visited December 1, 2020).
42. Shi, *supra* note 24, at 108.
43. Shitong Qiao, *Small Property, Big Market: A Focal Point Explanation*, 63 Am. J. Comp. L. 197 (2015).
44. 黄贝街道办事处 [Huangbei Street-Level Government], 碧波社区"天景花园业委会"从深圳走向了全国 [*The HoA of Skyview Garden in Crystal Wave Neighborhood Has Walked Toward the Country from Shenzhen*], Luohu Government Online (September 20, 2010), www.szlh.gov.cn/qgbmxxgkml/hbjdbsc/zwxx/gzdt/201009/t20100920_9731155.htm.
45. Qiao, *Small Property, Big Market, supra* note 43.
46. One factor that makes the manipulation more likely than in other Chinese cities is the Special Economic Zone (SEZ) legislative power that Shenzhen is granted by the central government: As a SEZ, Shenzhen has the so-called SEZ legislative power (特区立法权). Following the constitution and principles of national laws, it can change or adapt national laws and regulations to its local situations. Whether courts should apply national laws or the SEZ legislation when they are in conflict with each other is not entirely clear. *See, e.g.*, He Jiahua (何家华), 特区立法权的实践状况和社会效果——以深圳为例 [*The Practice and Consequence of SEZ Legislation: A Case Study of Shenzhen*], 《南海法学》 [South China Sea Law Review], no. 3, 2017. 100–110.
47. Interview No. SZ-HO-091118-11.
48. The developer had not provided homeowners with real estate certificates because it had not paid the government for land use rights, meaning that ZJJ could not exercise his right of exit. Liu Wu (柳五), 深圳景洲大厦：中国业主维权的标本 [*Shenzhen Jinghzhou Mansion: China's Fossil of Homeowners Defending Their Rights*], China Reform (2005), http://star.news.sohu.com/s2005/yezhu.shtml.
49. 宪法修正案(1999) [Amendment to the Constitution of the People's Republic of China (1999)] (adopted at the Second Session of the Ninth National People's Congress and promulgated for implementation by the Announcement of the National People's Congress on March 15, 1999) (Chinalawinfo).
50. HoCs did not have legal standing in court at the time. Interview No. SZ-HO-xxxx18*-18, 39.
51. Interview No. SZ-HO-091118-11.

52. SZ-HO-091118-11. Shenzhen Housing Administration (深住〔2004〕35号). 深圳市物业管理招投标专家库管理暂行办法 [Provisional Measures on the Administration of Expert Database on Real Estate Management Bidding], No. 35, April 8, 2004, Article 3. In Shenzhen real estate management bidding, evaluation experts must be chosen from the Shenzhen Real Estate Management Bidding Evaluation Expert Database.
53. Chen Min (陈敏), 邹家健：中国第一业主 [*Zhou Jiajian: China's No.1 Homeowner*], 《中国改革》 [China Reform] (May 17, 2005), http://news.sohu.com/20050517/n225604351.shtml.
54. Interview No. SZ-HO-091118-11.
55. Chen, *supra* note 41.
56. Interview No. SZ-HO-091118-11.
57. Property Law, *supra* note 1, art. 74.
58. Interview No. SZ-HO-091118-11. The transition always took time, and, in one case, the old company simply declined to submit the money.
59. 深圳市组织机构代码管理办法 [The Administrative Measures of Shenzhen Municipality on Institution Codes (2005 Revision)] (promulgated by Shenzhen City Government September 17, 1994, amended April 28, 2005) art. 4 (Chinalawinfo).
60. *Id.*
61. Interview No. SZ-HO-091118-11.
62. *Id.*
63. Interview No. SZ-HO-xxxx18*-18.
64. Zhen Jinghui (甄静慧), 范国振73岁老人的10年维权路 [*The 10 Years' Rights-Defending Journey of Fan Guozhen, a 73-Year-Old Man*], Nanfeng Chuang (February 3, 2010), http://focus.news.163.com/10/0203/10/5UJGHFR800011SM9.html.
65. 深圳市福田区南天一花园业主委员会与深圳市城市建设开发（集团）公司等房屋侵权纠纷再审案 [Shenzhen Futian District Nantianyi Garden Homeowner Committee v. Shenzhen Municipal Construction and Development Co., Ltd., Retrial of Real Estate-Related Tort Dispute] (PRC Sup. People's Ct. 2013) (China Judgement Online) [hereinafter *Sup. People's Ct. Nantianyi Garden Tort Dispute*].
66. 深圳市福田区南天一花园业主委员会与深圳市城市建设开发（集团）公司等房屋侵权纠纷再审案 [Shenzhen Futian District Nantianyi Garden Homeowner Committee v. Shenzhen Municipal Construction and Development Co., Ltd., Retrial of Real Estate-Related Tort Dispute] (PRC Sup. People's Ct. 2013), on file with author [hereinafter *Sup. People's Ct. Nantianyi Garden Tort Dispute*].
67. *Id.*
68. *Id*; 深圳经济特区住宅区物业管理条例 [Shenzhen Special Economic Zone Regulation on Residential Real Estate Management], Articles 47 and 48, Shenzhen People's Congress Standing Committee, July 11, 1994.
69. *Id.*
70. *Id.*
71. *Id.*
72. 深圳市福田区南天一花园业主委员会与深圳市城市建设开发（集团）公司等房屋侵权纠纷 [Nantianyi HoC v. Shenzhen Municipal Construction Corporation], Shenzhen Intermediate People's Court (广东省深圳市中级人民法院民事判决书（2007）深中法民重字第2号), March 2, 2010, on file with the author.

73. 深圳市福田区南天一花园业主委员会与深圳市城市建设开发（集团）公司等房屋侵权纠纷 [Nantianyi HoC v. Shenzhen Municipal Construction Corporation], Guangdong Province High People's Court (广东省高级人民法院民事判决书（2010）粤高法民一终字第114号), July 6, 2011, on file with the author.
74. 13年官司输了，业主维权精神赢了 [*A 13-year Legal Case Lost, while the Homeowners' Spirit of Right-Defending Won*], NANFANG CITY NEWSPAPER (February 28, 2014), http://news.ifeng.com/gundong/detail_2014_02/28/34270518_0.shtml.
75. 深圳市福田区南天一花园业主委员会与深圳市城市建设开发（集团）公司等房屋侵权纠纷再审案 [S Nantianyi HoC v. Shenzhen Municipal Construction Corporation] (PRC Sup. People's Ct. 2013), on file with the author.
76. Shenzhen Special Economic Zone Regulation on Residential Real Estate Management, *supra* note 68, art. 47 and 48.
77. At the same time, however, the SPC also held that because the condominium complex in this case had been developed at the end of the 1980s, the 2007 Property Law and related judicial interpretations did not apply, leaving it unclear whether homeowners in more recent condominium complexes have property rights over undeveloped land within their community boundaries. *Id. See* also SPC Press Conference on the Shenzhen Property Dispute (最高法就深圳房屋侵权纠纷案相关问题答记者问), www.chinapeace.gov.cn/chinapeace/c28648/2014-02/21/content_11732376.shtml.
78. While the foregoing series of litigation was ongoing in the local courts, the Land and Urban Planning Agency of Futian District, where FGZ's neighborhood was located, issued a real estate certificate for the disputed building to the developer after it paid the land use fee. Under FGZ's leadership, the HoC sued the agency for revoking its certificate, and the Shenzhen Court upheld its claim that the agency could not decide a property rights claim during ongoing litigation. Shenzhen Nantianyi Huayuan Yeweihui v. Shenzhen Shi Guihua yu Guotu Ziyuan Ju (深圳南天一花园业委会 v.深圳市规划与国土资源局) [Shenzhen Nantianyi Garden Homeowners Committee v. Shenzhen Housing Administration] (Shenzhen Intermediate People's Ct. August 25, 2008), on file with the author.
79. Zhen, *supra* note 64.
80. *Id.*
81. *Id.*
82. List of the Forum topics and dates (on file with the author).
83. 深圳：首期业主论坛开坛 热议业主自治模式 [*Shenzhen: The First Homeowner Forum Was Held, Participants Discussed Self-Governance of Homeowner*], JINGBAO (June 26, 2012), www.sxbailesy.com/2012/0626/1729.html.
84. *Id.*
85. 深圳业主论坛宗旨：在时代的夹缝中"架桥" [*The Motto of Shenzhen Homeowner Forum: Bridge the Gap in this Era*], ZHANG JIN'S BLOG (June 25, 2012), http://blog.sina.com.cn/s/blog_500ad625010143u9.html.
86. 张晋(Zhang Jin), 感恩有你，一路同行 [*Be Grateful for Your Company*], WECHAT ACCOUNT SHETOUSHE (June 27, 2017), https://mp.weixin.qq.com/s/l05dIHiiSitvLm3hhV6iGw.
87. *Id.*
88. Shentoushe (深透社), "历史告诉未来"深圳业主论坛五周年庆典记 [*Let History Speak to Future, the 5th Anniversary of Shenzhen Homeowner Forum*], SHENZHEN CENTER OF PROMOTING TRANSPARENT AND HARMONIOUS COMMUNITIES (June 27, 2017), https://mp.weixin.qq.com/s/dYPZcV8vDwOd6-LiVrFssg.

89. Wang Fei (王飞), "深透社"揭牌成立——深圳本土第一家职业化业主自治社会组织成立 [*Shenzhen Centre of Promoting Transparent and Harmonious Communities Was Founded – Shenzhen's First Professional Homeowner Self-Governance Organization*], 《住宅与房地产》 [SHENZHEN HOUSING AND REAL ESTATE MAGAZINE], no. 4, 2016, at 67.
90. 深透社成立大会于3月6日在市民中心成功举行 [*SZHC Was Launched at the Shenzhen Civic Centre on March. 6*], SZHC (March 7, 2016), https://mp.weixin.qq.com/s/7vMROx85nd49peYu-VI1mg.
91. 在时代的夹缝中构架沟通的桥梁——在深圳华南和谐社区发展中心成立大会上的致辞 [*Build a Bridge of Communication in the Squeezed Middle – Speech in the Opening Ceremony of Shenzhen Southern China Center of Harmonious Community Development*], ZHANG JIN'S BLOG (November 22, 2015), http://blog.sina.com.cn/s/blog_500ad6250102wdtf.html.
92. *supra* note 90.
93. *Id.*
94. Wang, *supra* note 89.
95. Interview No. SZ-HO-xxxx18*-18; SZHC, 国家行政学院4位专家调研深透社 [*4 Experts From National Administration School Conducted Research on SZHC*], SZHC (December 12, 2016), https://mp.weixin.qq.com/s/lM54ox8fcy3bJvhfV6j4IQ.
96. Interview No. SH-HO-062918-8.
97. Chen Yingfang (陈映芳), 行动力与制度限制：都市运动中的中产阶层 [*Ability of Action and Institutional Constraints: Middle Class in the Urban Movement*], 4 《社会学研究》 [SOCIOLOGY STUDY] 1 (2006).
98. Property Law, *supra* note 1, art. 74.
99. Interview No. SH-HO-062818-6, 20–21.
100. Regulations on Real Estate Management, art. 30, 38, and 39.
101. *See* Chapter 6.
102. Interview No. SH-HO-062918-9.
103. Property Law, art. 70, 73, and 74.
104. Interview No. SH-HO-062618-5; Fang Daohang (房导航), 涨不了的上海房价涨车位 [*Restriction on Shanghai Housing Price Cannot Prevent Rising Price of Parking Lot*], ZHIHU (August 13, 2018), https://zhuanlan.zhihu.com/p/34506080 (last visited December 5, 2021).
105. Interview No. SH-HO-062918-8. For a similar case, *see* Interview No. SH-HO-062618-5.
106. *See, e.g.*, Kevin J. O'Brien & Rongbin Han, *Path to Democracy? Assessing Village Elections in China*, 18 J. CONTEMP. CHINA 359 (2009); Liangjiang Li & Kevin J. O'Brien, *The Struggle Over Village Elections*, in THE PARADOX OF CHINA'S POST-MAO REFORMS 129 (Merle Goldman, Roderick MacFarquhar, eds., 1999); John James Kennedy, *The Face of "Grassroots Democracy" in Rural China: Real Versus Cosmetic Elections*, 42 ASIAN SURV. 456 (2002).
107. *See, e.g.*, Interview No. SH-HO-110218-15, 11; SH-HO-092418-13 & SH-HO-062618-4 (Both interviewees mentioned that some homeowners blocked the gate of the housing complex to protest against the parking regulation passed by the two-thirds super majority).
108. Interview No. SH-HWM-062418-2, 13-23.
109. Interview No. SH-HO-062918-8.

110. *See, e.g.*, Richard A. Epstein, *The Allocation of the Commons: Parking on Public Roads*, 31 J. Legal Stud. S515 (2002).
111. Interview No. SH-HWM-062418-2, 29.
112. As revealed by a search in the China Judicial Decisions Online, the SPC database, HoAs in Shanghai initiated more administrative litigations than their counterparts in Shenzhen and Beijing did from 2014 to 2017. (Search results on file with the author.)
113. 罗全福因核发业主大会、业主委员会备案证行政行为一案 [*In re* Luo Quanfu suing the administrative act that approved and issued the documentation certificate for homeowner convention and homeowner committee] (Shanghai 1st Intermediate People's Court, January 29, 2016).
114. WeChat Record from HB, Shanghai Homeowner and Founder of Mass Ant (June 26, 2018) (on file with author).
115. Transcript of Interview No. SH-HO-062918-8, at 28.
116. *Id.*, at 1–2.
117. *Id.*, at 1.
118. *Id.*, at 2.
119. *Id.*, at 11.
120. *Id.*, at 30.
121. *Id.*, at 3.
122. *Id.*, at 22.
123. *Id.*, at 8.
124. *Id.*, at 22.
125. *Id.*, at 22–23.
126. WeChat record from AJ, Intern in Mass Ant (December 14, 2018) (on file with author).
127. A list of offline meeting themes, on file with the author.
128. *See, e.g.*, HB strictly enforced the online group by kicking out a group member who shared a link of a crowdfunding platform to collect medical fees for his seriously ill daughter. WeChat record from HB (November 7, 2018) (on file with author).
129. WeChat records from HB (June 20, 2018 & June 26, 2018) (on file with author).
130. Interview No. SH-HO-141218-17.

6 The Origin of Self-governed Communities in Authoritarian Cities

1. Richard RW Brooks, and Carol M. Rose. Saving the Neighborhood: Racially Restrictive Covenants, Law, and Social Norms (2013); Robert C. Ellickson, Order Without Law: How Neighbors Settle Disputes (1991); Raghuram Rajan, The Third Pillar: How Markets and the State Leave the Community Behind (2019); Barak D. Richman, Stateless Commerce: The Diamond Network and the Persistence of Relational Exchange (2017).
2. Francis Fukuyama, Trust: The Social Virtues and The Creation of Prosperity (1995); Robert D. Putnam, Making Democracy Work: Civic Traditions in Modern Italy (1993); Robert D. Putnam, Bowling Alone: The Collapse and Revival of American Community (2000).
3. Robert C. Ellickson, *Property in Land*, 102 Yale L. J. 1315, 1335–1338 (1993).

4. Lisa Bernstein, *Opting out of the Legal System: Extralegal Contractual Relations in the Diamond Industry*, 21 J. Legal Stud. 115 (1992); Avner Greif, Institutions and the Path to the Modern Economy: Lessons from Medieval Trade (2006); Janet T. Landa, *A Theory of the Ethnically Homogeneous Middleman Group: An Institutional Alternative to Contract Law*, 10 J. Legal Stud. 349 (1981); Richman, *supra* note 1.
5. Lisa Bernstein, *Private Commercial Law in the Cotton Industry: Creating Cooperation through Rules, Norms, and Institutions*, 99 Mich. L. Rev. 1724 (2001); Lisa Bernstein, *Private Ordering, Social Capital and Network Governance in Procurement Contracts: A Preliminary Exploration*, 7 J. Legal Stud. 561 (2015); Robert C. Ellickson, *When Civil Society Uses an Iron Fist: The Roles of Private Associations in Rulemaking and Adjudication*, 18 Am. L. & Econ. Rev. 235 (2016).
6. Elinor Ostrom, Governing the Commons: The Evolution of Institutions for Collective Action 61–88 (1990); Richman, *supra* note 1, 120–125.
7. Alexis De Tocqueville, Democracy in America 101 (James T. Schleifer trans.)(2010).
8. *Id.*, 102.
9. Patricia H. Collins, *The New Politics of Community*, 75 Am. Soc. Rev. 7 (2010).
10. Suzanne Mettler, *Bringing the State Back In to Civic Engagement: Policy Feedback Effects of the GI Bill for World War II Veterans*, 96 Am. Pol. Sci. Rev. 351 (2002).
11. Theda Skocpol, Marshall Ganz, and Ziad Munson, *A Nation of Organizers: The Institutional Origins of Civic Voluntarism in the United States*, 94 Am. Pol. Sci. Rev. 527 (2000); Richard Brooks, and Timothy W. Guinnane, *The Right to Associate and the Rights of Associations: Civil-Society Organizations in Prussia, 1794–1908, in* Organizations, Civil Society, and the Roots of Development 291 (Naomi R. Lamoreaux and John Joseph Wallis eds., 2017).
12. Christopher Capozzola, Uncle Sam Wants You: World War I and the Making of the Modern American Citizen (2008); Skocpol, Ganze & Munson, ibid.
13. Theda Skocpol, *The Elite and Popular Roots of Contemporary Republican Extremism, in* Upending American Politics: Polarizing Parties, Ideological Elites, and Citizen Activists from the Tea Party to the Anti-Trump Resistance 3 (Theda Skocpol, Caroline Tervo eds., 2020).
14. Anne Applebaum, Iron Curtain: The Crushing of Eastern Europe (2012).
15. Evan Schofer, and Marion Fourcade-Gourinchas, *The Structural Contexts of Civic Engagement: Voluntary Association Membership in Comparative Perspective*, 66 Am. Soc. Rev. 806 (2001).
16. Jessica C. Teets, *Let Many Civil Societies Bloom: The Rise of Consultative Authoritarianism in China*, 213 China Q. 19 (2013).
17. Andrew Mertha, *Fragmented Authoritarianism 2.0: Political Pluralization in the Chinese Policy Process*, 200 The China Quarterly 995 (2009); Anthony J. Spires, *Contingent Symbiosis and Civil Society in an Authoritarian State: Understanding the Survival of China's Grassroots NGOs*, 117 Am. J. Soc. 1 (2011).
18. Tocqueville, *supra* note 7.

19. Lily L. Tsai, Accountability Without Democracy: Solidary Groups and Public Goods Provision in Rural China (2007).
20. Rajan, *supra* note 1, xxii.
21. Tocqueville, *supra* note 7, 102.
22. Putnam, Making Democracy Work, *supra* note 2.
23. Putnam, Bowling Alone, *supra* note 2.
24. Daniel Immerwahr, Thinking Small: The United States and the Lure of Community Development (2015).
25. Jacob T. Levy, *Pluralism without Privilege: Corps Intermédiaires, Civil Society, and the Art of Association*, *in* Organizations, Civil Society, and the Roots of Development (Naomi R. Lamoreaux and John Joseph Wallis eds., 2017)
26. Dylan Riley, *Civic Associations and Authoritarian Regimes in Interwar Europe: Italy and Spain in Comparative Perspective*, 70 Am. Soc. Rev. 288 (2005).
27. Daniel C. Mattingly, The Art of Political Control in China (2019).
28. *Id.*
29. Luigi Tomba, The Government Next Door: Neighborhood Politics in Urban China (2014).
30. Teets, *supra* note 16; Spires, *supra* note 17.
31. Yongshun Cai & Zhiming Sheng, *Homeowners' Activism in Beijing: Leaders with Mixed Motivations*, 215 China Q. 513 (2013); Zhengxu Wang, et al., *Leadership in China's Urban Middle Class Protest: The Movement to Protect Homeowners' Rights in Beijing*, 214 China Q. 411 (2013); Ngai Ming Yip, *Housing Activism in Urban China: The Quest for Autonomy in Neighbourhood Governance*, 34 Housing Stud. 1635 (2019).
32. Benjamin L. Read, *Democratizing the Neighborhood? New Private Housing and Homeowner Self-Organization in Urban China*, 49 China J. 31 (2003).
33. Tomba, *supra* note 29.
34. Reed, *supra* note 32.
35. Dietrich Rueschemeyer, Peter B. Evans, and Theda Skocpol, eds., Bringing the State Back In (1985); Theda Skocpol, *Bringing the State Back in: Retrospect and Prospect The 2007 Johan Skytte Prize Lecture*, 31 Scandinavian Pol. Stud. 109 (2008).
36. Shitong Qiao, *The Authoritarian Commons: Divergent Paths of Neighborhood Democratization in Three Chinese Megacities*, 71 Am. J. Comp. L. 388 (2023).
37. Douglas D. Heckathorn, *Respondent-Driven Sampling: A New Approach to the Study of Hidden Populations*, 44 Soc. Probs. 174 (1997).
38. David P. Lindstrom, *How Representative Are Snowball Samples? Using the Ethnosurvey to Study Guatemala–US Migration*, 666 Annals Am. Acad. Pol. & Soc. Sci. 64 (2016); Alexander Kroll, et al., *Mitigating the Negative Effects of Emotional Labor: A Study of Disaster Response and Recovery Workers after the 2010 Haiti Earthquake*, 34 Governance 87 (2021).
39. Jens Hainmueller, *Entropy Balancing for Causal Effects: A Multivariate Reweighting Method to Produce Balanced Samples in Observational Studies*, 20 Pol. Analysis 25 (2012); Rory Truex, *The Returns to Office in a "Rubber Stamp" Parliament*, 108 Am. Pol. Sci. Rev. 235 (2014).
40. Susan S. Silbey, *The Sociological Citizen: Pragmatic and Relational Regulation in Law and Organizations*, 5 Reg. & Governance 1 (2011).

41. Qiao, *supra* note 36.
42. Interview No. SH-HO-062818-7.
43. *Id.*
44. Interview No. SH-HO-062818-6.
45. *See* Table A.3 in the Appendix.
46. I construct an alternative measure of homeowners' activism based on the number of hours spent on neighborhood affairs per week. Respondents who work zero to ten hours are then coded as nonactivists and the rest who work over ten hours as activists.
47. *See* Table A.3 in the Appendix.
48. Descriptive statistics show that 75 percent of homeowner activists report that they would comply with a legally passed majority decision if they were on the losing side of the voting process, and then seek to change the decision through legal means. Nonetheless, only 67 percent of ordinary homeowners chose the option. The difference is statistically significant. Instead, 18 percent of nonactivists chose to respect their individual freedom and not comply with the majority decision. Thirteen percent of them chose to challenge the decision by convening another meeting or through court.
49. For the mediation analysis method we used, *see* Kosuke Imai et al., *Unpacking the Black Box of Causality: Learning about Causal Mechanisms from Experimental and Observational Studies*, 105 AM. POL. SCI. REV. 765 (2011). When *Government collusion* is included in the model as the alternative measure of perception of government support for HoAs, it explains 29.4 percent of activists' political trust. Detailed results are reported in Table A.8 in the Appendix II.
50. Sonja Zmerli and Ken Newton, *Social Trust and Attitudes Toward Democracy*, 72 PUB. OPINION Q. 706 (2008).
51. Mark S. Granovetter, *The Strength of Weak Ties*, 78 AM. J. SOCIO. 1360 (1973).
52. Zmerli and Newton, *supra* note 50.

7 Neighborhood Governance during China's COVID Lockdowns

1. Fang Ning (房宁), 抗疫斗争彰显中国制度优势 [The Fight Against the Pandemic Showed the Advantage of the Chinese Government], 《人民日报》 [PEOPLE'S DAILY], September 17, 2020, www.xinhuanet.com/politics/2020-09/17/c_1126503619.htm.
2. Hualing Fu, *Pandemic Control in China's Gated Communities*, in HOW COVID-19 TOOK OVER THE WORLD: LESSONS FOR THE FUTURE WITH COMPARATIVE PERSPECTIVES FROM HEALTH, POLITICS, AND SOCIO-ECONOMICS 9 (Christine Loh ed., 2022); Victor C. Shih, *China's Leninist Response to Covid-19 from Information Repression to Total Mobilization*, In CORONAVIRUS POLITICS: THE COMPARATIVE POLITICS AND POLICY OF COVID-19 67(SCOTT L. GREER, ET AL., EDS., 2021); Yuen Yuen Ang, *When COVID-19 Meets Centralized, Personalized Power*, 4 NAT. HUM. BEHAV. 445 (2020).
3. *See, e.g.*, Stephen Thomson & Eric C. Ip, *COVID-19 Emergency Measures and the Impending Authoritarian Pandemic*, J. L. & BIOSCIENCES, January–June 2020, at lsaa064.

4. Cissy Zhou, et al., *Inside Shanghai's COVID Lockdown Nightmare: China's Zero-COVID Policy Devastated the Commercial Capital*, NIKKEI ASIA, June 22, 2022, https://asia.nikkei.com/Spotlight/The-Big-Story/Inside-Shanghai-s-COVID-lockdown-nightmare.
5. Xi Jinping, (习近平), 习近平给武汉东湖新城社区全体社区工作者的回信 [Xi Jinping's Reply to All Community Workers in Wuhan's East Lake New Town Community], XINHUA NET, April 9, 2020, www.xinhuanet.com/politics/2020-04/09/c_1125832314.htm.
6. Benjamin L. Read, *Democratizing the Neighborhood? New Private Housing and Home-Owner Self-organization in urban China*, 49 CHINA J. 31 (2003).
7. *See, e.g.*, Peter Hessler, *What Chinese People Think of Their Government's "Zero COVID" Policy*, www.newyorker.com/news/news-desk/what-chinese-people-think-of-their-governments-zero-covid-policy.
8. *See, e.g.*, Frances Mao, *China Abandons Key Parts of Zero-Covid Strategy after Protests*, BBC, December 7, 2022, www.bbc.com/news/world-asia-china-63855508
9. *Id.*
10. Yutian An & Taisu Zhang, *Pandemic State-building: Chinese Administrative Expansion Since 2012*, YALE L. & POL'Y REV. (Forthcoming 2024) at 2, Available at SSRN: https://ssrn.com/abstract=4356026 or http://dx.doi.org/10.2139/ssrn.4356026.
11. *See infra* Section 7.1.2.
12. *Id.*
13. *Id.*
14. For the relationship between legibility and state capacity, *see* Melissa M. Lee, and Nan Zhang, *Legibility and the Informational Foundations of State Capacity*, 79 J. POLITICS 118 (2017).
15. JAMES C. SCOTT, SEEING LIKE A STATE: HOW CERTAIN SCHEMES TO IMPROVE THE HUMAN CONDITION HAVE FAILED (1998).
16. Sarah Zheng, *The Messy Afterlife of China's Covid Health Codes*, BLOOMBERG, August 16, 2023, www.bloomberg.com/news/articles/2023-08-16/china-begins-to-grapple-with-its-covid-data-collection-machine?embedded-checkout=true.
17. Interview No. CIWH01342523.
18. Yuan (Daniel) Chen et al., *Coproducing Responses to COVID-19 with Community-based Organizations: Lessons from Zhejiang Province, China*. 80 PUB. ADMIN. R. 866 (2020).
19. Haiqing Yu, *Living in the Era of Codes: A Reflection on China's Health Code System*, BIOSOCIETIES, Dec. 2022 at 1; Phoebe Zhang, *The Colour-coded Covid App that's Become Part of Life in China – Despite the Red Flags*, SOUTH CHINA MORNING POST (April 5, 2022), www.scmp.com/news/china/science/article/3173123/colour-coded-covid-app-thats-become-part-life-china-despite-red.
20. *See, e.g.*, *China Axes Travel Tracking App in Latest Easing of Covid Curbs*, CNBC, December 13, 2022, www.cnbc.com/2022/12/13/china-axes-travel-tracking-app-in-latest-easing-of-covid-curbs.html.
21. Interview No. CIWH0386723.
22. Interview No. CIWH0064623.
23. Interview No. CISZ00522723.
24. *Id.*

25. 广州：不以时空伴随划定密接，核酸检测不扩大范围 [Guangzhou will no longer classify "close contact in time and space" as close contacts, refrain from expanding the scope of compulsory COVID testing], 财新网 [Caixin Net], November 30, 2022, https://m.caixin.com/m/2022-11-30/101972493.html.
26. Interview No. CIWH0386723.
27. Interview No. CIWH00941123.
28. *Id.*
29. Interview No. CISZ00331123.
30. *Id.*
31. Jean Christopher Mittelstaedt, *The Grid Management System in Contemporary China: Grass-roots Governance in Social Surveillance and Service Provision*, 36 China Info. 3 (2022).
32. In 2013, the CCP Central Committee introduced a resolution on comprehensively deepening reform, which incorporated the concept of grid management. 中共中央关于全面深化改革若干重大问题的决定 [The Central Committee of the Communist Party of China's Decision on Some Major Issues Concerning Comprehensively Deepening Reforms] (promulgated by Third Plenary Session 18th Central Committee Communist Party China, November 12, 2013), www.ce.cn/xwzx/gnsz/szyw/201311/18/t20131118_1767104.shtml (Aiming toward grid-based management and socialized services, improve the grassroots comprehensive service management platform). It was reported that Wuhan and Shanghai were pioneers of the grid management system. Wang Xuezhu (王雪竹), 基层社会治理：从网格化管理到网络化治理[*Grassroots Social Governance: From Grid-based Management to Networked Governance*], 北京党建研究基地 [Research Centre for Beijing Party Building) (March 16, 2022), https://rcbpb.bac.gov.cn/news/voice/detail-c63-aid601.html. However, in Shanghai, residents seemed to be unaware of the existence of grid managers, indicating that they did not play a significant role in neighborhood governance. Interview No. CISH03241822.
33. Interview No. CIWH0175123.
34. Interview No. CIWH0205923.
35. Interview No. CIWH01242323.
36. Interview No. CISZ00631923.
37. Interview No. CIWH02251123.
38. Interview No. CISZ00331123.
39. *Id.*
40. *Id.*
41. *Id.*
42. Interview No. CISZ00631923.
43. Interview No. CIWH01242323; Interview No. CIWH01141823; Interview No. CIFS0015523.
44. Interview No. CIWH0205923.
45. Interview No. CISZ00422723.
46. *Id.*
47. *Id.*
48. Interview No. CISZ00331123.
49. *Id.*
50. *Id.*

51. 湖北14名新冠肺炎疫情防控一线牺牲人员被评定为首批烈士 [*Hubei's 14 Frontline Casualties in the Prevention and Control of the Noval Coronavirus Pneumonia Outbreak Were Assessed as the First Batch of Martyrs*], Xinhua Net, April 2, 2020, www.gov.cn/xinwen/2020-04/02/content_5498352.htm; 全国各地各族人民深切悼念抗击新冠肺炎疫情斗争牺牲烈士和逝世同胞 [*The People of All Ethnic Groups in All Parts of the Country Deeply Mourn the Martyrs and Compatriots Who Died in the Fight Against the Novel Coronavirus Pneumonia Epidemic*], Xinhua Net, April 4, 2020, www.xinhuanet.com/politics/2020-04/04/c_1125813957.htm.
52. Interview No. CISZ00331123.
53. *Id.*
54. *Id.*
55. *Id.*; *see* also 广州海珠区数百民众冲出封控区上街抗议与警方发生冲突 [Protesters Confronted Police in Haizhu District of Guangzhou], www.zaobao.com.sg/news/china/story20221116-1333559.
56. 守严守牢疫情防控的关键防线——全国城市社区党组织和广大党员全力打好疫情防控人民战争 [*Defend the Frontline of Pandemic Control: Community Party Organizations and Party Members Spare No Effort to Win the "People's War" of Stopping the Virus Spreading*], 新华社 [Xinhua Press] March 10, 2020, www.gov.cn/xinwen/2020-03/10/content_5489735.htm.
57. *Id.*
58. Interview No. CIWH02551223.
59. Interview No. CIWH01242323.
60. *Id.*
61. For research on the government's use of such thugs for other purposes before the pandemic, *see* Lynette H. Ong, *Thugs and Outsourcing of State Repression in China*. 80 China J. 94 (2018).
62. Interview No. CIFS0015523.
63. Interview No. CISZ00331123.
64. *Id.*
65. David Pierson et al., *China's Latest Source of Unrest: Unpaid "Zero Covid" Workers*, N. Y. Times, January 16, 2023, www.nytimes.com/2023/01/16/world/asia/china-covid-protests.html.
66. Interview No. CISZ00331123.
67. Interview No. CISZ00761523; Laura He, *China's Cities Are Running Out of Cash to Pay Huge Covid Lockdown Bills*, CNN, December 2, 2022, www.cnn.com/2022/12/02/economy/china-zero-covid-sustainability-debt-woes-intl-hnk/index.html#:~:text=They%20spent%2011.8%20trillion%20yuan,threat%20to%20China's%20economic%20health.
68. Interview No. CISH00862023.
69. Interview No. CIWH0396923.
70. *Id.*
71. Kenneth Lieberthal & Michel Oksenberg, Policy Making in China: Leaders, Structures, and Processes (1988); Andrew Mertha, *"Fragmented Authoritarianism 2.0": Political Pluralization in the Chinese Policy Process*, 200 China Q. 995 (2009).
72. Interview No. CIWH02551223.

73. Interview No. CISZ00331123.
74. Interview No. CISZ00631923.
75. Interview No. CISZ00331123; Interview No. CISH0207323.
76. Interview No. CIWH0175123.
77. Interview No. CIWH01242323.
78. Interview No. CIWH02251123.
79. *Id.*
80. Interview No. CIWH01141823.
81. Interview No. CIWH01542923.
82. Interview No. CIWH03152323.
83. 上海严打伪造买卖涉疫通行证违法犯罪 [*Shanghai Cracks Down on Illegal Crimes of Forging and Trading Epidemic-Related Permits*], SHANGHAI MUNICIPAL PUBLIC SECURITY BUREAU (May 1, 2022), https://gaj.sh.gov.cn/shga/wzXxfbGj/detail?pa=27cfd74b74a64343a2744fa74bed4a46e134015f1d110cf85fa654f099b205c182d91bf6eb1e07394f8d5649415718f5.
84. Interview No. CIWH02351123.
85. Interview No. CIZZ00412723; Interview No. CIZZ00512723.
86. Interview No. CIWH01141823.
87. Interview No. CISH00471523.
88. Robert Axelrod & William D. Hamilton, *The Evolution of Cooperation*, 211 SCIENCE 1390 (1981).
89. Interview No. CISH03241822.
90. ROBERT ELLICKSON, ORDER WITHOUT LAW (1991).
91. *See, e.g.,* 关于疫情防控期间社区团购相关法律问题的问答——嘉法涉疫法律适用问题系列研究之二 [*Q&A on Legal Issues Related to Community Group Buying During Epidemic Prevention and Control Period – Study Series on the Application of Law in Epidemic-related Matters by Jiafa, Part Two*], 上海嘉定法院 [SHANGHAI JIADING DIST. CT. WECHAT ACCOUNT], April 18, 2022, https://mp.weixin.qq.com/s?__biz=MzIwNzExNTI5MA==&mid=2649789680&idx=1&sn=156ca89ea244056929702baaba3d4e3f&scene=21#wechat_redirect.
92. Interview No. CIZZ00312823; Interview No. CIWH0375523; Interview No. CIWH01041223; Interview No. CIWH02251123.
93. Interview No. CISH03241822.
94. Interview No. CISH0338223.
95. Interview No. CISH00522723.
96. *Id.*
97. Interview No. CISH0137123.
98. Zhongjie Li et al., *Comprehensive Large-Scale Nucleic Acid–Testing Strategies Support China's Sustained Containment of COVID-19*, 27 NATURE MEDICINE 740 (2021).
99. Interview No. CIWH00332623.
100. Interview No. CISH01272223.
101. Interview No. CISH0177223.
102. Interview No. CIWH00131823.
103. Interview No. CIWH01342523.
104. Interview No. CIWH00131823.
105. *Id.*

106. *Id.*
107. *Id.*
108. *Id.*
109. *Id.*
110. Interview No. CIWH02251123.
111. Interview No. CIWH00451123.
112. *Id.*
113. Some scholars would call such an approach "the art of political control." DANIEL C. MATTINGLY, THE ART OF POLITICAL CONTROL IN CHINA (2020).
114. Interview No. CIZZ00412723.
115. *Id.*
116. Dake Kang, *Ignoring Experts, China's Sudden Zero-COVID Exit Cost Lives*, AP NEWS, March 23, 2023, https://apnews.com/article/zero-covid-exit-china-reopening-investigation-abridged-d7e7cf42b8f4b97e2744b640f431a7df.
117. Sabrina Tavernise, *China's Abrupt Reversal of "Zero Covid,"* N. Y. TIMES., January 17, 2023, www.nytimes.com/2023/01/17/podcasts/the-daily/china-zero-covid-outbreak-xi-jingping.html?showTranscript=1.
118. *See, e.g., Protests in Shanghai as Anger Mounts over China's "Zero-Covid" Lockdown Policy*, FRANCE24, November 27, 2022, www.france24.com/en/asia-pacific/20221127-protests-in-shanghai-as-anger-mounts-over-china-s-zero-covid-policy.
119. Yuan Li (袁莉), 那些年轻的抗议者 [Those Young Protesters: Why We Took to the Streets], 不明白播客 [BUMINGBAI PODCAST], November 29, 2022, https://github.com/bumingbaipod/podcast/blob/df97e856e557d25a8948b63424e6cdfee4410b49/EP-027-%E9%82%A3%E4%BA%9B%E5%B9%B4%E8%BD%BB%E7%9A%84%E6%8A%97%E8%AE%AE%E8%80%85-%E6%88%91%E4%BB%AC%E4%B8%BA%E4%BB%80%E4%B9%88%E8%A6%81%E4%B8%8A%E8%A1%97.md.
120. 上海汇贤居打响"自行解封"第一枪 [*Shanghai Huixianju Fired the First Shot of "Self-unsealing"*], 《联合早报》 [LIANHE ZAOBAO], May 24, 2022, www.kzaobao.com/shiju/20220524/117723.html.
121. *Id.*
122. *Id.*
123. 新冠疫情下的立法建议——多位学者呼吁再启紧急状态法立法 [*Legislative Proposals in the Context of the Novel Coronavirus Epidemic: A Number of Scholars Call for the Reintroduction of Emergency Law Legislation*], 《南方都市报》 [SOUTHERN METROPOLIS DAILY], March 14, 2020, https://m.mp.oeeee.com/a/BAAFRD000020200314283719.html.
124. *See* 全国人大常委会法工委就疫情防控有关法律问题再次发声 [The Legal Affairs Commission of the Standing Committee of the National People's Congress (NPC) spoke out again on legal issues related to epidemic prevention and control], 人大新闻网 [NATIONAL PEOPLE'S CONGRESS NEWS], March 6, 2020, http://npc.people.com.cn/n1/2020/0306/c14576-31619969.html.
125. Social Media Video: Volunteers in Shanghai's Xuhui District Refused to Come to the Door to Put Seals On (上海徐汇区志愿者拒绝上门贴封条), on file with the author.
126. *Id.*
127. Interview No. CIWH01141823.

128. *Id.*
129. Yan Senlin (颜森林), 一个北京小区被"临时管控"后争取解封的经过 [*A Beijing Neighborhood under "Temporary Control" and its Struggle to be Unblocked*], 中国数字时代 [China Digit. Times] (November 26, 2022), https://chinadigitaltimes.net/chinese/690149.html.
130. *Id.*
131. Interview No. CISZ00231023.
132. *Id.*
133. *Id.*
134. *Id.*
135. *Id.*
136. Fragrant Hill Homeowners' Association, 依法抗疫倡议书 [*Initiative to Fight Epidemics in Accordance with the Law*], No. XSMSYWH(2022)057, (November 29, 2022) (on file with the author).
137. Interview No. CISZ00231023.
138. *Id.*
139. Interview No. CIFS0015523; Interview No. CIWH00841023; Interview No. CIWH01141823; Interview No. CISH0137123.
140. Video: 北京市昌平区北七家镇枫树家园社区居民委员会办公室门口台阶上, 业主女子用喇叭向门口聚集的其他居民喊话 [On the steps in front of the office of the Maple Home Community Residents' Committee in Beiqijia Township, Changping District, Beijing, the Owner's Woman Used a Loudspeaker to Shout at Other Residents Gathered at the Doorway], (November 26, 2022) (on file with the author).
141. Interview No. CIWH00841023; Interview No. CIWH01141823.
142. Interview No. CIZZ00112923.
143. Interview No. CIFS0015523.
144. *See Shanghai Huixianju Fired the First Shot of "Self-unsealing," supra* note 120.
145. Interview No. CISH0147123.
146. 治安管理处罚法 [Law of Administrative Punishment on Public Security Offenses] (China), art. 83.
147. The Supreme People's Procuratorate publicized eighteen series of typical cases during Covid, which regularly include cases of disrupting government work (妨害公务罪). I examined all these cases and found that violently attacking a government worker was a common element.
148. Interview No. CIWH0386723.
149. Video: 2022年11月28日，上海某小区出现确诊病例，物业对整个小区进行封控，业主报警 [On November 28, 2022, There Was a Confirmed Case of the Disease in a Neighborhood in Shanghai, and the Property Owners Sealed Off the Entire Neighborhood, and the Owners Called the Police], on file with the author.
150. Interview No. CISZ00231023.
151. *Id.*
152. Fragrant Hill Homeowners' Association, 关于业主委员会发布《依法抗疫倡议书》的作废说明 [*Note on the Nullification of the Issuance of the Initiative to Fight the Epidemic in Accordance with the Law by the Fragrant Hill Mansion Homeowners' Association*] (on file with author)

153. Interview No. CISZ00231023. The HoC chairman was sneaky: He asked the government to draft the letter for him and then put the official seal of the HoA on such a letter immediately upon receiving it. The trick was the formality: The first letter was much more formal and longer with a document series number and the second one was much shorter, looked much more informal and in a rush.
154. *Id.*
155. 国家主席习近平发表二〇二三年新年贺词 [*President Xi Jinping Delivers a New Year's Address for the Year 2023*],中华人民共和国中央人民政府 [Central People's Government of the People's Republic of China], December 31, 2022, www.gov.cn/gongbao/content/2023/content_5736705.htm.
156. Social Media Video, *supra* note 125.
157. *Id.*
158. Social media video: 长风三村居民与书记对话, on file with the author.
159. *Id.*
160. *Id.*
161. *Id.*
162. *Id.*
163. James C. Scott, Weapons of the Weak: Everyday Forms of Peasant Resistance (1985).
164. *Id.*
165. *Id.* at Preface, xvi.
166. *See* Section 7.3.
167. Kevin J. O'Brien & Lianjiang Li, Rightful Resistance in Rural China (2006).
168. *How Xi Jinping is Mobilising the Masses to Control Themselves*, Economist, November 10, 2022, www.economist.com/china/2022/11/10/how-xi-jinping-is-mobilising-the-masses-to-control-themselves.
169. Mattingly, *supra* note 113.
170. Lynette H. Ong, Outsourcing Repression: Everyday State Power in Contemporary China (2022).
171. *Id.*
172. Rajat K. Ray, *Masses in Politics: The Non-Cooperation Movement in Bengal 1920–1922*, 11 Indian Econ. Soc. Hist. Rev. 343 (1974).

8 Contesting Party Leadership

1. 《人民日报》(People's Daily), "党政军民学，东西南北中，党是领导一切的" [The Party Leads Everything, in the Areas of Government, Military, Civilian Affairs, and Education, in the East, West, South, North, and Central Regions], 中国共产党新闻网 (CPC News) (February 14, 2022), http://dangjian.people.com.cn/n1/2022/0214/c117092-32351226.html.
2. *Id.*
3. Article One of the People's Republic of China Constitution (promulgated by the National People's Congress on December 4, 1982, amended by the National People's Congress on March 11, 2018).
4. Lauren Yu-Hsin Lin and Curtis J. Milhaupt, *Party Building or Noisy Signaling? The Contours of Political Conformity in Chinese Corporate Governance*, 50 J. Legal Stud. 187 (2021).

5. Ge Xin and Jie Huang, *Party Building in an Unlikely Place? The Adaptive Presence of the Chinese Communist Party in the Non-Governmental Organizations (NGOs)*, 31 J. Contemp. China 428 (2022).
6. Xiaojun Yan and Jie Huang, *Navigating Unknown Waters: The Chinese Communist Party's New Presence in the Private Sector*, 17 China Rev. 37 (2017).
7. 中共中央、国务院关于加强和完善城乡社区治理的意见 [The Central Committee of the Communist Party of China and the State Council's Opinions on Strengthening and Improving Urban and Rural Community Governance] (June 12, 2017), www.gov.cn/gongbao/content/2017/content_5204888.htm.
8. *Id.*
9. 中共中央办公厅印发《关于加强和改进城市基层党的建设工作的意见》 [The General Office of the Central Committee of the Communist Party of China has issued the Opinions on Strengthening and Improving the Work of Party Building at the Grassroots Level in Urban Areas] (May 8, 2019), www.gov.cn/zhengce/2019-05/08/content_5389836.htm.
10. 中共中央、国务院关于加强基层治理体系和治理能力现代化建设的意见 [Opinions of the Central Committee of the Communist Party of China and the State Council on Strengthening the Modernization of the Grassroots Governance System and Governance Capacity] (April 28, 2021).
11. *Id.*
12. *Id.*
13. 关于深化城市基层党建引领基层治理的若干措施(试行)中组发[2022]2号 [Several Measures (Pilot) on Deepening Urban Grassroots Party Building to Lead Grassroots Governance (Issued by the Organization Department, Political and Legal Affairs Commission, Ministry of Housing and Urban-Rural Development, Ministry of Civil Affairs on January 29, 2022)] (Zhong Zu Fa [2022] No. 2).
14. *See* 住房和城乡建设部等部门关于加强和改进住宅物业管理工作的通知 [建房规 (2020)10 号] [Notice from the Ministry of Housing and Urban-Rural Development and Other Departments on Strengthening and Improving Residential Property Management] [Jian Fang Gui (2020) No. 10] (December 5, 2020), www.gov.cn/zhengce/zhengceku/2021-01/05/content_5577326.htm.
15. In *Democracy by Petition*, Harvard political scientist Daniel Carpenter argues that in addition to institutional democracy, which focuses on elections and votes, there are procedural, organizational, and cultural facets of democracy. Petitions in nineteenth-century America contributed to all four facets of democracy but were particularly relevant for the last three. *See* Daniel Carpenter, Democracy by Petition: Popular Politics in Transformation, 1790–1870, 41 (2021).
16. 关于党建引领物业服务企业和业主委员会建设的指导意见的通知(京组通[2019]37号) [Notice on the Guidelines on Party Building Leading the Construction of Property Service Enterprises and Owners' Committees] (Jing Zu Tong [2019] No. 37) (promulgated by Organization Department of the Beijing Municipal Committee of the Communist Party of China on November 13, 2019); 关于进一步加强党建引领业主委员会建设的若干意见（上海） [Several Opinions on Further Strengthening Party Leadership in the Construction of Homeowners' Committees (Shanghai)] (promulgated by Shanghai Municipal Committee Organization Department on November 20, 2018), https://mp.weixin.qq.com/s/-K6d49-A30f-tlROKoEUbg; 深圳市住房和建设局关于推进住宅小区业主委员

会三年全覆盖的通知(深建物管〔2022〕24号) [Shenzhen Municipal Housing and Construction Bureau on Promoting the Three-Year Full Coverage of Owners' Committees in Residential Districts] (promulgated by the Shenzhen Municipal Bureau of Housing and Construction on April 18, 2022).

17. Several Opinions on Further Strengthening Party Leadership (Shanghai), *id.*
18. Notice on the Guidelines on Party Building (Beijing), *supra* note 16.
19. 提问标题： 成立业主委员会必须有党员人数过半 [Question Title: Half of the party members are required to set up an owners' association], 北京市住房和城乡建设委员会 [Beijing Municipal Commission of Housing and Urban-rural Development] (March 16, 2021), www.beijing.gov.cn/hudong/yonghu/static/zfhcxjsw/dayi/detail.html?searchCode=zfhcxjsw16156398346022349256; 北京市物业管理条例 [Regulation of the Beijing Municipality on Property Management] (promulgated by the Standing Committee of the People's Congress of the Beijing Municipality on March 27, 2020, effective on May 1, 2020), art. 3.
20. Interview with a Beijing homeowner activist, Beijing, March 21, 2023 (BJ001).
21. Interview with a Shanghai HoC leader, Shanghai, July 13, 2023 (SH003).
22. Interview with a Shanghai homeowner activist, Shanghai, July 1, 2023 (SH034).
23. Interview with a Shenzhen third-party organization leader, Shenzhen, March 9, 2023 (SZ001); interview with a chairperson of a homeowners' organization, Shenzhen, March 10, 2023 (SZ002); interview with a member of a homeowners' organization, Shenzhen, February 27, 2023 (SZ005).
24. Interview with a deputy community secretary, Shenzhen, February 27, 2023 (SZ004).
25. Carpenter, *supra* note 15, Preface.
26. *Id.*
27. *Id.*, at 31.
28. "Introduction into Politics," in Jerome Kohn ed., The Promise of Politics 97 (2005), cited in Carpenter, *supra* note 15, at 40.
29. 关于改进《关于做好"三个典型"培育工作的通知》的建议 [Suggestions for improving the Circular on the Cultivation of the "Three Typicals"] (promulgated by the Hefei Housing Security and Real Estate Administration on April 30, 2020), https://mp.weixin.qq.com/s/P9IQ9YlkVK56QG0tGz6YqA.
30. Interview with a leader of a Hefei-based homeowner organization, Hefei, March 10, 2023 (Interview No. HF002).
31. Interview No. HF002, *ibid*; Interview with a leader of a Hefei-based homeowner organization, Hefei, March 6, 2023 (HF003).
32. Interview No. HF003, *id.*
33. Interview No. HF002, *supra* note 30.
34. 联名信 安徽业主因党员比例、公共收益等问题通过信访上书安徽省省长 [Joint Letter of the Anhui Owners Petitioning the Anhui Governor Through Letters and Petitions over the Party Quota, Public Revenue, and More]. A screenshot of the online petition is on file with the author.
35. Interview No. HF002, *supra* note 30.
36. The full text of the petition, dated May 26, 2020, is on file with the author.
37. Interview No. HF002, *supra* note 30.
38. Screenshot of the reply, dated June 3, 2020, is on file with the author.
39. 刘媛媛 [Liu Yuanyuan], 社居委参与小区公共收益"共管"是否"共责"? 合肥市房产局回应 [Did the Neighborhood Committee Co-Manage Community Public

Revenue in an Act of "Shared Responsibility"? The Hefei Real Estate Bureau's Response], 《安徽商报》 [ANHUI BUSINESS NEWS], June 24, 2020, www.ahnews.com.cn/hefei/pc/con/2020-06/24/565_213954.html.

40. 中共中央关于全面深化改革若干重大问题的决定 [Decision of the Central Committee of the Communist Party of China on Several Major Issues Concerning the Comprehensive Deepening of Reform] (adopted at the Third Plenary Session of the 18th Central Committee of the Communist Party of China on November 12, 2013), www.gov.cn/jrzg/2013-11/15/content_2528179.htm; 《法制日报》 [LEGAL DAILY], 规范性文件合法性审核机制全面推行 [*The Mechanism for Reviewing the Legality of Normative Documents Is Fully Implemented*], 中华人民共和国司法部 [PRC MINISTRY OF JUSTICE] (August 8, 2019), www.moj.gov.cn/pub/sfbgw/qmyfzg/201908/t20190828_150366.html.
41. Legal Daily, *supra* note 40.
42. Ibid.
43. 新华社 [Xinhua News Agency], 关于国务院机构改革方案的说明 [*Explanation of the institutional reform program of the State Council*], 中华人民共和国中央人民政府 [PRC Central People's Government Website] (March 14, 2018), www.gov.cn/guowuyuan/2018-03/14/content_5273856.htm.
44. 朱宁宁 [Zhu Ningning], 宪法日，备案审查网络直通车正式开通：公民可一键提交审查建议 [On Constitution Day, the Record Review Network Was Officially Opened: Citizens Can Submit Review Proposals with a Single Keystroke], 澎湃 [THE PAPERS] (December 5, 2019), www.thepaper.cn/newsDetail_forward_5160957.
45. 规范性文件不合法，公民可提审查建议！广东人大加强备案审查力度 [*Citizens Can Make Review Proposals If Normative Documents Are Not Legal! Guangdong NPC Strengthens Record Review*], 《南方都市报》[SOUTHERN METROPOLIS DAILY] (May 7, 2019), https://static.nfapp.southcn.com/content/201905/07/c2197286.html.
46. Zhu, *supra* note 44.
47. Interview with an initiator of a homeowners' committee, Yinchuan, February 5, 2023 (Interview No. YC001).
48. 银川市司法局关于《规范性文件合法性审查申请书》的答复书 [Yinchuan Municipal Bureau of Justice's Reply to the Application for a Review of the Legality of Normative Documents] (September 30, 2022). The document is on file with the author.
49. 业主委员会组建、运行和管理的指导意见（试行）(银住建规发[2019]2号) [Guidelines on the Formation, Operation, and Management of Owners' Committees (for Trial Implementation) (Yinzhu Jianzhifa [2019] No. 2)] (promulgated by the Yinchuan Housing and Urban-Rural Development Bureau on January 4, 2023) (pre- and post-review versions). The document is on file with the author.
50. YC001, *supra* note 47.
51. Interview with an HoC Chairman, Huizhou, Sept.25, 2023 (Interview No. HuiZ001).
52. 惠州市住房和城乡建设局等部门《关于加强和改进住宅物业管理工作的通知》惠市住建[2021]141号 [The Huizhou Municipal Housing and Urban-Rural Development Bureau and Other Departments' Notice on Strengthening and Improving the Work of Residential Property Management] (Huizhou Municipal Housing and Construction [2021] No. 141). The document is on file with the author.

53. 惠州市住房和城乡建设局、中共惠州市委组织部《关于全面推进住宅小区党建提升城市基层治理现代化水平的实施意见》惠市住建[2021]158号 [The Huizhou Municipal Bureau of Housing and Urban-Rural Development and the Organization Department of the Huizhou Municipal Committee of the Communist Party of China (CPC) Implementing Opinions on Comprehensively Promoting Party Building in Residential Communities to Enhance the Modernization of Urban Grassroots Governance] (Huizhou City Housing Construction [2021] No. 158). The document is on file with the author.
54. Interview No. HuiZ001, *supra* note 51.
55. Id.
56. Reply of the Guangdong People's Congress Standing Committee, dated Sept 9, 2022. A screenshot of this reply is on file with the author.
57. 惠州市司法局回复电话的录音 [Recording of the Huizhou Municipal Department of Justice Response Call, July 10, 2022]. The recording is on file with the author.
58. 惠州市住房和城乡建设局等部门关于废止《关于加强和改进住宅物业管理工作的通知》的通知，惠市住建[2022]125号 [Notice of the Huizhou Municipal Housing and Urban-Rural Development Bureau and Other Departments on the Abolition of the Circular on Strengthening and Improving the Work of Residential Property Management] [Huizhou Municipal Housing and Construction (2022) No. 125]. The document is on file with the author.
59. 惠阳区淡水街道办社区建设办:关于湖滨花园小区现届业委会主任不是业主身份的问题的整改通知 [Neighborhood Building Office of Danshui Street of Huiyang District, Rectification notice on the non-homeowner status of the chairperson of the Lakeshore Garden HoC] (September 9, 2022). The document is on file with the author.
60. Interview No. HuiZ001, *supra* note 51.
61. 广东省人大常委会法制工作委员会备案审查处答复 [Reply of the Guangdong Provincial People's Congress Standing Committee of the Legislative Affairs Commission for the Record Review Division] (January 18, 2023). The document is on file with the author.
62. 惠州市住房和城乡建设局、中共惠州市委组织部：《关于落实〈关于全面推进住宅小区党建提升城市基层治理现代化水平的实施意见〉的补充通知》惠市住建[2022]179号 [The Huizhou Municipal Bureau of Housing and Urban-Rural Development and the Organization Department of the CPC Huizhou Municipal Committee: Supplementary Notice on the Implementation of the Opinions on Comprehensively Promoting Party Building in Residential Communities to Enhance the Modernization of Urban Grassroots Governance] (Huizhou City Housing Construction [2022] No. 179). The document is on file with the author.
63. 业委会主任与惠州市住建局法规科严科长沟通修改"业主大会和业主委员会指导规则" [HoC Chairman Communicated with Mr. Yan, Director of the Codes and Regulations Division of the Huizhou Municipal Housing and Urban Renewal Bureau, to revise the "Guidelines for Homeowner Associations and Homeowner Committees"], October 28, 2022. The recording is on file with the author.
64. 惠州市住房和城乡建设局、中共惠州市委组织部：《关于废止〈关于全面推进住宅小区党建提升城市基层治理现代化水平的实施意见〉等文件的通知》，惠市住建[2023]40号 [Huizhou Municipal Housing and Urban-Rural

Development Bureau, CPC Huizhou Municipal Committee Organization Department: On the Abolition of the Document Entitled “On the Comprehensive Promotion of Residential District Party Building to Enhance the Implementation of the Modernization of the Urban Grass-Roots Governance Level” and Other Documents Related to the Notice] [Huizhou City Housing and Construction [2023] No. 40]. The document is on file with the author.

9 Associations beyond Neighborhoods and Property

1. Richard Brooks & Timothy W. Guinnane, *The Right to Associate and the Rights of Associations: Civil-Society Organizations in Prussia, 1794–1908*, in ORGANIZATIONS, CIVIL SOCIETY, AND THE ROOTS OF DEVELOPMENT 291 (Naomi R. Lamoreaux & John Joseph Wallis eds., 2017).
2. LEE ANNE FENNELL, THE UNBOUNDED HOME: PROPERTY VALUES BEYOND PROPERTY LINES (2009).
3. *See,* e.g., Hongyan Gu, *Nimbyism in China: Issues and Prospects of Public Participation in Facility Siting*, 52 LAND USE POL’Y 527(2016).
4. Interview No. BJ-HO-080218-2.
5. *Id.*
6. Gu, *supra* note 3.
7. 陈幽鸿 (Chen Youhong), “深港西部通道接线工程”：环评事件中的博弈双赢 [Hong Kong-Shenzhen Western Corridor Link Project: A Win-Win Game in the EIA Incident], on file with the author.
8. *Id.*
9. Interview No. WH007.
10. Interview No. ZZ-HO-100618-2.
11. Interview No. HF002.
12. 成都市新兴社区发展中心 [Chengdu Xinxing Community Development Center], https://shop.quanming.me/app/index.php?i=4&c=entry&m=ewei_shopv2&do=mobile&r=diypage&id=472&v=164667.
13. Interview No. YC002.
14. Interview No. ZZ-HO-100618-1.
15. Interview No. ZZ-HO-100618-2.
16. *See* Section 9.3.2 of this chapter.
17. Interview No. BJ-HO-080518-5.
18. Interview No. BJ-HO-090720-17.
19. Interview No. BJ-HO-083020-18.
20. BJ-HO-090720-17, *supra* note 18.
21. Interview No. HF002.
22. Interview No. BJ-MC-041620.
23. *Id.*
24. *Id.*
25. Tianjin together with Shanghai, Beijing, and Chongqing are the four cities that are under the direct administration of the Chinese central government and administratively enjoy the status of provinces.
26. 《海南日报》 [Hainan Daily], 海南小区业委会成立比例不到三成 “难产”业委会 [*Hainan District Industry Committee Set Up Less Than 30% of The Proportion*

of "Difficult To Produce" Industry Committee], 新华网 [Xinhua Net], http://m.xinhuanet.com/hq/2019-07/19/c_1124771825.htm.

27. Similarly, in Liaoning, one of those "rust belt" provinces in northeast China, multiple city governments including Shenyang and Yinkou have been supportive for establishing citywide associations of HoAs as they urgently need homeowners to pay for the maintenance and upkeeping of neighborhoods built before the 1980s, in which time these cities were at the center of China's heavy industry. Establishing HoAs was a way to "develop a habit of paying for real estate management services" and "a spirit of taking care of their own neighborhoods." The problem in such cities is not too much homeowner mobilization but the opposite, too little mobilization while at the same time, individual homeowners blamed the government for not taking care of them in the increasing number of complaints filed.
28. Interview with a leader of an association of HoAs, Haikou, June 19, 2020, HK-HO-061920-1.
29. *See* Chapter 3, Section 3.2.2.
30. Interview No. ZZ-HO-100618-2.
31. 广东省华南和谐社区发展中心2017 年度年度检查报告书 [*Guangdong Province South China Harmonious Community Development Center 2017 Annual Inspection Report*], 广东省社会组织综合信息服务平台 [Guangdong Social Organization Comprehensive Information Service Platform], www.gdnpo.gov.cn/home/Pubbase/indexhjshow1new/gd001804301260003.
32. Interview No. SH-HO-020323-42.
33. *Id.*
34. *Id.*
35. *Id.*
36. 杜茂文 (Du Maowen), 我的竞选宣言[*My Election Manifesto*], on file with the author.
37. Interview No. BJ-HO-080518-5, supra note 17; *see* also 舒可心 (Shu Kexin), 民主从社区开始, 居住改变中国(上) [*Democracy Begins in the Community, Residence Transforms China (Volume 1)*], on file with the author.
38. 许志永的美好中国之五：把权利当真——竞选人大代表 [*Xu Zhiyong's Better China No. 5: Taking Rights Seriously – Running for the National People's Congress*], China Citizens Movement (February 19, 2020), https://cmcn.org/archives/46508.
39. *Id.*
40. *See,* e.g., David Kelly, *Citizen Movements and China's Public Intellectuals in the Hu-Wen era*, 79 Pacific Affairs 204 (2006).
41. 中央通讯社 [The Central News Agency], 在建设中反对，中国维权者许志永倡竞选2021 [*Providing Constructive Criticism, Chinese Human Rights Activist Xu Zhiyong Advocates Running For Election 2021*], Yahoo News (April 5, 2019), https://tw.news.yahoo.com/%E5%9C%A8%E5%BB%BA%E8%A8%AD%E4%B8%AD%E5%8F%8D%E5%B0%8D-%E4%B8%AD%E5%9C%8B%E7%B6%AD%E6%AC%8A%E8%80%85%E8%A8%B1%E5%BF%97%E6%B0%B8%E5%80%A1%E7%AB%B6%E9%81%B82021-060536592.html.
42. *See,* e.g., 周华 (Zhou Hua), 北京律师协会直选风波 [*Beijing Bar Association Direct Election Controversy*], 搜狐新闻[Sohu News] (October 14, 2008), https://news.sohu.com/20081014/n260012113.shtml; 孙红 (Sun Hong), 北京35名律师发

难要求直选，签名律师被解聘 [*Beijing's 35 Lawyers Lash Out for Direct Elections, Signing Lawyers Dismissed*], 搜狐新闻 [SOHU NEWS] (October 28, 2008), https://news.sohu.com/20081028/n260288413.shtml.

43. Interview No. BJ-LA-050919-4.
44. 第八届北京市律师代表大会第一次会议圆满结束 [*The First Meeting of the Eighth Beijing Lawyers' Congress Concluded Successfully*], 首都律师 [BEIJING LAWYER ASSOCIATION], www.beijinglawyers.org.cn/topic/1/beijing1.htm.
45. Interview No. BJ-LA-111423-5.

Conclusion: Democracy in China?

1 This argument goes beyond neighborhood governance. Another example is trade unions. Shanghai has mandated the direct election of grassroots trade unions since 2010. 肖堃涛在基层工会主席直接选举工作推进会上的讲话 (Xiao Kuntao's Speech at the Conference on the Promotion of Direct Elections of Grassroots Trade Unions), https://gov.eastday.com/renda/node5902/node5911/node6582/u1a1692385.html last visited August 1, 2024. 上海市总工会关于进一步推进基层工会主席直接选举工作的意见(沪工总组〔2010〕89号) (Opinion of the Shanghai Worker's Union on Further Promoting Direction Election of Grassroots Workers' Union Chairmen, No. 89, 2010), https://gov.eastday.com/renda/node5902/node5911/node6581/u1a1667051.html, last visited August 1, 2024. By 2011, 31 percent of the over 16,700 grassroots trade unions in Shanghai have held direct elections. 上海：推进基层工会创先争优 (Shanghai: A Model of Improving Grassroots Trade Unions), http://acftu.workercn.cn/c/2011/10/31/111031161916283373084.html, last visited March 3, 2021. As a comparison, in Guangdong province, which is a center of labor activism, by 2014 only 2 percent of the about 250,000 grassroots trade unions had held direct elections. 广东试点"民主选举"企业工会 (Guangdong Experimented with "Democratic Elections" of Trade Unions), www.gov.cn/xinwen/2014-07/02/content_2711085.htm, last visited March 3, 2021.

2 ALEXIS DE TOCQUEVILLE, DEMOCRACY IN AMERICA 891 (James T. Schleifer trans., 2010). A recent empirical study found that buying a home leads individuals to participate substantially more in local elections. Andrew B. Hall and Jesse Yoder, *Does Homeownership Influence Political Behavior? Evidence from Administrative Data* (Department of Political Science, Stanford University, working paper, 2019). In the context of developing countries, a recent study finds that in Congo citizens in neighborhoods where property was taxed were more likely to attend town hall meetings hosted by the government or submit evaluations of its performance than in neighborhoods where no such property tax existed. See Jonathan L. Weigel, *The Participation Dividend of Taxation: How Citizens in Congo Engage More with the State When It Tries to Tax Them*, 135 Q J ECON. 1849 (2020).

3 Shitong Qiao, *The Structure and Spirit of Chinese Property Law*, in THE ROUTLEDGE HANDBOOK OF PROPERTY, LAW AND SOCIETY (edited by Nicole Graham, Margaret Davies and Lee Godden, 2022), 52–60.

4 Estlund, Cynthia. *A New Deal for China's Workers?* Harvard University Press, 2017.

5 MICHAEL MANN, THE SOURCES OF SOCIAL POWER, VOLUME I: A HISTORY OF POWER FROM THE BEGINNING TO AD 1760 7 (1986).

6 Weijun Lai & Anthony J. Spires, *Marketization and Its Discontents: Unveiling the Impacts of Foundation-Led Venture Philanthropy on Grassroots NGOs in China*, 245 China Q. 72 (2021).
7 *See, e.g.*, Hyung-A Kim, Korea's Development under Park Chung Hee (2004).
8 *See, e.g.*, Andrew J. Nathan & Helena VS Ho, *Chiang Ching-kuo's Decision for Political Reform*, in Chiang Ching-kuo's Leadership in the Development of the Republic of China on Taiwan (Shao Chuan Leng ed., 1993): 31–61.
9 Kim, *supra* note 7.
10 Nathan & Ho, *supra* note 8.
11 Hanson, *Democracy and State Capacity*, *supra* note 206; Fortin, *Is There a Necessary Condition for Democracy*, *supra* note 206. This emphasis on state capacity is interestingly consistent with Sun Yat-sen's idea that a period of "political tutelage" goes before democracy, which has shaped political development in the Greater China area and resonated with political development in other areas too. *See*, e.g., Carlos Closa & Stefano Palestini, *Tutelage and Regime Survival in Regional Organizations' Democracy Protection: The Case of MERCOSUR and UNASUR*, 70 World Politics 443 (2018); Walter F. Weiker, Political Tutelage and Democracy in Turkey: The Free Party and its Aftermath (1973). For a more general discussion related to this, *see* Bruce Ackerman. Revolutionary Constitutions: Charismatic Leadership and the Rule of Law (2019).
12 For discussions of the negative impact of HoAs on broad urban governance, *see, e.g.*, Evan McKenzie, Privatopia: Homeowner Associations And the Rise of Residential Private Government (1994).
13 Wendell Pritchett & Shitong Qiao, *Exclusionary Megacities*, 91 S. Cal. L. Rev. 467 (2018).
14 Homeowners' exploitation of tenants is limited by two factors in China: First, migrant workers stay in small/informal property houses in the cities where they make a living. A major challenge to providing housing to the low-income migrant population is therefore how to legalize the informal housing sector. *See* Qiao, Chinese Small Property, *supra* note 185. Second, tenants who can afford rents in middle-class neighborhoods are usually members of the middle class who are on the path to becoming homeowners. The price-to-rent ratio in China is extremely high, reflecting a market of tenants instead of landlords. *See, e.g.*, Jing Wu et al., *Evaluating the Risk of Chinese Housing Markets: What We Know and What We Need to Know*, 39 China Econ. Rev. 91 (2016); Yangpeng Zheng, *Plunging Chinese Rental Yields Point to Property Bubbles in Major Cities*, South China Morning Post (July 18, 2017), www.scmp.com/business/china-business/article/2103116/plunging-chinese-rental-yields-point-property-bubbles-major. Therefore, Chinese urban tenants face a very different situation from their counterparts in the United States. For the problems of tenants in American cities, *see* Matthew Desmond, Evicted: Poverty and Profit in the American city (2016). For a book review, *see* Vicki Been & Leila Bozorg, *Spiraling: Evictions and Other Causes and Consequences of Housing Instability*, 130 Harv. L. Rev. 1408 (2017).
15 Raghuram Rajan, The Third Pillar: How Markets and the State Leave the Community Behind xxvii (2019). For balancing local democracy

and parochialism, *see* also Nestor M. Davidson, *The Dilemma of Localism in an Era of Polarization*, 128 YALE L.J. 954 (2019).

16 Tocqueville serves as a starting point for this article for many reasons. Readers who are concerned about the applicability or relevance of Tocqueville to China should be aware that his works are not only studied by Chinese intellectuals but read and recommended by prominent CCP leaders, primarily the Vice President and former head of the anti-corruption campaign Wang Qishan, *see, e.g.*, Cary Huang, *Tocqueville's Advice on French Revolution Captures Chinese Leaders' Attention*, SOUTH CHINA MORNING POST (January 22, 2013), www.scmp.com/news/china/article/1133212/tocquevilles-advice-french-revolution-captures-chinese-leaders-attention; Joseph Fewsmith, *De Tocqueville in Beijing*, 39 CHINA LEADERSHIP MONITOR 1 (2012), http://media.hoover.org/sites/default/files/documents/CLM39JF.pdf.

Bibliography

Books

Acemoglu, D. and Robinson, J. A. (2013). Why Nations Fail the Origins of Power, Prosperity, and Poverty. London: Profile Books.

(2019). The Narrow Corridor: States, Societies, and the Fate of Liberty. New York: Penguin Books.

Ackerman, B. A. (2019). Revolutionary Constitutions: Charismatic Leadership and the Rule of Law. Cambridge, MA: The Belknap Press of Harvard University Press.

Ang, Y. Y. (2016). How China Escaped the Poverty Trap. Ithaca, NY: Cornell University Press.

Applebaum, A. (2012). Iron Curtain: The Crushing of Eastern Europe, 1945–1956. London: Penguin.

Barzel, Y. (1997). The Economic Analysis of Property Rights. Cambridge: Cambridge University Press.

(2002). A Theory of the State Economic Rights, Legal Rights, and the Scope of the State. Cambridge: Cambridge University Press.

Brooks, R. R. and Rose, C. M. (2013). Saving the Neighborhood: Racially Restrictive Covenants, Law, and Social Norms. Cambridge, MA: Harvard University Press.

Capozzola, C. (2008). Uncle Sam Wants You: World War I and the Making of the Modern American Citizen. Oxford: Oxford University Press.

Carpenter, D. (2021). Democracy by Petition: Popular Politics in Transformation, 1790–1870. Cambridge, MA: Harvard University Press.

Chen, Y. (2009).社区治理的多元视角：理论与实践 [Dynamic Perspective of Social Governance: Theory and Practice]. Beijing: Peking University Press.

Chinese Academy of Social Sciences (中国社会科学院). (2013). 当代中国调查报告丛书：中国社会和谐稳定跟踪调查研究 [Contemporary China Investigation Report Series: A Follow-up Survey of Harmony and Stability of Chinese Society]. Beijing: China Social Sciences Press.

Coase, R. H. and Wang, N. (2012). How China Became Capitalist. Houndmills, Basingstoke, Hampshire: Palgrave Macmillan.

Corbin, J. and Strauss, A. (2008). Basics of Qualitative Research: Techniques and Procedures for Developing Grounded Theory, 3rd edn. London: SAGE Publications.

DESMOND, M. (2016). EVICTED: POVERTY AND PROFIT IN THE AMERICAN CITY. New York: Crown Publishers.

ELLICKSON, R. C. (1991). ORDER WITHOUT LAW: HOW NEIGHBORS SETTLE DISPUTES. Cambridge, MA: Harvard University Press.

ESTLUND, C. (2003). WORKING TOGETHER: HOW WORKPLACE BONDS STRENGTHEN A DIVERSE DEMOCRACY. Oxford: Oxford University Press.

(2017). A NEW DEAL FOR CHINA'S WORKERS? Cambridge, MA: Harvard University Press.

FENNELL, L. A. (2009). THE UNBOUNDED HOME: PROPERTY VALUES BEYOND PROPERTY LINES. New Haven, CT: Yale University Press.

FU, H. (2022). Pandemic Control in China's Gated Communities. In Loh, C. et al., eds, HOW COVID-19 TOOK OVER THE WORLD: LESSONS FOR THE FUTURE WITH COMPARATIVE PERSPECTIVES FROM HEALTH. Hong Kong: Hong Kong University Press, p. 9.

FU, H. and CHEN, W. (2020). AUTHORITARIAN LEGALITY IN ASIA: FORMATION, DEVELOPMENT AND TRANSITION. Cambridge: Cambridge University Press.

FUKUYAMA, F. (1996). TRUST: THE SOCIAL VIRTUES AND THE CREATION OF PROSPERITY. New York: Free Press.

(2014). POLITICAL ORDER AND POLITICAL DECAY: FROM THE INDUSTRIAL REVOLUTION TO THE GLOBALIZATION OF DEMOCRACY. London: Profile Books.

GALLAGHER, M. E. (2017). AUTHORITARIAN LEGALITY IN CHINA: LAW, WORKERS, AND THE STATE. Cambridge: Cambridge University Press.

GREIF, A. (2006). INSTITUTIONS AND THE PATH TO THE MODERN ECONOMY: LESSONS FROM MEDIEVAL TRADE. Cambridge: Cambridge University Press.

HE, B. (2007). RURAL DEMOCRACY IN CHINA: THE ROLE OF VILLAGE ELECTIONS. New York: Palgrave Macmillan.

HIRSCHMAN, A. O. (1970). EXIT, VOICE, AND LOYALTY; RESPONSES TO DECLINE IN FIRMS, ORGANIZATIONS, AND STATES. Cambridge, MA: Harvard University Press.

HOU, Y. (2019). THE PRIVATE SECTOR IN PUBLIC OFFICE: SELECTIVE PROPERTY RIGHTS IN CHINA. Cambridge: Cambridge University Press.

HSING, Y. (2010). THE GREAT URBAN TRANSFORMATION: POLITICS OF LAND AND PROPERTY IN CHINA. Oxford: Oxford University Press.

IMMERWAHR, D. (2018). THINKING SMALL: THE UNITED STATES AND THE LURE OF COMMUNITY DEVELOPMENT. Cambridge, MA: Harvard University Press.

KIM, H.-A. (2004). KOREA'S DEVELOPMENT UNDER PARK CHUNG HEE: RAPID INDUSTRIALIZATION, 1961–1979. London: Routledge.

KORNAI, J. and ROSE-ACKERMAN, S. (2004). BUILDING A TRUSTWORTHY STATE IN POST-SOCIALIST TRANSITION. New York: Palgrave Macmillan.

KORNAI, J., ROSE-ACKERMAN, S. and ROTHSTEIN, B. (2004). CREATING SOCIAL TRUST IN POST-SOCIALIST TRANSITION. New York: Palgrave Macmillan.

LAMOREAUX, N. R. and WALLIS, J. J. (2017). ORGANIZATIONS, CIVIL SOCIETY, AND THE ROOTS OF DEVELOPMENT. Chicago, IL: The University of Chicago Press.

LEI, Y.-W. (2019). THE CONTENTIOUS PUBLIC SPHERE: LAW, MEDIA, AND AUTHORITARIAN RULE IN CHINA. Oxford: Princeton University Press.

Lieberthal, K. G. and Oksenberg, M. (1988). Policy Making in China: Leaders, Structures, and Processes. Princeton, NJ: Princeton University Press.

Mann, M. (2012). The Sources of Social Power. Cambridge: Cambridge University Press.

Mattingly, D. (2019). The Art of Political Control in China. Cambridge: Cambridge University Press.

McAdams, R. (2015). The Expressive Powers of Law: Theories and Limits. Cambridge, MA: Harvard University Press.

McKenzie, E. (1994). Privatopia: Homeowner Associations and the Rise of Residential Private Government. New Haven, CT: Yale University Press.

Nathan, A. J. and Ho, H. V. (1993). Chiang Ching-kuo's Decision for Political Reform. In Leng, S. C., eds., Chiang Ching-kuo's Leadership in the Development of the Republic of China on Taiwan. Lanham, MD: University Press of America, pp. 31–61.

Nelson, R. H. (2005). Private Neighborhoods and the Transformation of Local Government. Washington, DC: Urban Institute Press.

North, D. C. (1990). Institutions, Institutional Change and Economic Performance. Cambridge: Cambridge University Press.

O'Brien, K. J. and Li, L. (2006). Rightful Resistance in Rural China. New York: Cambridge University Press.

Ober, J. (2018). Demopolis: Democracy before Liberalism in Theory and Practice. Cambridge: Cambridge University Press.

Ong, L. H. (2022). Outsourcing Repression: Everyday State Power in Contemporary China. New York: Oxford University Press.

Ostrom, E. (1990). Governing the Commons: The Evolution of Institutions for Collective Action. Cambridge: Cambridge University Press.

Putnam, R. D. (1993). Making Democracy Work: Civic Traditions in Modern Italy. Princeton, NJ: Princeton University Press.

(2001). Bowling Alone: The Collapse and Revival of American Community. New York: Touchstone.

Rajan, R. (2020). The Third Pillar: How Markets and the State Leave the Community Behind. New York: Penguin Books.

Richman, B. D. (2017). Stateless Commerce: The Diamond Network and the Persistence of Relational Exchange. Cambridge, MA: Harvard University Press.

Rothstein, B. (2011). The Quality of Government: Corruption, Social Trust, and Inequality in International Perspective. Chicago, IL: University of Chicago Press.

Rüschemeyer, D., Evans, P. B. and Skocpol, T. (2010). Bringing the State Back in. Cambridge: Cambridge University Press.

Scott, J. C. (1985). Weapons of the Weak: Everyday Forms of Peasant Resistance. London: Yale University Press.

(1998). Seeing like the State: How Certain Schemes to Improve the Human Condition Have Failed. New Haven, CT: Yale University Press.

Shi, T. (1997). Political Participation in Beijing. Cambridge, MA: Harvard University Press.

Standing Committee of the National People's Congress Legal Work Committee for Civil Law (全国人民代表大会常务委员会法制工作委员会民法室) (2007). 物权法立法背景与观点全集 [Collections of PRC Property Law Legislative Background and Opinions]. Beijing: Law Press.

Stasavage, D. (2021). The Decline and Rise of Democracy: A Global History from Antiquity to Today. Princeton, NJ: Princeton University Press.

Studwell, J. (2013). How Asia Works: Success and Failure in the World's Most Dynamic Region. New York: Grove Press.

Teets, J. C. (2014). Civil Society under Authoritarianism: The China Model. New York: Cambridge University Press.

Tocqueville, A. de (2012). Democracy in America, translated by Schleifer J. T. New York: Library of America Paperback Classics.

Tomba, L. (2014). The Government Next Door: Neighborhood Politics in Urban China. Ithaca, NY: Cornell University Press.

Tsai, L. L. (2007). Accountability without Democracy: Solidary Groups and Public Goods Provision in Rural China. Cambridge: Cambridge University Press.

Upham, F. K. (2018). The Great Property Fallacy: Theory, Reality, and Growth in Developing Countries. Cambridge: Cambridge University Press.

Weiker, W. (1973). Political Tutelage and Democracy in Turkey: The Free Party and Its Aftermath. Leiden: Brill.

Wu, Y. (吴莹) (2015). 社区何以可能:芳雅家园的邻里生活[How the Community is Possible: A Possible Analysis of a Commercial Residential Enclave's Neighboring]. Beijing: China Social Sciences Press.

Journal Articles, Book Chapters, and Working Papers

Alesina, A. and Giuliano, P. (2015). *Culture and Institutions*, 53 Journal of Economic Literature 898.

Alexander, G. S. (1989). *Dilemmas of Group Autonomy: Residential Associations and Community*, 75 Cornell L. Rev. 1.

Alexander, G. S. et al. (2008). *A Statement of Progressive Property*, 94 Cornell L. Rev. 743.

An, Y. and Zhang, T. (2023). *Pandemic State-building: Chinese Administrative Expansion Since 2012*, Yale L. & Poll'y Rev. (Forthcoming 2024) at 2, Available at SSRN: https://ssrn.com/abstract=4356026 or http://dx.doi.org/10.2139/ssrn.4356026

Ang, Y. Y. (2020). *When COVID-19 Meets Centralized, Personalized Power*, 4 Nat. Hum. Behav. 445.

Axelrod, R. and Hamilton, W. D. (1981). *The Evolution of Cooperation*, 211 Science 1390.

Bäck, H and Hadenius, A. (2008). *Democracy and State Capacity: Exploring a J-Shaped Relationship*, 21 Governance 1, 3.

Barzel, Y. and Sass, T. R. (1990). *The Allocation of Resources by Voting*, 105 Q. J. Econ. 745.

Been, V. and Bozorg, L. (2017). *Spiraling: Evictions and Other Causes and Consequences of Housing Instability*, 130 HARV. L. REV. 1408.

Beijing Department of Housing Management (1999). 关于业主委员会几个问题的探讨 [*Discussion on Several Issues of Owner's Committee*], 《中国房地产》 [CHINA'S REAL ESTATE], no. 10, 2.

Benjamin, S. M. (2005). *Evaluating E-Rulemaking: Public Participation and Political Institutions*, 55 DUKE L. J. 893.

Bernstein, L. (1992). *Opting out of the Legal System: Extralegal Contractual Relations in the Diamond Industry*, 21 J. LEGAL STUD. 115.

(2001). *Private Commercial Law in the Cotton Industry: Creating Cooperation through Rules, Norms, and Institutions*, 99 MICH. L. REV. 1724.

(2015). *Private Ordering, Social Capital and Network Governance in Procurement Contracts: A Preliminary Exploration*, 7 J. LEGAL STUD. 561.

Brooks, R. and Guinnane, T. W. (2017). The Right to Associate and the Rights of Associations: Civil-Society Organizations in Prussia, 1794–1908. In Lamoreaux, N. and Wallis, J., eds., ORGANIZATIONS, CIVIL SOCIETY, AND THE ROOTS OF DEVELOPMENT. Chicago, IL: University of Chicago Press, pp. 291–329.

Cai, Y. and Sheng, Z. (2013). *Homeowners' Activism in Beijing: Leaders with Mixed Motivations*, 215 CHINA Q. 513.

Chen, P. (陈鹏) (2013). 国家-市场-社会三维视野下的业委会研究 – 以B市商品房社区为例 [*A Study on Homeowners' Committees from the Perspective of Nation, Market and Society – Based on a Case of Commodity Housing Community in City B*], 《公共管理学报》 [JOURNAL OF PUBLIC MANAGEMENT], no. 10, 75.

Chen, W (陈雯) (2003). 论业主委员会的法律地位及制度完善 [*On the Legal Status and System Perfection of the Homeowners' Association*], 《政法学刊》 [JOURNAL OF POLITICAL SCIENCE AND LAW], no. 5, 41–43.

Chen, Y. (陈映芳) (2006). 行动力与制度限制：都市运动中的中产阶层 [*Ability of Action and Institutional Constraints: Middle Class in the Urban Movement*], 《社会学研究》 [SOCIOLOGY STUDY], no. 4, 1.

Chen, Y. (陈幽泓) (2012). "小区宪法"是社会契约中最基本最重要的规定 [*Neighborhood Constitution is the Most Fundamental Regulation in Social Contract*], 6 《和谐社区通讯》.

China Governance and Media Monitoring Center (中国政务舆情监测中心) (2015). 社会治理的上海一号课题是怎么做的 [*How was a Shanghai No. 1 Research Investigation on Social Governance Launched?*], 5《领导决策信息》 [INFORMATION FOR DECIDERS MAGAZINE], no. 5, 26–27.

Clarke, D. (2014). *China's Stealth Urban Land Revolution*, 62 AM. J. COMP. L. 323.

Closa, C. and Palestini, S. (2018). *Tutelage and Regime Survival in Regional Organizations' Democracy Protection: The case of MERCOSUR and UNASUR*, 70 WORLD POLITICS 443.

Cohen, M. (1927). *Property and Sovereignty*, 13 CORNELL L. Q. 9.

Collins, P. H. (2010). *The New Politics of Community*, 75 AM. SOC. REV. 7.

Dagan, H. and Heller, M. A. (2000). *The Liberal Commons*, 110 YALE L. J. 549, 581–582.

Davidson, N. M. (2019). *The Dilemma of Localism in an Era of Polarization*, 128 YALE L. J. 954.

Ellickson, R. C. (1982). *Cities and Homeowners Associations*, 130 U. PA. L. REV. 1519.

(1993). *Property in Land*, 102 YALE L. J. 1315, 1335–1338.

(1998). *New Institutions for Old Neighborhoods*, 48 DUKE L. J. 75.

(2016). *When Civil Society Uses an Iron Fist: The Roles of Private Associations in Rulemaking and Adjudication*, 18 AM. L. & ECON. REV. 235.

Eppinger, M. (2015). *Property and Political Community: Democracy, Oligarchy, and the Case of Ukraine*, 47 GEO. WASH. INT'L L. REV. 825.

(2018). *Cold-War Commons: Tragedy, Critique, and the Future of the Illiberal Problem Space*, 19 THEORETICAL INQUIRIES IN LAW 457, 488.

Epstein, R. A. (1988). *Covenants and Constitutions*, 73 CORNELL L. REV. 906.

(2002). *The Allocation of the Commons: Parking on Public Roads*, 31 J. LEGAL STUD. S515.

Fennell, L. A. (2012). *The Problem of Resource Access*, 126 HARV. L. REV. 1472.

Fewsmith, J. (2012). *De Tocqueville in Beijing*, 39 CHINA LEADERSHIP MONITOR 1, http://media.hoover.org/sites/default/files/documents/CLM39JF.pdf.

Fortin, J. (2012). *Is There a Necessary Condition for Democracy? The Role of State Capacity in Postcommunist Countries*, 45 COMP. POLIT. STUD. 903.

Foster, S. R. (2011). *Collective Action and the Urban Commons*, 87 NOTRE DAME L. REV. 57.

Foster, S. R. and Iaione, C. (2015). *The City as a Commons*, 34 YALE L. &POL'Y REV. 281.

Frug, G. E. (1980). *The City as a Legal Concept*, 93 HARV. L. REV. 1057.

(1981). *Cities and Homeowners Associations: A Reply*, 130 U. PA. L. REV. 1589.

Garnett, N. S. (2011). *Managing the Urban Commons*, 160 U. PA. L. REV. 1995.

Gillette, C. P. (1994). *Courts, Covenants, and Communities*, 61 U. CHI. L. REV. 1375.

Gilson, R. J. and Milhaupt, C. J. (2011). *Economically Benevolent Dictators: Lessons for Developing Democracies*, 59 AM. J. COMP. L. 227.

Granovetter, M. S. (1973). *The Strength of Weak Ties*, 78 AM. J. SOCIO. 1360.

Greif, A. (1994). *Cultural Beliefs and the Organization of Society: A Historical and Theoretical Reflection on Collectivist and Individualist Societies*, 102 JOURNAL OF POLITICAL ECONOMY 912.

Gu, H. (2016). *Nimbyism in China: Issues and Prospects of Public Participation in Facility Siting*, 52 LAND USE POL'Y 527.

Guan, B. and Cai, Y. (2015). *Interests and Political Participation in Urban China: The Case of Residents' Committee Elections*, 15 THE CHINA REVIEW 95.

Gulati, R., Wohlgezogen, F. and Zhelyazkov, P. (2012). *The Two Facets of Collaboration: Cooperation and Coordination in Strategic Alliances*, 6 ACADEMY OF MANAGEMENT ANNALS 531.

Guo, Y. (郭莹) and Wu, A. (吴爱民) (2014). 我国城市居民自治分析 [*An Analysis of Self-Governance of City Residents in Our Country*], 《四川行政学院学报》 [JOURNAL OF SICHUAN ADMINISTRATION INSTITUTE], no. 6, 17–21.

Hainmueller, J. (2012). *Entropy Balancing for Causal Effects: A Multivariate Reweighting Method to Produce Balanced Samples in Observational Studies*, 20 POL. ANALYSIS 25.

Hall, A. B. and Yoder, J. (2019). *Does Homeownership Influence Political Behavior? Evidence from Administrative Data* (Department of Political Science, Stanford University, working paper).

Hanson, J. K. (2015). *Democracy and State Capacity: Complements or Substitutes?*, 50 STUD. COMP. INT. DEV. 304.

Hardin, G. (1968). *The Tragedy of the Commons*, 162 SCIENCE 1243.

He, J. (何家华) (2017). 特区立法权的实践状况和社会效果- 以深圳为例 [*The Practice and Consequence of SEZ Legislation: A Case Study of Shenzhen*],《南海法学》[South China Sea Law Review], no. 3, 100–110.

Heckathorn, D. D. (1997). *Respondent-Driven Sampling: A New Approach to the Study of Hidden Populations*, 44 Soc. Probs. 174.

Heller, A. M. (1998). *The Tragedy of the Anticommons: Property in the Transition from Marx to Markets*, 111 Harv. L. Rev. 621.

Hendrix, S. C. (2010). *Measuring State Capacity: Theoretical and Empirical Implications for the Study of Civil Conflict*, 47 J. Peace Res. 273.

Hildebrandt, T. (2011). *The Political Economy of Social Organization Registration in China*, China Q. 970.

Hills, Jr., R. M. (2003). *The Constitutional Rights of Private Governments*, 78 NYUL Rev. 144.

Hills, Jr., R. M. and Qiao, S. (2016). *Voice and Exit as Accountability Mechanisms: Can Foot-Voting Be Made Safe for the Chinese Communist Party*, 48 Colum. Hum. Rts. L. Rev. 158, 162–171.

Hills, Jr., R. M. and Schleicher, D. (2015). *Planning an Affordable City*, 101 Iowa L. Rev. 91, 96.

(2020). *Building Coalitions Out of Thin Air: Transferable Development Rights and "Constituency Effects" in Land Use Law*, 12 J. Legal Analysis 79.

Imai, K. et al. (2011). *Unpacking the Black Box of Causality: Learning about Causal Mechanisms from Experimental and Observational Studies*, 105 Am. Pol. Sci. Rev. 765.

Kan, H. Y., Forsyth, A. and Rowe, P. (2017). *Redesigning China's Superblock Neighbourhoods: Policies, Opportunities and Challenges*, 22 Journal of Urban Design 757.

Kang, X. and Han, H. (2005). 分类控制：当前中国大陆国家与社会关系研究 [*The System of Differential Controls: A Study of the State-society Relationship in Contemporary China*],《社会学研究》[Sociological Research], no. 6, 73.

Katz, L. (2011). *Governing Through Owners: How and Why Formal Private Property Rights Enhance State Power*, 160 U. Pa. L. Rev. 2029.

Kelly, D. (2006). *Citizen Movements and China's Public Intellectuals in the Hu-Wen Era*, 79 Pacific Affairs 204.

Kennedy, D. J. (1995). *Residential Associations as State Actors: Regulating the Impact of Gated Communities on Nonmembers*, 105 Yale L. J. 761.

Kennedy, J. J. (2002). *The Face of "Grassroots Democracy" in Rural China: Real Versus Cosmetic Elections*, 42 Asian Surv. 456.

Kornhauser, L. A. (2004). *Governance Structures, Legal Systems, and the Concept of Law*, 79 Chi.-Kent L. Rev. 355, 362.

Kroll, A. et al. (2021). *Mitigating the Negative Effects of Emotional Labor: A Study of Disaster Response and Recovery Workers after the 2010 Haiti Earthquake*, 34 Governance 87.

La Porta, R. et al. (1999). *The Quality of Government*, 15 J. Law. Econ. Organ. 222.

Lai, W. and Spires, A. J. (2021). *Marketization and Its Discontents: Unveiling the Impacts of Foundation-Led Venture Philanthropy on Grassroots NGOs in China*, 245 China Q. 72.

Landa, J. T. (1981). *A Theory of the Ethnically Homogeneous Middleman Group: An Institutional Alternative to Contract Law*, 10 J. Legal Stud. 349.

Lee, M. M. and Zhang, N. (2017). *Legibility and the Informational Foundations of State Capacity*, 79 J. Politics 118.

Lei, Y. (2016). *Freeing the Press: How Field Environment Explains Critical News Reporting in China*, 122 Am. J. Sociol. 1.

Levy, J. T. (2017). Pluralism without Privilege: Corps Intermédiaires, Civil Society, and the Art of Association. In Lamoreaux, N. and Wallis, J., eds., Organizations, Civil Society, and the Roots of Development. Chicago, IL: University of Chicago Press, pp. 83–108.

Li, Fan. (李凡) (2013). 深圳人大代表选举事件及其对中国基层人大选举改革的意义 [The Election of Representatives of Shenzhen People's Congress and Its Impact on the Reform of China's Grassroots Election of People's Congresses] In Yan, J. (闫健) and Yu, K. (俞可平) eds., 《民主选举: 中国的民主治理理论与实践》 [China's Democracy Management: Theory and Practice], Beijing: Central Compilation & Translation Press, p. 159.

Li, L. and O'Brien, K. J. (1999). The Struggle Over Village Elections. In Goldman, M. and MacFarquhar, R., eds., The Paradox of China's Post-Mao Reforms. Cambridge, MA: Harvard University Press, p. 129.

Li, Z. et al. (2021). *Comprehensive Large-Scale Nucleic Acid–Testing Strategies Support China's Sustained Containment of COVID-19*, 27 Nature Medicine 740.

Lieberthal, K. (1992). Introduction: The Fragmented Authoritarianism Model and Its Limitations. In Lieberthal, K. and Lampton, D. M., eds., Bureaucracy, Politics, and Decision Making in Post-Mao China. Berkeley: University of California Press, pp. 1–30.

Lin, G. (林国强) (1996). 业主委员会的性质地位与权利义务 [*The Nature, Status, Rights and Obligations of Homeowners' Associations*], 《中国房地产》 [China's Real Estate], no. 11, 40–42.

Lin, L. Y. and Milhaupt, C. J. (2021). *Party Building or Noisy Signaling? The Contours of Political Conformity in Chinese Corporate Governance*, 50 J. Legal Stud. 187.

Lindstrom, D. P. (2016). *How Representative Are Snowball Samples? Using the Ethnosurvey to Study Guatemala-US Migration*, 666 Annals Am. Acad. Pol. & Soc. Sci. 64.

Liu, C. (刘长森) (2002). 论业主委员会的性质及法律地位 (*On the Nature and Legal Status of Homeowners' Association*), 《中国房地产》 [China's Real Estate], no. 5, 28–31.

Lyle, H. F. and Smith, E. A. (2014). *The Reputational and Social Network Benefits of Prosociality in an Andean Community*, 111 Proc. Natl. Acad. Sci. U.S.A. 4820.

Mann, M. (1984). *The Autonomous Power of the State: Its Origins, Mechanisms and Results*, 25 European Journal of Sociology 185.

Martinez-Bravo, M. et al. (2017). *The Rise and Fall of Local Elections in China: Theory and Empirical Evidence on the Autocrat's Trade-off*. No. w24032. National Bureau of Economic Research.

Merle, A. (2014). *Homeowners of Beijing, Unite! The Construction of a Collective Mobilisation*, China Perspect. 7.

Merrill, T. W. (2017). *Property and Sovereignty, Information and Audience*, 18 Theoretical Inq. L. 417.

Merrill, T. W. and Smith, H. E. (2000). *Optimal Standardization in the Law of Property: The Numerus Clausus Principle*, 110 Yale L. R. 1.

(2001). *The Property/Contract Interface*, 101 COLUM. L. REV. 773.

Mertha, A. (2009). *Fragmented Authoritarianism 2.0: Political Pluralization in the Chinese Policy Process*, 200 CHINA Q. 995.

Mettler, S. (2002). *Bringing the State Back in to Civic Engagement: Policy Feedback Effects of the GI Bill for World War II Veterans*, 96 AM. POL. SCI. REV. 351.

Mittelstaedt, J. (2022). *The Grid Management System in Contemporary China: Grass-roots Governance in Social Surveillance and Service Provision*, 36 CHINA INFO. 3.

Myerson, R. B. (2017). *Village Communities and Global Development* (African Development Bank, Abidjan, Côte d'Ivoire, Working Paper Series N° 300).

Nelson, R. H. (1998). *Privatizing the Neighborhood: A Proposal to Replace Zoning with Private Collective Property Rights to Existing Neighborhoods*, 7 GEO. MASON L. REV. 827.

North, D. C. and Weingast, B. R. (1989). *Constitutions and Commitment: The Evolution of Institutions Governing Public Choice in Seventeenth-Century England*, 49 J. ECON. HIST. 803.

O'Brien, K. J. and Han, R. (2009). *Path to Democracy? Assessing Village Elections in China*, 18 J. CONTEMP. CHINA 359.

Ong, L. H. (2018). *Thugs and Outsourcing of State Repression in China*. 80 CHINA J. 94.

Ostrom, V., Tiebout, C. M. and Warren, R. (1961). *The Organization of Government in Metropolitan Areas: A Theoretical Inquiry*, 55 AM. POLIT. SCI. REV. 831.

Pedriana, N. and Stryker, R. (2004). *The Strength of a Weak Agency: Enforcement of Title VII of the 1964 Civil Rights Act and the Expansion of State Capacity, 1965–1971*, 110 AM. J. SOCIOL. 709.

People's Bank of China. (2020). 2019 年中国城镇居民家庭资产负债情况调查报告 [*Survey Report on Household Assets and Liabilities of Chinese Urban Residents in 2019*], 《中国金融》 [CHINA FINANCE], Apr. 24, 2020.

Pritchett, W. and Qiao, S. (2018). *Exclusionary Megacities*, 91 S. CAL. L. REV. 467.

Qi, Q. (齐颀) (1999). 运作不规范权益难保障– 本市业主委员会建立和运行情况透视 [*Irregular Operation, Difficult to Protect Rights and Interests – The Establishment and Operation of Homeowners' Committee in Shanghai*], 《上海人大月刊》 [SHANGHAI PEOPLE'S CONGRESS MONTHLY JOURNAL], no. 9, 16–17.

Qiao, S. (2017). *Rights-Weakening Federalism*, 102 MINN. L. REV. 1671.

(2017). The Evolution of Property Law in China: Stick by Stick? In Chang, Y., Shen, W. and Wang, W., eds., PRIVATE LAW IN CHINA AND TAIWAN: LEGAL AND ECONOMIC ANALYSES. Cambridge: Cambridge University Press, pp. 182–211.

(2018). *Fragmented Laws, Contingent Choices: The Tragicomedy of the Village Commons in China*, 29 DUKE J. COMP. & INT'L L. 235.

(2022). The Structure and Spirit of Chinese Property Law. In Graham, N., Davies, M. and Godden, L. eds., THE ROUTLEDGE HANDBOOK OF PROPERTY, LAW AND SOCIETY. Oxford, New York: Routledge, pp. 52–60.

(2023). *The Authoritarian Commons: Divergent Paths of Neighborhood Democratization in Three Chinese Megacities*, 71 AM. J. COMP. L. 388.

Ray, R. K. (1974). *Masses in Politics: The Non-Cooperation Movement in Bengal 1920–1922*, 11 INDIAN ECON. SOC. HIST. REV. 343.

Read, B. L. (2003). *Democratizing the Neighborhood? New Private Housing and Home-Owner Self-Organization in Urban China*, 49 CHINA J. 31.

Riley, D. (2005). *Civic Associations and Authoritarian Regimes in Interwar Europe: Italy and Spain in Comparative Perspective*, 70 AM. SOC. REV. 288.

Rose-Ackerman, S. (2001). *Trust and Honesty in Post-Socialist Societies*, 54 KYKLOS 415.

(2001). *Trust, Honesty and Corruption: Reflection on the State-Building Process*, 42 EUR. J. SOC. 526.

Rose, C. (1968). *The Comedy of the Commons: Custom, Commerce, and Inherently Public Property*, 53 U. CHI. L. REV. 711.

(1998). *The Several Futures of Property: Of Cyberspace and Folk Tales, Emission Trades and Ecosystems*, 83 MINN. L. REV. 129, 155.

Rosser, E. (2013). *The Ambition and Transformative Potential of Progressive Property*, 101 CAL. L. REV. 107.

Schofer, E. and Fourcade-Gourinchas, M. (2001). *The Structural Contexts of Civic Engagement: Voluntary Association Membership in Comparative Perspective*, 66 AM. SOC. REV. 806.

Schragger, R. C. (2001). *The Limits of Localism*, 100 MICH. L. REV. 371, 388.

Silbey, S. S. (2011). *The Sociological Citizen: Pragmatic and Relational Regulation in Law and Organizations*, 5 REGUL. GOV. 1.

Singer, J. W. (2013). *Property as the Law of Democracy*, 63 DUKE L. J. 1287.

Shih, V. C. (2012). China's Leninist Response to Covid-19 from Information Repression to Total Mobilization. In Greer, S. L. et al., eds, CORONAVIRUS POLITICS: THE COMPARATIVE POLITICS AND POLICY OF COVID-19. Ann Arbor, MI: University of Michigan Press, p. 67.

Skocpol, T. (2020). The Elite and Popular Roots of Contemporary Republican Extremism. In Skocpol, T. and Tervo, C., eds., UPENDING AMERICAN POLITICS: POLARIZING PARTIES, IDEOLOGICAL ELITES, AND CITIZEN ACTIVISTS FROM THE TEA PARTY TO THE ANTI-TRUMP RESISTANCE. New York: Oxford University Press, p. 3.

Skocpol, T. (2008). *Bringing the State Back in: Retrospect and Prospect The 2007 Johan Skytte Prize Lecture*, 31 SCANDINAVIAN POL. STUD. 109.

Skocpol, T., Ganz, M. and Munson, Z. (2000). *A Nation of Organizers: The Institutional Origins of Civic Voluntarism in the United States*, 94 AM. POL. SCI. REV. 527.

Smith, H. E. (2012). *Property as the Law of Things*, 125 HARV. L. R. 1691.

Soifer, H. (2008). *State Infrastructural Power: Approaches to Conceptualization and Measurement*, 43 STUD. IN COMP. INT'L DEV. 231.

Spires, A. J. (2001). *Contingent Symbiosis and Civil Society in an Authoritarian State: Understanding the Survival of China's Grassroots NGOs*, 117 AM. J. SOCIOL. 1.

Stern, S. M. (2008). *Residential Protectionism and the Legal Mythology of Home*, 107 MICH. L. REV. 1093.

(2011). *Reassessing the Citizen Virtues of Homeownership*, 111 COLUM. L. REV. 890.

Sun, X. (孙宪忠) (2003). 如何处理《物业管理条例》中的业主委员会和社区立法中的居民委员会之间关系 [*On How to Deal with the Relationship Between Homeowners' Associations Defined in the Property Management Regulation and Residents Committee in the Community Legislation*], 《中国物业管理》[CHINA REAL ESTATE MANAGEMENT], no. 2, 19.

Tang, Y. (汤艳文) (2004). 不完全契约形态:转型社会的社区治理结构– 以上海康健地区业主委员会的发展为例 [*Incomplete Contract Form: The Community*

Governance Structure of a Transitional Society – Taking the Development of the Owners Committee of Shanghai Kangjian District as an Example], 《上海行政学院学报》[Journal of Shanghai Administration Institute], no. 2, 68–78.

Tao, J. L. and McCabe, B. C. (2012). *Where a Hollow State Casts No Shadow: Homeowner Associations in Local Governments*, 42 Am. Rev. Pub. Admin. 678.

Teets, J. C. (2013). *Let Many Civil Societies Bloom: The Rise of Consultative Authoritarianism in China*, 213 China Q. 19.

Thomson, S. and Ip, E. C. (2020). *COVID-19 Emergency Measures and the Impending Authoritarian Pandemic*, 7 J. L. & Biosciences 1–13.

Truex, R. (2014). *The Returns to Office in a "Rubber Stamp" Parliament*, 108 Am. Pol. Sci. Rev. 235.

Tushnet, M. (2014). *Authoritarian Constitutionalism*, 100 Cornell L. Rev. 391, 448.

Upham, F. (2015). *The Paradoxical Roles of Property Rights in Growth and Development*, 8 Law & Dev. Rev. 253, 264.

Wang, C. (王成义) (2019). 深圳特区立法权：历史、学理和实践 [*An Analysis on the Delegated Legislative Power in Shenzhen Special Economic Zone: History, Theory and Practice*], 《地方立法研究》[Local Legislation Journal], no. 1, 1.

Wang, F. and Cooper, T. L. (2008). *Chinese Homeowners' Associations: A School of Democracy*, Pa Times, Feb. 2008, 4.

Wang, Z. et al., (2013). *Leadership in China's Urban Middle Class Protest: The Movement to Protect Homeowners' Rights in Beijing*, 214 China Q. 411.

Weigel, J. L. (2020). *The Participation Dividend of Taxation: How Citizens in Congo Engage More with the State When It Tries to Tax Them*, 135 Q J Econ. 1849.

Wu, J. et al. (2016). *Evaluating the Risk of Chinese Housing Markets: What We Know and What We Need to Know*, 39 China Econ. Rev. 91.

Wyman, K. M. (2013). *Problematic Private Property: The Case of New York Taxicab Medallions*, 30 Yale J. on Reg. 125.

Xin, G. and Huang, J. (2022). *Party Building in an Unlikely Place? The Adaptive Presence of the Chinese Communist Party in the Non-Governmental Organizations (NGO)*, 31 J. Contemp. China 428.

Xu, T. (许涛) (2007). 全国"有产者"联合起来？ – 全国业主委员会联合组织调查 [*All "Property-owners" Unite? National Survey of Homeowners' Associations*], 《住宅与房地产》[Residential Property and Real Estate], no. 1, 8–10.

Yan, X. and Huang, J. (2017). *Navigating Unknown Waters: The Chinese Communist Party's New Presence in the Private Sector*, 17 China Rev. 37.

Yip, N. M. (2019). *Housing Activism in Urban China: The Quest for Autonomy in Neighbourhood Governance*, 34 Housing Stud. 1635.

Yu, H. (2022). *Living in the Era of Codes: A Reflection on China's Health Code System*, BioSocieties, Dec. 2022 at 1.

Yuan, Z. et al., (2011). *The Rise of The Middle Class in The People's Republic of China* (ADB Economics Working Paper Series No. 247, 2011).

Yun, X. (向云) (2011). 中国内地第一个业主委员会诞生始末 [*The Birth of the First Homeowners' Association in Mainland China*], 《中国物业管理》[China Property Management], no. 5, 17–19.

Zeng, J. (曾建华) (2005). 金湖新村业主委员会有起诉的权利吗？ [*Does the Homeowners' Association of Jinhu New Village Have the Right to Sue?*], 《现代物业》[Modern Property Management], no. 3, 34–41.

Zhang, T. (2009). *Why the Chinese Public Prefer Administrative Petitioning over Litigation*, 3 SOCIOL. STUD. 139.

Zhang, T. and Ginsburg, T. (2019). *China's Turn Toward Law*, 59 VA. J. INT'L L. 306.

Zmerli, S. and Newton, K. (2008). *Social Trust and Attitudes Toward Democracy*, 72 PUB. OPINION Q. 706.

Laws, Regulations, and Administrative Documents

中华人民共和国宪法 [The PRC Constitution]

中华人民共和国立法法 [Legislation Law of the People's Republic of China] (promulgated by National People's Congress on Mar. 15, 2000, effective on July 1, 2000).

中华人民共和国民法典 [Civil Code of the People's Republic of China], adopted at the Third Session of the Thirteenth National People's Congress on May 28, 2020.

中华人民共和国物权法 [Property Law] (promulgated by National People's Congress, Mar. 16, 2007, effective Oct. 1, 2007).

中华人民共和国城市居民委员会组织法 [Organic Law of the PRC Urban Residents Committee] (promulgated by Standing Committee of the National People's Congress, Dec. 26, 1989).

中华人民共和国物业管理条例 [Regulation on Real Estate Management] (promulgated by State Council, June 8, 2003, amended Mar. 19, 2018).

中华人民共和国治安管理处罚法 [Law of Administrative Punishment on Public Security Offenses].

全国人民代表大会和地方各级人民代表大会选举法(2015(修正)) [Election Law for the National People's Congress and Local People's Congresses at All Levels (2015 Amendment)] (promulgated by the Standing Committee of the National People's Congress, Aug. 29, 2015) (Chinalawinfo).

中华人民共和国地方各级人民代表大会和地方各级人民政府组织法 [Organization Law of the People's Republic of China for Local People's Congresses at All Levels and Local People's Governments at All Levels] (amended by Standing Committee of the National People's Congress, Aug. 29, 2015).

中华人民共和国城市街道办事处组织条例 [Organic Regulation of the Urban Street-Level Offices] (promulgated by Standing Committee of the National People's Congress, Dec. 31, 1954, abolished June 27, 2009).

中华人民共和国城市居民委员会组织条例 [Organic Regulation of the Urban Residents Committee] (promulgated by Standing Committee of the National People's Congress, Dec. 31, 1954, abolished Jan. 1, 1990).

中华人民共和国地方各级人民政府机构设置和编制管理条例 [Regulation on the Organization Establishment and Staffing Administration of Local People's Governments at All Levels] (promulgated by National People's Congress, Mar. 15, 2000).

中共中央关于制定国民经济和社会发展第十个五年计划的建议 [Proposal of the Central Committee of the Communist Party of China on Formulating the Tenth Five-Year Plan for National Economic and Social Development] (promulgated by the Central Committee, Oct. 11, 2000).

中共中央关于全面深化改革若干重大问题的决定 [The Central Committee of the Communist Party of China's Decision on Some Major Issues Concerning Comprehensively Deepening Reforms] (promulgated by Third Plenary Session 18th Central Committee of the Communist Party of China, Nov. 12, 2013), www.ce.cn/xwzx/gnsz/szyw/201311/18/t20131118_1767104.shtml.

中共中央、国务院关于加强和完善城乡社区治理的意见 [The Central Committee of the Communist Party of China and the State Council's Opinions on Strengthening and Improving Urban and Rural Community Governance] (June 12, 2017), www.gov.cn/gongbao/content/2017/content_5204888.htm.

中共中央、国务院关于加强基层治理体系和治理能力现代化建设的意见 [Opinions of the Central Committee of the Communist Party of China and the State Council on Strengthening the Modernization of the Grassroots Governance System and Governance Capacity] (Apr. 28, 2021).

中共中央办公厅印发《关于加强和改进城市基层党的建设工作的意见》 [The General Office of the Central Committee of the Communist Party of China has issued the Opinions on Strengthening and Improving the Work of Party Building at the Grassroots Level in Urban Areas] (May 8, 2019), www.gov.cn/zhengce/2019-05/08/content_5389836.htm.

中共中央关于全面深化改革若干重大问题的决定 [Decision of the Central Committee of the Communist Party of China on Several Major Issues Concerning the Comprehensive Deepening of Reform] (Adopted at the Third Plenary Session of the 18th Central Committee of the Communist Party of China on Nov. 12, 2013), www.gov.cn/jrzg/2013-11/15/content_2528179.htm.

关于进一步深化城镇住房制度改革、加快住房建设的通知 [Notice on Further Deepening the Reform of the Urban Housing System and Speeding Up Housing Construction] (promulgated by the State Council, July 3, 1998) (国发(1998)23号).

关于深化城镇住房制度改革的决定 [Deepening the Reform of the Urban Housing System] (promulgated by the State Council, July 18, 1994) (国发[1994]43号).

业主大会和业主委员会指导规则 [Guiding Rules of Homeowners' Associations and Homeowners' Committees] (promulgated by Ministry of Housing and Urban-Rural Development, 2009), www.gov.cn/gzdt/2009-12/17/content_1489296.htm.

国民经济和社会发展第十个五年计划城镇化发展重点专项规划 [The Tenth Five-Year Plan for the National Economic and Social Development Key Special Plan for Urbanization Development] (promulgated by the State Planning Commission, Aug. 7, 2001).

建设部关于宣传、贯彻《物业管理条例》的通知 [Notice of the Ministry of Construction on the Promotion and Implementation of the *Property Management Regulations*] (promulgated by June 12, 2003) (建住房[2003]122号).

业主大会和业主委员会指导规则 [Guiding Rules of Homeowners' Associations and Homeowners' Committees] (promulgated by the Ministry of Housing and Urban-Rural Development, 2009).

住房和城乡建设部等部门关于加强和改进住宅物业管理工作的通知[建房规(2020)10号] [Notice from the Ministry of Housing and Urban-Rural Development and Other Departments on Strengthening and Improving Residential Property

Management] [Jian Fang Gui (2020) No. 10] (Dec. 5, 2020), www.gov.cn/zhengce/zhengceku/2021-01/05/content_5577326.htm.

北京市住宅区业主大会和业主委员会指导规则京建发〔2010〕739 号 [Beijing Guiding Rules of Homeowners' Associations and Homeowners' Committees] (promulgated by Beijing Department of Housing and Urban-Rural Development, 2010).

关于加强本市住宅小区业主大会、业主委员会规范化建设的若干意见 [The Opinions on Enhancing the Normalization Construction of Owner Conventions and Owner Committees of Residential Areas in This Municipality] (promulgated by Shanghai Municipal Housing Guarantee and Houses Administration, Nov. 16, 2009, effective Nov. 16, 2009) (Chinalawinfo).

关于印发《北京市住宅专项维修资金使用审核标准》的通知 [Notice on Beijing Municipal Audit Standards of Using Housing Maintenance Funding] (promulgated by Beijing Housing and urban-rural development Committee Jan. 7, 2013), www.bjjs.gov.cn/bjjs/fwgl/fwaqysb/fwaqsbglfxxx/323991/index.

深圳市住房和建设局关于推进住宅小区业主委员会三年全覆盖的通知(深建物管〔2022〕24号) [Shenzhen Municipal Housing and Construction Bureau on Promoting the Three-Year Full Coverage of Owners' Committees in Residential Districts] (promulgated by the Shenzhen Municipal Bureau of Housing and Construction on Apr. 18, 2022).

关于加强和改进城市基层党的建设工作的意见 [On Strengthening and Improving Urban Grassroots Party Construction], CCP Central Committee Office (中共中央办公厅), Nov. 8, 2019, www.gov.cn/zhengce/2019-05/08/content_5389836.htm.

上海市居住物业管理条例 [Regulations of Shanghai Municipality on Residential Property Management] (promulgated by Shanghai People's Congress, June 9, 1997, effective July 1, 1997, abolished Apr. 1, 2004) (Chinalawinfo).

上海市加强住宅小区综合管理三年行动计划（2007—2009年） [Three-Year Action Plan (2007–2009) of Shanghai Municipality for Enhancing the Comprehensive Administration of Residential Quarters] (promulgated by Shanghai Housing, Land, and Resources Administration, June 5, 2007, effective June 5, 2007) (Chinalawinfo).

上海市住宅物业管理规定 [Provisions of Shanghai Municipality on Residential Property Management] (promulgated by Standing Committee of the Shanghai People's Congress, Dec. 23, 2010, effective Apr. 1, 2011) (Chinalawinfo).

上海市住宅小区建设"美丽家园"三年行动计划 (2018–2020) [Shanghai Three-Year-Action-Plan of "Constructing Beautiful Homes" in Residential Neighborhoods] (promulgated by the Shanghai City Government, Feb. 8, 2018), www.shanghai.gov.cn/nw2/nw2314/nw2319/nw12344/u26aw55185.html.

深圳市物业管理招投标专家库管理暂行办法 [Provisional Measures on the Administration of Expert Database on Real Estate Management Bidding], No. 35, Apr. 8, 2004.

深圳经济特区房地产转让条例 [Regulations of Shenzhen Special Economic Zone on Transfer of Real Estate] (promulgated by Standing Committee of the Shenzhen People's Congress, July 24, 1993, effective Oct. 1, 1993, revised June 30, 1999) (Chinalawinfo).

深圳经济特区物业管理条例 [Regulations of the Shenzhen Special Economic Zone on Realty Management] (promulgated by Standing Committee of the Shenzhen People's Congress, Oct. 17, 2007, effective Jan. 1, 2008) (Chinalawinfo).

深圳市人民政府关于印发深圳市物业专项维修资金管理规定的通知 [Shenzhen City Government's Notice on rules of Shenzhen Housing Maintenance Funding Management] (promulgated by Shenzhen City Government, Sept. 10, 2010), www.sz.gov.cn/zfgb/2010/gb714/201009/t20100929_1590798.htm.

深圳市房地产开发项目停车位建设及处分管理办法(征求意见稿) [Regulation on Shenzhen Real Estate Developing Plan Parking Space Construction and Management (Draft for Public Consultation)] (promulgated by the Shenzhen City Department of Land and Urban Planning, Dec. 2, 2014), www.sz.gov.cn/cn/xxgk/zfxxgj/tzgg/201412/t20141202_2720846.htm.

深圳市组织机构代码管理办法 [The Administrative Measures of Shenzhen Municipality on Institution Codes (2005 Revision)] (promulgated by Shenzhen City Government, Sept. 17, 1994, amended Apr. 28, 2005) (Chinalawinfo).

北京市物业管理办法 [Beijing Municipal Real Estate Management Regulations] (promulgated by Beijing Municipal Government, Apr. 6, 2010, effective Oct. 1, 2010).

北京市物业管理条例 [Regulation of the Beijing Municipality on Property Management] (promulgated by the Standing Committee of the People's Congress of the Beijing Municipality, Mar. 27, 2020, effective May 1, 2020).

关于《中华人民共和国民法典（草案）》的说明 [Explanation of the Draft of the Civil Code of the People's Republic of China], May 22, 2020, www.gov.cn/xinwen/2020-05/22/content_5513931.htm#1.

关于党建引领物业服务企业和业主委员会建设的指导意见的通知(京组通[2019]37号) [Notice on the Guidelines on Party Building Leading the Construction of Property Service Enterprises and Owners' Committees] (Jing Zu Tong [2019] No. 37) (promulgated by Organization Department of the Beijing Municipal Committee of the Communist Party of China, Nov. 13, 2019).

关于改进《关于做好"三个典型"培育工作的通知》的建议 [Suggestions for improving the Circular on the Cultivation of the "Three Typicals"] (promulgated by the Hefei Housing Security and Real Estate Administration, Apr. 30, 2020), https://mp.weixin.qq.com/s/P9IQ9YlkVK56QG0tGz6YqA.

关于进一步加强党建引领业主委员会建设的若干意见（上海） [Several Opinions on Further Strengthening Party Leadership in the Construction of Homeowners' Committees (Shanghai)] (promulgated by Shanghai Municipal Committee Organization Department, Nov. 20, 2018), https://mp.weixin.qq.com/s/-K6d49-A30f-tlROKoEUbg.

关于进一步做好本市既有多层住宅加装电梯工作的若干意见(沪建房管联〔2019〕749号) [Several Opinions on Further Improving the Installation of Elevators in Existing Multistory Residential Buildings in This City] (Document No. 749, issued by the SHDHC et al., Nov. 22, 2019).

关于深化城市基层党建引领基层治理的若干措施(试行)中组发[2022]2号 [Several Measures (Pilot) on Deepening Urban Grassroots Party Building to Lead Grassroots Governance (Issued by the Organization Department, Political and Legal Affairs Commission, Ministry of Housing and Urban-Rural Development, Ministry of Civil Affairs on Jan. 29, 2022)] (Zhong Zu Fa [2022] No. 2).

关于印发《关于进一步贯彻实施〈上海市住宅物业管理规定〉的若干意见》的通知 [Notice on Issuing "Several Opinions on Further Implementing the Shanghai Residential Property Management Regulations"] (promulgated by the SHDHC, May 18, 2021), www.shqp.gov.cn/xiay/xyzwgk/sqgl/20221105/1039182.html.

上海市关于调整本市既有多层住宅加装电梯业主表决比例的通知 [Notice from the Shanghai Municipal Government Regarding the Adjustment of the Voting Ratio of Owners in Existing Multistory Residential Buildings for Elevator Installation] (promulgated by the SHDHC, Dec. 31, 2020), https://zjw.sh.gov.cn/fwgl/20210104/5d4c3520e32143bd8d77ec2a2ca9182d.html.

上海市总工会关于进一步推进基层工会主席直接选举工作的意见(沪工总组〔2010〕89号) (Opinion of the Shanghai Worker's Union on Further Promoting Direction Election of Grassroots Workers' Union Chairmen, No. 89, 2010), www.shzgh.org/renda/node5902/node5911/node6581/u1a1667051.html, last accessed Mar. 3, 2021.

深圳经济特区物业管理条例 [Shenzhen Special Economic Zone Property Management Regulations] (promulgated by the First People's Congress of Shenzhen, June 18, 1994).

业主大会议事规则(沪房地资物[2008]389 号) [Homeowners General Assembly Meeting Rules] (promulgated by Shanghai Municipal Housing and Land Resources Administration, June 25, 2008).

Cases and Judicial Documents

最高人民法院关于金湖新村业主委员会是否具备民事诉讼主体资格请示一案的复函 [Supreme People's Court, Reply on the Case Concerning whether the Homeowners' Association of Jinhu New Village Has the Qualifications to Be the Subject of Civil Proceedings] (民立他字第46号), Aug. 20, 2003.

最高人民法院对十三届全国人大五次会议第7017号建议的答复 (The SPC's Response to Suggestion No. 7017 of the Fifth Session of the 13th National People's Congress), July 28, 2022, https://tyjrswj.beijing.gov.cn/fwzl/jxfw/202302/t20230206_2912283.html.

上海市高级人民法院关于业主委员会行政诉讼主体资格问题的解答 (2006年7月24日) [Shanghai High People's Court's Explanation regarding the Qualification of HoCs in Administrative Litigation (July 24, 2006)].

罗全福因核发业主大会、业主委员会备案证行政行为一案 [*In re* Luo Quanfu suing the administrative act that approved and issued the documentation certificate for homeowner convention and homeowner committee] (Shanghai 1st Intermediate People's Court, Jan. 29, 2016).

深圳市福田区南天一花园业主委员会与深圳市城市建设开发（集团）公司等房屋侵权纠纷再审案 [Shenzhen Futian District Nantianyi Garden Homeowner Committee v. Shenzhen Municipal Construction and Development Co., Ltd., Retrial of Real Estate-Related Tort Dispute] (PRC Supreme People's Court 2013) (China Judgement Online).

北京市高级人民法院关于印发《北京市高级人民法院关于审理物业管理纠纷案件的意见(试行)》的通知 (京高法发[2003]389号) [The Notice of the Beijing High People's Court on Issuing the "Opinions on the Trial of Property Management Dispute Cases by the Beijing High People's Court (Trial)" (2003) (No. 389)].

包燕谷等与上海市闵行区银桥花园业主委员会（第二届）等业主撤销权纠纷一审民事判决书，上海市闵行区人民法院民事判决书 (2021) 沪0112民初45367号 [Bao Yangu and Others v. The Second Yinqiao Garden HoC in Minhang District, Shanghai, and Others, Shanghai Minhang District People's Court, Minchu No. 45367 (2021)].

北京市朝阳区慧忠北里三塔楼小区业主委员会诉北京市朝阳区人民政府大屯街道办事处，北京市高级人民法院行政裁定书 (2023)京行申 1648 号 [SantalouHoC v. Datun Street Office of Chaoyang District People's Government, Beijing High People's Court Xingcai No. 1648 (2023)].

北京市朝阳区吉利家园小区业主委员会与北京市朝阳区人民政府太阳宫地区办事处其他二审行政判决书，北京市第三中级人民法院行政判决书(2014)三中行终字第1379号 [JilijiayuanHoC v. the Taiyanggong District Office of the Chaoyang District People's Government, Beijing Third Intermediate People's Court, Xingzhong No. 1379 (2014)].

北京市石景山区西引力小区业主委员会与北京市石景山区人民政府八角街道办事处等其他再审审查与审判监督行政裁定书，北京市第一中级人民法院行政裁定书(2020)京01行申5号 [XiyinliHoC v. Bajiao Street Office of Shijingshan District Government, Beijing First Intermediate People's Court, Xingshen No. 5 (2020)].

陈亮等诉上海市闵行区锦绣江南陶然居业主委员会（第五届）业主撤销权纠纷案上海市闵行区人民法院民事判决书(2021)沪0112民初22494号 [Chen Liang and others v. HoC (Fifth Session) of Jinxiu Jiangnan Taoranju Community in Minhang District, Shanghai Minhang District People's Court, Minchu No. 22494 (2021)].

董光亮等与上海市普陀区名都花园业主委员会业主撤销权纠纷一审民事判决书上海市普陀区人民法院民事判决书 (2021)沪0107民初11293号 [Dong Guangliang and others v. HoC of Mingdu Garden Community in Putuo District, Shanghai, Shanghai Putuo District People's Court, Minchu No. 11293 (2021)].

郭文利等与上海市松江区山的院子花园业主大会业主撤销权纠纷一审民事判决书，上海市松江区人民法院(2021)沪0117民初16661号 [Guo Wenli and others v. HoA of Shandeyuan Garden in Songjiang District, Shanghai, Shanghai Songjiang District People's Court, Minchu No. 16661 (2021)].

何冰、深圳碧桂园盛孚物业服务有限公司业主撤销权纠纷民事二审民事判决书广东省深圳市中级人民法院民事判决书(2021)粤03民终2750号 [He Bing v. Shenzhen Country Garden Shengfu Property Service Co., Ltd., Shenzhen Intermediate People's Court, Minzhong No. 2750 (2021)].

刘彦成与上海市闵行区高兴花园二至四街坊业主委员会（第三届）业主撤销权纠纷民事二审案件民事判决书上海市第一中级人民法院判决（2021）沪01民终16424号 [Liu Yancheng v. HoC of the Second to Fourth Neighborhoods of Xingxing Garden, Minhang District, Shanghai (Third Session), Shanghai First Intermediate People's Court, Min Zhong No. 16424 (2021)].

罗媚媚等与上海市浦东新区大华锦绣华城14街区业主委员会业主撤销权纠纷二审案件二审民事判决书上海市第一中级人民法院（2020）沪01民终11488号 [Luo Meimei and others v. HoC of Block 14, DahuaJinxiuHuacheng in Pudong, Shanghai, Shanghai First Intermediate People's Court, Minzhong No. 11488 (2020)].

马丽敏、深圳市罗湖区港逸豪庭第一届业主委员会业主撤销权纠纷二审民事判决书广东省深圳市中级人民法院民事判决书(2018)粤03民终12106号

[Ma Limin v. the First HoC of GangyiHaoting Community in Luohu District, Shenzhen, Guangdong Shenzhen Intermediate People's Court, Minzhong No. 12106 (2018)].

欧阳志斌、深圳市世外桃源物业管理有限公司物业服务合同纠纷民事二审民事判决书 (2021)粤03民终7275号 [Ouyang Zhibin v. Shenzhen Shiwai Taoyuan Property Management Co., Ltd., Guangdong Shenzhen Intermediate People's Court, Minzhong No. 7275 (2021)].

上海豪都房地产开发经营有限公司与上海市青浦区徐泾镇捷克住宅小区业主大会等业主撤销权纠纷民事一审案件民事判决书上海市闵行区人民法院民事判决书 (2021)沪0112民初22494号 [Shanghai Haodu Real Estate Development and Operation Co., Ltd. v. HoA of Czech Residential Community in Xujing Town, Qingpu District, Shanghai, Shanghai Minhang District People's Court, Minchu No. 22494 (2021)].

上海豪都房地产开发经营有限公司与上海市青浦区徐泾镇捷克住宅小区业主大会等业主撤销权纠纷民事一审案件民事判决书， 上海市青浦区人民法院(2022)沪0118民初4870号 [Shanghai Haodu Real Estate Development and Operation Co., Ltd. v. HoA of Czech Residential Community in Xujing Town, Qingpu District, Shanghai, Shanghai Qingpu District People's Court, Minchu No. 4870 (2022)].

上海骏丰嘉房地产开发有限公司业主撤销权纠纷二审民事判决书上海市第二中级人民法院民事判决书 (2020)沪02民终3424号 [Shanghai Junfeng Jia Real Estate Development Co., Ltd. v. HoA of JunfengJiastian and Jiafenghui, Jiading District, Shanghai, Shanghai Second Intermediate People's Court, Minzhong, Minzhong No. 3424 (2020)].

上海市浦东新区艺泰安邦业主委员会与徐伟芬业主撤销权纠纷二审案件二审民事判决书， 上海市第一中级人民法院民事判决书 (2020)沪01民终7473号 [YitaiAnbangHoC in Pudong, Shanghai v. Xu Weifen, Shanghai First Intermediate People's Court, Minzhong No. 7473 (2020)].

上海伟栋房地产开发有限公司与上海市松江区久阳文华府邸小区业主大会业主撤销权纠纷案上海市松江区人民法院民事判决书(2015)松民三(民)初字第1014号 [Shanghai Weidong Real Estate Development Co., Ltd. v. HoA of JiuyangWenhuaFudi Community in Songjiang District, Shanghai, Shanghai Songjiang District People's Court, Minchu No. 1014 (2015)].

深圳市宝安区泰华豪园第三届业主委员会诉深圳泰华物业管理有限公司物业管理合同纠纷案，广东省深圳市宝安区人民法院 (2016)粤0306民初2241号 [The Third HoC of TaihuaHaoyuan Community in Bao'an District, Shenzhen v. Shenzhen Taihua Property Management Co., Ltd., Guangdong Shenzhen Bao'an District People's Court, Minchu No. 2241(2016)].

深圳市宝安区泰华豪园第三届业主委员会与郭超勇业主撤销权纠纷上诉案，广东省深圳市中级人民法院 (2016)粤03民终11216号 [The third HoC of TaihuaHaoyuan Community in Bao'an District, Shenzhen v. Guo Chaoyong, Guangdong Shenzhen Intermediate People's Court, Minzhong No. 11216 (2016)].

深圳市龙华区玉华花园小区第三届业主委员会、梁逊策业主撤销权纠纷二审民事判决书， 广东省深圳市中级人民法院民事判决书(2019)粤03民终31830号 [The third HoC of Yuhua Garden Community in Longhua District, Shenzhen v. Liang Xunce, Guangdong Shenzhen Intermediate People's Court, Minzhong No. 31830 (2019)].

深圳市罗湖区中航凯特公寓第二届业主委员会等与叶其亮物业服务合同纠纷上诉案,广东省深圳市中级人民法院民事判决书(2017)粤03民终1037号 [Kate Condominium HoC v. Ye Qiliang et al, Shenzhen Intermediate People's Court, Minzhong No. 1037 (2017)].

谢湘华与上海市闵行区未明园业主委员会(第五届)业主撤销权纠纷民事一审案件民事判决书上海市闵行区人民法院民事判决书（2021）沪0112民初32511号 [XieXianghua v. HoC (Fifth Session) of Weimingyuan Community in Minhang District, Shanghai, Shanghai Minhang District People's Court, Minchu No. 32511 (2021)].

郑重与上海市闵行区丽华公寓小区业主委员会等业主撤销权纠纷,上海市闵行区人民法院民事判决书(2022)沪0112民初27268号 [Zheng Zhong v. Lihua Apartment Complex HoC in Minhang District, Shanghai, Minhang District People's Court in Shanghai, Minchu No. 27268 (2022)].

Index

www.ingramcontent.com/pod-product-compliance
Lightning Source LLC
LaVergne TN
LVHW062209200926
848484LV00006B/1356

* 9 7 8 1 1 0 8 8 4 0 2 7 9 *